ARIS AND PHILLIPS CLASSICAL TEXTS

EURIPIDES
Iphigenia in Tauris

Edited with introduction, translation and commentary

by

M. J. Cropp

SECOND EDITION

LIVERPOOL UNIVERSITY PRESS

First published 2023 by
Liverpool University Press
4 Cambridge Street
Liverpool
L69 7ZU

www.liverpooluniversitypress.co.uk

Copyright © 2023 M. J. Cropp

The right of Martin J. Cropp to be identified as the author of this book has been asserted by him in accordance with the Copyright, Designs and Patents Act 1988.

All rights reserved. No part of this book may be reproduced, stored in a retrieval system, or transmitted, in any form or by any means, electronic, mechanical, photocopying, recording, or otherwise, without the prior written permission of the publisher.

British Library Cataloguing-in-Publication data
A British Library CIP record is available

ISBN 978-1-83764-432-2 cased
ISBN 978-1-83764-431-5 paperback
ISBN 978-1-83764-270-0 e-book

Printed in the UK by CPI Group (UK) Ltd, Croydon CR0 4YY

Cover image: Iphigenia and her attendants prepare to receive the captives at the temple of Artemis. Wall-painting from Pompeii, House of Caecilius Iucundus, now in Naples (Museo Archeologico Nazionale, cat. no. 111439). Public Domain.

CONTENTS

Preface	v
Introduction	
Plot and themes	1
Mythical and cultic background	17
Iphigenia and Orestes	17
The Taurians	22
Artemis and Iphigenia at Brauron	27
Artemis Tauropolos at Halai	31
Theatre and dramatic setting	34
The chorus in the drama	37
Date and contemporary plays	40
The play in Antiquity and beyond	42
Greek text and critical apparatus	50
Iphigenia in Tauris	
Hypothesis	54
Text and translation	56
Commentary	149
Abbreviations and references	273
Indexes	295

PREFACE

The first edition of this book was published in the year 2000, when *Iphigenia in Tauris* was one of Greek tragedy's less studied and less well understood plays; the most recent commentaries were those of Maurice Platnauer (1938) and Hans Strohm (1949), both mainly philological. Since then approaches to the play have been broadened and transformed by studies of Greek tragedy as a genre and of related aspects of Greek culture, theatre history, religion and cults, archaeology, Black Sea studies, iconography and reception. Full commentaries have been published by Poulheria Kyriakou (2006), Letitia Parker (2016) and Christine and Luc Amiech (2017),[1] and extensive studies by Matthew Wright (2005, with *Helen* and *Andromeda*) and Isabelle Torrance (2019). This revision of my own work is indebted to all of these and to reviewers of the first edition who suggested a number of corrections and improvements.

Martin Cropp, Calgary   March 2023

---

[1] Emily Kearns's edition in the Cambridge 'Green and Yellow' series was about to be published as I completed this revision.

INTRODUCTION

PLOT AND THEMES

Iphigenia in Tauris rewrites the myths of Iphigenia and Orestes and gives them new endings, combining the two in a play which focuses on rescues, redemptions and restorations.[1] The heirs of the troubled dynasty of Argos are released from its tribulations, Iphigenia returns to the Hellenic world from exile in a barbarous realm and her own traumatic past, and Orestes is freed at last from persecution by Erinyes bent on punishing him for killing his mother. The women of the Chorus are redeemed from slavery, and the goddess Artemis quits the Taurians and their primitive rites for a better home and a more civilized cult in Greece. The Taurian king Thoas renounces wrath, pursuit and vengeance along with the goddess's image.

The plot travels to these conclusions from a beginning mired in suffering, grief and near-despair. In her prologue speech Iphigenia recalls how her father offered her in sacrifice to Artemis as the price for launching his expedition against Troy, and how the goddess put a deer in her place and carried her to the faraway land of the Taurians on the southern coast of the Crimea. She has served Artemis as her priestess from some fifteen years, sharing her exile with a group of enslaved Greek women who assist her in the sanctuary and form the play's Chorus. Together they must sacrifice to the goddess the few unfortunate Greek men who wander into the Taurians' realm (1–39). No word of her has travelled back to Greece, and although she has heard of the sack of Troy she knows nothing of the disastrous returns of the Greek contingents, her father's murder by Clytemnestra and Aegisthus and Orestes' vengeance on them. What she does know, or thinks she knows, is that her family is ruined and Orestes dead, for she has misunderstood a dream which really

---

[1] On Euripides' development of the myth see below, pp. 6–8. The play's title is Latin for *Iphigenia amongst the Taurians*, but 'Tauris' has long since become a geographical term (cf. French *Iphigénie en Tauride* etc.). The ancient name for the region was ἡ Ταυρικὴ (γῆ), e.g. Hdt. 4.99.5, [Scylax], *Periplous* 68, Diodorus 4.44.7: cf. *IT* 85, 1454. The play's original title was no doubt simply Ἰφιγένεια (as Aristotle calls it, *Poetics* 1454a7 etc.) and ἡ ἐν Ταύροις added later to distinguish it from Euripides' posthumously produced *Iphigenia at Aulis* (ἡ ἐν Αὐλίδι Ἰφιγένεια, *Poet.* 1454a32).

2   INTRODUCTION

means that he is alive and will soon stand before her as a victim for Artemis (42–66). As she prepares to lament her brother's death with libations, Orestes reaches the sanctuary with his loyal comrade and cousin Pylades. Acquitted at Athens but still harried by some dissident Erinyes, he is pursuing the last hope of redemption which Apollo has offered him: to steal the Taurian image of Artemis and bring it to Attica. Though daunted by his task and uncertain of Apollo's purpose, he is persuaded by Pylades to persist and hide until nightfall before attempting to break into the temple (67–122).

The Chorus comes to the temple, summoned by Iphigenia to assist in her libations, and their entrance song merges with her despairing laments over Orestes, her family's extinction and her own tribulations (123–235). Then a herdsman interrupts with portentous news. He and some others have found two Greek strangers lurking by the shore, watched one of them suffering a fit of madness and captured them after a spirited battle; Iphigenia can now relish an opportunity to kill Hellenes in retaliation for her own suffering at Aulis (236–339). She resolves to do so, but her vengefulness recedes as recollections of Aulis lead her to think of her lost family and to question whether the gods can really desire human sacrifices such as the Taurians offer them (342–91).

As the captives are brought to the temple the Chorus sings an excited song about their possible identity and their voyage, adding their own wishes for the punishment of Helen, who caused the Trojan War and Iphigenia's suffering, and for their own release from captivity (392–455). Then the captives are brought in and a long and elaborate dramatic process begins which will lead finally to the reunion of Orestes and Iphigenia. Moved by sympathy as she thinks of her lost brother, Iphigenia overcomes Orestes' truculence and gets from him news of the aftermath of the Trojan War, including the terrible history of her own family and, crucially, the fact that her brother is still alive; so she declares her dream false (still not understanding its real meaning) and her vengeful feelings towards the captives are finally dispelled (456–577). Orestes however has avoided identifying himself and Iphigenia has said nothing about her own identity, so it occurs to her to release him so that he can take a letter to her brother in Argos with news of herself and a plea for rescue. Orestes nobly insists that she should send Pylades on this mission while he remains to suffer sacrificial death. Iphigenia agrees, and the killing of brother by sister now seems inevitable (578–642). While she goes to fetch the letter, the comrades make their farewells and Orestes resists

INTRODUCTION 3

Pylades' wish to stay and die with him, requiring him instead to return to Greece and ensure the continuation of the Pelopid line by having sons with Electra, his sister now married to Pylades (643–722). When Iphigenia returns, however, she decides that she can only ensure the safe delivery of her message by reciting it to Pylades, and in doing so she at last names Orestes. Pylades delivers the letter instantly to its amazed recipient, and Orestes assures Iphigenia of his identity by describing heirlooms linked to the family's past (723–826). Seconded by Orestes, Iphigenia sings a song of joy and relief mixed with trepidation about their prospects of escape (827–99).

The difficult business of carrying off the image of Artemis must now be faced, but Iphigenia first insists on hearing more of Orestes' recent history, and we learn more of the events at Athens which led to his continued pursuit by the recalcitrant Erinyes (900–88). After some anxious discussion she contrives a scheme which, with the Chorus's connivance and Artemis's favour, may rescue them all. She will pretend that the captives and the image of Artemis must be purified from their blood-pollution at the seashore; thus they can reach the ship without interference and make good their escape (989–1088). A nostalgic song of the Chorus covers the preparations for this manoeuvre and reinforces Iphigenia's plea for Artemis's support (1089–1152). When Thoas arrives to see the sacrifice of the captives completed he is easily taken in by Iphigenia's pretence and despatches the ritual procession to the seashore complete with captives and image, though also with an escort (1153–1233). The Chorus sings again, praising Apollo and his Delphic authority (1234–83), then one of Thoas's men rushes in to report that the Greeks have eluded and fought off their escort and launched their ship, but were then driven back to the beach by a violent wind and wave so that they now lie at the Taurians' mercy (1284–1421).

As Thoas prepares to pursue and slaughter the fugitives (1422–34), the goddess Athena intervenes to forbid the pursuit and reveal the destined end of Orestes' mission. He must take the image of Artemis to Halai on the eastern coast of Attica and found a sanctuary for Artemis where a special ritual will commemorate his near-death. Iphigenia will serve as the goddess's priestess at nearby Brauron and after her death will have a tomb there and herself receive cult. The loyal women of the Chorus must also be permitted to return to Greece (1435–74). Thoas accepts the goddess's commands, and Orestes and his companions are

4 INTRODUCTION

free to sail for Attica, the knots of his and Iphigenia's destinies unravelled, their sufferings giving way to good fortune.

The novelty of this plot is matched by the ingenuity of the play's structure.[2] As in many of Euripides' later plays, the action is twofold: first the events leading up to the recognition (*anagnôrisis*), which in a startling reversal (*peripeteia*) reunites Iphigenia and Orestes just as she is about to kill him, and then the intrigue by which they overcome dangers and impediments and make their escape to Greece. The process of recognition and intrigue, descended ultimately from Homer's *Odyssey*, had its own special pleasures for a Greek theatre audience.[3] In *Iphigenia* the elaborately crafted recognition occupies fully a quarter of the play, and the threat of disaster which it averts, with one long-lost relative about to be killed by another, was calculated to stir in the audience the tragic emotions of pity and fear in the most poignant way, but without subjecting them to the repellent reality of a fatal deed.[4] The recognition and escape-planning together are an almost seamless dramatic process,

---

[2] On the play's structure and deployment of plot motifs see especially Strohm 18–37, Burnett 1971, 47–72.

[3] See throughout the Commentary on 456–1088. For the importance of recognition and reversal in creating tragic effect, see Aristotle, *Poetics* 1450a33–35, 1452a12–b8, 1454a2–9, 1455b32–34. In the second of these passages *Iphigenia* is Aristotle's example of the kind of complex plot in which recognition combined with reversal leads from ill fortune to good, while Sophocles' *Oedipus* represents the type leading from good to ill. Aristotle's perception of serious moral dimensions in *Iphigenia* is discussed by White 1992 and Belfiore 1992.

[4] Cf. *Poetics* 1453b26–54a9, where Aristotle commends the plots of Euripides' *Cresphontes* and *Iphigenia* (for *Cresphontes* see Collard–Cropp–Lee 1995, 121f.). On Aristotle's (and tragedy's) preference for skirting the most painful kinds of tragic experience see Murnaghan 1995. We can observe the increasing and increasingly artificial elaboration of these near-catastrophic plots. In *Cresphontes* (composed in the mid-420s) the hero returns home disguised as his own killer and is almost killed in revenge by his mother before he is recognized. In *Iphigenia* Orestes and Iphigenia are each unknown to the other. In *Ion* Creusa and Ion are unknown to each other and each nearly kills the other. In the probably Hellenistic plot summarized in Hyginus, *Fab.* 100, Telephus wins his unrecognized mother Auge's hand in marriage, but she is unwilling to marry and tries to kill him, and he retaliates by trying to kill her (see Cropp 2021, 394–98). The plot summarized in Hyginus, *Fab.* 122 is a 'sequel' to *Iphigenia* in which Electra nearly kills Iphigenia thinking she has actually sacrificed Orestes (Cropp 2021, 404–6). Hyginus, *Fab.* 190, 'Theonoe' summarizes an even more convoluted plot (Cropp 2021, 407–10). Belfiore 2000 documents the prevalence of violence and threats of violence amongst *philoi* ('friends') throughout Greek tragedy.

INTRODUCTION 5

starting from Iphigenia's first meeting with the captives (467) and punctuated only by a brief interlude as the letter is fetched (642–56) and by the climactic reunion celebration (827–99). Orestes, Pylades and (but for her one brief absence) Iphigenia are on stage throughout this process, while the Chorus hardly participates.[5] Starting from their confrontation in ignorance and despair – each convinced the other is dead, Iphigenia determined to kill her captive, Orestes resigned to dying – the drama brings brother and sister gradually together and creates the setting for their high-spirited escape from adversity.

The impact of the recognition and reversal is continually enhanced by suspense and dramatic irony. The risk that Iphigenia will kill her brother is made vivid in her dream (42–58), which shows her preparing to sacrifice him and so sets a puzzle: how can the dream be fulfilled without her actually killing him?[6] Her own misunderstanding of the dream complicates the problem, for so long as she thinks Orestes is dead she cannot begin to guess that he is one of her prisoners, and is at first more determined to kill him because of her own grief. Even when Orestes tells her that Orestes is alive, the risk of her killing him recedes slowly as he still avoids identifying himself and insists that he rather than Pylades should be sacrificed. Yet frequent reminders of fortune's instability, the difficulty of reading the gods' nature and intentions, and the frailty of human understanding foreshadow the reversal. Right after hearing Iphigenia's dream of Orestes' supposed death we see him alive and well. Orestes and Pylades are bombarded by the Taurians' rocks yet mysteriously protected from them (328f.). Iphigenia puzzles over the nature of Artemis – bloodthirsty as the Taurians believe, or humane as her own survival and instincts suggest? Orestes distrusts Apollo, but Pylades asserts the god's will and the value of courageous persistence.[7]

---

[5] A long dramatic development with the Chorus's part abbreviated and subordinated to the action is characteristic of late fifth-century tragedy, e.g. *Helen* 528–1106, *Orestes* 356–806, S. *Electra* 516–1057, *Philoctetes* 219–675, *OC* 254–666. *Iphigenia* has only three self-contained choral songs (392–455, 1089–1152, 1234–83).

[6] Cf. Hamilton 1978, 283–88. On the complexities of the dream and its interpretation see the Commentary (42–66 n.) with Mirto 1994, 56–70 and Trieschnigg 2008.

[7] See 91–115 with Commentary on 91, 92, 105; also 711–24, and 902–8. This last speech, Pylades' call to action after the recognition, is significantly his last in the play. From here on Orestes shares his confidence in Apollo and Artemis (1012–16), though he must rely on Iphigenia to find the means of escape.

6 INTRODUCTION

When Iphigenia's dream comes true she complains that it was false, while Orestes blames the divine guidance which has in fact brought them face to face (569–71) and accuses Apollo of neglect just as Iphigenia brings out the letter which will seal their reunion (711–28).

The play's mythical basis deepens the emotional impact of the near-disaster and the recognition. Iphigenia and Orestes belong to a family doomed to tragic suffering, have themselves shared in the suffering and seem destined to replicate it yet again. Repeated evocations of Iphigenia's sacrifice and Orestes' matricide and persecution by the Erinyes[8] are interwoven with reflections on the family's earlier disasters, Orestes' supposed death, the extinction of the house, the gods' hostility, Helen's guilt and the losses of the Trojan War.[9] Ominous comparisons are suggested. Clytemnestra's dream portending the return of Orestes is refigured in Iphigenia's dream portending his survival (and both fail to recognize him when he appears).[10] Electra's mourning and libations for Agamemnon are transformed into Iphigenia's mourning and libations for Orestes,[11] and Agamemnon's sacrifice of his daughter into her threatened sacrifice of her brother.[12]

In these various ways the play portrays the couple struggling through impediments and uncertainties to escape from their tragic past and its latest crisis. Their hard-won transition to a post-tragic future is symbolized in the recognition tokens, celebrated in the reunion scene and reflected in symmetries between the play's later and earlier action. The Herdsman's report of Orestes' capture showed Orestes at the mercy of the Erinyes, seemingly led to destruction by Apollo, fighting manfully but vainly against the Taurians, and crying out defiantly as he faced up to inevitable death (320–22). The matching Messenger's report of the escape is almost a re-run of this, but now no Erinyes threaten, the Taurians cannot overpower the Hellenes and the cry from the ship

---

[8] The sacrifice of Iphigenia is evoked in her prologue speech, the Parodos, her speech responding to the Herdsman's news and her dialogue with Orestes (538–41, 563–66); Orestes' plight in his prologue scene, the Herdsman's report and (again) his dialogue with Iphigenia (511f., 555–60).

[9] See especially 10–14, 44–58, 143–202, 230–35, 348–58, 439–46, 517–71.

[10] See the Commentary, introductory note on lines 42–66.

[11] See the Commentary, introductory note on lines 123–235.

[12] 344–60; cf. 609–35 (Iphigenia remembers her lost brother while explaining how she will supervise her captive's death and care for his corpse) and 866–72 (retrospective recognition of the danger).

INTRODUCTION 7

anticipates a successful escape (1385–89). Even the wind and wave threatening final entrapment (like the entrapment at Aulis which led to Iphigenia's sacrifice) are promptly quashed. The solemn procession of the Chorus assisting Iphigenia's funeral ritual for her brother (123–36) is mirrored in her mock-ritual exit with disguised captives and entourage (1222–29), the captives themselves bound and escorted just as when they arrived (456–60). The outward and homeward voyages are evoked in the choral songs which flank the central dramatic sequence (392–455, 1089–1152).

In extending and combining the myths of Iphigenia and Orestes, Euripides was building especially on Aeschylus's *Oresteia*, and improving on it.[13] In Aeschylus's trilogy Iphigenia died at Aulis and the tragic history of the House of Atreus ended in Orestes' acquittal in his trial before the Areopagus court at Athens. Euripides' *Electra*, produced probably a few years before *Iphigenia*,[14] maintained these basic features while portraying the matricide not as a necessary evil but as a tragic error flowing as much from Electra's obsession with vengeance and Orestes' moral inexperience as from Apollo's lack of concern for the human agents of his justice. In *Iphigenia* the heroine's undetected survival suggests that the revenge murders which stemmed from her supposed death at Aulis were unneeded,[15] just as in *Helen* (in a very similar dramatic pattern) the real Helen's

---

[13] See especially Caldwell 1974–75, Sansone 1975, Zeitlin 2005.

[14] See pp. 40–42 below.

[15] Kyriakou (22f., 298) denies this, arguing that the text hardly mentions revenge for Iphigenia as a motive for Clytemnestra's killing of Agamemnon and hints only at her adultery with Aegisthus (926f.). That would be a reversion to the tradition of the *Odyssey*, but we can reasonably assume the revenge motive in a play so engaged with the tradition established by the *Oresteia*. According to Kyriakou (23), 'there is no evidence that any pre-Euripidean source attributed the murder of Agamemnon exclusively or primarily to his wife's wish to avenge the sacrifice of their daughter'. But that is exactly what Clytemnestra declares as her motive in Aeschylus's *Agamemnon* (1406, 1412–20, 1431–33), and the heartrending account of the sacrifice in that play's parodos (*Ag.* 104–257) is pointless if the sacrifice is not to be understood as central to her motivation. The sacrifice is her first justification in Euripides' *Electra* (1018–29) and her whole justification in Sophocles' *Electra* (525–51), although in both cases Electra rejects it. Pindar, *Pyth.* 11.22–25 poses the question, sacrifice or adultery? In *Iphigenia*, mention of this topic before the recognition would have caused Iphigenia to be identified prematurely, and a later mention of any justification for Clytemnestra would have detracted from the righteousness of Orestes' revenge (cf. Kyriakou on 924–27).

8   INTRODUCTION

sojourn in Egypt implies the needlessness of the Trojan War fought over her phantom. A sense of regret for the terrible consequences of human ignorance and misdirected emotion displaces the deep concern with the revenge process itself and its relationship with justice which dominated the earlier plays. The impasse created by Orestes' killing of his own mother, a morally unacceptable act of justice, is recognized, for example, in Iphigenia's reaction when she first hears of it ('Alas, how well did he perform a righteous wrong!', 559) as well as in the Erinyes' division into two factions and Orestes' own continued sense of guilt.[16] Euripides' shaping of the myth offers three ways of alleviating this impasse. First, Iphigenia's survival and the dissociation of Artemis from human sacrifices confirm that the killings of Agamemnon and (consequently) Clytemnestra need not and should not have happened. Secondly, Orestes' longer and harder route to his final acquittal supplies a fuller atonement and an added element of restoration since he retrieves Iphigenia and 'redeems' Artemis. Lastly, the damage done is compensated by additional long-term benefits, the creation of the cults of Artemis at Halai and Brauron.[17] While the damage portrayed in the *Oresteia* myth remains, along with the human and divine fallibility which it represents, these are now balanced by a further, less pessimistic episode. Iphigenia and Orestes face predicaments modelled on those which have gone before but avoid replicating the earlier disastrous choices, partly through following their own more humane instincts and partly through the unforeseeable turn of events which finds 'fortune' and the impetus of divine will now working in their favour.

The theme of *tuchê*, the prevailing uncertainty of human experience, is prominent in the play.[18] The word *tuchê*, literally a 'hit', could denote either a stroke of fortune, or fortune in general, or the power of fortune

---

The topic is therefore treated equivocally, but that does not make it irrelevant for the audience, who might well see allusions to it in lines 553 and 927.

[16] It is notable that the play does not even mention the more justified killing of Aegisthus, nor his role in the killing of Agamemnon (see lines 543–59). For indications of Orestes' sense of guilt see e.g. 281–91 (with Commentary on 281–300), 546, 554, 940f.

[17] See further below, pp. 27–34.

[18] Cf. Matthiessen 1964, 180–85; Burnett 1971, 65–69; Mirto 1994, 62f., 96f.; Amiech LXXVI–LXXX. On *tuchê* in Euripides in general: Giannopoulou 1999–2000, 257–61; Wright 2005, 372–80; Lloyd 2013.

INTRODUCTION 9

(sometimes seen as a divine being).[19] The relationship between *tuchê* and the power and will of the gods was always and inevitably uncertain in Greek belief, but in Iphigenia the two remain closely if obscurely linked. *Tuchê* is not here a self-willed and capricious deity, but rather the aspect of unexpectedness in a complex pattern of events, including divine forces, which humans must handle with flexibility and initiative. Thus Iphigenia seeing the captives before her reflects, 'Who can know who will have fortunes (*tuchai*) such as these? All of the gods' designs are obscure in outcome, and no one can know anything for sure, for fortune (*tuchê*) leads us astray into ignorance' (475–78). In other words, what happens to us is so variable and unpredictable that we can never know what to expect next, nor why what happens happens, not because there are no gods' designs and no pattern but because the designs and the pattern are obscure and complicated. In the same vein after the recognition she sings of being subjected to a new crisis through some daimon's stroke of fortune' (*tuchê*, 865f.), Pylades advises 'not to let go of fortune (*tuchê*) but seize the moment', and Orestes agrees: 'I reckon this is fortune's business as well as our own. When someone is determined it's likely the divine power will show more strength' (907–11). Thus the play's drama of ignorance presupposes directions of events and divine influences on them to which human intelligence has limited access. The unexpected must always be expected and, as Pylades insists at the lowest point of Orestes' fortunes, 'extreme adversity does on occasion (ὅταν τύχῃ, 'when it happens') bring extreme reverses' (721f.).

In these circumstances humans must manage their luck and their relations with the gods as best they can, despite their limitations. The realisation of this is an important ethical element in the play. Pylades' positive attitude is a foil for the pessimism of Orestes, who needs his comrade's exhortation to keep him from despair as they reach the temple (102–22), resigns himself to *tuchê* with complaints about Apollo's betrayal as the sacrifice approaches (489, 570f., 711–15), and is only fully restored to constructive action by the recognition. At this point Orestes realises that Apollo must be favouring their escape (1012–16), and Iphigenia devises a way of turning ritual practice and Orestes'

---

[19] For 'strokes of fortune' see 89, 475, 648, 867, 875, 907, 1065, 1067 with Commentary on 865–67, and for fortune generally 478, 489, 501, 909. For brief surveys of the concept and the deity see 'Tyche' in *LIMC* VIII or *The Oxford Classical Dictionary*.

10 INTRODUCTION

pollution to their advantage (1029–49),[20] praying persuasively to Artemis about their common interests (1082–88) while the Chorus predicts that Apollo and Pan will assist the return voyage (1125–31). Athena's intervention at the end confirms the human intuitions and initiatives which have preceded it; the happy outcome involves collaboration between gods and humans, and on their joint recognition of 'what must be'.[21]

Iphigenia, Orestes and Pylades collaborate with and shape their better fortune, and so seem to deserve it, not only by sensing the turn of events and acting positively but by behaving humanely and in particular exercising the affection, interdependence and loyalty which they owe to each other as *philoi* ('friends' or 'loved ones'). The instinctive humanity and attachment to family which Iphigenia shows in her grief at Orestes' supposed death, her revulsion from human sacrifices and revenge, her sisterly response to the unrecognized captives (472–75) and her pity for Agamemnon and Clytemnestra (545–59) shape her plan to send the letter which brings about the recognition and persuade her to renounce her resentment of Agamemnon's role in her sacrifice in the interests of brother and family (991–95). Orestes and Pylades display touching altruism in their concern and affection for each other (597–608, 674–722). These exemplary displays of *philia* and self-sacrifice reverse the pattern of strife and kin-killing among the descendants of Pelops as Orestes, Pylades and Iphigenia all in turn refuse to impose death on each other and choose to accept it for themselves.[22]

These human efforts remain perilously subordinate to divine purposes and natures which cannot be fully known and may have their own conflicts, inconsistencies or limits. This remains a tragic undercurrent in a play which leans towards optimism.[23] The point is clearest in the case of

---

[20] The escape plan depends essentially on Iphigenia's female ingenuity and use of her authority as priestess of Artemis (McClure 2017; Torrance 2019, 71f.).

[21] Human understanding of 'what must be' depends on the superior understanding of gods such as Apollo and Athena: see 1438–39 n., 1486.

[22] 603–8, 674f., 687–92, 1004–9. On *philia* and adherence to moral standards in misfortune as basic themes in the play see Belfiore 1992, 374f. and 2000, 21–38; White 1992, 236f.; Kyriakou 10f., 30–34. The *philia* shown by the three characters, and especially the dependence of the youthful Orestes on Pylades and Iphigenia, is well summed up by Mastronarde 2010, 285–87. See also Torrance 2019, 72f., and on the parallels between the situations of Orestes and Iphigenia, Sansone 1975, 283–87; Zeitlin 2011, 454–56.

[23] Cf. Mirto 1994, 96.

INTRODUCTION 11

Apollo, whose use of Orestes to punish Clytemnestra was criticized in *Electra* and is not vindicated in *Iphigenia*.[24] Here the Fury-ridden Orestes is a casualty of the god's enforcement of justice and has received the guidance he needs for his deliverance only by blackmailing the god with a threat to die in his sanctuary (972–78). Athena may in the end justify Apollo's policy in terms of its outcomes and the requirements of destiny (1438–41), but as in the near-contemporary *Ion* this does not cancel the impression of the god's remoteness and unconcern for human suffering. The Third Stasimon (1234–83) sums up his relationship with his worshippers in a suggestively ambivalent way. On the one hand, its light-hearted narrative congratulates the god for violently attaining his power and authority at Delphi and foreshadows his success in redeeming Orestes. On the other hand it reveals how, by persuading Zeus to suppress Earth-born dreams which revealed to mortals the divinely ordained truths of past, present and future, he has monopolized these truths and now dispenses encouragement to his humble worshippers at his own discretion and in return for his own enrichment and aggrandizement.

This ambivalent view of Apollo is at least in part a reflection of his superior power and his role as oracular god and dispenser of justice, closely associated with the will of Zeus and with larger necessities and patterns of events which allow little regard for human individuals. Moreover, the play is not directly concerned with Apollo's relationship with Athens, whereas it is concerned with the incorporation of his sister Artemis into the Athenian cult system and works with some determination to relegate the negative aspects of this goddess to the realms of the past, the foreign, the mythical and the symbolic.[25] Whether Artemis really demanded Iphigenia's sacrifice is left unclear; the demand was due to Calchas's interpretation of Agamemnon's vow and the weather conditions at Aulis,[26] whereas the goddess herself intervened to rescue

---

[24] On Apollo's interdependence with Orestes and his need for vindication as instigator of the matricide see Zeitlin 2005, 201–8, 2011, 454. On his enigmatic influence throughout the action of the play leading to the foundation of the cult at Halai, Kavoulaki 2009, 237–44; Amiech LXXIII–LXXVI.

[25] On the play's complex portrayal of Artemis see especially Sourvinou-Inwood 1997, 171–75, 2003, 31–40; Kyriakou 13–15; Zeitlin 2011, 452, 459f., 462–66; Bremmer 2013, 99f.; Amiech LVI–LXI.

[26] See lines 15–25 with Commentary. Both the cause of the delay and the identification of Iphigenia as Artemis's required victim depend on Calchas's interpretation. Iphigenia blames her sacrifice on Calchas and Odysseus (cf. 531–35) along with Helen and Menelaus for whose sake she was killed (13f., 354–60,

12 INTRODUCTION

Iphigenia (15–30).[27] In the course of the play the Taurians' enthusiasm for human sacrifice is contrasted with Iphigenia's reluctance and doubts,[28] with recollections of the goddess's mercy, and with the attachment to a life-affirming Artemis which both Iphigenia and the Chorus celebrate, while Artemis herself appears tacitly willing to abandon the Taurians and take her place in the blessed community of Athens.[29] The goddess who emerges in the perceptions of its Hellenic characters is compatible with the benevolent and caring figure imaged in the fourth-century reliefs at Brauron and addressed there in the offerings of grateful mothers, even if her primitive destructive potential continues to be recognized in its myths and rituals.[30]

This positive impression is reinforced when Athena, the patroness of Attica, proclaims at the end of the play that cults at Halai and Brauron are to be the lasting outcome of Orestes' mission.[31] Euripides here reformulates the outcome of Aeschylus' *Eumenides*, in which Athena asserted the acquittal of Orestes and persuaded the Erinyes to accept a civic role within the Athenian community. The introduction of the Erinyes to Athenian

---

521–25; similarly the Chorus, 439–46, and Orestes, 566). She is sympathetic to Agamemnon despite her horror in recollecting his part in her sacrifice (211f., 359–71, 565, 853f., 864), regrets his death (549–53) and ultimately feels 'no rancour at the man who killed me' (992f.). The influence of Calchas and Odysseus in enforcing the sacrifice is heavily emphasized in the later *Iphigenia at Aulis*.

[27] Iphigenia recognizes this at the outset (28–30) and later (783–85, 1082f.).

[28] For the Taurians human sacrifice is a lawful practice (*nomos*: 35, 38, 277, 586, 1189) and presumably pleasing to Artemis (e.g. 243f., 334f.). Iphigenia performs her duties accordingly (35–39, 467–71, 1189), and even the victims accept the *nomos* (490f., 585–87). Yet she does so reluctantly and pities the victims (36f., 344–47, 479–81, 617–20, 774–76), and questions whether this is what the goddess really could or should want (see 380–91 with Commentary).

[29] 1012–16, 1082–88, 1230–33. The Chorus's second song celebrates the civilized cult of Artemis on the Athenian-controlled island of Delos (already existing at this mythical time, apparently) in contrast with the primitive Taurian cult (1096–1105). The Taurians might continue to worship the goddess in their own way after losing her image (hence the cult described by Herodotus, pp. 19f. below), but that would still be barbarous and from the Greek point of view 'wrong'.

[30] Sourvinou-Inwood (1997, 171–75; 2003, 31–40) rightly stresses that the play's account of Artemis is exploratory, but Athenian tragedies about Athens do tend to share with other forms of Athenian public discourse a basic optimism about the gods' benevolence towards Athens (»» R. Parker 1997, esp. 150).

[31] For historical information on these cults and their rituals see below, pp. 27–34.

INTRODUCTION   13

cult which Aeschylus invented is matched by Euripides' invention of the introduction to Athenian cult of the Taurian Artemis and the heroine Iphigenia. Other plays of Euripides likewise use Athena to validate politically significant outcomes (a tradition of friendship between Athens and Argos in *Suppliant Women*, Athenian origins for the Hellenic tribes in *Ion*, the roles of Erechtheus and his family in Athenian history and cult in *Erechtheus*), while others again seem designed to project Athenian claims of cultural hegemony in the Greek world by depicting the incorporation of panhellenic figures such as Iphigenia into Attic cults.[32]

The play's allusions to the orderly ritual world of contemporary Athens, set against the perversions of the Taurians' ritual world and of Pelopid history, reinforce its mythical message of transformation, of a better order emerging from the disorder of the distant past.[33] The value of rightly deployed ritual and the power of symbolic action to condition the relations of humans with gods are emphasized when the play shows the primitive practices of the mythical past being refashioned as, or replaced by, symbolic acts.[34] Orestes and Pylades confront the altar but do not die, for Iphigenia manipulates ritual procedures and a pre-sacrificial purification to bring about their escape; all that remains of the sacrifice of Orestes for future time is this story and the blood-letting ritual at Halai (1458–61). In the Choes ritual the Athenians devise a way of receiving the polluted Orestes hospitably, and their success in handling the crisis is likewise remembered in a ritual event (947–60). Orestes himself, with Apollo's and Athena's guidance, transfers the Taurian Artemis from a barbaric cult to a constructive place in the Attic cult system (1086–88, 1449–57). The results of such ritual negotiation are also celebrated in the play's evocations of some of the leading Greek cults of Euripides' own time: the great festivals of Hera at Argos and Athena at Athens, the

---

[32] See especially Krummen 1993 discussing *Oedipus at Colonus*, *Suppliant Women* and *Iphigenia in Tauris* and Kowalzig 2006 discussing *Hippolytus*, *Heracles*, *Ajax* and *Oedipus at Colonus*. Krummen 214–18 notes a possible element of 'religious fortification' in the association of gods and heroes with locations in Attica, which might have been particularly relevant in the period when *Iphigenia* was produced.

[33] Sourvinou-Inwood usefully describes such allusions as 'zooming devices' which pick out for the tragedian's audience the relevance to their own world of the play's mythistorical events.

[34] See especially Sansone 1975; Wolff 1992; Goff 1999; Sourvinou-Inwood (n. 30 above). The last three note that these conclusions are not entirely certain or stable; the ritual world of the present still retains elements of the past.

14 INTRODUCTION

comforting beauties of the Delian sanctuary, the wealth and authority of Delphi.[35] In the choral songs above all, Iphigenia's servants recall the physical beauties of Greece and yearn for the dance-filled festivals they enjoyed as girls.[36] These positive images of ritual activity and well-managed relations with the gods may have had a particular resonance for the Athenian audience in the troubled period when Iphigenia was first produced.[37]

Some recent studies take a negative view of the play's outcomes.[38] Iphigenia, it is argued, is denied a return to home and normal life and will remain unmarried and childless in Artemis's service, to be honoured after her death with the relics of fatal childbirths. Civilized Hellas is not entirely different from the Taurian land, as her sacrifice at Aulis and Orestes' matricide (which shocks Thoas, 1174) show. Orestes' future happiness and security are not explicitly assured, and he remains diminished by the matricide even if he is formally freed from it. More radically, the play has been seen as insisting on uncertainty and illusion as a constant and menacing condition of human life.[39] These are understandable reactions in a modern reader, but it is unlikely that they would have been shared by many in Euripides' audience, for whom (as noted above) the play's events belonged to a remote and formative stage of their own past.[40] Iphigenia and Orestes are indeed damaged by their experiences and their family's history, ignorant of their destinies and subjected to unknowable divine purposes,[41] but from the recognition onwards the mood of the play is increasingly positive as they find their way out of their predicament and sense with increasing confidence that their sufferings are giving way to good fortune; none of the characters doubts that this is so. The

---

[35] *IT* 221–24, 1094–1105, 1234–82.

[36] *IT* 133–36, 398–401, 452–55, 1138–52.

[37] Cf. Krummen cited above (n. 32).

[38] See especially Masaracchia 1984; Goff 1999; Stern-Gillet 2001; Said 2002; Zeitlin 2005 (cf. 2019, 454–56); Wright 2005, 357–62; Torrance 2019, 31–43; Duranti 2022.

[39] Wright in his close study of Euripides' escape-tragedies (*Iphigenia, Helen, Andromeda*) places them 'among Euripides' most pessimistic tragedies, depicting humans not unlike ourselves struggling to comprehend a world which confounds and disappoints' (Wright 2005, 337).

[40] For recent positive evaluations of the outcome see Sourvinou-Inwood 2003, 31–40; Lefkowitz 2016, 89–98; Latifses 2019; Budelmann 2019.

[41] See above, pp. 8f.

INTRODUCTION   15

Chorus's parting words ('Go on your way in your good fortune etc.' 1490f.) are especially telling as a conclusion spoken by a representative group of Athenian citizens responding to the outcomes proclaimed to its Athenian audience by the patron goddess of Athens.[42] The cults at Halai and Brauron are validated, Iphigenia is compensated by her attachment to the cult of Artemis. Athena perhaps verified Orestes' future in her speech,[43] but even if she did not, nothing suggests that he will not find the respite from his ordeals promised to him by Apollo, much as he may have doubted this himself in the earlier part of the play.[44] In short, the play's focus is on its main characters' passing from ill fortune to *eudaimonia*, as Aristotle recognized. The human uncertainties and subjection to the gods and fortune which it dramatizes were accepted as the normal conditions of human life in Greek poetry from the *Iliad* onwards and were not necessarily grounds for unrelieved pessimism. Ignorance with its complications, crises and resolutions is the essence of the plots of New Comedy.

The play's balancing of tragic suffering with positive outcomes is reflected in the complexities of its mood, tone and design. Euripides advertises his creative treatment of the story with meta-dramatic references to tragic conventions and to the history of the Oresteia myth in earlier literature and drama. Mythical innovations are presented in ways which advertise their newness, especially by contrasting them with established mythology.[45] Narrative and dramatic motifs such as dream, lamentations and libations are creatively adapted,[46] recognition and planning artfully and sentimentally elaborated,[47] report scenes incongruously framed and stocked with mock-epic combats described by naive Taurians, who unlike most tragic messengers draw the wrong conclusions from what they have

---

[42] Thoas himself agrees (1481f.). Already in the Second Stasimon the Chorus has foreseen Iphigenia reaching Attica after a joyous, divinely escorted voyage (1123–31).

[43] See Commentary on lines 1467–71.

[44] Even in the much darker *Electra* Orestes is promised the same release from his past and ultimate *eudaimonia*, exiled from Argos but founder of a city in Arcadia (*El.* 1273–75, 1291).

[45] See e.g. the Commentary on 902–1088 (adaptation of the Orestes story), 947–60 (aetiology of the Choes ritual), 1234–83 (the myth of Apollo's establishment at Delphi).

[46] See Commentary notes on 42–66, 123–235.

[47] See above, pp. 4–6 with notes.

16   INTRODUCTION

witnessed.[48] If these features advertise the play's imaginative and indeed imaginary basis, its tone is further varied by the colouring of tragedy's standard ingredients with other less typically tragic elements. The motif of the hero's quest to a faraway land and discovery of his long-lost sister is drawn from folktale and in Greek literature is more associated with romance than tragedy.[49] The situation in which stranded Hellenes outwit primitive, isolated and threatening natives also has folktale origins and was much used in Athenian satyr-plays.[50] The sentimentally handled recognition, with opportunities for revelation declined and Iphigenia refusing to recognize what is happening, has humorous elements which appear more pervasively in Euripides' *Ion* and *Helen* and were to become stock features of New Comedy and its Roman derivatives.[51]

This variety of ingredients puts in question the status of *Iphigenia* and similar plays as tragedies and has produced a variety of alternative labels: romantic, prosatyric, melodramatic, comic, tragicomic, and so on. These are useful in identifying features which colour the play and distinguish it from many others, but they risk simplifying and distorting our perceptions of it, for as the number of alternatives suggests, none of them sums up its character completely. Moreover, we know relatively little about how the genre of tragedy was defined in Euripides' time, and what we do know suggests that some of the criteria which seem obvious to us, such as narrative type and emotional tone, may not have been crucial. We do not know, for example, that the humour and sentimentality of the recognition scene of *Iphigenia* were considered in some way 'untragic', or that such elements would have seemed like intrusions from other genres. Tragedy in the fifth century may well have been a much more open field for narrative and dramatic experimentation than the prescriptions of Aristotle's *Poetics* suggest, and Euripides not so much a subversive revolutionary as a pioneer in the exploration of tragedy's potential.[52]

---

[48] See Commentary notes on 236–391, 301–35, 328–29, 1284–1434, 1327–1419, 1414–19.

[49] Caldwell 1974–75.

[50] Cf. especially Burnett 1971, 71f. and Sutton 1972 (though his suggestion that *Iphigenia* was a prosatyric play like *Alcestis* is to be rejected).

[51] On *IT*, *Ion* and *Helen* as precursors of New Comedy see especially Knox 1970 and Segal 1995.

[52] The issues raised here are discussed at length by Wright 2005, 6–43; Mastronarde 2010, 44–62.

INTRODUCTION   17

Euripides' new resolution of the story, with its focus on restoration for Iphigenia and Orestes and rehabilitation for their sponsoring gods, is obviously not 'tragic' by the unrelenting standards of Sophocles' *Oedipus* or Euripides' own *Heracles* or *Bacchae*, but this does not in itself detach *Iphigenia* from the realm of tragedy. Tragedy's essential premiss of human vulnerability to weakness, error and the pressures of events and larger powers remains. Greek tragedies often and in various ways find some accommodation for the resulting human sufferings which they portray by balancing them with good outcomes, or conversely by suggesting that human good cannot be achieved without cost. Aeschylus's *Oresteia* and Danaid trilogies portrayed the whole process of better emerging painfully and incompletely from worse. Herodotus's tragically patterned account of Croesus ends with Apollo's miraculous rescue of the humbled king as he faces death on the pyre.[53] Sophocles' Oedipus finds some compensation for his evil destiny, albeit in a separate and much later play, in his death and heroization on Attic soil at Colonus. In plays as different as *Heracles, Ion* and *Iphigenia* Euripides too shows legendary figures ruined or threatened by the perilous conditions of their existence and close relationships with the gods but settled finally and with mutual benefit into the humane domain of Athenian myth and cult.

MYTHICAL AND CULTIC BACKGROUND

Iphigenia and Orestes. The mythical Iphigenia was partly a figure of poetry, the princess sacrificed by her father to allow the conquest of Troy and retrieval of Helen, and partly a subordinate figure connected with the cults and myths of Artemis. In the archaic period these two aspects were already intertwined. She is not mentioned in the Homeric poems, but that may be because her story did not suit the purposes of these epic narratives.[54] The earliest notices of her and the sacrifice come from three

---

[53] Hdt 1.26–56, 69–91.

[54] *Iliad* 1.106–8, where Agamemnon accuses Calchas of always having given him bad advice, is hardly an allusion to the sacrifice although it might suggest that the poet was aware of the story. Iphianassa, named as a living daughter of Agamemnon in *Iliad* 9.145 and 287 (and later in the *Cypria* and Sophocles' *Electra*) is clearly not to be identified with Iphigenia. On these issues see Davies 2019, 147–49.

18 INTRODUCTION

poems composed probably in the early to mid-sixth century.[55] The Hesiodic *Catalogue of Women*, a genealogical poem compiled from earlier traditions, related that Agamemnon and Clytemnestra had a daughter named Iphimedê whom the Achaeans sacrificed to Artemis on the day when they sailed for Troy,[56] but adds that this was

> a phantom (eidôlon): her self the deer-slaying archeress rescued very easily, and anointed her head with lovely ambrosia, so that her flesh should be unperishing, and made her immortal and ageless for all her days. The tribes of men now call her Artemis of the Wayside (Einodia), attendant (propolos) of the famed archeress.[57]

The phrasing of this might suggest that Iphigenia's survival was added at some point to a tradition which once included only her sacrifice, but more probably it was an essential part of the myth and was suppressed in tragic versions of the story in which she was supposed to have died.[58] At any rate, it was taken for granted by Stesichorus in his *Oresteia*, a lyric narrative which was important in shaping the story of Orestes. According to our much later source, Stesichorus 'following Hesiod [said] that Agamemnon's daughter Iphigenia is the deity now called Hecatê'.[59] The name Hecatê here is presumably an interpretation of the *Catalogue*'s Artemis E(i)nodia,[60] and Stesichorus may also have talked of an *eidôlon* (as he famously did in the case of Helen), but it is not clear how, or in how much detail, he told the story. Compared with this, our information about the *Cypria*, an epic poem which told the story of the Trojan War up to the beginning of the *Iliad*, is more complete. According to the (again

---

[55] On the date of the *Catalogue* see the useful but unattributed Wikipedia article, 'Catalogue of Women'; for Stesichorus, Davies–Finglass 2014, 1–6, and for the *Cypria* Davies 2019, 6–8.

[56] The name Iphimedê/Iphimedeia is etymologically distinct from Mycenean I-pe-me-de-ja, a goddess's name which appears in a Linear B tablet of about 1200 BC (Pylos Tn 316), although the legendary heroine might nevertheless have come to be associated with the cult of that goddess. The meaning of I-pe-me-de-ja and her function(s) are however uncertain: cf. Ventris–Chadwick 1983, 286–88, Neumann 1985, Rocchi 1996, *LIMC* V.1, 'Iphigenia', p. 706.

[57] Hesiod fr. 23(a).15–26 Merkelbach–West.

[58] See Dowden 1989, 17; Bonnechere 1994, 41f.; Henrichs 2013, 137f.

[59] Stesichorus fr. 178 Finglass = 215 *PMGF*. The source is a Herculaneum papyrus fragment of Philodemus, *On Piety*.

[60] The two were readily identified with each other (»» Davies–Finglass 2014, 502). Pausanias 1.43.1 refers to the *Catalogue*'s Artemis Einodia as Hecatê (Hesiod fr. 23(b) Merkelbach–West).

INTRODUCTION   19

much later) summary which provides most of our knowledge of this poem,

> When the expedition had gathered for the second time at Aulis [after an abortive first excursion to Mysia], Agamemnon shot a deer while hunting and claimed to be excelling Artemis. The goddess took umbrage and held them back from their voyage by sending storms. Calchas explained the goddess's wrath and told them to sacrifice Iphigenia to Artemis, so they sent for her on the pretext of marriage with Achilles and set about sacrificing her. But Artemis snatched her away, transported her to the Taurians and made her immortal, setting a deer on the altar instead of the girl.[61]

Thus the *Cypria* included some details (Artemis's wrath and a reason for it, the delay by storms, Calchas's advice, the pretended marriage, and probably Iphigenia's transportation to the Taurians)[62] which might or might not have been known to the poet of the *Catalogue* and might or might not have been addressed by Stesichorus, and differed from the *Catalogue* in having Iphigenia replaced by a deer rather than an *eidôlon*. Iphigenia's narrative of her own experience in *IT* 10–34 reflects much of the *Cypria*'s account but differs on the reason for Artemis's wrath, on the weather conditions at Aulis, and in having Iphigenia surviving among the Taurians as a mortal servant of Artemis. In *Iphigenia* also, though not necessarily in the *Cypria*, the substitution of the deer does not prevent the Achaeans from believing that Iphigenia herself has died.

Iphigenia's survival and deification are taken for granted in the *History* of Herodotus, who describes the Taurians' customs in his account of the Scythian response to the Persian invasion of c. 513 BC (Hdt. 4.103):

> [The Taurians] sacrifice to the Maiden (Parthenos) shipwrecked men and any Greeks they capture by putting out to sea after them, in the following way. After consecrating the victim they strike his head with a club. Some say they then push the body down from the cliff (the sanctuary stands on a cliff) and impale the head. Others agree about the head but say the body is not pushed from the cliff but buried in the ground. This deity to whom they sacrifice is said by the Taurians themselves to be Agamemnon's

---

[61] *Cypria*, *GEF* p. 75, in a summary included in Proclus's *Chrestomatheia*, a kind of literary handbook probably compiled in the 2nd C AD (West 2013, 4–16).

[62] That the *Cypria* mentioned the Taurians has been doubted (e.g. Burnett 1971, 73, Hall 1989b, 111, S. West 2019, 32), but they were probably known to Greek explorers and settlers around the Black Sea when the *Cypria* was composed and conveniently identified with the mythical land to which Iphigenia had been sent.

20   INTRODUCTION

daughter Iphigenia. As for their defeated enemies, they treat them as follows. Each cuts off a head, takes it away to his house, fixes it on a long pole and positions it high above the house, usually over the chimney. They say these act as guardians of the household as they hang there. They get their living generally from brigandage and war.

Herodotus did not know the Taurians at first hand, and what he says about them is limited to a few exotic features based on hearsay.[63] He omits the fact that in his own time there was a Greek settlement at Chersonesos on the Taurian coast, where Greeks had interacted with Taurians for nearly a hundred years (below, p. 24). Parthenos is a Greek name for the Taurians' maiden goddess whose worship had been adopted and Hellenized at Chersonesos.[64] The equation with Iphigenia was obviously not made by the Taurians (though they might have accepted it when asked) but was easily enough made by Greek settlers who had heard of a deified Iphigenia dwelling in the area.

Unlike the sources reviewed above, earlier Attic tragedy generally did not mention Iphigenia's survival or her deification. Aeschylus's *Oresteia*, Euripides' *Electra* and Sophocles' *Electra* all rely on the assumption that she died at Aulis (as does Pindar in *Pythian* 11.22f.). This is compatible with her having survived undetected, but no such revelation is made by Apollo or Athena in Aeschylus's *Eumenides*, nor by Castor in the final scene of Euripides' *Electra*.[65] Aeschylus's *Iphigenia* and Sophocles'

---

[63] See for example McInerney 2014, 293, S. West 2019, 34–39, and on the historical Taurians below, pp. 22–27.

[64] There is no evidence for a Taurian cult apart from Herodotus's statement. For the cult at Chersonesos see Dana 2007, 171–77; Braund 2018, 15–17, 28–60; Lo Monaco 2018, 408–28, 576–81. She was the city's patron and protectress, seen like Artemis as both a life-giving figure and a virginal huntress but not explicitly identified as Artemis (the identification is seen only in later writers influenced by Euripides: Dionysius Scytobrachion *FGH* 32 F 14.109 (in Diodorus 4.44.7), Strabo 12.2.3 etc.). Strabo 7.4.2 describes a temple in the city and on a nearby promontory a sanctuary with an ancient image (*xoanon*, 87–88 n.; for the approximate location see Braund 2018, 19f.). The goddess's importance at Chersonesos is evident from many inscriptions (see especially *IOSPE* I² 343, 344, 352, 401 = *IOSPE* III (online) 51, 1, 8, 100) and from its coinage (»» Guldager Bilde 2003). Other Parthenos cults are attested in the Aegean, Caria and (best attested) Neapolis in Thrace (now Kavala): see *LIMC* VIII.1, 'Parthenos', Lo Monaco 411–23, 427, 581–83.

[65] In *Agamemnon* 248 the old men of the chorus say that they did not see and cannot tell what happened when the death-blow was struck. Cunningham 1994

INTRODUCTION   21

Iphigenia probably told the story of her sacrifice similarly.[66] Euripides' *Iphigenia at Aulis*, one of the plays produced after his death, ended with the substitution of the deer, but the original ending is lost and we cannot tell if it included a revelation of Iphigenia's transition to a distant land.[67] When Euripides composed his play, then, there were two strands to the tradition: either Iphigenia was rescued and deified (as in the earlier poets and Herodotus) or she died or at least seemed to have died at Aulis (as in most tragedies).[68] Euripides diverges from both of these by having her survive as a mortal priestess of Artemis amongst the Taurians and then bringing her back to Greece to continue her service to Artemis at Brauron where she will eventually die and become a recipient of cult. He connects her return with Orestes' quest for the image of Artemis and seems to indicate that the quest was a new development of the myth of Orestes when he twice makes Orestes explain at length that Apollo sent him to steal the image of Artemis when some Erinyes continued to persecute him after his acquittal at Athens (77–92, 970–78.). By extending Orestes' story in this way Euripides unravelled and redirected the tradition of Aeschylus's *Oresteia*, which ends with all of the Erinyes accepting Orestes' acquittal, a home on the Areopagus and a beneficial presence in the Athenian community while Orestes returns to Argos to

---

suggests that her survival could have been revealed in *Proteus*, the satyr-play of the *Oresteia*.

[66] See S. Radt in *TrGF* 3.213f. and 4.270f. The suggestion that Sophocles' *Iphigenia* included her transportation to the Taurians depends on a very insecure guess linking this play with some later mythographic summaries (Hyginus, *Fab.* 98, Apollodorus, *epit.* 3.21f.). It has also been suggested that Sophocles' *Chryses*, which may have preceded *Iphigenia in Tauris*, involved Thoas's pursuit of Iphigenia and Orestes and his death at the hands of the younger Chryses (Agamemnon's son by the Chryseis of *Iliad* 1), but again this depends on an improbable identification of Sophocles' plot in a later handbook (Hyginus, *Fab.* 120.5 and 121: see Cropp 2021, 399–403).

[67] In the extant inauthentic ending a messenger reports that she disappeared as the sacrificial blow was struck and a deer sent by Artemis died in her place. In what seems to be a fragment of the lost real ending (fr. 857 Nauck² = fr. i Diggle, in Aelian, *NA* 7.39) Artemis announces that she will send the deer but that the Achaeans will think they are sacrificing Iphigenia. See further Stockert 1992, 79–87, Collard–Morwood 2017, II.621–23.

[68] As Bonnechere (1994, 41) notes, these are not mutually exclusive. In both cases Iphigenia's mortal life ends, and her apparent death at Aulis does not exclude her having survived in some supernatural manner.

22 INTRODUCTION

reclaim his kingdom.[69] It is possible that a cult legend connecting Orestes with the bringing of the image to Halai already existed, for the story follows a pattern in which a cult's alien features are said to have originated long ago in a faraway barbarian land and to have been brought into a Greek community by an outsider on a special mission.[70] But even if that is so, it was probably Euripides who blended this with a purposeful reformulation of Aeschylus's account of Orestes and of the story of Iphigenia. The final product, bringing Iphigenia to Brauron and Artemis to Halai through Orestes' quest for purification and linking all this with the cults and cult features of both sanctuaries is an impressive example of his creativity in the poet's traditional role as maker of myths.

The Taurians. Our only description of the Taurians before Euripides is in Herodotus's superficial account. This may well have been the basis for Euripides' description, but there are also differences.[71] Herodotus's Taurians are thoroughly uncivilized and violent; no polis or temple is

---

[69] The Aeschylean conclusion is subverted in various ways in other plays of Euripides. At the end of *Electra* (a few years earlier than *Iphigenia*) Castor predicts a single conclusive trial at Athens, but Orestes is to be exiled from Argos and must found the city of Oresteion in Arcadia (*El.* 1249–75). In the later *Orestes* the hero is tried and condemned to death at Argos but rescued by Apollo to spend a year's exile in Arcadia, face trial and acquittal at Athens, and return to govern his ancestral kingdom (*Or.* 1643–65).

[70] See Graf 1979. Some of these legends connect Orestes similarly with other cults, but the sources for these are much later than Euripides. (There may however be early evidence for Orestes and Iphigenia bringing the Taurian image to Sicily. A fragmentary terra cotta plaque from Francavilla near Sicilian Naxos, dated to the 460s (*LIMC Supp.*, 'Orestes' no. 9/'Iphigenia' no. 2) shows a small image of Artemis standing on the poop of a ship with a male and a female figure standing on the shore. For the interpretation see Parra 1991–92 and 2005, 423–25.)

[71] Some of the 'barbarous' features of Euripides' Taurians seem to recall those described by Herodotus. The latter impale the heads of their sacrificed victims and either throw their bodies from the cliff where the sanctuary is located or bury them in the ground. Euripides' Taurians fix the heads on the front of the temple (75 n.), and Thoas threatens to hurl the recaptured fugitives 'down some rough rockface' or impale them (*IT* 1429f.). Such differences are more likely adaptations from Herodotus than taken from some other now unknown source(s). As Bremmer notes (2013, 98), 'all elements [of Herodotus's description] in some way return in [Euripides'] play'; cf. Hall 1989b, 111f., Lo Monaco 2018, 430f. Contrary opinions: Kyriakou 21 n. 14; Wright 2005, 164–66; Braund 2018, 66; Porucznik 2021, 153–66.

INTRODUCTION 23

mentioned and they sacrifice to their maiden goddess (Parthenos) by killing the victims crudely and abusing their corpses. Euripides' play is set in a remote mythical past and his Taurians are correspondingly mythical and adapted to the purposes of the play. His Taurians have a polis (a civic community, 38 n.) and a fine columned temple, both in Hellenic style.[72] They sacrifice human victims, but their goddess has the Greek name Artemis[73] and they sacrifice in the Hellenic manner, lustrating the victim, cutting his throat and draining the blood onto the altar. Victims' heads are displayed on the temple front (75 n.), but Iphigenia can expect to prepare Orestes' body for cremation in the heroic manner before his remains are consigned to 'a broad chasm in the rock' (625–35 n.). Thoas is happy to supervise the human sacrifices and is capable of barbarous cruelty (1429–30 n.), but he is pious and respectful towards the priestess Iphigenia (1153–1221). These more civilized features make the Taurians suitable owners of the image and cult of Artemis which are destined to be established in a Hellenic form at Halai (below, pp. 31–33), as Thoas himself accepts when he submits to Athena's commands in the final scene (1475–85).

The real Taurians are now usually identified with the so-called Kizil-Koba culture for which there is substantial archaeological evidence.[74] Their name is found only in Greek sources, perhaps adapted from a local name. They occupied the rugged southern coast and hinterland of the Crimea (in Greek terms, the Tauric Chersonese), and were probably of Iranian or pre-Iranian stock, arriving from the Caucasus in the late second millennium as the first settlers of this area. In Euripides' time they were an agro-pastoral people (those who discover Orestes and Pylades are herding cattle on the seashore, 252–55) and used cave dwellings and cliff refuges extensively. The most notable features of the archaeological record are their large cave sanctuaries and grave areas with massive stone markers and large sunken stone coffins for multiple burials. The Taurians

---

[72] They also understand and speak Greek, but that is conventional for Greek tragedy. The Taurians' foreignness is not marked in their language in the play (»» Bacon 1961, 115–20; Colvin 1999, 74–87).

[73] The name Parthenos never occurs in Euripides' text. Iphigenia prays to Artemis as 'maiden daughter (παρθένε) of Zeus and Leto' (1230), but that is not an allusion to the name.

[74] The Taurians: Leskov 1980; Hind 1983–84, 85 and 1992–93, 99; Nikolaenko 2006, 152–55; Hall 2013, 65–68; Braund 2018, 38–41; Guldager Bilde et al. 2020, 447.

24   INTRODUCTION

remained distinct from the Scyths who dominated the Crimean steppe from the mid-seventh century (displacing the Cimmerians) and influenced Taurian culture especially in metal-work, weaponry and the use of horses. There is no physical evidence of their practising human sacrifice; what Herodotus says about this may be due to his assimilating them to Scythians although he knew that they were ethnically distinct (Hdt. 4.99f.).

Greek settlement on the northern Black Sea coasts was concentrated in the wealthier areas of the Bug–Dniepr and Dniestr estuaries in the northwest (where Milesians settled the island now known as Berezan in the later seventh century and Olbia on the Bug estuary in the early sixth) and to the east of the Crimea on the shores of the Cimmerian Bosporus (the entrance to the Sea of Azov, Greek Lake Maiotis) where numerous settlements from the early sixth century onwards were welded into the Bosporan kingdom and ruled dynastically (later under Roman protection) down to the mid-fourth century AD[75] In the rest of the Crimea Greek settlement started later and remained sparse, with Milesian settlements at Theodosia on the south-east coast and Kerkinitis on the west coast. At the south-western tip the site of Chersonesos (now part of modern Sevastopol) seems to have been used by traders from Heraclea and Sinope (Megarian and Milesian colonies on the southern Black Sea coast) in the late sixth century and later developed as a *polis* with control of an increasingly large rural territory.[76] Here it seems that a local goddess was adopted by the Greek settlers as their chief protector under the Greek name Parthenos (Maiden).[77] It is the site of Chersonesos, loosely imagined in its pre-Greek condition, which is the setting for Euripides' play.

---

[75] Greek Black Sea settlements: Trejster–Vinogradov 1993; Tsetskhladze 1994; Tsetskhladze (ed.) 1998; Boardman 1999, 238–64, 281f.; Guldager Bilde et al. 2020. The Bosporan Kingdom: Hind 1994; Braund 2018, 1–8; Gallo 2020, 11 n. 1. Athens attempted to establish influence in the Black Sea area in the 430s and 420s (Meiggs 1972, 197–99, 328f.).

[76] For the late 6th-century archaeological evidence see e.g. Zolotarev 2003, 603–7; Nikolaenko 2006, 153f. There is no clear evidence for a permanent Greek community before the 420s, not long before the production of *Iphigenia* (Gallo 2020, 15–19).

[77] See above, note 64 on the Parthenos cult at Chersonesos and the relationship between this and the Greek cults of Artemis and Iphigenia.

INTRODUCTION   25

The Taurians subsisted for centuries after Euripides' time as neighbours of the Greek inhabitants,[78] occupying the coast and hinterland between Chersonesos and Theodosia and interacting productively with Greek communities in the coastal and agricultural areas. They appear occasionally in the Greek and Roman historical record as fierce and piratical barbarians (no doubt a biased view),[79] and in literature they remained a byword for human sacrifices thanks mainly to the portrayals of Herodotus and Euripides.[80] For Euripides' audience they were remote enough to be viewed mythically like the Ethiopians, especially in a story set in the Greeks' own largely mythical heroic age long before the Black Sea settlements were planted. We find them also coopted into the myth of the Argonauts as relatives of the Colchians, who occupied the eastern coast of the Black Sea in what is now Georgia. King Aietes of Colchis was said to have had a brother Perses king of the Taurians, both being sons of the sun-god Helios. Perses' daughter Hecate married her uncle Aietes and became the mother of the witches Medea and Circe. Jason and the Argonauts visited the Taurians as they sailed to Colchis. The traditional fire-breathing bulls (Greek *tauroi*) guarding the Fleece were redefined as fierce Taurians hired by Aietes. All this may have been invented after Euripides' time,[81] but there are notable allusions to the Argonaut expedition in Orestes' voyage through the Symplêgades and across the Black Sea in the play's First Stasimon (392–455) and striking similarities between Orestes' and Jason's missions to barbarian lands and their reliance on a woman's aid for survival and escape.[82]

---

[78] Xenophon's descriptions of encounters between his Greek mercenary force and the mountain tribes on the south coasts of the Black Sea about 400 BC offer a suggestive comparison (Xen. *Anab.* 4.6–5.4).

[79] Diodorus 20.25.2 (piracy suppressed by a late 4th-century Bosporan ruler); *IOSPE* I² 352.5–15 = *IOSPE* III (online) 8.5–15 with bibliography (subjugation by a general of Mithradates VI, cf. Strabo 7.4.2f.); Appian 12.53 (support for Mithradates VI against Rome); Tacitus, *Annals* 12.17 (attack on part of a Roman expeditionary force stranded on the Taurian coast, 49 AD); *CIRB* 39, 40, 1008, 1237 (Taurians subdued/pacified by Bosporan rulers, 1st–3rd C AD; also Bowersock–Jones 2006). For the later history of Chersonesos see Gallo 2020, 19–24.

[80] e.g. ps.-Scymnus, *Periodos* 831–34, Clement of Alexandria, *Protrepticus* 3.42.3, Achilles Tatius, *Leucippe and Clitophon* 8.2.3; cf. Braund 2018, 29f.

[81] The sources are Hellenistic: Dionysius Scytobrachion, *FGrH* 32 F 1a (in Schol. Ap. Rhod. 3.200), Diodorus 4.44.7–4.48.4.

[82] Sansone 2000, 169f. adds some relevant details.

26   INTRODUCTION

The semi-mythical Taurians of Euripides' play, like the Scythians of Herodotus,[83] are systematically different from Greeks, both threatening and inferior to them. Like the great wanderers Heracles, Odysseus and Jason, Orestes must overcome an alien people with Hellenic courage and adaptability. For Iphigenia (and for the Chorus whose situation mirrors hers) the Taurian land is a site of captivity and separation from home. For Artemis they are a 'wrong' environment, offering improper worship. Images of passing through the Symplêgades and crossing the Unwelcoming Sea to a barren land evoke the threatening alienness of this world.[84] The Taurians themselves show no sign of commerce with other peoples[85] or with the laws of hospitality, seeing Greek seafarers as victims to be hunted down for sacrifice and mutilating their bodies. Other 'primitive' features are their technological and military inferiority, lack of religious insight and gullibility.[86] These features add up to a general unGreekness of the kind which we find projected onto 'barbarian' peoples by Greek writers of the fifth century and later as the Greeks used barbarian 'difference' more or less consciously for their own self-definition and (for the most part) self-justification.[87] But besides adding some civilized features (as noted above), Euripides at some points treats the Greek/ barbarian polarity with sophisticated irony or ambivalence. The Taurians we meet in the play are simple and ignorant rather than debased, far from corruption by wealth or luxury, and surprisingly amenable. The Herdsman and the Messenger are observant and eloquent (though easily misled) and appreciate their adversaries' finer points. Thoas trusts Iphigenia, cares for his community and cheerfully accepts Athena's instructions at the end. It is even suggested that Greeks might excel barbarians in criminality and treachery.[88] But if Euripides hints paradoxically at the artificiality of Greek prejudices against barbarians, it remains difficult (as so often with this playwright of the sophistic era) to see beyond this and

---

[83] Cf. Hartog 1980, Part 1.

[84] See especially *IT* 93f., 123–25, 218f., 241f., 393–402, 422–38, 886–90.

[85] It is Hellenic enterprise and risk-taking that bring the occasional trader from Greece to the Taurians' 'unwelcoming land': see especially 399–421.

[86] Technology etc. 303–5, 323–33, 1364–78; religion esp. 243–45, 385–91, 1416–19; gullibility 1153–1221, 1327–44 and Commentary on 336–39. Many of the Taurians' deficiencies are shared with mythical subhumans such as Homer's Cyclopes.

[87] See especially Hartog 1980, Hall 1989b.

[88] See Commentary on 1174, 1205.

INTRODUCTION 27

identify a committed critique underlying the rhetorical and dramatic effects.[89]

Artemis and Iphigenia at Brauron. According to the play, Iphigenia became the first priestess of Artemis at Brauron in Attica, where she was buried on her death and afterwards honoured with dedications of clothing from women who had died in childbirth (*IT* 1462–67), while Orestes delivered the image of the Taurian Artemis to Halai and founded a temple for Artemis Tauropolos there, instituting a ritual in which blood was drawn from a man's throat during the Tauropolia festival to compensate for his own unfulfilled sacrifice (1446–61). The dramatic relevance of this culmination in the founding of two important Attic cults has been mentioned above (pp. 12–15).

Brauron lay at the mouth of the Erasinos river some 30 km east of Athens and about 12 km south of Araphen (the modern port of Rafina). In the Bronze Age it was a flourishing harbour town, remembered in later Athenian tradition as one of the twelve towns merged by Theseus into the Attic state. Resettled some time after the collapse of the Mycenean civilization, it flourished in the archaic and classical periods until flooding left the sanctuary virtually abandoned before the end of the third century BC Evidence of post-Mycenean cultic activity begins in the Geometric period when much of the Greek cult system of the archaic and classical eras was beginning to take shape. The sanctuary lay at the foot of the Mycenean acropolis.[90] Its chief features were an early fifth-century temple of Artemis (replacing one probably founded by the sixth-century tyrant Peisistratos[91] and destroyed by the Persians in 480) and a pi-shaped stoa built incompletely only a few years before the first production of

---

[89] Opinions on this issue vary. Hall (1989b, 211–23) argues that Euripides' sub-version of the Greek/barbarian polarity is a 'rule-proving exception' which shows only that the polarity 'was such a fundamental dogma as to produce striking rhetorical effects on being inverted' (222). Others see a more serious challenge to the assumption of Greek superiority over other peoples: see especially Said 1984; Stern-Gillet 2001; Wright 2005, 177–202; Torrance 2019, 57–68, 77f.

[90] Site and remains: Papadimitriou 1963; Kahil 1963 (pottery); Kondis 1967; Themelis 1971 and 2002; Osborne 1985, 154–57; Hollinshead 1985, 432–35; Travlos 1988, 55–80; Ekroth 2003, 60, 102–18; Goette 2005; R. Parker 2005, 228–30; Nielsen 2009, 93–101; Calame 2009; Lo Monaco 2018, 493–506; Chatzivasiliou 2019, 207–10. The acropolis itself appears to have been a sanctuary and pilgrimage site in the Mycenean period (Kalogeropoulos 2019).

[91] Photius *β* 264 Theodoridis, '*Βραυρωνία*'.

28   INTRODUCTION

Iphigenia. The stoa was flanked on two sides by ten rooms, of which nine were equipped with benches and tables for 99 diners. In the hillside twenty-five metres from the temple entrance was an old cave sanctuary flanked by two small sacred buildings. The supposed shrine of Iphigenia, to which Euripides seems to allude at the end of the play, may have been located in this area, but there is no material evidence for the identification.[92]

The classical Artemis was a goddess of fecundity in vegetation, animals and humans, and was closely connected with the natural cycle of child-bearing, child-rearing and maturation. This aspect was an important feature of the cult at Brauron.[93] Offerings found there include images of boys and girls bringing thank-offerings to the goddess and pottery depicting the girls' rituals known as the *arkteia*, while inscriptions record women's dedications of clothing and adornments. Some fine fourth-century reliefs show Artemis receiving offerings from grateful families and displaying her benevolence and concern. The practice of offering to Iphigenia the clothing of women who had died in childbirth, for which this play is our only evidence,[94] seems designed to distance the goddess herself from the more destructive side of her nature. Yet Artemis remained fundamentally both a giver and a taker of life, sponsoring and sharing in men's hunting and warfare, and in some cults receiving sacrifices of animals and blood on a massive scale.[95]

At least from the later sixth century the cult at Brauron had an important place in the Athenian religious system. An old sanctuary of Artemis on the Acropolis of Athens became, at least by the late fifth century, a metropolitan office housing deposits and records from the coastal sanctuary.[96] The festival of the Brauronia was celebrated in a

---

[92] See Commentary on lines 1464–67.

[93] Hadzisteliou Price 1978, 121f., 205f., Lo Monaco 2018, 496–98.

[94] See further the Commentary on lines 1464–67.

[95] The iconography of Artemis in the early archaic period tends to suggest a ferocious figure developed from Near Eastern models, strongly differentiated from the kourotrophic and animal-protecting Aegean nature goddess (Marinatos 1998). The most violent festival of Artemis was the Laphria at Patrai (Pausanias 7.18.11–13); see further Graf 1985, 411–17. Close to the time of Euripides' play the poet Timotheus, who came from Miletus, could describe the goddess in his *Artemis* in terms of ecstasy and destructive madness (θυιάδα φοιβάδα μαινάδα λυσσάδα: Timotheus fr. 2(b) *PMG* in Plutarch, *Mor.* 170a).

[96] For the Brauronion in Athens see Pausanias 1.23.7; Linders 1972, 2 n. 3, 70 n. 22; Osborne 1985, 154–56; R. Parker 1996, 73f.; Hurwit 1999, 197f.

INTRODUCTION   29

grand form every fourth year, like the Panathenaea and other great festivals,[97] and probably included a procession from the city to the coastal sanctuary. The most distinctive feature of the activities at Brauron was the *arkteia*, a pre-marriage rite in which young girls were dedicated to Artemis and acted as 'bears' (*arktoi*) while wearing a saffron-yellow chiton (*krokôtos*).[98] A similar ritual was performed at Artemis's sanctuary at Mounychia in the Piraeus area.[99] Commemorative pottery from these and a few other sanctuaries of Artemis in Attica shows groups of girls, naked or clothed in chitons, some carrying wreaths or branches, some dancing or running towards or away from an altar, while mature women supervise.[100] Fragments of one vase from Brauron show naked girls running away from a bear, and a male and a female figure each with a bear's head or mask.[101] A myth explained that a female bear protected by

---

[97] [Aristot.] *Ath. Pol.* 54.7, Hesychius β 1067 Latte, cf. Hdt. 6.138, Ar. *Lys.* 645; R. Parker 2005, 230–32.

[98] The main literary sources are Schol. Ar. *Lys.* 645, Harpocration α 235 (citing Lysias fr. 303 Carey) and δ 16, Suda α 3958; *ThesCRA* II.119–21 lists sources and iconography. Recent discussions (amongst many): Kahil 1983, 1988; Lloyd-Jones 1983, 91–101; Osborne 1985, 157–72; Brulé 1987, 179–262 and 1990; Sourvinou-Inwood 1988 and 1990; Dowden 1989, 26–42; Kearns 1989, 29–32; Bonnechere 1994, 26–38; Fowler 1995, 9–12; Faraone 2003; R. Parker 2005, 232–48; Calame 2009, 88–92; Nielsen 2009, 78–80; see also n. 102 below. Clement 1934 interpreted a late 2nd C inscription from Pagasae in Thessaly as referring to local girls serving Artemis as fawns and suggested that a similar practice at Aulis might lie behind the legend of Iphigenia's near-sacrifice there (cf. Dowden 1989, 41f., 47; Bonnechere 1994, 45), but the obscure word νεβεύσασα, now attested in a dozen Thessalian inscriptions, is unrelated to νέβροι, 'fawns' (see now Graninger 2007).

[99] Sources for the *arkteia* at Mounychia: Schol. Ar. *Lys.* 645, Harpocration α 235 (see previous note). Site: Palaiokrassa 1991; Chatzivasiliou 2019, 212–15.

[100] For these *kratêriskoi* (small two-handled goblets) and illustrations see especially Kahil 1977, 1983, 1988; Hamilton 1989; Reeder (ed.) 1995, 321–28; R. Parker 2005, 234–37, Nielsen 2009, 81–93. The fewer dedications found at the other sites may have come from girls who had participated at Brauron or Mounychia. Those found at Halai apparently do not have the figured iconography seen elsewhere (below, n. 121). Chatzivasiliou 2019, 205–7 questions whether all the figured scenes are related to the *arkteia*.

[101] Kahil 1977, 1983, 237f., 1988; Reeder (ed.) 1995, 327f. They see a depiction of the myth of Callisto and her son Arkas whom Artemis killed in the form of bears, but a bear-ritual seems more likely (cf. Nielsen 2009, 88). Evidence for sacrifices of bears and dedications of bear images at Greek sanctuaries is collected by Bevan 1987.

30 INTRODUCTION

Artemis had been tamed by the local people but killed by the brother(s) of a girl who had been blinded by the bear when she baited it; Artemis punished the people with a famine which was only relieved when they instituted the *arkteia* to be performed by all their daughters before they could be married.[102] A similar myth at Mounychia told that Artemis demanded the sacrifice of a girl in return for the bear's death, and that Embaros circumvented this by hiding his daughter in the sanctuary and sacrificing a goat dressed as the girl, thereby becoming the first priest of the cult there.[103] The myth of Iphigenia's sacrifice at Aulis, another coastal sanctuary of Artemis, had some similar features: Agamemnon offended Artemis (in one version by killing a sacred deer) and was obliged to offer his marriageable daughter in atonement, but the goddess spared the girl by substituting a deer.[104] A competing Athenian tradition, probably created in the fourth century, placed the sacrifice of Iphigenia at Brauron and made the substituted animal a bear.[105] The *arkteia* seems to have functioned as a rite of passage, the girls living in Artemis's wild realm and meeting a symbolic death before the onset of menstruation, although its original purpose may have been simply to gain the goddess's favour for their lives and future child-bearing.

How and when Iphigenia came to be associated with the cult at Brauron remains uncertain. Euripides' description is our earliest evidence of her cult there or anywhere else. There is no definite archaeological evidence (the identification of her shrine is conjectural, as noted above) and no early evidence of a role for her in the mythology of the *arkteia*. Her connections with other cults of Artemis could have been inspired by Euripides' play.[106] Euripides might, then, have invented her connection

---

[102] Sources for the aetiological myth at Brauron: Schol. Ar. *Lys.* 645, Suda α 3958. 'All their daughters' must in practice have been (or become) a fairly small group representing the Athenian community (Bonnechere 1994, 172f.; R. Parker 2005, 233f.).

[103] For the aetiological myth at Mounychia see Pausanias Att. ε 35 Erbse ≈ Photius ε 692, Suda ε 937 etc.; Brelich 1969, 248f. The relationship between the myths at Mounychia, Brauron and Aulis is discussed by Sale 1975; Dowden 1989, 20–23; Bremmer 2002, 39–42.

[104] See further the Commentary on lines 20–21.

[105] Phanodemus, *FGrH* 325 F 14, cf. Schol. Ar. *Lys.* 645.

[106] The evidence for these comes from Pausanias in the second century AD: a burial site and *herôon* of Iphigenia at Megara, Paus. 1.43.1; a sanctuary of 'Artemis Iphigenia' at Hermione, Paus. 2.35.1; an old image of Iphigenia in the sanctuary of Artemis at Aigeira, Paus. 7.26.5. These and similar cases are

INTRODUCTION 31

with Brauron,[107] but it seems unlikely that he would have invented a substantial feature of a major Athenian cult and more likely that he was providing an aetiology for something that already existed.[108] If so, two ways of explaining a pre-existing cult of Iphigenia at Brauron have been proposed. In all versions of the myth in which she survives her sacrifice, including Euripides' play, Iphigenia eventually becomes a cult-receiving acolyte of Artemis. A figure with her chthonic character (associations with earth, birth and death), a share in an Olympian goddess's sanctuary and rituals and a tomb in the sanctuary where she was supposedly once the goddess's priestess might then belong to the type of the 'faded goddess', a prehistoric deity subordinated to an Olympian one (like Hecatê or the birth goddess Eileithuia),[109] retaining a special function within her cult and redefined in myth as originally human, in this case the legendary girl sacrificed to Artemis for the sake of the great expedition against Troy. Alternatively, recent studies have focused on the sacrifice and near-death of Iphigenia as the myth's defining feature. A number of cult-related myths (including that of Embaros's daughter at Mounychia) involve girls somehow associated with Artemis being transformed into animals such as deer or bears and undergoing death or near-death. These girls (it is argued) can be seen as mythical models for the 'deaths' which symbolized the end of their virginity for those girls who were dedicated to Artemis in rites such as the *arkteia*.[110]

Artemis Tauropolos at Halai. The cult of Artemis Tauropolos at Halai was distinct from the cult at Brauron, although there are some notable

---

surveyed by Brulé 1987, 186–200. Locations of Iphigenia's death and burial further afield are linked with later elaborations of Euripides' story.

[107] For this possibility see especially Ekroth 2003

[108] See the Commentary on lines 1464–67 with notes 40 and 41 there. Despinis (2005) reconstructs the much-discussed 'Götterrelief' found at Brauron in 1958 (Brauron Inv. NE 1180) and dated very near the time of the production of *IT* as showing the foundation of the cult with (in its now missing part) Orestes and Iphigenia bringing the Taurian image to Brauron (rather than Halai as in Euripides). For the relief see also Vikela 2015, 218 with Taf. 53 (**Tr** 2) and pp. 11f., 81f., 175–77.

[109] Or a minor functional figure or 'aspect' of Artemis (or a predecessor): see e.g. Kearns 1989, 32f.

[110] Summary statements of this view: Brulé 1987, 260f.; Dowden 1989, 46f., 1990, 31f., 2011, 489–92; Sourvinou-Inwood 1990, 52f.; Bonnechere 1994, 35–38, 164–80.

32   INTRODUCTION

similarities and Euripides' myth suggests a connection between them.[111] The sanctuary was beside the saltwater lagoon at Halai Araphenides (modern Loutsa), between Araphen and Brauron. Its central feature was a small temple built probably in the fifth century.[112] The worship of Artemis Tauropolos, which Euripides connects quite artificially with the Taurians,[113] was in fact widespread especially in Asia Minor.[114] The title 'bull-minder' associates her with the powerful figure of the bull (*tauros*),[115] with imposing and curing madness[116] and probably with male sexuality and the protection and testing of young men classified as 'bulls' as they approached the status of mature hunters and warriors.[117] Athena's instruction that the festival at Halai should include the ritual drawing of blood from a male victim's throat in compensation for the unfulfilled sacrifice of Orestes probably provided an origin (*aition*) for a real ritual in which young men underwent an initiatory mock death comparable with that of the girl-'bears' at Brauron.[118] Our other main evidence for the rituals at the Tauropolia, however, strikes a different note.[119] The plot of Menander's comedy *Epitrepontes* (*Arbitration-Seekers*, c. 300 BC) stems from the rape of a girl by a drunken youth during the festival's all-night revels, and surviving fragments of the play describe finely dressed girls dancing and playing together accompanied by musicians.[120] Halai, moreover, is one of the sanctuaries where *kratêriskoi* similar to those

---

[111] Strabo 9.1.22 locates and distinguishes the two. Cult and similarities with Brauron: Bonnechere 1994, 48–52; Bathrellou 2012, 160–66.

[112] Site and excavations: see Commentary on lines 1453–57.

[113] Commentary on lines 1453–57.

[114] Cults of Artemis Tauropolos: Lo Monaco 2018, 529–58, 622–36; cf. Graf 1979 and 1985, 413; Guldager Bilde 2003, 167–69. For Artemis's associations with Asia Minor see Burkert 1985, 149.

[115] Bull-associations and iconography: *LIMC* II, 'Artemis' nos 700–5, Lo Monaco 2018, 532–34, 538–44.

[116] Cf. S. *Ajax* 172 and other evidence adduced by Lloyd-Jones 1983, 96f.

[117] Brelich 1969, 245f.; Graf 1979; Lloyd-Jones 1983, 97, 98–101.

[118] See *IT* 1458–61 with Commentary.

[119] For the meagre evidence for the festival see R. Parker 2005, 241f. (with n. 101), 481; Bathrellou 2012, 166–70; Furley 2013, 174f. Hesychius τ 251, 'Ταυροπόλια' is uninformative.

[120] Menander, *Epitrepontes* 445–520, cf. 863, 1118–20; for the girls' 'playing' see line 478.

INTRODUCTION 33

from Brauron and Mounychia have been found.[121] Thus girls and their rites seem strongly represented at Halai, just as boys are strongly represented in the dedications to Artemis at Brauron. Either the Artemis of both places was always concerned with both sexes, or the characters of the two sanctuaries became assimilated in the classical period.[122] The cult statue of Artemis at Brauron could at least in later times be identified with the Taurian image which Orestes brought.[123]

The elements of violence and death in the myths and rituals of Artemis are present in the story of Iphigenia, who was herself a victim of the goddess, supervises human sacrifices to her amongst the Taurians, rescues her brother from a sacrificial death, and must help to 'tame' the Taurian goddess by bringing her to Greece. This story, moreover, reflects the pattern of the cult myths in which an angered goddess demands the death of a girl approaching marriage (Iphigenia herself is a mock bride) but commutes her death into animal sacrifice and commemorative ritual. In her suspended maidenhood Iphigenia first faces an aberrant human sacrifice in a long-ago Greek realm, then lives in a faraway barbarian realm where such sacrifices are normal, and finally returns to become associated with a Greek realm which recognizes human sacrifice only in symbols and where Artemis presides over an orderly construction of female lives. Iphigenia's association with Artemis is both the source of her hardships and the basis of her salvation, as she herself recognizes at the point in the play when this salvation begins to take shape.[124]

---

[121] Bathrellou however reports that the *kratêriskoi* found at Halai have patterned decorations like those from Brauron and elsewhere but not the figured iconography usually associated with the *arkteia* (Bathrellou 2012, 163f.).

[122] Identification of the Brauronian goddess with Artemis Tauropolos is unlikely (see e.g. Dowden 1989, 26 with n. 31). Lloyd-Jones 1983, 97 thought of parallel cults originally concerned with males (Halai) and females (Brauron). Their common features are noted by Brelich 1969, 246; Bonnechere 1994, 49f.; Furley 2013, 175; Lo Monaco 2018, 497f.

[123] For this identification in the 5th century see Despinis (above, n. 108); Lo Monaco 2018, 498–501, 506. Pausanias 3.16.7–11 (cf. 1.33.1) names other places which in his day claimed to possess the original image, including the sanctuary of Artemis Orthia at Sparta which was also a centre for male initiation rituals. For the locations see Graf 1979; Guldager Bilde 2003, 166f. with map; Hall 2013, 135–50; Lo Monaco 506–28, 597–616. The Lydian sanctuary of Artemis Anaitis mentioned by Pausanias 3.16.8 was in or near Philadelphia (Burrell 2005).

[124] See especially *IT* 782–87, 1082–88, 1230–33, 1398–1402.

34 INTRODUCTION

Orestes' mythical career follows a similar path. Persecuted by the Erinyes he suffers madness and wandering, faces death amongst the Taurians, escapes through flight, and is finally restored to normality. The symbolic nature of these experiences is advertised in the play when he recounts the aetiology of the Choes ritual,[125] and in its occasional hints that his troubles and fears, real as they are for him, will be overcome with the support of his divine patron Apollo.[126] Orestes, then, could be seen as a precursor of the young men who passed through a symbolic death in the cult at Halai, as Iphigenia was for the girls at Brauron.[127]

THEATRE AND DRAMATIC SETTING[128]

In the original production three actors shared the play's seven speaking roles, accompanied by a chorus of fifteen and numerous extras. The leading actor who played the long and difficult part of Iphigenia with its sung passages (143–77, 203–35, 827–99) almost certainly took the role of Athena as well, thus announcing the conclusion of Iphigenia's story. The second and third actors probably played either *(a)* Orestes/Thoas and Pylades/Herdsman/Pylades/Messenger or *(b)* Orestes/Herdsman/Orestes/ Messenger and Pylades/Thoas. The second scheme would be more burdensome for the second actor, but either way it will have been the same actor who delivered the two closely matched report speeches. Extras in the earlier scenes include some male temple servants, who assist in Iphigenia's libation ceremony and probably remain until dismissed to help prepare the sacrifice of Orestes, and the herdsmen who bring Orestes and Pylades from Thoas to Iphigenia.[129] More Taurians accompany Thoas when he comes to the temple (1153), some of whom will escort the procession to the shore (1205, 1208) while one goes to alert the city (1211) and the rest stay with Thoas and react with him to the Messenger's

---

[125] See further the Commentary on *IT* 947–60.

[126] *IT* 67–122 n., 104f., 114–22, 328–29 n., 711–24 with 723–24 n.

[127] This is not to say that Euripides' plot was determined by a pattern of ritual initiation, as argued by Tzanetou 1999–2000 (criticized by Kyriakou 27f.; Wright 2005, 356; Amiech 330f.), but rather that the symbolic perils and survival of those undergoing the rites of passage at Brauron and Halai could be seen as anticipated in the mythical experiences of Iphigenia and Orestes.

[128] See also Kyriakou 37–39, Ketterer 2013.

[129] See stage directions with Commentary at lines 143, 167f., 456ff., 642 (638 n.), 725f.

INTRODUCTION   35

report (1422–34). Temple servants are also part of the procession, carrying the adornments of Artemis's image, sacrificial lambs, torches and other ritual equipment (1223–25; extras would have played the veiled Orestes and Pylades at this point). Thus Taurians are present (either speaking or mute) for most of the play and absent only when the Hellenes must be allowed privacy, namely in the two opening scenes (1–142), the recognition and planning (727–1088) and the two choral songs which follow the planning and deception scenes (1089–1152, 1234–83).

Despite its remote barbarian setting, the play seems to envisage the temple of Artemis as a Greek one in Doric style with stout walls, imposing doors, ornamented façade and surrounding columns.[130] In its first production in the Theatre of Dionysus the façade of the Taurian temple was probably represented by a painted backdrop covering the front of the stage building (*skênê*) while the building's central door served as the door of the temple. In front of this, probably off-centre near the rear edge of the orchestra, stood the sacrificial altar which Orestes and Pylades notice as they approach (72f.), a permanent symbol of the character of the Taurian sanctuary.[131] The temple's interior is unseen but dramatically relevant, as the interior of the stage building often is in Greek tragedies. It is Iphigenia's home[132] and houses both the image of Artemis which is the object of Orestes' quest and the altar on which his body is to be burned (626). It is thus a source of destruction and salvation, reflecting the dual character of Artemis herself. Orestes and Pylades approach as temple robbers (110–12), reach it as sacrificial victims, and finally enter it under the protection of Iphigenia and Artemis. What comes out of the temple is more important in the end: first the letter mediating the reunion of brother and sister, then the image of the goddess herself with her priestess and the veiled captives abandoning the place of human sacrifice. Up to that point Iphigenia herself as priestess and keeper

---

[130] For the physical features of the temple see especially 74f., 96–101, 113f., 128f., 405f. with Commentary on these passages and the discussions of Miller 1929–32, I.105–17; Bacon 1961, 132–37.

[131] Given its function and size, it is not likely to have been very close to the temple front or the *skênê* door. On the other hand, it need not have been placed at the centre of the orchestra since it was not a focus for any dramatic action, unlike the altars in suppliant plays and other sites of ritual action where the central position was important (cf. Rehm 1988; Poe 1989, 116–30; Wiles 1997, 66–86).

[132] See Commentary on 65–66.

36INTRODUCTION

of the temple-keys has controlled all access.[133] As she prepares to leave it she sends Thoas inside to cleanse a temple now deprived of the goddess's presence (1215f.).

The action of the play, though basically simple, is subtly dramatic, especially in the gradual bringing together of Iphigenia and Orestes which culminates in their mutual embrace (827–41) and in the contrasting movements of arrival and departure noticed above. A wealth of unseen action is evoked by the songs and movements of the Chorus and by the narrative speeches of the Herdsman, Orestes and the Messenger. Ritual actions are a particular leitmotif. Iphigenia re-lives her own sacrifice in three different keys (24–29, 359–77, 853–64), dreams of sacrificing Orestes (50–58) and gives him a preview of the ritual which awaits him (617–26), while as a counterpoint the sacrifice of Helen is imagined by Iphigenia (357f.) and danced by the Chorus (439–46). The procession and libations for the 'dead' Orestes (123–202) are balanced by the saving procession to the shore for his purification and restoration to life (1222–33).[134] A meticulous oath exchange between Iphigenia and Pylades leads to the recognition (743–52), and formal prayers from Iphigenia to Artemis close the scenes of planning and departure from the temple (1082–88, 1230–33). Dancing, religious celebration and sacred narrative dominate the second and third choral songs.

As we have noticed already, the remote and barren Taurian environment is continually evoked by the play's poetry and contrasted with the comforts of Hellas.[135] The temple overlooks the sea (1196), and one of the theatre's two side-entrances is used for access to and from the Taurians' settlement (including Thoas's dwelling) and beyond that the shore where at some distance Orestes and Pylades have moored their ship, are captured by the herdsmen and make their escape at the end.[136]

---

[133] See Commentary on 130–32.

[134] The veiling of Orestes and Pylades and the projected cleansing at the sea-shore (cf. Commentary on 1039) are motivated by the need for purification but also suggest an initiation ritual bringing the initiands through mock-death (which all three principals have faced) to a purer, more enlightened life. Cf. Burnett, 1971, 63 and p. 33 with n. 127 above.

[135] Above, pp. 25f.

[136] This is Side-entrance B in my translation. It must lead both to and from the shore (67, 122, 1233, 1284) and to and from the Taurians' settlement and Thoas's house (236, 343, 456, 1153) since *(a)* at 236 the Chorus guesses that the Herdsman is coming from the shore when in fact he has come *via* Thoas's house, and *(b)* at 1209–12 the procession is to go through the settlement on its way to the

INTRODUCTION 37

The shore and the world beyond are carefully shaped in words for the audience's imagination. The shore is not only the place of the Hellenes' arrival, capture and escape but a marginal zone where the power of Artemis is strongly felt (as in the coastal areas where her sanctuaries such as Aulis, Halai, Brauron and Mounychia were sited) and supernatural powers operate rather freely – the Erinyes maddening Orestes, divine protection of Orestes and Pylades from the Taurians' missiles (328f.), the final assaults of wind and wave. Beyond the shore and repeatedly evoked are the Black or 'Unwelcoming' Sea (*Axeinos Pontos*) and the Clashing Rocks (*Symplêgades*), which cut off the Taurians from civilization and make their land inaccessible.[137] The First Stasimon evokes the thrill and challenge of the sea journey, while the second contrasts the ship's expected safe return under divine protection with the miseries of the Chorus's own voyage into slavery. Dreams and memories of life in distant Hellas sustain the Chorus and Iphigenia in their hopes for release.[138] For these humans, impassable paths by land are the only alternative to the treacherous sea (884–91), and winged escape is something the Chorus can only imagine (1138–42). For gods, on the other hand, the sky is an open domain and in this play a channel of divine influence on human events: the image of Artemis fell to the Taurians from heaven (88), Iphigenia was transported by Artemis 'through the radiant sky' (29f.), and Athena flies in to impose the final resolution before departing in the same way.

THE CHORUS IN THE DRAMA

As in most of the extant plays of Euripides, the Chorus is not central to the play's action and serves mainly to witness and react to events in sympathy with its leading character. Sung parts are limited to the Parodos (shared with Iphigenia), three odes and a brief lament for the fates of Orestes and Pylades (643–56) which stands in place of an ode punctuating the long dramatic sequence which culminates in the reunion and

---

shore. Side-entrance A gives access from the temple precincts and is used only for the entrance of the Chorus (123) and probably for its final exit after bidding farewell to Iphigenia and her companions.

[137] See the Commentary on lines 124–25, 393–97. On the connotations of the Black Sea and the Taurian shore: Buxton 1992; Said 2002, 51–54; Wright 2005, 202–25; Hall 2013, 47–68; Kowalzig 2013, 186–90.

[138] Cf. 44f., 133–36, 221–24, 447–55, 1089–1105, 1138–52.

38   INTRODUCTION

planning of the escape.[139] The Chorus notably does not contribute to the reunion celebration (827–99). Iphigenia introduces it as a group of enslaved Greek women assigned to her as temple-servants by king Thoas (63f.). Further details are sketched in the Parodos, the first and second choral odes and a few other brief interventions. They are young unmarried women from notable families, sold into slavery after the capture of their city and transported to the Taurian land. Their situation is thus parallel to Iphigenia's and they identify with her in several ways: longing for their lost home and the normal lives of well-born young women, resentment at their service in a barbarous cult requiring human sacrifices, sympathy with the afflictions of Iphigenia's family, hatred of Helen for provoking the Trojan War and Iphigenia's sacrifice, amazement at the revelation of Orestes' identity and the reunion of brother and sister.[140] Their loyalty to Iphigenia leads naturally to their collaboration with her escape plan, and they risk punishment by Thoas until Athena rewards their loyalty by ordering their return to Greece.[141] Athena may or may not have added something about their future lives,[142] but if she did it will have been brief and unspecific. The play is purposefully vague about the location of the women's home city and the details of its capture. What matters is the women's separation from and final return to the life, culture and rituals of the Hellenic world as a whole.

While the Chorus is mostly a witness of the play's events, it was nonetheless central to its conception and performance in the Athenian theatre. Tragedy was fundamentally a choral genre, and its choruses share to some extent the functions of non-dramatic choruses which addressed their audiences directly, contextualizing the play's narrative and

---

[139] Elsewhere the Chorus announces the captives' arrival in recited anapaests (456–66) and closes the play with an anapaestic response to Athena's settlement (1490–96). It or its leader speaks in iambics when introducing the Herdsman (236f.), reacting to his report, the news from Argos, the reunion, Orestes' explanation of his mission and the report from the shore (340f., 576f., 900f., 987f., 1420f.) and contributing to the escape plot (1075–77, 1156, 1288–1301).

[140] Nostalgia etc., lines 132–36, 447–55, 576f., 647–49 and much of the Second Stasimon. Resentment at service in the Taurian cult, 463–66, 1113–16. Sympathy for Iphigenia and her family, 186–202, 987f. Hatred of Helen, 439–46. Reaction to the reunion, 900f.

[141] Collaboration, lines 1056–78, 1284–1301. Thoas's threat, 1431–34. Athena's resolution, 1467–69, 1482f.

[142] The text at this point is probably defective: see Commentary on lines 1467–71.

INTRODUCTION 39

prompting its audience's reactions.[143] Once established in the orchestra, a tragic chorus was usually present throughout the play. It remained in character so long as it was engaged with the dramatic action but could transcend this identity in the odes which it sang (and danced) in elevated poetic language at major pauses in the action, with actors absent or at least inactive.[144] In the First Stasimon of *Iphigenia* the Chorus speculates about the reasons for the Greek captives' voyage to the remote land of the Taurians, imagines their passage and ends by wishing that a ship could have brought Helen to be sacrificed or someone who might rescue themselves. All of this responds to the dramatic situation, but the song's allusions to the myths of Io and Achilles, a gnomic reflection on the dangers of wealth-seeking and an exuberant lyrical description of the voyage are not particularly in character for this group of enslaved women and additionally serve the poet's purpose of reinforcing the themes and mood of the play's opening scenes and the characterization of Iphigenia. The Second Stasimon balances the first as the women sing of their nostalgia for the joyous rituals of their girlhood and compare the divinely escorted voyage home which Iphigenia can now expect with their own continued endurance of exile amongst the Taurians. Again this responds to the dramatic situation but goes beyond it thematically as the women focus on the beauties of Delos (the religious centre of the Athenian empire) and the ship's arrival with Iphigenia and the Taurian image in 'the Athenians' bright land' (1130f.), and then re-enact the joyous dancing of their youth which typifies the orderly communal life of Greece. Lastly, the Third Stasimon, sung as the escape begins, is an elaborate, formally independent hymnic narrative telling how Apollo gained control of Delphi and of human access to divine truths through his oracle there. Here the Chorus becomes (as in real, non-dramatic hymns) the voice of the poet's wisdom and mythical knowledge, playing on the theme of divine truth and affirming the dominance of the Olympian god which will ultimately ensure Iphigenia's return to Hellas, the settlement of Artemis in Attica and Orestes' release from the Erinyes.

---

[143] On tragic choruses in general see Gagné–Hopman 2013, 18–28 with the relevant essays in that volume, Calame 2017; on Euripidean choruses Mastronarde 2010, 88–152, and for aspects of the chorus in *Iphigenia* Swift 2010, 205–18, Kowalzig 2013 (esp. 198–210), Taddei 2015, Torrance 2019, 47–55.

[144] Iphigenia was probably present but inactive during the First Stasimon (see note on lines 386–91). For the others the Chorus is alone.

40   INTRODUCTION

DATE AND CONTEMPORARY PLAYS[145]

There is no direct evidence for the production date of *Iphigenia*, but technical considerations make it likely that it was produced in 414 or 413. First, it includes some trochaic tetrameters (lines 1203–33), a metre which Euripides used regularly in the last dozen years of his life but not, apparently, earlier; those in *Heracles*, *Trojan Women* (415), *Iphigenia* and *Helen* (412) are climactic and relatively brief, whereas those in the latest plays are used more diversely and are more elaborate.[146] Secondly, in his later career Euripides used resolution in the long positions of iambic trimeters (the standard metre of tragic dialogue and speeches) with increasing freedom and variety; statistical analysis of this trend suggests a fairly confident dating of each of the extant plays to within about five years and favours the following order for the plays between *Hippolytus* (428) and *Orestes* (408): *Andromache* 425–421, *Suppliant Women* 424–420, *Hecuba* 423–418, *Electra* 422–417, *Heracles* 421–416, *Trojan Women* 419–413 (actually 415), *Ion* 418–413, *Iphigenia in Tauris* 417–412, *Helen* 413–408 (actually 412), *Phoenician Women* 414–408 (actually 409±2).[147] An equally important guide is the increasing variety of rhythmic effects which Euripides introduced by using new word-shapes and word-breaks involving resolution in the trimeter. This qualitative criterion largely confirms the quantitative analysis, putting *Iphigenia* later than *Electra*, *Heracles* and *Trojan Women*, very close to *Ion*, and earlier than *Helen* and *Phoenician Women*.[148] Lastly, Euripides' use of so-called 'choriambic dimeters' (aeolic cola with choriambic ending) seems less developed in *Iphigenia* than in *Helen*.[149] These two plays are very similar in their myths and dramatic design. Each has a Greek princess vanishing at the start of the Trojan War, stranded among barbarians, reunited with her long-lost brother (Orestes) or husband (Menelaus), and escaping with him back to Greece. Each proceeds from

---

[145] See also Kyriakou 39–41 and in more detail Parker lxxvi–lxxx.

[146] See Commentary on lines 1203–33.

[147] See Cropp–Fick 1985, 5–8, 23 (Table 3.5).

[148] Dale 1967, xxiv–xxviii explains the findings of Zielinski 1925, 133–240 and discusses some key indicators. Full data in Cropp–Fick 1985, 60–63 and preceding lists. Marshall (2009, 141–45) argues that the metrical evidence allows a date as early as 419, but the qualitative criteria in particular tell against this (cf. Parker lxxix–lxxx).

[149] Itsumi 1982, 63, 69; cf. Parker lxxix, xciii ('polyschematists').

INTRODUCTION   41

the heroine's despair (believing brother/husband dead) through a confrontation based on this misconception to recognition, escape planning,
deception of the barbarian king and escape with a final complication
resolved by an intervening god.[150] There are many textual similarities,
especially in the scenes where the escape plans are designed, executed
and reported. Few scholars have been prepared to place two so similar
plays in the same year,[151] and most have inferred that the flamboyant,
fanciful, less smoothly constructed and less tragic *Helen* exploits a
dramatic pattern already established in *Iphigenia*.[152] Those disagreeing[153]
have been influenced to some extent by the assumption that *Electra*,
which preceded *Iphigenia*,[154] was produced in 413, but that assumption is
now widely discredited.[155]

Elements of *Iphigenia* may be reflected in the final scene of
Aristophanes' *Thesmophoriazusae* (usually dated 411, otherwise 410), in
which Euripides rescues his kinsman from captivity amongst the women
celebrating the Thesmophoria (*Thesm.* 1160–1226). Euripides has got the
kinsman into trouble by sending him to act the part of Telephus (hero of
his *Telephus*, 438 BC) and defend Euripides' reputation against the
women's criticisms. He has twice tried without success to rescue him by
enacting scenes from his own plays, first as Menelaus rescuing Helen
(*Helen*, 412), then as Perseus rescuing Andromeda (*Andromeda*, also
412). In the briefer closing scene he becomes an old woman named
Artemisia (~ Artemis?) and rescues his kinsman (~ Iphigenia?) by
seducing his Scythian guard (~ Thoas?) with the offer of a few moments
of bliss with a young prostitute named Elaphion ('Fawn', alluding to the
deer substituted at Aulis?). These comparisons can perhaps be extended.
In *Thesm.* 1160–72 Euripides appeals to a responsive Chorus, like

---

[150] Systematic comparisons were made by Ludwig 1954, Matthiessen 1964, 16–
62, 127–37, both concluding that *Helen* is the later play.

[151] e.g. Hose 1995, 14–17, 190–97. Wright (2005, 44–55) argues that *Iphigenia*
was produced with *Helen* and *Andromeda* in 412 to make a trilogy focused on the
theme of escape, perhaps with *Cyclops* as the satyr-play.

[152] See e.g. Bruhn 11ff., Grégoire 100–106; also Ludwig and Matthiessen
(n. 150).

[153] e.g. Zielinski 1925, 308–13, Perrotta 1928 and others listed by Lesky 1983,
410 n. 214.

[154] This assumption is plausible even without the metrical evidence since *Electra*
treats the trial of Orestes at Athens as final (*El.* 1250–75, 1288–91).

[155] For details see Cropp 2013, 31f.

42INTRODUCTION

Iphigenia in *IT* 1056–77; in *Thesm.* 1171 he needs to fool the Scythian, as Iphigenia needs to persuade Thoas in *IT* 1049; and in *Thesm.* 1217–26 the Chorus misdirects the Scythian's pursuit, rather as the Chorus tries to mislead the Messenger in *IT* 1293–1301. Taken together, these comparisons suggest that Aristophanes might have been alluding specifically to Euripides' scene.[156]

THE PLAY IN ANTIQUITY AND BEYOND[157]

The only traces of the impact of *Iphigenia*'s first production are Aristophanes' parodies of lines 1–2 in *Frogs* and 32–33 in the lost *Women of Lemnos*, and perhaps of the escape scene in *Thesmophoriazusae*,[158] but its early popularity is evident in fourth-century vase-paintings (see below), and Aristotle's repeated uses of it as an example in his discussions of plot structure confirm that it was both well known and highly regarded.[159] This play rather than *Iphigenia at Aulis* is probably the *Iphigenia* of Euripides chosen for reperformance at the Great Dionysia of 341 BC with the renowned actor Neoptolemos in the title role,[160] and it was probably performed widely around the Greek world, though direct evidence is lacking. No other Greek tragedy on this theme is known,[161] but there was at least one burlesque version, by Rhinthon in

---

[156] Bobrick 1991 makes the case for connecting the relevant characters with those of *Iphigenia*; see also Wright 2005, 50–52. Kyriakou 41–43 disputes it. On the relevance of Euripides' escape plots to Aristophanes' presentation of the Scythian in *Thesm.* see Hall 1989a (she compares the roles of the two choruses in misleading the barbarians, 52 n. 71).

[157] Hall 2013 is an extensive and lively study of the play's rich and diverse reception down to recent times. For the period to 1800 see also Gliksohn 1985. Briefer surveys: Mills 2015; Parker xl–lx; Torrance 2019, 99–121 and for antiquity Kyriakou 41–47. For further detail see the notes to this section.

[158] See the Commentary on lines 1–5 and 32–33, and above, pp. 41f.

[159] *Poetics*, chapters 14, 16, 17; cf. notes 3 and 4 above.

[160] *IG* II² 2320, col. II.1–4, from the Didascaliae inscription listing productions at the Dionysia (*TrGF* I, pp. 13, 25f., Millis–Olson 2012, 65–67. The title role of this play is much more attractive for a star actor than any of the major roles in *Iphigenia at Aulis*.

[161] 'Polyidus the sophist', mentioned by Aristotle as having improved on the Euripides' recognition by having Orestes compare his own sacrifice with Iphigenia's (*Poetics* 1455a6–8, b9–12), is included in *TrGF* I as no. 78 but was either the well-known dithyrambist Polyidus of Selymbria or an otherwise unknown critic. Hall 2013, 71–76 assumes that Aristotle was referring to a

INTRODUCTION   43

the third century,[162] and the Latin tragedy *Iphigenia* of Cn. Naevius (late 3rd C BC), of which one line survives, may have been based on Euripides' Taurian play (there is no real evidence for a tragedy of Pacuvius on this subject).[163] The probably much later 'Charition mime', of which 149 lines survive more or less complete on papyrus, is a crude parody in which Charition, serving as a priestess somewhere beyond the Indian Ocean, is rescued by her brother and his shipmates who get her gobbledygook-speaking captors drunk.[164] Tragic plots providing sequels to Iphigenia and extending the adventures and tribulations of Orestes and his sister still further are known to us through the Latin myth-handbook of Hyginus and the fragments of Latin tragedies which probably had Greek originals.[165] Other elaborations of the myth proliferated as Greek cities around the Hellenistic and later Greek world connected cults and place-names with the wanderings of Orestes and Iphigenia.[166]

---

tragedy, but see now Carrara 2020. Nothing but the title is known of an *Orestes and Pylades* by Timesitheos (*TrGF* I no. 214, Suda τ 613).

[162] Rhinthon fr. 6 *PCG*.

[163] For Naevius Maltby–Slater 2022, 274–77. The scene of Pacuvius which Cicero admires in *Fin.* 2.79, 5.63 and *Amic.* 7.24, in which Orestes rejected Pylades' attempt to save him from death by identifying himself as Orestes, is best assigned to his *Chryses* (see n. 165 below). Hall assumes that it came from an adaptation of *IT* (Hall 2013, 93–101, 299; cf. Torrance 2019, 109f.), and the same assumption underlies the frequent introduction of the identity contest into 17th/18th C adaptations of *IT* (explicitly, for example, in John Dennis's preface to his *Iphigenia* of 1699). In the Taurian context Thoas expects to see both captives sacrificed and has no reason to worry about their identity. Hall also assumes that the play in question was Pacuvius's *Orestes*, but the evidence for such a play is minimal (see Schierl 2006, 6) and those who accept it usually make it an adaptation of Aeschylus's *Eumenides* or Euripides' *Orestes* (D'Anna's case for *Eumenides* is elaborated by Degiovanni 2011).

[164] P. Oxy. 413. Text and translation in Rusten–Cunningham 2002, 357f., 376–89. Full discussion in Hall 2013, 116–34.

[165] Hyginus, *Fab.* 121 seems to summarize the original of Pacuvius's *Chryses* (See Schierl 2006, 192–239; Cropp 2021, 399–403 with n. 66 above on the suggestion that this was Sophocles' *Chryses*). Hyginus, *Fab.* 122 (n. 4 above) may perhaps be linked similarly with Accius's almost wholly lost *Children of Agamemnon* (see Dangel 2002, 169, 325; Cropp 2021, 404–6).

[166] See the references in note 123 above.

44   INTRODUCTION

Reflections of Euripides' play in Hellenistic poetry are sparse and idiosyncratic.[167] The earliest extant author after Aristotle who gives us any sense of its dramatic and emotional appeal is Ovid, who used Euripides' story in *Tristia* 4.4.63–88 and at greater length in *Ex Ponto* 3.2.39–96. In both poems the exiled Ovid appeals for loyal assistance from his friends by recalling the exemplary mutual loyalty of Orestes and Pylades which brought them safety and restoration.[168] Both passages concentrate on the play's plot up to the joyous moment of the recognition with emphasis on the pathos of the impending sacrifice, and both evoke visual details from Euripides' scenes such as the temple of Artemis, the bloodstained altar before its double doors, the binding of the captives' hands behind their backs, the letter and the embrace sealing the recognition.[169] Friendship is also the theme of Lucian's dialogue *Toxaris* (2nd C AD), in which the Scythian Toxaris explains that the mutual loyalty of Orestes and Pylades has earned them hero worship in Scythia.[170] This and other elements of the play are recalled diffusely and indirectly in prose literature of the Roman period, especially the romantic narratives of Greek novels.[171]

A rich visual tradition also depicts dramatic and emotional highlights of the play, with broad artistic licence.[172] Fourteen vase-paintings from the fourth century BC (one Attic, the rest South Italian) share Aristotle's interest in the recognition sequence, showing the captives' arrival before Iphigenia, Iphigenia describing the sacrificial ritual to the condemned Orestes, or in eight examples her handing the letter to Pylades.[173] Several

---

[167] Euphorion fr. 91 Powell/85 Lightfoot (see footnote to 1464–67 n.); Lycophron, *Alexandra* 183–201, 323–26; Nicander in Antoninus Liberalis 27. Sansone 2000 observes reflections of Euripides' plot and narrative details in Apollonius's *Argonautica*.

[168] Ovid's admiring narrator in *Ex Pont.* 3.2. is a Taurian. On this theme in Ovid, and others see Hall 2013, 100–110. Fantham 1992 and Ingleheart 2010 examine Ovid's use of Euripides' text in detail.

[169] *Trist.* 4.4.63f., 72f. (altar), 79f. (embrace), *Ex Pont.* 3.2.49–54 (temple and altar), 72 (hands bound behind backs), 89–92 (letter).

[170] *Toxaris* 1–8; cf. Hall 2013, 106f., 114–16.

[171] Hall 2013, 113f.

[172] See above all *LIMC* V, 'Iphigeneia' with *LIMC Supp.*, 'Iphigeneia'.

[173] Vases, *LIMC* nos 14, 15, 19–29, *LIMC Supp.* add. 1; Cambitoglou 1975; Taplin 2007, 149–56; Jucker 1998, 107–14, 124–28; Hall 2013, 72–91 and 2019, 306–11.

INTRODUCTION 45

elaborate wall-paintings from Pompeii and Herculaneum and a sadly damaged example from one of the terrace houses at Ephesus (2nd C AD) focus on the arrival of the captives or their departure for the seashore with Iphigenia bringing the image out of the temple.[174] These and other scenes – Orestes' madness, his farewell to Pylades, the recognition, the battle at the shore with the fugitives' embarkation – are seen on some twenty sarcophagi and other relief sculptures, including frieze sarcophagi showing three or four separate scenes, most often the captives' arrival, the recognition and the battle and embarkation.[175] Visual and literary traditions merge in poetic and rhetorical descriptions of works of art (*ecphrases*) such as an epigram describing Iphigenia's reaction on first seeing the captives:

> *Iphigenia rages, but the sight of Orestes*
> *restores her to sweet recollection of their kinship.*
> *She nurses her resentment, and beholds her brother;*
> *pity and rage together sway her gaze.*[176]

The elder Pliny mentions a famous painting by Timomachus of Byzantium which may be the art-work described here and may also be reflected in one of the most impressive (though now incomplete) Pompeii wall-paintings.[177] Lucian's *Toxaris* features an imaginary series of wall-

---

[174] Wall-paintings, *LIMC* nos 52, 53, 58–64; Jucker 1998, 117–21, 132–35; Hall 2013, 95–100 and 2019, 316–18.

[175] Sarcophagi and other reliefs, *LIMC* nos 26, 54, 56, 57, 67–84; Jucker 1998, 114–17, 128–32; Bielfeldt 2005; Bonanno Aravantinos 2008, 80–85, 90–109 (with photos and additions to *LIMC*); Hall 2013, 150–57 and 2019, 321–25; on frieze sarcophagi in general, Newby 2011. Bielfeldt studies the featuring of Roman virtues (*virtus, pietas, amicitia*) in the presentation of scenes from Euripides' story on Roman sarcophagi. A bronze crater from ancient Dionysopolis (now Balčik near Varna in Bulgaria, *LIMC* no. 85) is decorated similarly, though in one scene Pylades surprisingly writes down Iphigenia's message as she dictates it to him.

[176] *Anth.Plan.* 128. The words μαίνεται ('rages') and μανία ('rage') do not imply that she is possessed by Dionysiac madness as Hall 2013, 97 assumes. They can denote any kind of intense passion, here her resentment of those responsible for her sacrifice which hardens her heart against Orestes and Pylades when she hears of their capture but is relaxed as soon as she sees them (*IT* 342–60, 472–81). The epigram thus reflects the Euripidean scene closely, though with some exaggeration of Iphigenia's state of mind. On other ecphrastic treatments of tragic scenes see Hall 114–16.

[177] Timomachus: Pliny, *NH* 35.49. Pliny makes him a contemporary of Julius Caesar, but an earlier Hellenistic date is possible. On this and the possible

46   INTRODUCTION

paintings in a corridor of the Scythian temple dedicated to Orestes and Pylades: on one side the voyage, shipwreck, capture and preparation for sacrifice, and opposite these the battle at the shore and the victorious heroes sailing away with Iphigenia and the divine image.

The text of *Iphigenia in Tauris* was almost lost in late antiquity and ultimately survived only in the manuscript copied for Demetrius Triclinius at Thessaloniki in the early fourteenth century (below, p. 50). Medieval Latin literature generally focused on the sacrifice at Aulis, with little attention to the Taurian episode except in allusions to Pylades' attempt to be identified as Orestes, which was not directly derived from Euripides' play.[178] The first printed edition of Euripides' plays, the Aldine of 1503, prompted rather limited interest,[179] but the play's exotic elements made it a rich source for imitation and adaptation in the period between 1670 and 1800, which produced more than a dozen plays and twice that number of operas under various titles.[180] These works typically used the basics of Euripides' plot but manipulated and elaborated it freely, especially in the first half of this period when a profusion of scenarios and incidents added romantic and/or political dimensions.[181]

---

reflection in the Pompeii wall-painting see Gutzwiller 2004, 344, 355. The wall-painting (*LIMC* no. 52: Naples, National Archaeological Museum no. 111439) is shown in part on the cover of this book..

[178] See note 163 above. One such allusion is Dante's in *Purgatorio* 13.31f. On the medieval period in general see Gliksohn 1985, 56–59; Hall 2013, 158f.; Parker xlvii–xlviii.

[179] Notably an Italian translation by Alessandro Pazzi de' Medici (1524: Parker xlviii) and a much elaborated version with the title *Oreste* by Giovanni Ruccellai (1520s: Hall 2013, 161–66; Mills 2015, 262; Parker xlix–l).

[180] Reid 1993, I.605–7 provides a fairly full list; a few more operas in Rossi 2007, 26–28. Surveys in Hall 2013, 175–201; Mills 2015, 262–67; Parker l–lix; Torrance 2019, 101–7, 111–14, 119f. Studies: Heitner 1964; Gliksohn 1985, 153–221. On the Greek tragic tradition in opera, Napolitano 2012.

[181] One example: in Lagrange-Chancel's *Oreste et Pilade, ou Iphigénie en Tauride* (1697) Thoas is a usurper who has planned to marry the rightful heiress Thomiris but now loves the priestess Iphigenia and tries to marry off Thomiris to a neighbouring ruler. Oracles have warned him that he will be killed by a Greek named Orestes, and when Orestes and Pylades are captured he fears that one of them is Orestes. Orestes conceals his identity but, resolved to die for his crime, tells Iphigenia that he is Clytemnestra's killer, thus compelling Pylades to identify him so as to prevent Iphigenia from avenging her mother by killing her brother. After the reunion Thomiris assists their flight, disguising Iphigenia as herself and helping Orestes and Pylades to carry off the image of the goddess. The play ends

INTRODUCTION 47

A classicizing reaction is best represented by the two works which have had lasting influence, Gluck's *Iphigénie en Tauride* (first performed in Paris in May 1779)[182] and Goethe's *Iphigenie auf Tauris* (first performed at Weimar six weeks earlier).[183]

Gluck's opera (or *tragédie lyrique*) approximates tragic form while intensifying the emotions and revising the religious elements of Euripides' plot. A continuous action is set at the temple of Diana, a chorus of enslaved Greek women assists Iphigenia, there are incidental secondary choruses, and the goddess descends at the end to direct the outcome. The Furies' assault on Orestes is staged, with Orestes dreaming so that they are still imagined figures. The recognition is postponed until Iphigenia is about to strike the death blow and Orestes recalls her own death at Aulis.[184] Thoas becomes a central and menacing figure, convinced by oracles that he will die if he does not sacrifice all captured strangers, terrified of punishment after death and justly killed by Pylades.[185] Iphigenia is torn between the demand for human sacrifices and her intuition that they cannot be wanted by the goddess, and wishes

---

with Pylades and Iphigenia married, Thoas killed by Orestes and the Greeks sailing away to safety while Thomiris takes her place as ruler of Tauris. Jean Racine had contemplated a version with Iphigenia abducted from Aulis by pirates before her sacrifice and wooed by Thoas's son despite his father's objections, but he only completed a sketch of the first act (on this see Jurgensen 1977).

[182] The libretto was adapted by Nicolas-François Guillard from a play of Claude Guimond de La Touche (1757). On the opera see especially Ewans 2007, 31–53; Goldhill 2010; Hall 2013, 183–205; also Heitner 1964, 304–6; Gliksohn 1985, 177–84; Colombati 2008.

[183] First written in prose; the verse text was completed in 1787. On the play see Brendel 1950; Matthiessen 2000; Lee 2003; Hall 2013, 206–16; also Heitner 1964, 306–8; Gliksohn 1985, 172–77; Hughes 2007, 120–26; Torrance 2019, 102–5, 112–14, 120.

[184] This follows the recommendation of Polyidus as reported by Aristotle (above, n. 161). The letter device thus serves only to dispatch Pylades to the shore, whence he will return with his men to kill Thoas and rescue Iphigenia and Orestes at the end.

[185] Thoas is usually more central in 17th/18th-century works than the Euripidean Thoas. In Gluck's opera (as in La Touche's play) his belief in the oracles is sincere and only shown by the outcome to be against nature (in Vaubertrand's anti-clerical *Iphigénie en Tauride* (1757) he has invented them himself as a means of control). His death is not unusual and anticipated in Lucian's *Toxaris*.

48 INTRODUCTION

to die on learning that Orestes is dead.[186] Much is made of the mutual devotion of Orestes and Pylades, and Orestes himself longs for death until the goddess declares that his remorse is enough to free him from his matricidal guilt.

Goethe's play represents a more radical reshaping of the Euripidean myth in terms of a humane morality. It has a classic five-act structure with a cast limited to the four central characters and Arkas, a minister of Thoas sympathetic to Iphigenia. The text consists largely of scenes in which the characters ponder their circumstances and debate their obligations to themselves and each other. Thoas is an honourable man who has treated Iphigenia kindly and ended the practice of human sacrifice at her request, but he is now tempted to require the sacrifice of the two recently captured Greeks if she will not accept his offer of marriage (his wish to remarry is intensified by the recent loss of his only son). Iphigenia feels an overwhelming attachment to home and family, and when Orestes identifies himself and reveals that he has killed their mother she realises she must betray Thoas in order to save her brother and end the family curse. Orestes, wracked by guilt, still insists on a sacrificial death until a vision of his dead family members reconciled in the Underworld convinces him that finding his sister means salvation and an end to the Furies' persecution. Iphigenia now sets about deceiving Thoas, reluctantly, with the pretended purification and theft of the divine image,[187] but she cannot bring herself to conceal the truth from Thoas and can only appeal to him not to impede their departure. Conflict between Greeks and Taurians leads to a confrontation between Thoas and Orestes, but Iphigenia intercedes, Thoas stays the conflict, and Orestes realises that he has misunderstood Apollo's instruction: the sister he must retrieve is not Apollo's but his own, and by releasing Iphigenia Thoas will fulfil the goddess's plan of preserving her for the salvation of her family. Thoas concedes, and as they part Iphigenia promises continuing guest-friendship between Taurians and Greeks.[188] Her purity has prevailed, the goddess's

---

[186] Her dream of killing Orestes seems confirmed when (still unnamed) he tells her that the matricide Orestes 'has met the death he has long sought' (*a rencontré la mort qu'il a longtemps cherchée*), meaning of course the death he now faces.

[187] The deception is planned by Pylades, not by Iphigenia as in Euripides' play.

[188] The ending is ambivalent. When Orestes and Iphigenia beg Thoas to do the right thing he responds with a curt 'Then go!' (*So geht!*), and his parting words are just 'Farewell' (*Lebt wohl!*). But he presumably gives Iphigenia his right hand

INTRODUCTION 49

image remains with the Taurians, now freed from the taint of human blood, and Iphigenia returns, not to Brauron but to Argos and the life from which her sacrifice had separated her.

Goethe's idealizing vision almost put an end to more conventional adaptations of the Taurian story and long held an authoritative place in German and wider European culture. The twentieth century, however, saw reactions against the underlying assumptions of both Euripides' and Goethe's plays. One of these is that the curse on the descendants of Tantalus could be ended, whether by the bringing of the image of Artemis to Greece (Euripides) or by the reunion of Orestes and Iphigenia (Goethe). The distinguished Mexican writer Alfonso Reyes, who spent much of his life abroad after his father was killed in a political conflict, rejected these optimistic outcomes in his verse drama *Ifigenia Cruel* (1924).[189] His Ifigenia has no memory of her past and longs to recover it, but when Orestes arrives and prompts her to do so she is so horrified by their family's history and the cyclical violence which permeates it that she refuses to return to Greece and chooses to continue serving the goddess and the sacrificial rite with which she now identifies herself. Reyes's text also subverts the traditional polarity of Greek (or European) over barbarian, portraying Orestes and his company as aggressive intruders threatening the peaceful pastoral life of the Taurian (or Mesoamerican) people. This polarity is denied again in works reacting against the barbarity of the Nazi regime with its appropriation of Goethe as a champion of Aryan culture,[190] and in more recent works challenging other elements of European politics and colonialism.[191] Another feature of the myth in its conventional form – Iphigenia's acceptance of her subordination to the needs of her family, and willingness even to forgive the father who sacrificed her – has been subverted in recent feminist productions of

---

to accept her pledge as she has requested, and his curtness may suggest regret rather than resentment.

[189] Bietolini 2008; Barrenechea 2012; Hall 2013, 275–81

[190] Hall 2013, 217–30; Mills 2015, 267f.; also Aretz 1999, 357–462 (on Gerhard Hauptmann's *Atriden-Tetralolgie* including *Iphigenie in Delphi*); Hermann 2005, 27–53 (Hauptmann) and 54–75 Fassbinder's *Iphigenie auf Tauris von Johann Wolfgang Goethe*); Secci 2008, 138–42 (Hauptmann) and 142f. (two plays of Ilse Langner).

[191] Mills 2015, 269, 283f.; cf. Hermann 2005, 76–92 (on Jochen Berg's *Im Taurerland*) and 93–120 (on Volker Braun's *Iphigenie in Freiheit*), Hall 2013, 287–92 (on the Australian Louis Nowra's *The Golden Age*).

50 INTRODUCTION

the play and recastings of her story.[192] Euripides' creation will no doubt continue to be a rich source of appropration, reinterpretation and controversy.

GREEK TEXT AND CRITICAL APPARATUS

The complete text of *Iphigenia in Tauris*, as of the other eight so-called alphabetic plays of Euripides,[193] has survived through a single manuscript now in Florence (**L** = Laurentianus plut. 32.2, early 14th C), which includes all of the extant plays of Euripides except *Trojan Women* and the second half of *Bacchae*, all those of Sophocles except *Oedipus at Colonus*, the Byzantine Triad of Aeschylus (*Persians*, *Seven against Thebes*, *Prometheus*) and Hesiod's *Works and Days*. The text of *IT* was written by Nicolaus Triclines and used as a working copy by a relative of his, the Byzantine scholar Demetrius Triclinius (**Tr**). Nicolaus included a few variant readings and marginal notes, and Demetrius added many notes and alterations to the text, often basing them on an understanding of metre which was incomplete but still remarkable for his time. Another early 14th-century manuscript **P**, now partly in Florence (Laurentianus conv. soppr. 172) and partly in the Vatican Library (Palatinus gr. 287, including *IT*) was copied directly from **L** so far as the alphabetic plays are concerned and has no special value except that it often preserves original readings in **L** which are now unclear, especially where Triclinius altered its text after **P** was copied from it.[194] The two later manuscripts listed below, Paris gr. 2817 and 2887, were also copied from **L**.

---

[192] For details see Hall 2013, 264–73, Mills 2015, 281f., Torrance 2019, 115–17.

[193] *Helen, Electra, Heracles, Heraclidae, Suppliant Women, Ion, Iphigenia at Aulis, Cyclops*. The Greek titles all begin with the letters Ε, Η, Ι or Κ (Ἑλένη, Ἠλέκτρα, Ἡρακλῆς, Ἡρακλεῖδαι, Ἱκέτιδες, Ἴων, Ἰφιγένεια, Κύκλωψ), probably because they survive from a collection in which the plays were grouped alphabetically.

[194] **L** and **P** are fully described by Turyn 1957, 222–64; see also Zuntz 1965, 126–40. Complete digital images of the manuscripts can be found on the websites of the Medicean Library in Florence and the Vatican Library in Rome. Facsimiles of the Euripidean sections were published by J. A. Spranger (1920, 1939–46) and are available in some major university libraries (in England at Cambridge, London and Oxford). For **P**'s dependence on **L** and Triclinius's work on **L** see especially Zuntz 1965 and (with reference to *Electra*) Donzelli 1989, 70–86. Parker xcvii–cvi provides an excellent survey of the history of the text from Euripides' time to the Renaissance and of the more important printed editions starting with the Aldine of 1503. See also Finglass 2020.

INTRODUCTION 51

Other evidence for the text includes:

(a) Papyrus fragments, all very incomplete:[195]

Π[1] P. Hamb. 118 fr. a col. i, 3rd–2nd C BC (Hamburg: lines 51–66)

Π[2] P. Hibeh 1.24 frs a–m, 3rd C BC (Cambridge: lines 174–191, 245–255, 272–286, 581–595, 600–629)

Π[3] P. Köln 7.303 (superseding P. Köln 5.211), 3rd–4th C AD (Cologne: lines 350–356)

Π[4] P. Berol. Inv. 21133 (now BKT IX.34), 1st–2nd C AD (Berlin, ed. G. Parassoglou, *Hellenika* 34 (1982–83) 479–80, 584: lines 946–955)

Π[5] P. Oxy. 67.4565, 2nd C AD (Oxford: lines 1340–52, 1367–78)

(b) Testimonia: i.e. quotations, citations, paraphrases and anthologized extracts found in a variety of ancient and medieval texts of other authors, collections, reference books, etc. Details of these are given in the apparatus of Sansone's edition.

Fuller information about the manuscripts, textual tradition and modern discussions and conjectures can be found in the editions of Sansone, Diggle and Parker.[196] My own apparatus is largely confined to significant departures from L's text and continuing uncertainties.

The following symbols etc. are used in the text and apparatus:

[ ] word(s) in **L** judged to be inauthentic additions to Euripides' text

⟨ ⟩ conjectural supplements to **L**'s text

† † word(s) in **L** judged corrupt but not corrected

L ms. Laurentianus plut. 32.2

L[sl] superscript in **L** (see Parker cii)

L[ac] L before correction by its copyist, Nicolaus Triclines (see above)

L[pc] L after correction by its copyist

⟨**L**⟩ original reading of **L** inferred from **P**

Π[1–5] one of the papyri listed above

---

[195] Essentials of the papyri are detailed in Carrara 2009, respectively nos 15, 13, 119, 87, 78. Online images and and data are available for Π[1] (Papyrus-Sammlung Hamburg), Π[3] (Kölner Papyri), Π[4] (Berliner Papyrusdatenbank) and Π[5] (Oxyrhynchus Online).

[196] Older conjectures are listed in the Appendix to the edition of R. Prinz and N. Wecklein (1898); see also Diggle 1994, 521f. For Livineius see Battezzato 2000, 346.

52 INTRODUCTION

P   ms. Vaticanus Palatinus gr. 287

p   correction in **P** (late 15th C)

Paris. 2817   ms. Parisinus gr. 2817 (copied from **L** c. 1500 with a few emendations: see Sansone VIII)

Paris. 2887   ms. Parisinus gr. 2887 (copied from **L** c. 1500 with a few emendations: see Sansone VIII)

Tr   alteration in **L** by Triclinius

Sansone IX–XIII lists editions, commentaries and studies of the text which are referred to by authors' names in my apparatus. For more recent items see the relevant notes in my commentary.

IPHIGENIA IN TAURIS

ΥΠΟΘΕΣΙΣ ΙΦΙΓΕΝΕΙΑΣ ΤΗΣ ΕΝ ΤΑΥΡΟΙΣ

Ὀρέστης κατὰ χρησμὸν ἐλθὼν εἰς Ταύρους τῆς Σκυθίας μετὰ Πυλάδου παραγενηθεὶς τὸ παρ' αὐτοῖς τιμώμενον τῆς Ἀρτέμιδος ξόανον ὑφελέσθ-αι προῃρεῖτο. προελθὼν δ' ἀπὸ τῆς νεὼς καὶ μανείς, ὑπὸ τῶν ἐντοπίων ἅμα τῷ φίλῳ συλληφθεὶς ἀνήχθη κατὰ τὸν παρ' αὐτοῖς ἐθισμόν, ὅπως τοῦ τῆς Ἀρτέμιδος ἱεροῦ σφάγιον γένωνται. τοὺς γὰρ καταπλεύσαντας ξένους ἀπέσφαττον...*(several lines left blank in ms. L)*....

ἡ μὲν σκηνὴ τοῦ δράματος ὑποκεῖται ἐν Ταύροις τῆς Σκυθίας· ὁ δὲ χορὸς συνέστηκεν ἐξ Ἑλληνίδων γυναικῶν, θεραπαινίδων Ἰφιγενείας. προλογίζει δὲ Ἰφιγένεια.

τὰ τοῦ δράματος πρόσωπα· Ἰφιγένεια, Ὀρέστης, Πυλάδης, χορός, βουκόλος, Θόας, ἄγγελος, Ἀθηνᾶ.

---

2 παραγενηθεὶς ⟨L⟩P παραγενόμενος Tr   3 μανείς Wilamowitz φανεὶς L   ἐντοπίων ⟨L⟩P ἐγχωρίων Tr   11 Ἀθηνᾶ ed. Aldin. Ἀθηνᾶ Ἀπόλλων L

OUTLINE OF *IPHIGENIA IN TAURIS*[1]

Orestes in obedience to an oracle went to the land of the Taurians in Scythia with Pylades and when he arrived there planned to steal the image of Artemis which they revered. He went ashore from the ship and suffered a fit of madness, and he and his friend were caught by the local people and brought in according to their custom to be sacrificed in the sanctuary of Artemis. For they used to slaughter those foreigners who had landed there...*(the rest of the plot-summary is lost)*....

The play is set amongst the Taurians in Scythia. The Chorus consists of Hellenic women, servants of Iphigenia. Iphigenia speaks the prologue.

The play's characters: Iphigenia, Orestes, Pylades, Chorus, Herdsman, Thoas, Messenger, Athena.

---

[1] The first paragraph is the beginning of a narrative summary of a kind which circulated in antiquity in mythological handbooks and are seen more fully in a collection now sometimes known as 'Tales from Euripides'. Such summaries are attached to most of Euripides' plays in the medieval manuscripts, and several papyri of the so-called 'Tales' are known. The identifications of setting, Chorus, prologue-speaker and characters derive from the hypothesis attributed to Aristophanes of Byzantium, who apparently provided this with other information and some very brief critical comments when he edited Euripides in Alexandria about the end of the third century BC This kind of information is preserved somewhat more fully in the manuscripts of most of the select plays of Euripides (i.e. the non-alphabetic plays, cf. Introduction, p. 50), e.g. *Alcestis, Orestes.* »» Parker 51f.

ΙΦΙΓΕΝΕΙΑ Η ΕΝ ΤΑΥΡΟΙΣ

ΙΦΙΓΕΝΕΙΑ
Πέλοψ ὁ Ταντάλειος ἐς Πῖσαν μολὼν
θοαῖσιν ἵπποις Οἰνομάου γαμεῖ κόρην,
ἐξ ἧς Ἀτρεὺς ἔβλαστεν, Ἀτρέως δ' ἄπο
Μενέλαος Ἀγαμέμνων τε, τοῦ δ' ἔφυν ἐγώ,
τῆς Τυνδαρείας θυγατρὸς Ἰφιγένεια παῖς,   5
ἣν ἀμφὶ δίνας ἃς θάμ' Εὔριπος πυκναῖς
αὔραις ἑλίσσων κυανέαν ἅλα στρέφει
ἔσφαξεν Ἑλένης οὕνεχ', ὡς δοκεῖ, πατὴρ
Ἀρτέμιδι κλειναῖς ἐν πτυχαῖσιν Αὐλίδος.
ἐνταῦθα γὰρ δὴ χιλίων νεῶν στόλον   10
Ἑλληνικὸν συνήγαγ' Ἀγαμέμνων ἄναξ,
τὸν καλλίνικον στέφανον Ἰλίου θέλων
λαβεῖν Ἀχαιοῖς τούς θ' ὑβρισθέντας γάμους
Ἑλένης μετελθεῖν, Μενέλεῳ χάριν φέρων.
δεινῇ δ' ἀπλοίᾳ πνευμάτων τ' οὐ τυγχάνων   15
ἐς ἔμπυρ' ἦλθε, καὶ λέγει Κάλχας τάδε·
'Ὦ τῆσδ' ἀνάσσων Ἑλλάδος στρατηγίας
Ἀγάμεμνον, οὐ μὴ ναῦς ἀφορμίσῃς χθονὸς
πρὶν ἂν κόρην σὴν Ἰφιγένειαν Ἄρτεμις
λάβῃ σφαγεῖσαν· ὅ τι γὰρ ἐνιαυτὸς τέκοι   20
κάλλιστον ηὔξω φωσφόρῳ θύσειν θεᾷ.
παῖδ' οὖν ἐν οἴκοις σὴ Κλυταιμήστρα δάμαρ
τίκτει' (τὸ καλλιστεῖον εἰς ἔμ' ἀναφέρων)
'ἣν χρή σε θῦσαι.' καί μ' Ὀδυσσέως τέχναις
μητρὸς παρείλοντ' ἐπὶ γάμοις Ἀχιλλέως.   25
ἐλθοῦσα δ' Αὐλίδ' ἡ τάλαιν' ὑπὲρ πυρᾶς
μεταρσία ληφθεῖσ' ἐκαινόμην ξίφει·
ἀλλ' ἐξέκλεψέ μ' ἔλαφον ἀντιδοῦσά μου
Ἄρτεμις Ἀχαιοῖς, διὰ δὲ λαμπρὸν αἰθέρα
πέμψασά μ' ἐς τήνδ' ᾤκισεν Ταύρων χθόνα,   30

3 δ' ἄπο Badham   δὲ παῖς L   6 δίνας Monk -αις L   13 Ἀχαιοῖς Lenting -οὺς L
14 ἑλένης p ἑλένη (i.e. -η) L   15 δεινῇ δ' ἀπλοίᾳ Rauchenstein (δ' Barnes) δειν** (-ῆς
TrP) τ' ἀπλοίας L   18 ἀφορμίσῃς Kirchhoff -η L   20 λάβῃ Matthiae λάβοι L
28 ἐξέκλεψέ μ' Reiske ἐξέκλεψεν L

56

IPHIGENIA IN TAURIS

The scene is the entrance to the temple of the Taurian Artemis. In front of it is a large, bloodstained altar. Iphigenia enters from the temple, alone.

IPHIGENIA

Pelops son of Tantalus went to Pisa with his swift mares and wedded Oenomaus's daughter. Atreus was her offspring; from Atreus sprang Menelaus and Agamemnon, who begot me, child of Tyndareus's daughter, Iphigenia.[5] By the eddies which Euripus with its dense breezes stirs together, churning the dark swell, my father because of Helen slaughtered me – so it is believed – for Artemis in the famous vales of Aulis.

For at that place lord Agamemnon had assembled a Hellenic force of a thousand ships,[11] wanting to get for the Achaeans the glorious crown of victory over Troy and avenge the violation of Helen's marriage, for Menelaus's satisfaction. But when the voyage was terribly delayed and he did not get winds for it,[15] he resorted to burnt offerings, and Calchas made this pronouncement: 'O you who hold this high command of Hellas, Agamemnon, never will you launch your ships from land till Artemis receives your daughter Iphigenia, slaughtered.[20] For you vowed to offer to the light-bearing goddess the fairest product that the year should bear. Now in your house your wife Clytemnestra has a child' (thus he awarded me the prize for beauty!) 'whom you must offer.' And so, through Odysseus's trickery, they took me from my mother to be married to Achilles.[25] When I came to Aulis, I was lifted high in my misery over the altar, ready for the sword; but Artemis stole me away, giving the Achaeans a deer in my place, and bringing me through the radiant sky she settled me here in the Taurians' land,[30] where Thoas rules,

Euripides

οὗ γῆς ἀνάσσει βαρβάροισι βάρβαρος
Θόας, ὃς ὠκὺν πόδα τιθεὶς ἴσον πτεροῖς
ἐς τοὔνομ' ἦλθε τόδε ποδωκείας χάριν,
ναοῖσι δ' ἐν τοῖσδ' ἱερέαν τίθησί με·
ὅθεν νόμοισιν οἷσιν ἥδεται θεὰ   35
Ἄρτεμις ἑορτῆς, τοὔνομ' ἧς καλὸν μόνον –
τὰ δ' ἄλλα σιγῶ τὴν θεὸν φοβουμένη·
θύω γὰρ ὄντος τοῦ νόμου καὶ πρὶν πόλει,
ὃς ἂν κατέλθῃ τήνδε γῆν Ἕλλην ἀνήρ.
[κατάρχομαι μέν, σφάγια δ' ἄλλοισιν μέλει   40
ἄρρητ' ἔσωθεν τῶνδ' ἀνακτόρων θεᾶς.]
  ἃ καινὰ δ' ἥκει νὺξ φέρουσα φάσματα
λέξω πρὸς αἰθέρ', εἴ τι δὴ τόδ' ἔστ' ἄκος.
ἔδοξ' ἐν ὕπνῳ τῆσδ' ἀπαλλαχθεῖσα γῆς
οἰκεῖν ἐν Ἄργει, παρθενῶσι δ' ἐν μέσοις   45
εὕδειν, χθονὸς δὲ νῶτα σεισθῆναι σάλῳ,
φεύγειν δὲ κἄξω στᾶσα θριγκὸν εἰσιδεῖν
δόμων πίτνοντα, πᾶν δ' ἐρείψιμον στέγος
βεβλημένον πρὸς οὖδας ἐξ ἄκρων σταθμῶν.
μόνος δ' ἐλείφθη στῦλος, ὡς ἔδοξέ μοι,   50
δόμων πατρῴων, ἐκ δ' ἐπικράνων κόμας
ξανθὰς καθεῖναι, φθέγμα δ' ἀνθρώπου λαβεῖν,
κἀγὼ τέχνην τήνδ' ἣν ἔχω ξενοκτόνον
τιμῶσ' ὑδραίνειν αὐτὸν ὡς θανούμενον,
κλαίουσα. τοὔναρ δ' ὧδε συμβάλλω τόδε·   55
τέθνηκ' Ὀρέστης, οὗ κατηρξάμην ἐγώ·
στῦλοι γὰρ οἴκων παῖδές εἰσιν ἄρσενες,
θνῄσκουσι δ' οὓς ἂν χέρνιβες βάλωσ' ἐμαί.
[οὐδ' αὖ συνάψαι τοὔναρ ἐς φίλους ἔχω·
Στροφίῳ γὰρ οὐκ ἦν παῖς ὅτ' ὠλλύμην ἐγώ.]   60
  νῦν οὖν ἀδελφῷ βούλομαι δοῦναι χοὰς
ἀποῦσ' ἀπόντι (ταῦτα γὰρ δυναίμεθ' ἄν)
σὺν προσπόλοισιν ἃς ἔδωχ' ἡμῖν ἄναξ

---

35 νόμοισιν οἷσιν Herwerden νόμοισι τοῖσιδ' ⟨L⟩P (τοῖσιν Tr)   37 after 41 Markland ('perhaps'), after 40 Stinton (deleting 38–39, 41)   40–41 del. Stedefeldt (38–39 Murray, 38–39, 41 Diggle, *alii alia*)   45 παρθενῶσι δ' ἐν μέσοις Valckenaer, Markland παρθένοισι δ' ἐν μεσαις L   50 ἐλείφθη Paris. 2887 ἐλήφθη L   54 ὑδραίνειν Musgrave ὕδραινον L   58 οὓς Scaliger ὡς L   βάλωσ' ἐμαί Canter βάλωσί με L   59–60 del. Monk 62 ἀποῦσ' ἀπόντι Badham (παροῦσ' ἀπόντι Canter) παροῦσα παντὶ L

Iphigenia in Tauris

barbarian over barbarians, who running with wing-swift speed of foot has gained the name because of his swiftness, and placed me as priestess in her temple here. And so by the laws of the festival which please the goddess Artemis,[35] a festival whose name alone is fair – but the rest I hold in silence, fearing the goddess. For by the law that stands for this community long since, I sacrifice any Greek man who lands on this shore. [*I perform the consecration, but the slaughter is a task for others,*[40] *unspoken of, within the goddess's precincts here.*]

Now I will tell to the sky the strange new apparitions this night has brought me, if this be any remedy. I seemed in my sleep to be removed from this land and living in Argos, and sleeping in the midst of the maidens' apartment;[45] then the earth's surface, it seemed, was shaken by a tremor, and I was fleeing, and standing outside I saw the cornice of the palace falling and the whole roof from column-tops down thrown in ruins to the ground. One column alone was left, it seemed to me,[50] from our ancestral palace, and from its capital it sent down auburn hair and took a human's voice; and I observing this stranger-killing art of mine, was sprinkling it with water as one about to die, weeping as I did so. And this is how I interpret the dream:[55] Orestes is dead, and he was the one I consecrated; for male children are the pillars of their houses, and all those sprinkled by my lustrations die. [*Neither can I connect the dream with friends; for Strophius had no son when I was dying.*][60]

Now therefore I mean to offer libations to my brother, absent one to absent one – this I can do for him – together with the servants whom the king gave me, Hellene women. But for

Euripides

Ἑλληνίδας γυναῖκας. ἀλλ' ἐξ αἰτίας
οὔπω τινὸς πάρεισιν· εἶμ' ἔσω δόμων 65
ἐν οἷσι ναίω τῶνδ' ἀνακτόρων θεᾶς.

ΟΡΕΣΤΗΣ
ὅρα· φυλάσσου μή τις ἐν στίβῳ βροτῶν.

ΠΥΛΑΔΗΣ
ὁρῶ· σκοποῦμαι δ' ὄμμα πανταχῇ στρέφων.

Ορ. Πυλάδη, δοκεῖ σοι μέλαθρα ταῦτ' εἶναι θεᾶς,
  ἔνθ' Ἄργοθεν ναῦν ποντίαν ἐστείλαμεν; 70
Πυ. ἔμοιγ', Ὀρέστα· σοὶ δὲ συνδοκεῖν χρεών.
Ορ. καὶ βωμός, Ἕλλην οὗ καταστάζει φόνος;
Πυ. ἐξ αἱμάτων γοῦν ξάνθ' ἔχει θριγκώματα.
Ορ. θριγκοῖς δ' ὑπ' αὐτοῖς σκῦλ' ὁρᾷς ἠρτημένα;
Πυ. τῶν κατθανόντων γ' ἀκροθίνια ξένων. 75
  ἀλλ' ἐγκυκλοῦντ' ὀφθαλμὸν εὖ σκοπεῖν χρεών.
Ορ. ὦ Φοῖβε, ποῖ μ' αὖ τήνδ' ἐς ἄρκυν ἤγαγες
  χρήσας, ἐπειδὴ πατρὸς αἷμ' ἐτεισάμην
  μητέρα κατακτάς, διαδοχαῖς δ' Ἐρινύων
  ἠλαυνόμεσθα φυγάδες ἔξεδροι χθονός, 80
  δρόμους τε πολλοὺς ἐξέπλησα καμπίμους,
  ἐλθὼν δέ σ' ἠρώτησα πῶς τροχηλάτου
  μανίας ἂν ἔλθοιμ' ἐς τέλος πόνων τ' ἐμῶν
  [οὓς ἐξεμόχθουν περιπολῶν καθ' Ἑλλάδα]·
  σὺ δ' εἶπας ἐλθεῖν Ταυρικῆς μ' ὅρους χθονός, 85
  ἔνθ' Ἄρτεμίς σοι σύγγονος βωμοὺς ἔχει,
  λαβεῖν τ' ἄγαλμα θεᾶς ὅ φασιν ἐνθάδε
  ἐς τούσδε ναοὺς οὐρανοῦ πεσεῖν ἄπο,
  λαβόντα δ' ἢ τέχναισιν ἢ τύχῃ τινὶ
  κίνδυνον ἐκπλήσαντ' Ἀθηναίων χθονὶ 90
  δοῦναι (τὸ δ' ἐνθένδ' οὐδὲν ἐρρήθη πέρα),
  καὶ ταῦτα δράσαντ' ἀμπνοὰς ἕξειν πόνων.
  ἥκω δὲ πεισθεὶς σοῖς λόγοισιν ἐνθάδε
  ἄγνωστον ἐς γῆν ἄξενον. σὲ δ' ἱστορῶ,
  Πυλάδη (σὺ γάρ μοι τοῦδε συλλήπτωρ πόνου), 95
  τί δρῶμεν; ἀμφίβληστρα γὰρ τοίχων ὁρᾷς

65 εἶμ' ἔσω Hermann εἴς μ' εἴσω (L)P (ἐς ἔμ' Tr) 68 πανταχῇ Monk -οῦ L 73 θριγκώματα Valckenaer, Ruhnken τριχώματα L 76 (Πυ.) Reiske Ορ. L 75 γ' ἀκροθίνια
Hermann τἀκρο- L 84 del. Markland 86 σοι Kirchhoff σὺ L σῇ p

60

Iphigenia in Tauris

some reason they are not yet here; I'll go inside this dwelling[65] in which I live, in the temple of the goddess.

Iphigenia exits into the temple. Orestes and Pylades enter conversing, furtively and unaccompanied, by Side-entrance B and approach the temple.

ORESTES

Look out, take care, in case there's someone on the path.

PYLADES

I'm looking; I'm peering about in all directions.

Or. Pylades, do you think this is the goddess's temple, for which we set our course by ship from Argos?[70]

Pyl. I do, Orestes, and you should think so too.

Or. And this the altar that Hellene blood drips down on?

Pyl. Its copings at any rate are brown with bloodstains.

Or. And right below the copings you see spoils hanging?

Pyl. Indeed, choice pickings from the strangers who have died here.[75] But I must look all around and explore thoroughly.

(He explores while Orestes speaks.)

Or. O Phoebus, what is this net you have led me into now with your instruction, when I'd avenged my father's murder by killing my mother and was being driven by the Erinyes' pursuit in exile from the land,[80] and had completed many rounding laps, and came and asked you how I might reach an end of my wheeling madness and my ordeals [*through which I was struggling, wandering over Hellas*]: you said I must go to the borders of the Taurian land,[85] where your sister Artemis possesses altars, and take the goddess's image which they say fell here into this sanctuary from the sky, and once I'd taken it, either by craft or by some stroke of luck, must complete the peril and give it to the Athenians' land[90] (of what would come after that, nothing was said), and having done all this would have respite from my ordeals. And I have come, persuaded by your words, here to an unknown and unfriendly country. *(Turning to Pylades)* And now I ask you, Pylades (for you are my comrade in this task),[95] what shall we do? You see these

Euripides

ὑψηλά· πότερα κλιμάκων προσαμβάσεις
ἐμβησόμεσθα; πῶς ἂν οὖν λάθοιμεν ἄν;
ἢ χαλκότευκτα κλῆθρα λύσαντες μοχλοῖς
†ὧν οὐδὲν ἴσμεν†; ἢν δ' ἀνοίγοντες πύλας   100
ληφθῶμεν ἐσβάσεις τε μηχανώμενοι,
θανούμεθ'. ἀλλὰ πρὶν θανεῖν νεὼς ἔπι
φεύγωμεν ᾗπερ δεῦρ' ἐναυστολήσαμεν.
Πυ. φεύγειν μὲν οὐκ ἀνεκτὸν οὐδ' εἰώθαμεν,
τὸν τοῦ θεοῦ δὲ χρησμὸν οὐκ ἀτιστέον.   105
ναοῦ δ' ἀπαλλαχθέντε κρύψωμεν δέμας
κατ' ἄντρ' ἃ πόντος νοτίδι διακλύζει μέλας
νεὼς ἄπωθεν, μή τις εἰσιδὼν σκάφος
βασιλεῦσιν εἴπῃ κᾆτα ληφθῶμεν βίᾳ.
ὅταν δὲ νυκτὸς ὄμμα λυγαίας μόλῃ,   110
τολμητέον τοι ξεστὸν ἐκ ναοῦ λαβεῖν
ἄγαλμα, πάσας προσφέροντε μηχανάς.
†ὅρα δέ γ' εἴσω τριγλύφων ὅποι κενὸν
δέμας καθεῖναι†· τοὺς πόνους γὰρ ἀγαθοὶ
τολμῶσι, δειλοὶ δ' εἰσὶν οὐδὲν οὐδαμοῦ.   115
οὔτοι μακρὸν μὲν ἤλθομεν κώπῃ πόρον,
ἐκ τερμάτων δὲ νόστον ἀροῦμεν πάλιν.
Ορ. ἀλλ' εὖ γὰρ εἶπας, πειστέον· χωρεῖν χρεὼν
ὅποι χθονὸς κρύψαντε λήσομεν δέμας.
οὐ γὰρ τὸ τοῦδε γ' αἴτιον γενήσεται   120
πεσεῖν ἄχρηστον θέσφατον· τολμητέον.
μόχθος γὰρ οὐδεὶς τοῖς νέοις σκῆψιν φέρει.

ΧΟΡΟΣ
εὐφαμεῖτ' ὦ
πόντου δισσὰς συγχωρούσας
πέτρας ἀξείνου ναίοντες.   125
ὦ παῖ τᾶς Λατοῦς
Δίκτυνν' οὐρεία,

97 κλιμάκων Kayser δωμάτων L   προσαμβάσεις Barnes πρὸς ἀμβ- L   98 ἐμβησόμεσθα
Blomfield **βησ- L^ac ἐκβησ- L^pc or Tr, P   ἂν p (ἂν Tr, om. L)   λάθοιμεν Sallier μάθοιμεν L   105 οὐκ ἀτιστέον Valckenaer οὐ κακιστέον L (οὐδὲ...κακιστεύσομεν Malalas 5.32
Thurn)   111 τοι ⟨L⟩P τὸ Tr   116–17 (Πυ.) Hardion Ορ. L del. Dindorf   118 χωρεῖν
χρεὼν Scaliger χώρει νεκρῶν L   120 τοῦδε Weil τοῦ θεοῦ L   123–42 Χο. Tyrwhitt
123–36 Ιφ., 137–42 Χο. L   125 ἀξείνου Markland εὐξείνου L

Iphigenia in Tauris

high enclosing walls. Shall we get onto scaling-ladders? How then could we avoid being seen? Or shall we force the bronze-made doors with crowbars and †*of which we know nothing*†? But if we are caught trying to open the doors[100] and contriving our entry, we will die. No, before we die let's flee on board the ship by which we voyaged here.

Pyl. Fleeing is intolerable and not our way, and we must not dishonour the god's instruction.[105] Let's leave the temple and hide ourselves in the caves which the dark sea washes through with its surf, away from the ship, in case someone should see the vessel and tell the local rulers, and we be forcibly taken. But when the face of murky night appears,[110] we must nerve ourselves and muster all contrivances to get the carved image out of the temple. †*Yet see inside the triglyphs to where there is a space for letting down one's body*†. Noble men face up to ordeals, while cowards count for nothing anywhere.[115] We surely have not sailed so long a route, only to launch a homeward voyage from its end.

Or. Yes, your advice is good and I must take it. We must go to some nearby place where we can hide ourselves and lie low. I for my part will not be responsible for the[120] oracle going unfulfilled; we must be bold. Young men are never excused from any exertion.

Orestes and Pylades exit by Side-entrance B. The Chorus enters in procession by Side-entrance A, singing, and approaches the temple.

CHORUS

Be silent, all you
who dwell by the twin converging
rocks of the Unwelcoming Sea![125]
O daughter of Leto,
mountain-roaming Dictynna,

63

Euripides

πρὸς σὰν αὐλάν, εὐστύλων
ναῶν χρυσήρεις θριγκούς,
ὁσίας ὅσιον πόδα παρθένιον   130
κληδούχου δούλα πέμπω,
Ἑλλάδος εὐίππου πύργους
καὶ τείχη χόρτων τ' εὐδένδρων
ἐξαλλάξασ' Εὐρώπαν,   135
πατρῴων οἴκων ἕδρας.
ἔμολον· τί νέον; τίνα φροντίδ' ἔχεις;
τί με πρὸς ναοὺς ἄγαγες ἄγαγες,
ὦ παῖ τοῦ τᾶς Τροίας πύργους
ἐλθόντος κλεινᾷ σὺν κώπᾳ   140
χιλιοναύτᾳ μυριοτευχεῖ
†Ἀτρειδᾶν τῶν κλεινῶν†;

Ιφ.   ἰὼ δμωαί,
δυσθρηνήτοις ὡς θρήνοις
ἔγκειμαι, τᾶς οὐκ εὐμούσου   145
μολπᾶς ἀλύροις ἐλέγοις – αἰαῖ –
ἐν κηδείοις οἴκτοισιν.
ἆται μοι συμβαίνουσ', ἆται
σύγγονον ἀμὸν κατακλαιομένᾳ,
τοίαν ἰδόμαν ὄψιν ὀνείρων   150
νυκτὸς τᾶς ἐξῆλθ' ὄρφνα.
ὀλόμαν ὀλόμαν·
οὐκ εἴσ' οἶκοι πατρῷοι·
οἴμοι ⟨μοι⟩ φροῦδος γέννα·   155
φεῦ φεῦ τῶν Ἄργει μόχθων.
ἰὼ δαῖμον,
μόνον ὅς με κασίγνητον συλᾷς,
Ἅιδᾳ πέμψας, ᾧ τάσδε χοὰς
μέλλω κρατῆρά τε τὸν φθιμένων   160
ὑγραίνειν γαίας ἐν νώτοις,
παγάς τ' οὐρειᾶν ἐκ μόσχων

---

130 ὁσίας ὅσιον etc. Seidler πόδα παρθένιον ὅσιον ὁσίας L   133 εὐίππου p   τᾶς εὐίππου L
138 ἄγαγες ἄγαγες Tr   ἄγες ἄγες L   141 χιλιοναύτᾳ ed. Aldin. -α L   μυριοτευχεῖ Barnes
-τεύχοις L   -τευχοῦς L   lacuna before 142, Hermann   143 ἰὼ Seidler   ὦ L
146 μολπᾶς Bothe   μολπᾶς βοὰν L   αἰαῖ Nauck   ἒ ἒ L   148 ἆται μοι Diggle   αἵ μοι L
150 τοίαν Elmsley   ζωᾶς οἵαν L   155 ⟨μοι⟩ Hermann   158 μόνον ὅς Bothe   ὃς τὸν
μόνον L   159 ᾧ ed. Hervag.   ὦ L   161 ὑγραίνειν Blaydes ὑδραίνειν L

Iphigenia in Tauris

to your court, to the gilded copings
of your fine-columned temple,
I walk in this holy maiden-procession,[131]
servant of your holy key-keeper,
far from the ramparts and towers
of horse-rich Hellas and Europe
with its lushly wooded pastures,[135]
where lies my ancestral home.
I have come: what is new, what concern do you have?
Why have you brought me, brought me to the temple,
O daughter of him who went to Troy's ramparts
with that famous fleet[140]
of a thousand ships, ten thousand armaments
†*of the famous sons of Atreus*†?

Iphigenia has by now entered from the temple with some attendants,
one of whom carries a golden libation-jug. She sings in response to the
Chorus.

Iph.   Ah servants,
how painful the lamentations
I am immersed in, the lyreless plaints
of this unmusical song – *aiai* – [146]
amid funereal keening.
Disasters come upon me, disasters
as I grieve for my brother,
such a vision of apparitions have I seen[150]
in this night whose darkness has just passed.
I am lost, I am lost!
Gone is my ancestral house!
Oimoi, moi, my family is no more![155]
Alas, alas, those ordeals at Argos!
Ah daimon,
you who rob me of my only brother,
sending him to Hades! For him I shall pour
on earth's surface these libations,
this bowl belonging to the dead,[160]
milk from young mountain-heifers

Euripides

Βάκχου τ' οἰνηρὰς λοιβὰς
ξουθᾶν τε πόνημα μελισσᾶν,   165
ἃ νεκροῖς θελκτήρια χεῖται.
ἀλλ' ἔνδος μοι πάγχρυσον
τεῦχος καὶ λοιβὰν Ἅιδα.
ὦ κατὰ γαίας Ἀγαμεμνόνιον   170
θάλος, ὡς φθιμένῳ τάδε σοι πέμπω.
δέξαι δ'· οὐ γὰρ πρὸς τύμβον σοι
ξανθὰν χαίταν, οὐ δάκρυ' οἴσω.
τηλόσε γὰρ δὴ σᾶς ἀπενάσθην   175
πατρίδος καὶ ἐμᾶς, ἔνθα δοκήμασι
κεῖμαι σφαχθεῖσ' ἁ τλάμων.

Χο.   ἀντιψάλμους ᾠδὰς ὕμνων τ'
Ἀσιητᾶν σοι βάρβαρον ἀχάν,   180
δέσποιν', ἐξαυδάσω,
τὰν ἐν θρήνοισιν μοῦσαν
νέκυσιν μέλεον, τὰν ἐν μολπαῖς
Ἅιδας ὑμνεῖ δίχα παιάνων.   185
οἴμοι τῶν Ἀτρειδᾶν οἴκων·
ἔρρει φῶς σκήπτρων, ⟨ἔρρει⟩·
οἴμοι πατρῴων οἴκων.
ἦν ἐκ τῶν εὐόλβων Ἄργει
βασιλέων ⟨τᾶς νῦν ἄτας⟩ ἀρχά·   190
μόχθος δ' ἐκ μόχθων ἄσσει
⟨   ⟩
δινευούσαις ἵπποις πταναῖς,
ἀλλάξας δ' ἐξ ἕδρας ἱερὸν
⟨   ⟩ ὄμμ' αὐγᾶς
Ἅλιος. ἄλλοτε δ' ἄλλα προσέβα   195
χρυσέας ἀρνὸς μελάθροις ὀδύνα,

166 χεῖται Nauck κεῖ∗∗∗ L (i.e. κεῖται altered to κεῖτ' by Tr)   173 πρὸς τύμβον Heath πάρος τύμβου L   175 τηλο]θι Π²?   176 δοκήμασι Porson δοκίμα L   177 σφαχθεῖσ' ἁ probably Π² ( ]σα α τλ[ ), conj. Markland σφαχθεῖσα L   178–202 Χο. Hermann 178–85 Χο., 186–202 Ιφ. L   178–79 ὕμνων τ' Ἀσιητᾶν Bothe ὕμνον τ' Ασιήταν L (]ον τε α[Π²)   180 ἀχάν Nauck ἰαχάν L   181 δέσποιν' ρ δέσποινά γ' L (τ' P)   182 θρήνοισιν Markland -οισι L -οις P ( ]ς Π²)   186 οἴκων TrP -ον L   187 σκῆπτρόν τ' Burges ⟨ἔρρει⟩ England   189 ἦν Murray τίν' L   190 ⟨τᾶς νῦν ἄτας⟩ Diggle   lacuna before 192, Dindorf   192 ἵπποις Markland -σι L (-σιν TrP)   193 ἐξ ἕδρας Elmsley ἐξέδρασ' L   194 ⟨μετέβασ'⟩ Paley   195 ἄλλοτε Jacobs ἄλλοις L

Iphigenia in Tauris

and Bacchus's vinous liquor
and the labour of humming bees,[165]
things that are poured as comforts for the dead.

    (turning to an attendant)

Now hand me the vessel all of gold
with its liquid prepared for Hades.

    (pouring the libation)

O scion of Agamemnon beneath the earth,[170]
I send you these libations, you who are dead.
Accept them, for I shall bring to your tomb
no auburn hair, no tear.
Far have I been removed from the homeland,[175]
yours and mine, where as people believe
I lie slaughtered, poor afflicted one.

Chor.   Antiphonal songs and barbarian clamour
of Asian chants I shall cry forth
in response to you, mistress,[181]
that mournful music for the dead
conveyed in dirges, music that Hades
chants in songs distinct from paeans.[185]
Oimoi, the house of the Atreids!
Gone is the glory of its royal power, gone!
Oimoi, the ancestral house!
From the prosperous kings at Argos
was the beginning ⟨*of this present ruin*⟩;[190]
and trouble surges out of troubles
⟨   *one or more lines lost*   ⟩
with circuiting winged mares,
and Helios shifting it from its seat
⟨ *one or two words lost* ⟩ his eye's sacred brightness.
At different times a different anguish has come[195]
from the golden lamb upon the house,

Euripides

†φόνος ἐπὶ φόνῳ, ἄχεα ἄχεσιν†.
ἔνθεν τῶν πρόσθεν δμαθέντων
ἐκβαίνει ποινὰ Τανταλιδᾶν   200
εἰς οἴκους, σπεύδει δ᾽ ἀσπούδαστ᾽
ἐπὶ σοὶ δαίμων ⟨   ⟩.

Ιφ.   ἐξ ἀρχᾶς μοι δυσδαίμων
δαίμων †τᾶς ματρὸς ζώνας†
καὶ νυκτὸς κείνας· ἐξ ἀρχᾶς   205
λόχιαι στερρὰν παιδείαν
Μοῖραι συντείνουσιν θεαί·   207
ἃν πρωτόγονον θάλος ἐν θαλάμοις   209
Λήδας ἁ τλάμων κούρα   210
σφάγιον πατρῴᾳ λώβᾳ
καὶ θῦμ᾽ οὐκ εὐγάθητον
†ἔτεκεν ἔτρεφεν† εὐκταίαν.
ἱππείοις ⟨δ᾽⟩ ἐν δίφροισι
ψαμάθων Αὐλίδος ἐπέβασαν   215
νύμφαν μ᾽, οἴμοι, δύσνυμφον
τῷ τᾶς Νηρέως κούρας· αἰαῖ.
νῦν δ᾽ ἀξείνου πόντου ξείνα
δυσχόρτους οἴκους ναίω,
ἄγαμος ἄτεκνος ἄπολις ἄφιλος,   220
ἁ μναστευθεῖσ᾽ ἐξ Ἑλλάνων,   208
οὐ τὰν Ἄργει μέλπουσ᾽ Ἥραν   221
οὐδ᾽ ἱστοῖς ἐν καλλιφθόγγοις
κερκίδι Παλλάδος Ἀτθίδος εἰκὼ
⟨καὶ⟩ Τιτάνων ποικίλλουσ᾽, ἀλλ᾽
αἱμόρραντον δυσφόρμιγγα   225
ξείνων αἱμάσσουσ᾽ ἄταν,
οἰκτράν τ᾽ αἰαζόντων αὐδὰν
οἰκτρόν τ᾽ ἐκβαλλόντων δάκρυον.
καὶ νῦν κείνων μέν μοι λάθα,

---

197 del. Hartung   ἄχεα ⟨τ᾽⟩ ἄχεσιν Barnes   200 ἐκβαίνει ποινὰ etc. Monk   Τανταλιδᾶν ἐκβαίνει ποινά γ᾽ L   202 ⟨   ⟩ Hartung   204 several words lost after δαίμων, Diggle   206 λόχιαι Hermann   λοχείαν L   208 after 220, Scaliger   213 ἔτεκεν κἄτρεφεν Seidler   214 ἱππείοις Markland -σιν L   ⟨δ᾽⟩ Heath   216 νύμφαν (Scaliger) μ᾽ England νύμφαιον L   224 ⟨καὶ⟩ Tyrwhitt   225 αἱμόρραντον Bothe αἱμορράντων L   226 ἄταν Bothe ἄταν βωμούς L   227–28 αὐδὰν | οἰκτρόν Tyrwhitt οὐδ᾽ ἄνοικτρόν L

Iphigenia in Tauris

†*murder on murder, griefs on griefs*†.
Thence retribution for those slain before
emerges against the Tantalids' house,[200]
and the daimon pursues abhorrent designs
⟨ *one or two words lost* ⟩ upon you.

Iph. From the start the daimon has been baneful for me,
†*from my mother's womb*†
and that night when I was born. From the start[205]
the divine Moirai who attended my birth
drew tight a hard childhood for me.
I was the firstborn scion
that Leda's ill-used daughter in her chamber[210]
†*gave birth to, nurtured*†,
victim for a father's atrocity,
a joyless sacrifice promised by his vow.
In a horse-drawn carriage
they set me on the sands of Aulis,[215]
an ill-wedded bride – *oimoi* –
for Nereus's daughter's son – *aiai*.
And now, a guest of the Unwelcoming Sea,
I dwell in a barren home,
no marriage, no children, no city, no loved ones,[220]
I who had suitors from amongst the Hellenes,[208]
not singing Hera at Argos,[221]
nor on the sweet-voiced loom
picking out with my shuttle the likeness
of Attic Pallas and the Titans, but now
inflicting a bloody fate,[225]
unfit for the lyre, on strangers
wailing with piteous cries,
casting forth piteous tears.
Yet now I have no thought of them

Euripides

    τὸν δ' Ἄργει δμαθέντ' ἀγκλαίω   230
    σύγγονον ὃν ἔλιπον ἐπιμαστίδιον,
    ἔτι βρέφος, ἔτι νέον, ἔτι θάλος
    ἐν χερσὶν ματρὸς πρὸς στέρνοις τ'
    Ἄργει σκηπτοῦχον Ὀρέσταν.   235

Χο. καὶ μὴν ὅδ' ἀκτὰς ἐκλιπὼν θαλασσίους
    βουφορβὸς ἥκει σημανῶν τί σοι νέον.

ΒΟΥΚΟΛΟΣ
    Ἀγαμέμνονός τε καὶ Κλυταιμήστρας τέκνον,
    ἄκουε καινῶν ἐξ ἐμοῦ κηρυγμάτων.
Ιφ. τί δ' ἔστι τοῦ παρόντος ἐκπλῆσσον λόγου;   240
Βο. ἤκουσιν ἐς γῆν κυανέας Συμπληγάδας
    πλάτῃ φυγόντες δίπτυχοι νεανίαι,
    θεᾷ φίλον πρόσφαγμα καὶ θυτήριον
    Ἀρτέμιδι. χέρνιβας δὲ καὶ κατάργματα
    οὐκ ἂν φθάνοις ἂν εὐτρεπῆ ποιουμένη.   245
Ιφ. ποδαποί; τίνος γῆς σχῆμ' ἔχουσιν οἱ ξένοι;
Βο. Ἕλληνες· ἓν τοῦτ' οἶδα κοὐ περαιτέρω.
Ιφ. οὐδ' ὄνομ' ἀκούσας οἶσθα τῶν ξένων φράσαι;
Βο. Πυλάδης ἐκλήζεθ' ἅτερος πρὸς θατέρου.
Ιφ. τῷ ξυζύγῳ δὲ τοῦ ξένου τί τοὔνομ' ἦν;   250
Βο. οὐδεὶς τόδ' οἶδεν· οὐ γὰρ εἰσηκούσαμεν.
Ιφ. ποῦ δ' εἶδετ' αὐτοὺς κἀντυχόντες εἵλετε;
Βο. ἄκραις ἐπὶ ῥηγμῖσιν ἀξένου πόρου.
Ιφ. καὶ τίς θαλάσσης βουκόλοις κοινωνία;
Βο. βοῦς ἤλθομεν νίψοντες ἐναλίᾳ δρόσῳ.   255
Ιφ. ἐκεῖσε δὴ 'πάνελθε, ποῦ νιν εἵλετε
    τρόπῳ θ' ὁποίῳ· τοῦτο γὰρ μαθεῖν θέλω.
    [χρόνιοι γὰρ ἥκουσ', οὐδέ πω βωμὸς θεᾶς
    Ἑλληνικαῖσιν ἐξεφοινίχθη ῥοαῖς.]
Βο. ἐπεὶ τὸν ἐκρέοντα διὰ Συμπληγάδων   260
    βοῦς ὑλοφορβοὺς πόντον εἰσεβάλλομεν,

---

230 δμαθέντ' ἀγκλαίω Weil δμαθέντα κλαίω L   237 σημανῶν ed. Aldin. σημαίνων L
238 τε Reiske παῖ L   241 κυανέας Συμπληγάδας Bentley -αν -α L   246 σχῆμ' Monk
ὄνομ' L (ονομ[Π², τοὔνομα Malalas 5.33 Thurn)   250 τῷ ξυζύγῳ Elmsley τοῦ -ου L
252 ποῦ Musgrave πῶς L κἀντυχόντες Reiske (καν[Π²) καὶ τυχ- L   253 ἄκραις Plut.
Mor. 602a ἀκταῖσιν L εὐξείνου πόντου Plut. (ευξε[Π²)   256 ποῦ Bothe πῶς L
258–59 del. Monk   258 οἶδ' ἐπεὶ Seidler   260 ἐκρέοντα Elmsley εἰσ- L

Iphigenia in Tauris

but weep for the brother now laid low[230]
in Argos, whom I left sucking at the breast,
still an infant, still young, still a tender child
in his mother's arms, on her bosom,
Argos's sceptred ruler, Orestes.[235]

A herdsman approaches by Side-entrance B.

Chorus (speaking) But look, here comes a cowherd leaving the sea-
shore to tell you of something new.

HERDSMAN
Daughter of Agamemnon and Clytemnestra, listen to the
strange new report I have to make!

Iph. And what is so amazing in what you have to tell?[240]

Herd. New arrivals have reached our land, a pair of young men
escaped from the dark Symplêgades on their ship, a welcome
sacrifice and offering for the goddess Artemis. You cannot be
too soon in preparing your lustrations and consecrations.[245]

Iph. Where are they from? What country's look do these strangers
have?

Herd. They are Hellenes; I know just that and nothing more.

Iph. You've not heard and cannot tell the strangers' names?

Herd. One of them was calling the other Pylades.

Iph. And what about his companion, what was *his* name?[250]

Herd. None of us knows; we did not hear it spoken.

Iph. But where did you see them, and come upon and catch them?

Herd. Right at the breakers' edge of the Unwelcoming Sea.

Iph. And what do cowherds have to do with the sea?

Herd. We went to wash our cows with briny water.[255]

Iph. Get back to telling me where you captured them, and in what
way; that's what I want to learn. [*They are late in coming, and
the goddess's altar has not yet been crimsoned with Hellenes'
flowing blood.*]

Herd. (expansively) As we were driving our woodland-grazing cattle
into the sea which flows out through the Symplêgades, there

Euripides

ἦν τις διαρρὼξ κυμάτων πολλῷ σάλῳ
κοιλωπὸς ἀγμός, πορφυρευτικαὶ στέγαι.
ἐνταῦθα δισσοὺς εἶδέ τις νεανίας
βουφορβὸς ἡμῶν, κἀνεχώρησεν πάλιν   265
ἄκροισι δακτύλοισι πορθμεύων ἴχνος.
ἔλεξε δ᾽· 'Οὐχ ὁρᾶτε; δαίμονές τινες
θάσσουσιν οἴδε.' θεοσεβὴς δ᾽ ἡμῶν τις ὢν
ἀνέσχε χεῖρα καὶ προσηύξατ᾽ εἰσιδών·
'Ὦ ποντίας παῖ Λευκοθέας, νεῶν φύλαξ,   270
δέσποτα Παλαῖμον, ἵλεως ἡμῖν γενοῦ,
εἴτ᾽ οὖν ἐπ᾽ ἀκταῖς θάσσετον Διοσκόρω,
ἢ Νηρέως ἀγάλμαθ᾽ ὃς τὸν εὐγενῆ
ἔτικτε πεντήκοντα Νηρήδων χορόν.'
ἄλλος δέ τις μάταιος, ἀνομίᾳ θρασύς,   275
ἐγέλασεν εὐχαῖς, ναυτίλους δ᾽ ἐφθαρμένους
θάσσειν φάραγγ᾽ ἔφασκε τοῦ νόμου φόβῳ,
κλυόντας ὡς θύοιμεν ἐνθάδε ξένους.
ἔδοξε δ᾽ ἡμῶν εὖ λέγειν τοῖς πλείοσιν,
θηρᾶν τε τῇ θεῷ σφάγια τἀπιχώρια.   280
   κἀν τῷδε πέτραν ἅτερος λιπὼν ξένοιν
ἔστη, κάρα τε διετίναξ᾽ ἄνω κάτω,
κἀνεστέναξεν, ὠλένας τρέμων ἄκρας,
μανίαις ἀλαίνων, καὶ βοᾷ κυναγὸς ὥς·
'Πυλάδη, δέδορκας τήνδε; τήνδε δ᾽ οὐχ ὁρᾷς   285
Ἅιδου δράκαιναν ὥς με βούλεται κτανεῖν
δειναῖς ἐχίδναις εἰς ἔμ᾽ ἐστομωμένη;
ἡ δ᾽ †ἐκ χιτώνων† πῦρ πνέουσα καὶ φόνον
πτεροῖς ἐρέσσει μητέρ᾽ ἀγκάλαις ἐμὴν
ἔχουσα, πέτρινον ὄγκον, ὡς ἐπεμβάλῃ.   290
οἴμοι, κτενεῖ με· ποῖ φύγω;' παρῆν δ᾽ ὁρᾶν
οὐ ταῦτα μορφῆς σχήματ᾽, ἀλλ᾽ †ἠλλάσσετο†
φθογγάς τε μόσχων καὶ κυνῶν ὑλάγματα
[ἃς φᾶσ᾽ Ἐρινῦς ἱέναι μιμήματα].
ἡμεῖς δὲ συσταλέντες ὡς †θανούμενοι†   295
σιγῇ καθήμεθ᾽· ὁ δὲ χερὶ σπάσας ξίφος,

---

265 κἀνεχώρησεν Blomfield κἀπ- L   281 ξένοιν Brodaeus -ην L   283 κἀνεστέναξεν
Monk κἀπ- L   290 ὄγκον Heimsoeth ὄχθον L ἄχθος Bothe   291 κτενεῖ p (κτανεῖ
Longin. 15.2) κτείνει L   292 ταῦτα Markland ταυτὰ (i.e. ταὐτὰ) L   294 del. Wilamowitz
295 θαμβ- L^sl θανουμένου Wilamowitz   296 χερὶ σπάσας Pierson περισπάσας L

Iphigenia in Tauris

was a hollow-fronted cleft bored out by the waves' continuous motion,[262] a purple-fishers' shelter. Here one of us cowherds caught sight of two young men, and retreated back to us,[265] navigating his way on tiptoe. 'Don't you see?', he said, 'some deities are sitting here.' Then one of us, a god-fearing man, lifted an arm and prayed as he looked upon them: 'O son of sea-goddess Leucothea, protector of ships,[270] lord Palaemon, be gracious to us, whether these be Zeus's twins sitting on the shore, or glories of Nereus who begot that well-born chorus of fifty Nereids.' But another man, foolish and bold in irreverence,[275] laughed at these prayers and insisted it was shipwrecked sailors sitting in the crevice for fear of our usual custom, having heard that we sacrifice strangers here. Most of us thought he was right and that we should hunt our country's customary victims for the goddess.[280]

Meanwhile one of the strangers had left the cave, and stood and tossed his head up and down, and howled aloud, his hands shaking, rambling in mad seizures, and cried out like a hunter: 'Pylades, have you spotted this one? And this[285] she-dragon from Hades, don't you see how she threatens to kill me, brandishing terrible snakes against me? And that one, breathing flame and gore †*from her garments*†, beats the air with her wings, holding in her crooked arms my mother, a rocky mass, to hurl it upon me.[290] Oh no, she'll kill me; where can I run to?' Yet to our vision there were no such figures, but †*he was getting in exchange?*† cattle's lowing and dogs' yelping [*sounds that they say the Erinyes emit as likenesses*].

Now we had drawn together, †*expecting to die*†,[295] and were sitting in silence. But he unsheathed his sword, leapt like

Euripides

μόσχους ὀρούσας ἐς μέσας λέων ὅπως,
παίει σιδήρῳ λαγόνας ἐς πλευράς ⟨θ'⟩ ἱείς,
[δοκῶν Ἐρινῦς θεὰς ἀμύνεσθαι τάδε,]
ὥσθ' αἱματηρὸν πέλαγος ἐξανθεῖν ἁλός.   300
κἀν τῷδε πᾶς τις ὡς ὁρᾷ βουφόρβια
πίπτοντα καὶ πορθούμεν' ἐξωπλίζετο,
κόχλους τε φυσῶν συλλέγων τ' ἐγχωρίους·
πρὸς εὐτραφεῖς γὰρ καὶ νεανίας ξένους
φαύλους μάχεσθαι βουκόλους ἡγούμεθα·   305
πολλοὶ δ' ἐπληρώθημεν οὐ μακρῷ χρόνῳ.
πίπτει δὲ μανίας πίτυλον ὁ ξένος μεθείς,
στάζων ἀφρῷ γένειον· ὡς δ' ἐσείδομεν
προύργου πεσόντα, πᾶς ἀνὴρ εἶχεν πόνον,
βάλλων ἀράσσων. ἅτερος δὲ τοῖν ξένοιν   310
ἀφρόν τ' ἀπέψη σώματός τ' ἐτημέλει
πέπλων τε προὐκάλυπτεν εὐπήνους ὑφάς,
καραδοκῶν μὲν τἀπιόντα τραύματα,
φίλον δὲ θεραπείαισιν ἄνδρ' εὐεργετῶν.
ἔμφρων δ' ἀνᾴξας ὁ ξένος πεσήματος   315
ἔγνω κλύδωνα πολεμίων προσκείμενον
[καὶ τὴν παροῦσαν συμφορὰν αὐτοῖν πέλας],
ᾤμωξέ θ'· ἡμεῖς δ' οὐκ ἀνίεμεν πέτροις
βάλλοντες, ἄλλος ἄλλοθεν προσκείμενοι.
οὗ δὴ τὸ δεινὸν παρακέλευμ' ἠκούσαμεν·   320
'Πυλάδη, θανούμεθ'· ἀλλ' ὅπως θανούμεθα
κάλλιστ'· ἕπου μοι φάσγανον σπάσας χερί.'
ὡς δ' εἴδομεν δίπαλτα πολεμίων ξίφη,
φυγῇ λεπαίας ἐξεπίμπλαμεν νάπας.
ἀλλ' εἰ φύγοι τις, ἅτεροι προσκείμενοι   325
ἔβαλλον αὐτούς· εἰ δὲ τούσδ' ὠσαίατο,
αὖθις τὸ νῦν ὑπεῖκον ἤρασσον πέτροις.
ἀλλ' ἦν ἄπιστον· μυρίων γὰρ ἐκ χερῶν
οὐδεὶς τὰ τῆς θεοῦ θύματ' ηὐτύχει βαλών.
μόλις δέ νιν τόλμῃ μὲν οὐ χειρούμεθα,   330
κύκλῳ δὲ περιβαλόντες ἐξεκόψαμεν

298 ⟨θ'⟩ Reiske   299 del. West   300 ὥσθ' Markland ὡς L   306 οὐ Nauck ἐν L ἐν
μικρῷ Tr   309 εἶχεν Heiland ἔσχεν L   317 del. Bothe   318 πέτροις Lˢˡ -ους L
327 αὖθις Schaefer (αὗτις Tr) οὗτις ⟨L⟩P   331 περιβαλόντες Reiske -βάλλοντες L
ἐξεκόψαμεν Bothe -κλέψαμεν L

74

Iphigenia in Tauris

a lion in amongst the cattle, and was striking them with his blade, thrusting at flanks and ribs, [*thinking he was thus fending off the divine Erinyes,*] so that the sea-swell bloomed with a blood-red foam.[300]

Meanwhile every one of us, seeing the cattle falling and being slaughtered, was arming himself, blowing on conchs and calling the locals together, for against these sturdy young strangers we reckoned herdsmen were no match in fighting;[305] and before long we were mustered in ample numbers. The stranger fell, throwing off the assault of madness, dripping foam down his chin; and when we saw him fallen at our mercy, every one went to work, pelting and pounding. But the other stranger[310] wiped off the foam and gave his body protection, shielding him with his well-woven cloak and watching out for the wounds that were coming his way, succouring his comrade with tender care. Then leaping up conscious once again from his fall,[315] the stranger recognized a threatening wave of foes falling upon them [*and the calamity now present close upon them*], and wailed aloud. But we did not let up, pelting them with stones, laying on from different sides.

At that point we heard this terrifying exhortation:[320] 'We are going to die, Pylades. Well, let's make sure we die in the noblest way! Draw your sword and follow me!' And when we saw our foes' two brandished swords, we fled and crowded into the rocky gullies. Still, when any fled, the others pressed forward[325] and bombarded them; and when they repelled these, those just then retreating would once again pound them with stones. Yet here was a wonder: countless hands were throwing, but no one was succeeding in hitting the goddess's victims. We subdued them finally with difficulty and not through our own valour.[330] We surrounded them and knocked

Euripides

πέτροισι χειρῶν φάσγαν', ἐς δὲ γῆν γόνυ
καμάτῳ καθεῖσαν. πρὸς δ' ἄνακτα τῆσδε γῆς
κομίζομέν νιν· ὁ δ' ἐσιδὼν ὅσον τάχος
ἐς χέρνιβάς τε καὶ σφαγεῖ' ἔπεμπέ σοι.   335
εὔχου δὲ τοιάδ', ὦ νεᾶνι, σοὶ ξένων
σφάγια παρεῖναι· κἂν ἀναλίσκῃς ξένους
τοιούσδε, τὸν σὸν Ἑλλὰς ἀποτείσει φόνον,
δίκας τίνουσα τῆς ἐν Αὐλίδι σφαγῆς.

Χο. θαυμάστ' ἔλεξας τὸν μανένθ', ὅστις ποτὲ   340
     Ἕλληνος ἐκ γῆς πόντον ἦλθεν ἄξενον.

Ιφ. εἶέν· σὺ μὲν κόμιζε τοὺς ξένους μολών,
     τὰ δ' ἐνθάδ' ἡμεῖς ὅσια φροντιούμεθα.
     ὦ καρδία τάλαινα, πρὶν μὲν ἐς ξένους
     γαληνὸς ἦσθα καὶ φιλοικτίρμων ἀεί,   345
     ἐς θοὐμόφυλον ἀναμετρουμένη δάκρυ,
     Ἕλληνας ἄνδρας ἡνίκ' ἐς χέρας λάβοις.
     νῦν δ' ἐξ ὀνείρων οἷσιν ἠγριώμεθα
     [δοκοῦσ' Ὀρέστην μηκέθ' ἥλιον βλέπειν]
     δύσνουν με λήψεσθ', οἵτινές ποθ' ἥκετε.   350
     καὶ τοῦτ' ἄρ' ἦν ἀληθές, ᾔσθημαι, φίλαι·
     οἱ δυστυχεῖς γὰρ τοῖσι δυστυχεστέροις
     αὐτοὶ κακῶς πράσσοντες οὐ φρονοῦσιν εὖ.
     ἀλλ' οὔτε πνεῦμα Διόθεν ἦλθε πώποτε,
     οὐ πορθμὶς ἥτις διὰ πέτρας Συμπληγάδας   355
     Ἑλένην ἐπήγαγ' ἐνθάδ' ἥ μ' ἀπώλεσεν
     Μενέλεών θ', ἵν' αὐτοὺς ἀντετιμωρησάμην,
     τὴν ἐνθάδ' Αὖλιν ἀντιθεῖσα τῆς ἐκεῖ,
     οὗ μ' ὥστε μόσχον Δαναΐδαι χειρούμενοι
     ἔσφαζον, ἱερεὺς δ' ἦν ὁ γεννήσας πατήρ.   360
     οἴμοι (κακῶν γὰρ τῶν τότ' οὐκ ἀμνημονῶ),
     ὅσας γενείου χεῖρας ἐξηκόντισα
     [γονάτων τε τοῦ τεκόντος ἐξαρτωμένη],
     λέγουσα τοιάδ'· Ὦ πάτερ, νυμφεύομαι

335 ἐς Valckenaer τε L   σφαγεῖ' Musgrave σφάγι' L   340 μανένθ' Kaehler, Lakon
φανένθ' L   343 ὅσια Reiske οἷα L   349 del. Nauck   351–53 del. F. W. Schmidt (351
del. Monk), present in Π³   351 ᾔσθημαι Platnauer (ᾐσθόμην Seager) ἠχθόμην L (η[Π³)
352 τοῖσι δυστυχεστέροις Wecklein   τοῖσιν εὐτυχεστέροις L (τοισιν[Π³)
353 πρασσο[ντες Π³ πράξαντες L   356 ἐπήγαγ' Haupt ἀπ- L ( ]πη[Π³)   359 οὗ
Pierson οἵ L   361 τότ' ed. Aldin. τοῦδ' L   363 del. West

Iphigenia in Tauris

the swords from their hands with rocks, and they sank to the ground, kneeling exhausted. Then we brought them to the ruler of our land, who took one look and sent them to you as fast as might be for consecration and slaughter.[335]

Pray, young lady, to have strangers like these for victims. If you kill such strangers as these, Hellas will be making amends for your murder and paying the price for your sacrifice at Aulis.

Chor. It's amazing, what you've told us about this man's madness, whoever he may be[340] who has come from Hellene land to Unwelcoming Sea.

Iph. Very well; go now and bring the strangers with you, and we will attend to our holy duties here.

(The Herdsman exits by Side-entrance B.)

O my long-suffering heart, in the past you were always gentle and compassionate towards strangers,[345] measuring out tears to match my kinship with them, whenever you received Hellenes into your hands. But now because of the dreams that have made me savage [*supposing Orestes no longer sees the sun*], you will find me unkind, whoever you are who have come here.[350] And this, then, was true, I now have learned, dear friends: the unfortunate, seeing others more unfortunate, faring badly themselves are not well disposed to them. But to this day no wind has come from Zeus,[354] no vessel bringing Helen, who destroyed me, and Menelaus through the Symplêgades, so I could make them pay, setting the Aulis here against that Aulis, where like a heifer the Danaans manhandled me for slaughter, and the sacrificer was the father who begot me.[360]

Alas (for I cannot forget the horrors of that day), how many times did I cast my hands at his cheek [*and at the knees of my father, clinging to them*], calling upon him: 'O father,

Euripides

νυμφεύματ' αἰσχρὰ πρὸς σέθεν· μήτηρ δ' ἐμὲ   365
σέθεν κατακτείνοντος Ἀργεῖαί τε νῦν
ὑμνοῦσιν ὑμεναίοισιν, αὐλεῖται δὲ πᾶν
μέλαθρον· ἡμεῖς δ' ὀλλύμεσθα πρὸς σέθεν.
Ἅιδης Ἀχιλλεὺς ἦν ἄρ', οὐχ ὁ Πηλέως,
ὅν μοι προτείνας πόσιν ἐν ἁρμάτων ⟨μ'⟩ ὄχοις   370
ἐς αἱματηρὸν γάμον ἐπόρθμευσας δόλῳ.'
ἐγὼ δὲ λεπτῶν ὄμμα διὰ καλυμμάτων
ἔχουσ' ἀδελφὸν οὔτ' ἀνειλόμην χεροῖν
ὃς νῦν ὄλωλεν, οὐ κασιγνήτῃ στόμα
συνῆψ' ὑπ' αἰδοῦς, ὡς ἰοῦσ' ἐς Πηλέως   375
μέλαθρα· πολλὰ δ' ἀπεθέμην ἀσπάσματα
ἐς αὖθις, ὡς ἥξουσ' ἐς Ἄργος αὖ πάλιν.
ὦ τλῆμον, εἰ τέθνηκας, ἐξ οἵων καλῶν
ἔρρεις, Ὀρέστα, καὶ πατρὸς ζηλωμάτων.
τὰ τῆς θεοῦ δὲ μέμφομαι σοφίσματα,   380
ἥτις βροτῶν μὲν ἤν τις ἅψηται φόνου
ἢ καὶ λοχείας ἢ νεκροῦ θίγῃ χεροῖν,
βωμῶν ἀπείργει μυσαρὸν ὡς ἡγουμένη,
αὐτὴ δὲ θυσίαις ἥδεται βροτοκτόνοις.
οὐκ ἔσθ' ὅπως ἂν ἔτεκεν ἡ Διὸς δάμαρ   385
Λητὼ τοσαύτην ἀμαθίαν. ἐγὼ μὲν οὖν
τὰ Ταντάλου θεοῖσιν ἑστιάματα
ἄπιστα κρίνω, παιδὸς ἡσθῆναι βορᾷ,
τοὺς δ' ἐνθάδ' αὐτοὺς ὄντας ἀνθρωποκτόνους
ἐς τὴν θεὸν τὸ φαῦλον ἀναφέρειν δοκῶ·   390
οὐδένα γὰρ οἶμαι δαιμόνων εἶναι κακόν.

Χο.   κυάνεαι,   *[στρ. α*
       κυάνεαι σύνοδοι θαλάσσας,
       ἵν' οἶστρος ὁ ποτώμενος Ἀργόθεν
       ἄξενον ἐπ' οἶδμα διεπέρασε ⟨πόντου⟩   395
       Ἀσιήτιδα γαῖαν
       Εὐρώπας διαμείψας.

---

365 ἐμὲ Reiske   ἐμὴ L   366 νῦν Heath, Tyrwhitt   νιν L   370 προτείνας Badham
προσεῖπας L   ⟨μ'⟩ Bothe   373 οὔτ' ἀνειλόμην Tyrwhitt τοῦτον εἱλόμην L   378 καλῶν
Reiske κακῶν L   384 αὐτὴ Portus αὕτη L   385 ἂν ἔτεκεν Bothe ἔτεκεν ἂν L   390 τὴν
anon. (in Markland) τὸν L   394 ἵν' Hermann ἦν L   ποτώμενος Tr πετόμενος L
395 ἄξενον Markland εὔξεινον L (-ξειν- Tr)   διεπέρασε ⟨πόντου⟩ Schoene διεπέρασεν L

Iphigenia in Tauris

you are making me the bride at an ugly wedding.[365] Now, as you kill me, my mother and the women of Argos are singing wedding songs for me, pipe music fills our palace – and I am perishing at your hands. Achilles, then, was Hades, not Peleus's son; you offered him to me as a husband, then brought me in a carriage[370] to a bloody wedding, deceitfully.' Hiding my face behind a delicate veil, I had not lifted my brother, who now is dead, in my arms, not shared a kiss with my sister; shame forbade me, for I was going, I thought, to Peleus's palace.[375] Many an embrace had I left for another time, when I should once again return to Argos.

Poor Orestes, if you are dead, what a fine and enviable heritage from your father you have lost! As for the goddess's sophistries, I deplore them.[380] When any mortal comes into contact with bloodshed, or touches childbirth or a corpse with their hands, she bars them from her altars, judging them polluted; yet she herself takes pleasure in human sacrifices. It's not possible that Zeus's consort[385] Leto could have given birth to such great ignorance! I for my part do not believe the story of Tantalus's feast for the gods, that they enjoyed a meal of his son. The people here, I think, being murderous themselves, ascribe their weakness to the goddess.[390] I do not think that any of the gods is evil.

Iphigenia remains while the Chorus sings:

Chor.   Dark, dark confluences of sea,   [Strophe 1
        where the gadfly flying from Argos
        crossed over the Unwelcoming ⟨sea⟩-swell,[395]
        passing to Asian land from Europe,

Euripides

τίνες ποτ' ἄρα τὸν εὔυδρον δονακόχλοον
λιπόντες Εὐρώταν 400
ἢ ῥεύματα σεμνὰ Δίρκας
ἔβασαν ἔβασαν ἄμεικτον αἶαν, ἔνθα κούρᾳ
Δίᾳ τέγγει
βωμοὺς καὶ περικίονας 405
ναοὺς αἶμα βρότειον;

ἢ ῥοθίοις [ἀντ. α
εἰλατίνας δικρότοισι κώπας
ἔστειλαν ἐπὶ πόντια κύματα
νάϊον ὄχημα λινοπόροις ⟨σὺν⟩ αὔραις, 410
φιλόπλουτον ἄμιλλαν
αὔξοντες μελάθροισιν;
φίλα γὰρ ἐλπὶς †γένετ' ἐπὶ πήμασι βροτῶν†
ἄπληστος ἀνθρώποις, 415
ὄλβου βάρος οἳ φέρονται
πλάνητες ἐπ' οἶδμα πόλεις ⟨τε⟩ βαρβάρους περῶντες,
κοινᾷ δόξᾳ·
γνώμα δ' οἷς μὲν ἄκαιρος ὄλ- 420
βου, τοῖς δ' ἐς μέσον ἥκει.

πῶς τὰς συνδρομάδας πέτρας, [στρ. β
πῶς Φινεϊδᾶν ἄϋπν-
ους ἀκτὰς ἐπέρα-
σαν, παρ' ἅλιον αἰγιαλὸν ἐπ' Ἀμφιτρί- 425
τας ῥοθίῳ δραμόντες,
ὅπου πεντήκοντα κορᾶν
Νηρήδων ⟨ – ◡ ⟩ χοροὶ
μέλπουσιν ἐγκύκλιοι,
πλησιστίοισι πνοαῖς 430
συριζόντων κατὰ πρύμν-
αν εὐναίων πηδαλίων,

399 δονακόχλοον ⟨L?⟩, Elmsley   -α TrP   403–4 κούρᾳ Δίᾳ τέγγει Elmsley κούρα δια-
τέγγει L   405–6 περικίονας ναοὺς Elmsley περὶ κίονας ναοῦ ⟨L⟩P (ναῶν Tr)   407 ἢ
Barnes ἢ L   εἰλατίνας...κώπας Reiske ἐλατίνοις...κώπαις L (εἰλ- Tr)   409 ἔστειλαν
Rauchenstein ἔπλευσαν L   410 ⟨σὺν⟩ Wecklein   414 ἐγένετ' ed. Aldin.   πήμασιν P
417 ⟨τε⟩ Tr   419 κοινᾷ δόξᾳ Bergk κοιναὶ δόξαι L   421 μέτρον Tucker   423 Φινεϊδᾶν
Rauchenstein Φινηΐδας L (-εΐ- Tr.)   425 παρ' ἅλιον Seidler παράλιον L   428 ⟨ἁβρὰ⟩
West   429 ἐγκύκλιοι Heath ἐγκυκλίοις L   430 καὶ πλησιστίοισι Tr (σὺν Diggle)

Iphigenia in Tauris

who then are these men who have left Eurotas's
beautiful waters and fresh green reeds,[400]
or Dirce's venerable streams,
and come, come to this unwelcoming land, where
for Zeus's daughter
altars and columned temples[405]
   are soaked with human blood?

Have they with double-pounding surges of pinewood oar *[Antistr. 1*
driven their naval vessel
over the sea's waves, with canvas-driving breezes,[410]
in ever more urgent quest of riches for their houses?
Cherished hope †*becomes to the affliction of mortals*†
insatiable for men.[415]
They gather a weight of wealth,
wandering over the sea, roving amongst barbarian peoples,
in common expectation;
but some men's judgment misses the measure of wealth,[420]
   while in others it finds a proper moderation.

How did they pass the converging rocks,   *[Strophe 2*
how pass the unsleeping
   shores of Phineus's sons,
   running past sea-swept coast
   on Amphitrite's surf,[426]
where choruses
of fifty Nereid maidens
circle and sing ⟨   ⟩,
as in sail-swelling gusts[430]
the embedded steering-oars
sing at the stern,

81

Euripides

αὔραισιν νοτίαις
ἢ πνεύμασι Ζεφύρου,
τὰν πολυόρνιθον ἐπ' αἰ- 435
αν, λευκὰν ἀκτάν, Ἀχιλῆ-
ος δρόμους καλλισταδίους,
ἄξεινον κατὰ πόντον;

εἴθ' εὐχαῖσιν δεσποσύνοις *[ἀντ. β*
Λήδας Ἑλένα φίλα 440
παῖς ἐλθοῦσα τύχοι
τὰν Τρῳάδα λιποῦσα πόλιν, ἵν' ἀμφὶ χαίταν δρόσον αἱματηρὰν
ἑλιχθεῖσα λαιμοτόμῳ
δεσποίνας χειρὶ θάνῃ, 445
ποινὰς δοῦσ' ἀντιπάλους.
ἥδιστ' ἂν δ' ἀγγελίαν
δεξαίμεσθ' Ἑλλάδος ἐκ
γᾶς πλωτήρων εἴ τις ἔβα
δουλείας ἐμέθεν 450
δειλαίας παυσίπονος.
⟨κἂν⟩ γὰρ ὀνείροισι συνείην δόμοις πόλει τε πατρῴ-
ᾳ, τερπνῶν ὕπνων ἀπόλαυ-
σιν, κοινὰν χάριν †ὄλβα†. 455

Χο. ἀλλ' οἴδε χέρας δεσμοῖς δίδυμοι
συνερεισθέντες χωροῦσι, νέον
πρόσφαγμα θεᾷ· σιγᾶτε, φίλαι·
τὰ γὰρ Ἑλλήνων ἀκροθίνια δὴ
ναοῖσι πέλας τάδε βαίνει, 460
οὐδ' ἀγγελίας ψευδεῖς ἔλακεν
βουφορβὸς ἀνήρ.
ὦ πότνι', εἴ σοι τάδ' ἀρεσκόντως
πόλις ἥδε τελεῖ, δέξαι θυσίας

433 αὔραισιν Heath -αις L   439 δεσποσύνοις Markland -ας L   442 χαίταν ed. Aldin. χαίτα (i.e. -ᾳ) L   447 δ' Hermann τήνδ' L   448 δεξαίμεσθ' Tr -μεθ' L   452 ⟨κἂν⟩ Herwerden (⟨καὶ⟩ Tr)   ὀνείροισι συνείην Fritzsche ὀνείρασι συμβαίην L   454 τερπνὰν Cropp (-ὴν Herwerden)   ὕπνων Hermann ὕμνων L   455 ὄλβου Dupuy ὄλβω (i.e. -ῳ) Tr 456–66 Χο. Bothe 456–62 Ιφ., 463–66 Χο. L   456 δίδυμοι Markland -οις L   458 θεᾷ Toup θεᾶς L

82

Iphigenia in Tauris

on southerly breezes
or Zephyr's breaths,
to the bird-thronged land,[435]
  the white shore, Achilles'
  fair running-ground,
  upon the Unwelcoming Sea ?

If only through my mistress's prayers   *[Antistrophe 2*
Leda's dear daughter Helen[440]
might come here,
having left Troy's city,
  so that, hair ringed with a bloody dew,
she might die by my mistress's stroke upon her throat,[445]
paying the penalty for her offences.
Most gladly too would I receive
the news, if from Hellas-land
some voyager arrived
to end these pains of slavery
that I in my misery endure.[451]
Even in dreams might I be joined
  with my home and native city,
  boon of pleasant slumbers,
  shared grace †*of bliss?*†.[455]

The Chorus chants as Orestes and Pylades enter by Side-entrance B, bound
and escorted by some of the Taurian herdsmen.

But here with hands tied tight together
the pair of them come,
a new sacrifice for the goddess. Be silent, friends!
Truly the choicest pickings of the Hellenes
are here approaching the altar,[460]
nor was the news the herdsman proclaimed untrue.
O Mistress, if it is pleasing to you
that this community performs these rites,

83

Euripides

ᾶς ὁ παρ᾽ ἡμῖν
νόμος οὐχ ὁσίας ἀναφαίνει.   466

Ιφ. εἶεν·
τὰ τῆς θεοῦ μὲν πρῶτον ὡς καλῶς ἔχῃ
φροντιστέον μοι. μέθετε τῶν ξένων χέρας,
ὡς ὄντες ἱεροὶ μηκέτ᾽ ὦσι δέσμιοι·
ναοῦ δ᾽ ἔσω στείχοντες εὐτρεπίζετε   470
ἃ χρὴ 'πὶ τοῖς παροῦσι καὶ νομίζεται.
φεῦ·
τίς ἄρα μήτηρ ἡ τεκοῦσ᾽ ὑμᾶς ποτε
πατήρ τ᾽; ἀδελφή δ᾽, εἰ γεγῶσα τυγχάνει,
οἵων στερεῖσα διπτύχων νεανιῶν
ἀνάδελφος ἔσται. τὰς τύχας τίς οἶδ᾽ ὅτῳ   475
τοιαίδ᾽ ἔσονται; πάντα γὰρ τὰ τῶν θεῶν
ἐς ἀφανὲς ἕρπει, κοὐδὲν οἶδ᾽ οὐδεὶς σαφές·
ἡ γὰρ τύχη παρήγαγ᾽ ἐς τὸ δυσμαθές.
πόθεν ποθ᾽ ἥκετ᾽, ὦ ταλαίπωροι ξένοι;
ὡς διὰ μακροῦ μὲν τήνδ᾽ ἐπλεύσατε χθόνα,   480
μακρὸν δ᾽ ἀπ᾽ οἴκων χρόνον ἔσεσθε δὴ κάτω.

Ορ. τί ταῦτ᾽ ὀδύρῃ κἀπὶ τοῖς μέλουσι νῷν
κακοῖς σὲ λυπεῖς, ἥτις εἶ ποτ᾽, ὦ γύναι;
οὔτοι νομίζω σοφὸν ὃς ἂν μέλλων κτανεῖν
οἴκτῳ τὸ δεῖμα τοὐλέθρου νικᾶν θέλῃ,   485
οὐδ᾽ ὅστις Ἅιδην ἐγγὺς ὄντ᾽ οἰκτίζεται
σωτηρίας ἄνελπις. ὡς δύ᾽ ἐξ ἑνὸς
κακὼ συνάπτει· μωρίαν τ᾽ ὀφλισκάνει
θνήσκει θ᾽ ὁμοίως. τὴν τύχην δ᾽ ἐᾶν χρεών.
ἡμᾶς δὲ μὴ θρήνει σύ· τὰς γὰρ ἐνθάδε   490
θυσίας ἐπιστάμεσθα καὶ γιγνώσκομεν.

Ιφ. πότερος ἄρ᾽ ὑμῶν †ἐνθάδ᾽ ὠνομασμένος†
Πυλάδης κέκληται; τόδε μαθεῖν πρῶτον θέλω.

Ορ. ὅδ᾽, εἴ τι δή σοι τοῦτ᾽ ἐν ἡδονῇ μαθεῖν.

Ιφ. ποίας πολίτης πατρίδος Ἕλληνος γεγώς;   495

---

466 ἀναφαίνει Bergk Ἕλλησι διδοὺς ἀναφαίνει L   467 ἔχῃ (i.e. -ῃ) TrP -ει or -οι L
470 ναοῦ Valckenaer -οὺς L   473 ἀδελφή δ᾽...τυγχάνει, Markland ἀδελφή τ᾽... τυγχάνει; L   477 σαφές Maas (σαφῶς Wecklein) κακόν L   481 ἔσεσθε δὴ Dobree ἔσεσθ᾽ ἀεὶ L
482 μέλουσι Kvíçala μέλλ- L   483 κακοῖς σὲ Housman κακοῖσι L   484 κτανεῖν Seidler
θανεῖν L   485 θέλῃ (i.e. -ῃ) TrP, Stob. 3.8.6 θέλει L   486 οὐδ᾽ Hermann οὐχ L   494 εἴ
τι Tr ἔστι LP

Iphigenia in Tauris

receive these sacrifices which the law of our own land declares unholy.[466]

Iph. Now then: first I must make sure that everything is right for the goddess. *(To the escort)* Release the strangers' hands – they are sacred and should no longer be tied up. Then go into the temple and prepare[470] what is needed and prescribed for our present task.

(They untie the prisoners' hands and enter the temple. Iphigenia turns to the prisoners.)

Ah! Who, I wonder, can be the mother that bore you, and your father? And your sister, if you have one – what a pair of young brothers she'll lose and be without! Who can know who will have fortunes[475] such as these? All of the gods' designs are obscure in outcome, and no one knows anything for sure, for fortune leads us astray into ignorance. Wherever have you come from, wretched strangers? You surely have sailed long and far to this land;[480] and long will you rest far from home in the earth below.

Or. Why lament and vex yourself over troubles that are our concern, lady, whoever you are? I find it foolish if someone who is going to kill tries to overcome the fear of that death with pity;[485] and foolish too if a man grieves at imminent death when he has no hope of rescue. He makes a pair of evils out of one, showing foolishness and perishing all the same. No, one should let fortune have its way. Sing us no dirges; we know about the sacrifices here and understand them.[491]

Iph. Which of you, then, †*named here*† is called Pylades? This I would like to know first.

Or. (indicating Pylades) This one, if learning it will give you pleasure.

Iph. Of what Hellenic land is he a citizen?[495]

Euripides

Op.	τί δ' ἂν μαθοῦσα τόδε πλέον λάβοις, γύναι;	
Ιφ.	πότερον ἀδελφὼ μητρός ἐστον ἐκ μιᾶς;	
Op.	φιλότητί γ'· ἐσμὲν δ' οὐ κασιγνήτω, γύναι.	
Ιφ.	σοὶ δ' ὄνομα ποῖον ἔθεθ' ὁ γεννήσας πατήρ;	
Op.	τὸ μὲν δίκαιον Δυστυχὴς καλοίμεθ' ἄν.	500
Ιφ.	οὐ τοῦτ' ἐρωτῶ· τοῦτο μὲν δὸς τῇ τύχῃ.	501
Op.	τὸ σῶμα θύσεις τοὐμόν, οὐχὶ τοὔνομα.	504
Ιφ.	τί δὲ φθονεῖς τοῦτ'; ἢ φρονεῖς οὕτω μέγα;	503
Op.	ἀνώνυμοι θανόντες οὐ γελώμεθ' ἄν.	502
Ιφ.	οὐδ' ἂν πόλιν φράσειας ἥτις ἐστί σοι;	505
Op.	ζητεῖς γὰρ οὐδὲν κέρδος ὡς θανουμένῳ.	
Ιφ.	χάριν δὲ δοῦναι τήνδε κωλύει τί σε;	
Op.	τὸ κλεινὸν Ἄργος πατρίδ' ἐμὴν ἐπεύχομαι.	
Ιφ.	πρὸς θεῶν· ἀληθῶς, ὦ ξέν', εἶ κεῖθεν γεγώς;	
Op.	ἐκ τῶν Μυκηνῶν ⟨γ'⟩, αἵ ποτ' ἦσαν ὄλβιαι.	510
Ιφ.	καὶ μὴν ποθεινός γ' ἦλθες ἐξ Ἄργους μολών.	515
Op.	οὔκουν ἐμαυτῷ γ'· εἰ δὲ σοί, σὺ τοῦθ' ὅρα.	516
Ιφ.	φυγὰς ⟨δ'⟩ ἀπῆρας πατρίδος, ἢ ποίᾳ τύχῃ;	511
Op.	φεύγω τρόπον γε δή τιν' οὐχ ἑκὼν ἑκών.	512
Ιφ.	ἆρ' ἄν τί μοι φράσειας ὧν ἐγὼ θέλω;	513
Op.	ὡς ἐν παρέργῳ τῆς ἐμῆς δυσπραξίας.	514
Ιφ.	Τροίαν ἴσως οἶσθ', ἧς ἁπανταχοῦ λόγος;	517
Op.	ὡς μήποτ' ὤφελόν γε μηδ' ἰδὼν ὄναρ.	
Ιφ.	φασίν νιν οὐκέτ' οὖσαν οἴχεσθαι δορί.	
Op.	ἔστιν γὰρ οὕτως, οὐδ' ἄκραντ' ἠκούσατε.	520
Ιφ.	Ἑλένη δ' ἀφῖκται δῶμα Μενέλεω πάλιν;	
Op.	ἥκει, κακῶς γ' ἐλθοῦσα τῶν ἐμῶν τινι.	
Ιφ.	καὶ ποῦ 'στι; κἀμοὶ γάρ τι προυφείλει κακόν.	
Op.	Σπάρτῃ ξυνοικεῖ τῷ πάρος ξυνευνέτῃ.	
Ιφ.	ὦ μῖσος – εἰς Ἕλληνας, οὐκ ἐμοὶ μόνῃ.	525
Op.	ἀπέλαυσα κἀγὼ δή τι τῶν κείνης γάμων.	
Ιφ.	νόστος δ' Ἀχαιῶν ἐγένεθ' ὡς κηρύσσεται;	
Op.	ὡς πάνθ' ἅπαξ με συλλαβοῦσ' ἀνιστορεῖς.	
Ιφ.	πρὶν γὰρ θανεῖν σε τοῦδ' ἐπαυρέσθαι θέλω.	
Op.	ἔλεγχ', ἐπειδὴ τοῦδ' ἐρᾷς, λέξω δ' ἐγώ.	530
Ιφ.	Κάλχας τις ἦλθε μάντις ἐκ Τροίας πάλιν;	

500 Δυστυχὴς Barthold δυστυχεῖς L   504, 503, 502 Barthold   503 ἢ Hermann ἢ L
510 ⟨γ'⟩ Monk   515–16 after 510, Platnauer   516 τοῦθ' ὅρα Jacobs τοῦτ' ἔρα L
511 ⟨δ'⟩ Scaliger

Iphigenia in Tauris

Or. And what good would you get from learning that, lady?
Iph. Are you brothers, both born from the same mother?
Or. Brothers in affection, but we are not siblings, lady.
Iph. And what name did the father who sired you give you?
Or. By rights I should be called Unfortunate.[500]
Iph. That's not what I'm asking; credit that to fortune.[501]
Or. It's my body you will sacrifice, not my name.[504]
Iph. But why grudge me this? Are you so very proud?[503]
Or. By dying unnamed I shall remain unmocked.[502]
Iph. You'll not even tell me what your city is?[505]
Or. No, your question offers me no profit when I'm about to die.
Iph. But what prevents you from granting me this as a favour?
Or. (relenting) I proclaim illustrious Argos as my homeland.
Iph. By the gods! That's really where you are sprung from, stranger?
Or. Yes, from Mycenae, a city that once was prosperous.[510]
Iph. Your arrival is longed for indeed if you come from Argos![515]
Or. Not to myself; if to you, you must judge for yourself.[516]
Iph. You left your homeland as an exile, or by what chance?[511]
Or. I'm a kind of exile, both unwilling and willing.[512]
Iph. Would you perhaps tell me something I want to hear?[513]
Or. Very well, as an aside from my ill fortune.[514]
Iph. You know perhaps of Troy, which they talk of everywhere?[517]
Or. Would I had never done so, even in a dream!
Iph. They say it is no more, destroyed by war.
Or. Yes, that is so; it is no idle report.[520]
Iph. Has Helen returned to Menelaus's house?
Or. She has, an evil return for one of my family.
Iph. And where is she now? She has long owed me payment for a wrong as well.
Or. She is living at Sparta with her former husband.
Iph. Hateful creature – to the Hellenes, not me alone![525]
Or. (ironic) I too have had some benefit from her marriage.
Iph. And the Achaeans' return came about as reported?
Or. How you pull everything together in your questioning!
Iph. Yes, I want to get some benefit from this before you die.
Or. Ask away, since that's what you want, and I will answer.[530]
Iph. Did a prophet called Calchas make the return from Troy?

Euripides

Op. ὄλωλεν, ὡς ἦν ἐν Μυκηναίοις λόγος.
Ιφ. ὦ πότνι' ὡς εὖ. τί γὰρ ὁ Λαέρτου γόνος;
Op. οὔπω νενόστηκ' οἶκον· ἔστι δ', ὡς λόγος.
Ιφ. ὄλοιτο, νόστου μήποτ' ἐς πάτραν τυχών.	535
Op. μηδὲν κατεύχου· πάντα τἀκείνου νοσεῖ.
Ιφ. Θέτιδος δ' ὁ τῆς Νηρῇδος ἔστι παῖς ἔτι;
Op. οὐκ ἔστιν· ἄλλως λέκτρ' ἔγημ' ἐν Αὐλίδι.
Ιφ. δόλια γάρ, ὡς ἴσασιν οἱ πεπονθότες.
Op. τίς εἶ ποθ'; ὡς εὖ πυνθάνῃ τἀφ' Ἑλλάδος.	540
Ιφ. ἐκεῖθέν εἰμι· παῖς ἔτ' οὖσ' ἀπωλόμην.
Op. ὀρθῶς ποθεῖς ἄρ' εἰδέναι τἀκεῖ, γύναι.
Ιφ. τί δ' ὁ στρατηγὸς ὃν λέγουσ' εὐδαίμονα;
Op. τίς; οὐ γὰρ ὅν γ' ἐγῷδα τῶν εὐδαιμόνων.
Ιφ. Ἀτρέως ἐλέγετο δή τις Ἀγαμέμνων ἄναξ.	545
Op. οὐκ οἶδ'· ἄπελθε τοῦ λόγου τούτου, γύναι.
Ιφ. μὴ πρὸς θεῶν, ἀλλ' εἴφ' ἵν' εὐφρανθῶ, ξένε.
Op. τέθνηχ' ὁ τλήμων· πρὸς δ' ἀπώλεσέν τινα.
Ιφ. τέθνηκε; ποίᾳ συμφορᾷ; τάλαιν' ἐγώ.
Op. τί δ' ἐστέναξας τοῦτο· μῶν προσῆκέ σοι;	550
Ιφ. τὸν ὄλβον αὐτοῦ τὸν πάροιθ' ἀναστένω.
Op. δεινῶς γὰρ ἐκ γυναικὸς οἴχεται σφαγείς.
Ιφ. ὦ πανδάκρυτος ἡ κτανοῦσα χὠ θανών.
Op. παῦσαί νυν ἤδη, μήδ' ἐρωτήσῃς πέρα.
Ιφ. τοσόνδε γ', εἰ ζῇ τοῦ ταλαιπώρου δάμαρ.	555
Op. οὐκ ἔστι· παῖς νιν ὃν ἔτεχ', οὗτος ὤλεσεν.
Ιφ. ὦ συνταραχθεὶς οἶκος· ὡς τί δὴ θέλων;
Op. πατρὸς θανόντος τήνδε τιμωρούμενος.
Ιφ. φεῦ·
	ὡς εὖ κακὸν δίκαιον ἐξεπράξατο.
Op. ἀλλ' οὐ τὰ πρὸς θεῶν εὐτυχεῖ δίκαιος ὤν.	560
Ιφ. λείπει δ' ἐν οἴκοις ἄλλον Ἀγαμέμνων γόνον;
Op. λέλοιπεν Ἠλέκτραν γε παρθένον μίαν.
Ιφ. τί δέ; σφαγείσης θυγατρὸς ἔστι τις λόγος;
Op. οὐδείς γε, πλὴν θανοῦσαν οὐχ ὁρᾶν φάος.
Ιφ. τάλαιν' ἐκείνη χὠ κτανὼν αὐτὴν πατήρ.	565
Op. κακῆς γυναικὸς χάριν ἄχαριν ἀπώλετο.

533 εὖ. τί Musgrave ἔστι L   538 ἄλλως Tr ἄλλως δὲ ⟨L⟩P   ἔγημ' ἐν Dupuy ἔγημεν L
539 ἴσασιν Nauck φασὶν L   543 εὐδαίμονα Markland εὐδαιμονεῖν L   553 θανών Tr
κτανών ⟨L⟩P   559 ἐξεπράξατο Elmsley εἰσ- L

Iphigenia in Tauris

Or. He is dead, so the word was in Mycenae.
Iph. O Mistress, how good that is! And what of Laertes' son?
Or. He has not yet reached home, but is living, so it is said.
Iph. May he perish and never get back to his homeland![535]
Or. No need to curse him; all his affairs are ailing.
Iph. And the Nereid Thetis's son, is he still living?
Or. No; that was a vain marriage he made at Aulis.
Iph. Yes, a false one, as those who have suffered from it know.
Or. Who are you? How keenly you search for news from Hellas![540]
Iph. I am from there; I was lost when still a child.
Or. So you rightfully long to know the news from there, lady.
Iph. And what of the general they call fortunate?
Or. Who is that? The one I know is not one of the fortunate.
Iph. A son of Atreus was called so, king Agamemnon.[545]
Or. I know nothing of him; leave that subject, lady!
Iph. No, by the gods! Speak out and satisfy me, stranger!
Or. The poor man is dead – and destroyed someone else as well.
Iph. He's dead? Through what misfortune? Wretched am I!
Or. Why lament at that? He surely was nothing to you?[550]
Iph. (composing herself) I'm lamenting the prosperity he once had.
Or. Yes, he perished terribly, slaughtered by his wife.
Iph. O lamentable – she who killed *and* he who died!
Or. Just stop there now. Don't ask any further questions.
Iph. This much more only: is the poor man's wife still living?[555]
Or. She is not. The son she bore became her killer.
Iph. O family in turmoil! Why did he do it?
Or. He was taking vengeance on her for his dead father.
Iph. Alas, how well he performed a righteous wrong!
Or. But gets no good fortune from the gods, though he acted justly.[560]
Iph. And does Agamemnon leave other offspring in the house?
Or. Yes, he has left a single daughter, Electra.
Iph. And what of his sacrificed daughter, is there word of her?
Or. None, but that she died and no longer sees the light.[564]
Iph. Unhappy one, and unhappy the father who killed her!
Or. She perished for the thankless sake of an evil woman.

Euripides

Ιφ. ὁ τοῦ θανόντος δ' ἔστι παῖς Ἄργει πατρός;
Ορ. ἔστ' ἄθλιός γε κοὐδαμοῦ καὶ πανταχοῦ.
Ιφ. ψευδεῖς ὄνειροι, χαίρετ', οὐδὲν ἦτ' ἄρα.
Ορ. οὐδ' οἱ σοφοί γε δαίμονες κεκλημένοι   570
    πτηνῶν ὀνείρων εἰσὶν ἀψευδέστεροι.
    [πολὺς ταραγμὸς ἔν τε τοῖς θείοις ἔνι
    κἀν τοῖς βροτείοις· ἓν δὲ λυπεῖται μόνον,
    ὅτ' οὐκ ἄφρων ὤν, μάντεων πεισθεὶς λόγοις,
    ὄλωλεν ὡς ὄλωλε τοῖσιν εἰδόσιν.]   575
Χο. φεῦ φεῦ· τί δ' ἡμεῖς οἵ τ' ἐμοὶ γεννήτορες;
    ἆρ' εἰσίν; ἆρ' οὐκ εἰσί; τίς φράσειεν ἄν;
Ιφ. ἀκούσατ'· ἐς γὰρ δή τιν' ἥκομεν λόγον,
    ὑμῖν τ' ὄνησιν, ὦ ξένοι, σπεύδουσ' ἅμα
    κἀμοί· τὸ δ' εὖ μάλιστά γ' ὧδε γίγνεται   580
    εἰ πᾶσι ταὐτὸν πρᾶγμ' ἀρεσκόντως ἔχει·
    θέλοις ἄν, εἰ σώσαιμί σ', ἀγγεῖλαί τί μοι
    πρὸς Ἄργος ἐλθὼν τοῖς ἐμοῖς ἐκεῖ φίλοις,
    δέλτον τ' ἐνεγκεῖν ἥν τις οἰκτίρας ἐμὲ
    ἔγραψεν αἰχμάλωτος, οὐχὶ τὴν ἐμὴν   585
    φονέα νομίζων χεῖρα, τοῦ νόμου δ' ὕπο
    θνήσκειν, τὰ τῆς θεοῦ τάδε δίκαι' ἡγούμενος;
    οὐδένα γὰρ εἶχον ὅστις ἀγγείλαι μολὼν
    ἐς Ἄργος αὖθις τάς ⟨τ'⟩ ἐμὰς ἐπιστολὰς
    πέμψειε σωθεὶς τῶν ἐμῶν φίλων τινί.   590
    σὺ δ' – εἶ γὰρ ὡς ἔοικας οὔτι δυσγενὴς
    καὶ τὰς Μυκήνας οἶσθα χοὓς ἐγὼ φιλῶ –
    σώθητι κεῖσε, μισθὸν οὐκ αἰσχρὸν λαβών,
    κούφων ἕκατι γραμμάτων σωτηρίαν.
    οὗτος δ', ἐπείπερ πόλις ἀναγκάζει τάδε,   595
    θεᾷ γενέσθω θῦμα χωρισθεὶς σέθεν.
Ορ. καλῶς ἔλεξας τἆλλα πλὴν ἕν, ὦ ξένη·
    τὸ γὰρ σφαγῆναι τόνδ' ἐμοὶ βάρος μέγα.

570–75 Ορ. Heath   569–75 Ιφ. L (572–75 Ορ. Tr)   570 οὐδ' Hermann οὔθ' L   572–75
del. Cropp (570–75 susp. Diggle)   572 θείοις Scaliger θεοῖς L   573 λείπεται Tr
579 σπεύδουσ' Musgrave σπουδῆς L   580 τὸ δ' Markland τόδ' L   ὧδε Porson οὕτω L
582 θέλοις Portus θέλεις L   587 τὰ Hermann (]τα τ[ο]υ θεου τ[Π²) γε L   τάδε Pierson
ταῦτα L   ἡγούμενος Hermann ἡγουμένης L   589 ⟨τ'⟩ Bothe   590 τινί Lˢˡ τινός L
591 οὔτι A. Y. Campbell   οὔτε L   οὐχί Diggle   592 ἐγὼ Markland κἀγὼ L   φιλῶ Musgrave θέλω L   593 κεῖσε Heimsoeth (σώθητ' ἐκεῖσε Musgrave) καὶ σὺ L (κα[Π²)

90

Iphigenia in Tauris

Iph. The dead king's son, is he now living at Argos?

Or. He lives a troubled life, nowhere and everywhere.

Iph. Deceptive dreams, farewell, you were nothing, then!

Or. Nor indeed are the gods who are called wise[570] more undeceiving than flighty dreams. [*There is much turmoil in divine affairs and in human ones; but he feels grief at one thing only, when not being foolish, persuaded by seers' pronouncements, he is ruined as those who know it know he is ruined.*][575]

Chor. Alas, and what of us, what of our parents? Are they alive, are they not? Who can tell us this?

Iph. *(to the prisoners)* Listen: I have just come upon a plan, pursuing both your advantage, strangers, and mine; and this is the best basis for good results,[580] if the same transaction is satisfying for all. Would you be willing, were I to rescue you, to go to Argos and take a message for me to my loved ones there, and carry a letter which a captive, taking pity on me, wrote, not[585] reckoning my hand guilty of his murder, but that he was dying by virtue of the law, thinking these rites of the goddess legitimate? I've had no one who could go and take news back to Argos and bring my letter, once safe, to one of my loved ones.[590] But you, it seems, are not of lowly birth and know Mycenae and those I love. So be saved and go there, getting no mean payment, your rescue for carrying these insubstantial writings. And since the community requires these things,[595] let your companion be a victim for the goddess without you.

Or. Your plan is excellent, stranger, but for one thing. The slaying of this man would be a great weight on me. I am the one who

Euripides

ὁ ναυστολῶν γάρ εἰμ' ἐγὼ τὰς συμφοράς,
οὗτος δὲ συμπλεῖ τῶν ἐμῶν μόχθων χάριν. 600
οὔκουν δίκαιον ἐπ' ὀλέθρῳ τῷ τοῦδ' ἐμὲ
χάριν τίθεσθαι καὐτὸν ἐκδῦναι κακῶν.
ἀλλ' ὣς γενέσθω· τῷδε μὲν δέλτον δίδου
(πέμψει γὰρ Ἄργος ὥστε σοι καλῶς ἔχειν),
ἡμᾶς δ' ὁ χρῄζων κτεινέτω. τὰ τῶν φίλων 605
αἴσχιστον ὅστις καταβαλὼν ἐς ξυμφορὰς
αὐτὸς σέσωται· τυγχάνει δ' ὅδ' ὢν φίλος
ὃν οὐδὲν ἧσσον ἢ 'μὲ φῶς ὁρᾶν θέλω.

Ιφ. ὦ λῆμ' ἄριστον· ὡς ἀπ' εὐγενοῦς τινος
ῥίζης πέφυκας, τοῖς φίλοις τ' ὀρθῶς φίλος. 610
τοιοῦτος εἴη τῶν ἐμῶν ὁμοσπόρων
ὅσπερ λέλειπται· καὶ γὰρ οὐδ' ἐγώ, ξένοι,
ἀνάδελφός εἰμι, πλὴν ὅσ' οὐχ ὁρῶσά νιν.
ἐπεὶ δὲ βούλῃ ταῦτα, τόνδε πέμψομεν
δέλτον φέροντα, σὺ δὲ θανῇ· πολλὴ δέ τις 615
προθυμία σε τοῦδ' ἔχουσα τυγχάνει.

Ορ. θύσει δὲ τίς με καὶ τὰ δεινὰ τλήσεται;
Ιφ. ἐγώ· θεᾶς γὰρ τήνδε συμφορὰν ἔχω.
Ορ. ἄζηλον, ὦ νεᾶνι, κοὐκ εὐδαίμονα.
Ιφ. ἀλλ' εἰς ἀνάγκην κείμεθ', ἣν φυλακτέον. 620
Ορ. αὐτὴ ξίφει κτείνουσα θῆλυς ἄρσενας;
Ιφ. οὔκ, ἀλλὰ χαίτην ἀμφὶ σὴν χερνίψομαι.
Ορ. ὁ δὲ σφαγεὺς τίς, εἰ τόδ' ἱστορεῖν με χρή;
Ιφ. ἔσω δόμων τῶνδ' εἰσὶν οἷς μέλει τάδε.
Ορ. τάφος δὲ ποῖος δέξεταί μ' ὅταν θάνω; 625
Ιφ. πῦρ ἱερὸν ἔνδον χάσμα τ' εὐρωπὸν πέτρας.
Ορ. φεῦ·
πῶς ἄν μ' ἀδελφῆς χεὶρ περιστείλειεν ἄν;
Ιφ. μάταιον εὐχήν, ὦ τάλας, ὅστις ποτ' εἶ,
ηὔξω· μακρὰν γὰρ βαρβάρου ναίει χθονός.
οὐ μήν, ἐπειδὴ τυγχάνεις Ἀργεῖος ὤν, 630
ἀλλ' ὧν γε δυνατὸν οὐδ' ἐγὼ 'λλείψω χάριν.
πολύν τε γάρ σοι κόσμον ἐνθήσω τάφῳ,

---

610 ὀρθῶς Tr ὀρθὸς L   618 τήνδε Π² (conj. Bothe) τῆσδε L   συμ[φο]ραν Π² προς-
τροπὴν L   619 ἄζηλον Bothe ἄζηλά γ' L   621 κτεινουσα Π² θύουσα L   622 οὔκ Tr
(and probably Π²) οὔκουν LP   623 τόδ' Diggle τάδ' L   626 πέτρας L   631 'λλείψω
Markland λείψω L

Iphigenia in Tauris

bears this cargo of misfortunes, while he is sailing with me because of my ordeals.[600] It would surely not be right, at the cost of his destruction, to do you this favour and escape from peril myself. Let it be this way, then: give him the letter – he'll take it to Argos, so all will be well for you – and let him who desires it kill me.[605] It brings great disgrace when a man has cast friends into adversity and survived himself; and this man is a friend whose life I value no less than my own.

Iph. O excellent nature – what a noble root you have grown from, and what proper friendship you show to your friends![610] May that brother of mine who still lives be such a man! For I too, strangers, am not without a brother, except insofar as he is not before my eyes. But since this is what you want, I'll send him with the letter, and you shall die. A great[615] desire for this possesses you, for some reason.

Or. But who will sacrifice me and dare the terrible deed?

Iph. I shall, for this is the fortune I have from the goddess.

Or. An unenviable one, young lady, and not a happy one.

Iph. But I am under compulsion, and must heed it.[620]

Or. Killing me with the sword yourself, female killing male?

Iph. No, but I'll sprinkle holy water around your head.

Or. And who will be the slaughterer, if I may ask this?

Iph. Those with that duty are in the building here.

Or. And what kind of burial will receive me when I die?[625]

Iph. A sacred fire inside, and a broad chasm in the rock.

Or. Alas, if only my sister's hand could prepare me for burial!

Iph. That's a vain wish, poor man, whoever you are, for she lives far from this barbarian land. Yet, since you are an Argive,[630] I too will not neglect to offer you what service I can. I'll give you much adornment for burial, and †*quench*† your body with

Euripides

ξανθῷ τ' ἐλαίῳ σῶμα σὸν †κατασβέσω†,
καὶ τῆς ὀρείας ἀνθεμόρρυτον γάνος
ξουθῆς μελίσσης ἐς πυρὰν βαλῶ σέθεν.   635
ἀλλ' εἶμι, δέλτον τ' ἐκ θεᾶς ἀνακτόρων
οἴσω. τὸ μέντοι δυσμενὲς μή μοὐγκαλῆς,
φυλάσσετ' αὐτούς, πρόσπολοι, δεσμῶν ἄτερ.
ἴσως ἄελπτα τῶν ἐμῶν φίλων τινὶ
πέμψω πρὸς Ἄργος ὃν μάλιστ' ἐγὼ φιλῶ,   640
καὶ δέλτος αὐτῷ ζῶντας οὓς δοκεῖ θανεῖν
λέγουσ' ἀπίστους ἡδονὰς ἀπαγγελεῖ.

Χο.   κατολοφύρομαί σε τὸν χερνίβων
       ῥανίσι μελόμενον ⟨μέλεον⟩ αἱμακταῖς.   645

Ορ.   ἀλλ' οὐ γὰρ οἶκτος ταῦτα χαίρετ', ὦ ξέναι.

Χο.   σὲ δὲ τύχας μάκαρος, ὦ νεανία,
       σεβόμεθ' ἐς πάτραν ὅτι πόδ' ἐμβάσῃ.

Πυ.   ἄζηλά τοι φίλοισι θνησκόντων φίλων.   650

Χο.   ὦ σχέτλιοι πομπαί·
       †φεῦ φεῦ διόλλυσαι –
       αἰαῖ, αἰαῖ – πότερος ὁ μέλλων;†
       ἔτι γὰρ ἀμφίλογα δίδυμα μέμονε φρήν,   655
       σὲ πάρος ἢ σ' ἀναστενάξω γόοις.

Ορ.   Πυλάδη, πέπονθας ταὐτὸ πρὸς θεῶν ἐμοί;

Πυ.   οὐκ οἶδ'· ἐρωτᾷς οὐ λέγειν ἔχοντά με.

Ορ.   τίς ἐστιν ἡ νεᾶνις; ὡς Ἑλληνικῶς   660
       ἀνήρεθ' ἡμᾶς τούς τ' ἐν Ἰλίῳ πόνους
       νόστον τ' Ἀχαιῶν τόν τ' ἐν οἰωνοῖς σοφὸν
       Κάλχαντ' Ἀχιλλέως τ' ὄνομα, καὶ τὸν ἄθλιον
       Ἀγαμέμνον' ὡς ᾤκτιρ' ἀνηρώτα τέ με
       γυναῖκα παῖδάς τ'. ἔστιν ἡ ξένη γένος   665
       ἐκεῖθεν Ἀργεία τις· οὐ γὰρ ἄν ποτε

633 κατασκεδῶ Geel   635 πυρὰν βαλῶ Canter   πῦρ ἐμβαλὼν L   636 τ' ἐκ Tr   τε LP
637 μή μοὐγκαλῆς Jackson (μή μοι 'γκαλῆς Kirchhoff)   μή μου λάβῃς L   642 λέγουσ'
ἀπίστους Portus   λέγουσα πιστὰς L   645 ⟨μέλεον⟩ Monk   646 ἀλλ' οὐ γὰρ οἶκτος ταῦτα
Weil   οἶκτος γὰρ οὐ ταῦτ, ἀλλὰ L   649 πόδ' Elmsley   ποτ' L   ἐμβάσῃ Seidler   ἐπεμβάσῃ L
650 ἄζηλά τοι Burges   ἄζηλα τοῖς L   651–57 Xo. Tr   651–52 Πυ., 653–57 Xo. ⟨L⟩P
652 ⟨δύο⟩ διολλῦσαι Bothe   654 μᾶλλον Musgrave   655 ἀμφίλογα ed. Brubach. ἀμφί-
φλογα L   μέμονε Lˢˡ μέμηνε L

Iphigenia in Tauris

yellow olive-oil, and on your pyre I'll pour the flower-dripped dew of the humming mountain-bee.[635]

Well, I must go and bring the letter from the goddess's temple. But lest you hold this hostility against me – servants, guard them here, but keep them unbound. Perhaps it's unexpected news I'll send to Argos for one of my loved ones, the one that I love most,[640] and this letter, telling him those whom he thinks died are living, will announce to him incredible joys.

Iphigenia exits into the temple. The Chorus sings a brief lament with Orestes and Pylades speaking in response.

Cho.   I cry in lamentation for you who are destined ⟨wretched one⟩ for the lustral water's bloody shower.[645]

Or.   No, this is nothing to be mourned. Be happy, strangers.

Chor.   And you, young man, we honour for your happy fortune, that you will set foot in your native land.

Pyl.   That is no enviable thing for a friend, when friends are dying.[650]

Cho.   O harsh dispatchings!
†*Ah, Ah, you are perishing –*
aiai, aiai – which the one about to?†
My mind still wavers in ambivalent purpose,[655] whether I'll first bemoan you, or you, with my laments.

Orestes and Pylades converse.

Or.   Pylades, do you have the same feeling, by heaven, as I do?

Pyl.   I do not know. You ask and I cannot answer.

Or.   Who is this young woman? How Hellenic[660] was her style in questioning us on the hard times at Troy and the Achaeans' return, on Calchas wise in bird-signs and famed Achilles! What sorrow she showed for poor Agamemnon, and questioned me also about his wife and children! This stranger[665] is an Argive by descent and comes from there, or she would never

95

Euripides

δέλτον τ' ἔπεμπε καὶ τάδ' ἐξεμάνθανεν
ὡς κοινὰ πράσσουσ' Ἄργος εἰ πράσσει καλῶς.

Πυ. ἔφθης με μικρόν, ταὐτὰ δὲ φθάσας λέγεις
πλὴν ἕν· τὰ γάρ τοι βασιλέων παθήματα 670
ἴσασι πάντες ὧν ἐπιστροφή τις ᾖ.
ἀτὰρ διῆλθον χἄτερον λόγον τινά.

Ορ. τίν'; ἐς τὸ κοινὸν δοὺς ἄμεινον ἂν μάθοις.

Πυ. αἰσχρὸν θανόντος σοῦ βλέπειν ἡμᾶς φάος.
κοινῇ δὲ πλεύσας δεῖ με καὶ κοινῇ θανεῖν. 675
καὶ δειλίαν γὰρ καὶ κάκην κεκτήσομαι
Ἄργει τε Φωκέων τ' ἐν πολυπτύχῳ χθονί·
δόξω δὲ τοῖς πολλοῖσι (πολλοὶ γὰρ κακοί)
προδοὺς σεσῶσθαι σ' αὐτὸς εἰς οἴκους μόνος,
ἢ καὶ φονεῦσαί σ' ἐπὶ νοσοῦσι δώμασιν 680
ῥάψας μόρον σοι σῆς τυραννίδος χάριν,
ἔγκληρον ὡς δὴ σὴν κασιγνήτην γαμῶν.
ταῦτ' οὖν φοβοῦμαι καὶ δι' αἰσχύνης ἔχω·
κοὐκ ἔσθ' ὅπως οὐ χρὴ συνεκπνεῦσαί μέ σοι
καὶ συσφαγῆναι καὶ πυρωθῆναι δέμας, 685
φίλον γεγῶτα καὶ φοβούμενον ψόγον.

Ορ. εὔφημα φώνει· τἀμὰ δεῖ φέρειν κακά,
ἁπλᾶς δὲ λύπας ἐξόν, οὐκ οἴσω διπλᾶς.
ὃ γὰρ σὺ λυπρὸν κἀπονείδιστον λέγεις
ταῦτ' ἔστιν ἡμῖν εἴ σε συμμοχθοῦντ' ἐμοὶ 690
κτενῶ. τὸ μὲν γὰρ εἰς ἔμ' οὐ κακῶς ἔχει,
πράσσονθ' ἃ πράσσω πρὸς θεῶν, λήγειν βίου.
σὺ δ' ὄλβιός τ' εἶ, καθαρά τ' οὐ νοσοῦντ' ἔχεις
μέλαθρ', ἐγὼ δὲ δυσσεβῆ καὶ δυστυχῆ.
σωθεὶς δέ, παῖδας ἐξ ἐμῆς ὁμοσπόρου 695
κτησάμενος, ἣν ἔδωκά σοι δάμαρτ' ἔχειν,
ὄνομά τ' ἐμοῦ γένοιτ' ἄν, οὐδ' ἄπαις δόμος
πατρῷος οὑμὸς ἐξαλειφθείη ποτ' ἄν.
ἀλλ' ἕρπε καὶ ζῆ καὶ δόμους οἴκει πατρός.
ὅταν δ' ἐς Ἑλλάδ' ἵππιόν τ' Ἄργος μόλῃς, 700

---

670 τοι Hermann τῶν L   671 ᾖ Hartung ἦν L   672 διῆλθον Porson διῆλθε L
673 μάθοις L^sl μάθης (i.e. -ῃς) L   675 δὲ πλεύσας Elmsley τ' ἔπλευσα L   679 σεσῶσθαι
σ(ὲ) Stinton (σεσῶσθαί σ(ε) Elmsley) σε σώζεσθ' L   680–81 φονεῦσαί σ'...ῥάψας Bergk
φονεύσας...ῥάψαι L   690 ταῦτ' (i.e. τὸ αὐτό) L. Dindorf   ταῦτ' L   692 λήγειν βίου
Markland λήσειν βίον L (λήγειν L^sl)

96

Iphigenia in Tauris

be sending the letter and making these enquiries as if she shares its good fortune if Argos fares well.

Pyl. You're a little ahead of me but are saying the same, except for one thing: the sufferings of kings[670] are surely known to everyone who gives them any thought. But there is another point too that I've considered.

Or. What is it? You'll learn better if you share it.

Pyl. It's shameful for me to go on living when you have died. I shared the voyage with you and should also share your death.[675] Cowardice and baseness will be imputed to me in Argos and in Phocis with its many valleys. The people at large will believe (low as they are) that I got home safely myself by betraying you, or even murdered you now that your family is in trouble,[680] plotting your fate in order to gain your kingdom, seeing that I'm married to your sister, its heiress. This makes me fearful and provokes my sense of shame; and it's surely right that I should breathe my last with you, be slaughtered and have my body burned with you,[685] when I am your friend and have this fear of censure.

Or. Don't say such things! I must bear my own troubles, but I won't bear double pains when they can be single. What you are calling grievous and contemptible is the same for me if I bring you, my fellow-toiler,[690] to your death. For my part it's no bad thing, faring as I fare at the gods' hands, to cease from life. But you are fortunate; your home is unsullied, not diseased, while mine is impious and unlucky. If you are saved, you can get sons from my sister,[695] whom I gave to you to have as your wife; my name can be known, nor would my ancestral house be childless and in time obliterated. No, go and live and dwell in your father's house. And when you come

Euripides

πρὸς δεξιᾶς σε τῆσδ' ἐπισκήπτω τάδε·
τύμβον τε χῶσον κἀπίθες μνημεῖά μοι,
καὶ δάκρυ' ἀδελφὴ καὶ κόμας δότω τάφῳ·
ἄγγελλε δ' ὡς ὄλωλ' ὑπ' Ἀργείας τινὸς
γυναικὸς ἀμφὶ βωμὸν ἁγνισθεὶς φόνῳ. 705
καὶ μὴ προδῷς μου τὴν κασιγνήτην ποτέ,
ἔρημα κήδη καὶ δόμους ὁρῶν πατρός.
καὶ χαῖρ'· ἐμῶν γὰρ φίλτατόν σ' ηὗρον φίλων,
ὦ συγκυναγὲ καὶ συνεκτραφεὶς ἐμοί,
ὦ πόλλ' ἐνεγκὼν τῶν ἐμῶν ἄχθη κακῶν. 710
ἡμᾶς δ' ὁ Φοῖβος μάντις ὢν ἐψεύσατο·
τέχνην δὲ θέμενος ὡς προσώταθ' Ἑλλάδος
ἀπήλασ' αἰδοῖ τῶν πάρος μαντευμάτων.
ᾧ πάντ' ἐγὼ δοὺς τἀμὰ καὶ πεισθεὶς λόγοις
μητέρα κατακτὰς αὐτὸς ἀνταπόλλυμαι. 715
Πυ. ἔσται τάφος σοι, καὶ κασιγνήτης λέχος
οὐκ ἂν προδοίην, ὦ τάλας, ἐπεί σ' ἐγὼ
θανόντα μᾶλλον ἢ βλέπονθ' ἕξω φίλον.
ἀτὰρ τὸ τοῦ θεοῦ σ' οὐ διέφθορέν γέ πω
μάντευμα, καίτοι γ' ἐγγὺς ἕστηκας φόνου· 720
ἀλλ' ἔστιν, ἔστιν ἡ λίαν δυσπραξία
λίαν διδοῦσα μεταβολάς, ὅταν τύχῃ.
Ορ. σίγα· τὰ Φοίβου δ' οὐδὲν ὠφελεῖ μ' ἔπη·
γυνὴ γὰρ ἥδε δωμάτων ἔξω περᾷ.

Ιφ. ἀπέλθεθ' ὑμεῖς καὶ παρευτρεπίζετε 725
τἄνδον μολόντες τοῖς ἐφεστῶσι σφαγῇ.
δέλτου μὲν αἴδε πολύθυροι διαπτυχαί,
ξένοι, πάρεισιν· ἃ δ' ἐπὶ τοῖσδε βούλομαι
ἀκοῦσατ'· οὐδεὶς αὐτὸς ἐν πόνοις ⟨τ'⟩ ἀνὴρ
ὅταν τε πρὸς τὸ θάρσος ἐκ φόβου πέσῃ. 730
ἐγὼ δὲ ταρβῶ μὴ ἀπονοστήσας χθονὸς
θῆται παρ' οὐδὲν τὰς ἐμὰς ἐπιστολὰς
ὁ τήνδε μέλλων δέλτον εἰς Ἄργος φέρειν.
Ορ. τί δῆτα βούλῃ; τίνος ἀμηχανεῖς πέρι;

714 ᾧ Tr ὦ LP   719 σ'...γέ Nauck (γ'...σέ Reiske) γ'...μέ L   720 κἄγγὺς Erfurdt
727 πολύθυροι Aristot. *Rhet.* 1407b35 πολύθρηνοι L   728 ξένοι Pierson -οις L
729 αὐτὸς Valckenaer αὐτὸς L ⟨τ'⟩ Köchly

Iphigenia in Tauris

to Hellas and horse-rearing Argos,[700] by this right hand of yours I charge you with this duty. Pile up a barrow, and place on it tokens of remembrance; let my sister offer tears and hair on the grave, and report how I perished at the hands of an Argive woman, purified by her at the altar for slaughter.[705] And never forsake my sister when you see your marriage alliance and my father's house destitute. And fare well! For of all my friends I have found you the dearest, my fellow hunts- man, fellow in upbringing, who have borne so much of the burden of my troubles.[710] But Phoebus, seer though he is, de- ceived me. He used a trick and drove me as far from Hellas as he could, in shame at his earlier pronouncements. I trusted my whole fate to him and obeyed his words, and killed my mother; and now I perish in my turn[715]

Pyl. You shall have a tomb, and I shall not betray my marriage with your sister, my poor friend; for I shall hold you dearer in death than in life. Still, the god's pronouncement has not yet destroyed you, though indeed you are standing close to death;[720] yet sure, O sure it is that extreme adversity does on occasion bring extreme reverses.

Or. Be quiet! Phoebus's words are giving me no help. Here is the woman now, coming out of the house.

Iphigenia re-enters from the temple, carrying her letter.

Iph. Be gone now, servants, and get[725] things ready inside for those in charge of the slaughter.

(They obey. Iphigenia turns to the prisoners.)

Here now is the many-leaved letter, strangers. But listen to what I want in addition to what we have agreed. No one is the same man both in trouble and when he escapes from fear and regains his nerve.[730] I fear that the one of you who will carry this letter to Argos may count my instructions for nothing once he has made his way home from this country.

Or. So what do you want? What is it that perplexes you?

Euripides

Ιφ. ὅρκον δότω μοι τάσδε πορθμεύσειν γραφὰς 735
πρὸς Ἄργος οἷσι βούλομαι πέμψαι φίλων.
Ορ. ἦ κἀντιδώσεις τῷδε τοὺς αὐτοὺς λόγους;
Ιφ. τί χρῆμα δράσειν ἢ τί μὴ δράσειν; λέγε.
Ορ. ἐκ γῆς ἀφήσειν μὴ θανόντα βαρβάρου.
Ιφ. δίκαιον εἶπας· πῶς γὰρ ἀγγείλειεν ἄν; 740
Ορ. ἦ καὶ τύραννος ταῦτα συγχωρήσεται;
Ιφ. ναί·
πείσω σφε, καὐτὴ ναὸς ἐσβήσω σκάφος.
Ορ. ὄμνυ· σὺ δ᾽ ἔξαρχ᾽ ὅρκον ὅστις εὐσεβής.
Ιφ. 'Δώσω', λέγειν χρή, 'τήνδε τοῖσι σοῖς φίλοις.'
Πυ. τοῖς σοῖς φίλοισι γράμματ᾽ ἀποδώσω τάδε. 745
Ιφ. κἀγὼ σὲ σώσω κυανέας ἔξω πέτρας.
Πυ. τίν᾽ οὖν ἐπόμνυς τοισίδ᾽ ὅρκιον θεῶν;
Ιφ. Ἄρτεμιν, ἐν ἧσπερ δώμασιν τιμὰς ἔχω.
Πυ. ἐγὼ δ᾽ ἄνακτά γ᾽ οὐρανοῦ, σεμνὸν Δία.
Ιφ. εἰ δ᾽ ἐκλιπὼν τὸν ὅρκον ἀδικοίης ἐμέ; 750
Πυ. ἄνοστος εἴην· τί δὲ σὺ μὴ σώσασά με;
Ιφ. μήποτε κατ᾽ Ἄργος ζῶσ᾽ ἴχνος θείην ποδός.
Πυ. ἄκουε δή νυν ὃν παρήλθομεν λόγον.
Ιφ. ἀλλ᾽ εὐθὺς ἔστω κοινὸς ἢν καλῶς ἔχῃ.
Πυ. ἐξαίρετόν μοι δὸς τόδ᾽· ἤν τι ναῦς πάθῃ, 755
χἠ δέλτος ἐν κλύδωνι χρημάτων μέτα
ἀφανὴς γένηται, σῶμα δ᾽ ἐκσώσω μόνον,
τὸν ὅρκον εἶναι τόνδε μηκέτ᾽ ἔμπεδον.
Ιφ. ἀλλ᾽ οἶσθ᾽ ὃ δράσω (πολλὰ γὰρ πολλῶν κυρεῖ);
τἀνόντα κἀγγεγραμμέν᾽ ἐν δέλτου πτυχαῖς 760
λόγῳ φράσω σοι πάντ᾽ ἀναγγεῖλαι φίλοις.
ἐν ἀσφαλεῖ γάρ· ἢν μὲν ἐκσώσῃς γραφήν,
αὐτὴ φράσει σιγῶσα τἀγγεγραμμένα.
ἢν δ᾽ ἐν θαλάσσῃ γράμματ᾽ ἀφανισθῇ τάδε,
τὸ σῶμα σώσας τοὺς λόγους σώσεις ἐμοί. 765
Πυ. καλῶς ἔλεξας τῶν τε σῶν ἐμοῦ θ᾽ ὕπερ.
σήμαινε δ᾽ ᾧ χρὴ τάσδ᾽ ἐπιστολὰς φέρειν
πρὸς Ἄργος ὅτι τε χρὴ κλυόντα σοῦ λέγειν.

---

744 τοῖσι σοῖς Seager τοῖς ἐμοῖς L   747 τοῖσιδ᾽ Markland -σιν L   752 ποδός Lᵖᶜ or Tr ποτέ (L?)P   754 εὐθὺς ἔστω κοινὸς Enger (ἔστω Fix, κοινὸς Markland) αὖτις ἔσται καινὸς L   763 αὐτὴ ed. Hervag.² αὕτη L   766 τε σῶν Haupt θεῶν L

100

Iphigenia in Tauris

Iph. Let him give me an oath that he will carry this letter[735] to Argos for those loved ones I want to send it to.

Or. And will you give the same kind of promise in return?

Iph. To do or not do what? Tell me what you mean.

Or. To release him alive from this barbarian land.

Iph. That's a fair demand; how else could he make his report?[740]

Or. And will the king also go along with this?

Iph. Yes, I'll persuade him, and I'll put the man on board myself.

Or. (to Pylades) Swear now – *(to Iphigenia)* and you dictate an oath that is suitably solemn.

Iph. (to Pylades) 'I will give', you must say, 'this letter to your loved ones'.

Pyl. To your loved ones I will deliver this document.

Iph. And I will see you safely past the Dark Rocks.[746]

Pyl. Which god do you call on as witness of this promise?

Iph. Artemis, in whose temple I hold office.

Pyl. And I the ruler of heaven, majestic Zeus.

Iph. And if you abandon your oath and do me wrong?[750]

Pyl. May I not get home – and you, if you do not see me safe?

Iph. May I never set foot in Argos so long as I live.

Pyl. Listen, though, to a point that we have overlooked.

Iph. Well, share it with us at once if it's for the good.

Pyl. Allow me this exception: if something happens to the ship,[755] and the letter disappears in the deep with the goods, and I salvage nothing but my self, this oath shall no longer be binding.

Iph. You know what I'll do, then (for more ways give more chances)? Everything that's written and contained in the folded letter[760] I'll tell to you in words for you to repeat to my loved ones. That makes things secure; if you save the letter, it will silently tell what is written in it. But if the written words disappear in the sea, by saving your self you'll save my words for me.[765]

Pyl. That's a good suggestion you've made, for both of us. But tell me for whom I'm to carry this letter to Argos, and what I should say after hearing it from you.

Euripides

Ιφ.	ἄγγελλ' Ὀρέστῃ παιδὶ τἀγαμέμνονος –	769
Πυ.	ὦ θεοί – Ιφ. τί τοὺς θεοὺς ἀνακαλεῖς ἐν τοῖς ἐμοῖς;	780
Πυ.	οὐδέν· πέραινε δ'· ἐξέβην γὰρ ἄλλοσε.	781
Ιφ.	Ὀρέσθ' ' (ἵν' αὖθις ὄνομα δὶς κλυὼν μάθῃς)	779
	'Η 'ν Αὐλίδι σφαγεῖσ' ἐπιστέλλει τάδε	770
	ζῶσ' Ἰφιγένεια, τοῖς ἐκεῖ δ' οὐ ζῶσ' ἔτι.'	
Πυ.	ποῦ δ' ἔστ' ἐκείνη; κατθανοῦσ' ἥκει πάλιν;	
Ιφ.	ἥδ' ἣν ὁρᾷς σύ· μὴ λόγων ἔκπλησσέ με.	
	'Κόμισαί μ' ἐς Ἄργος, ὦ σύναιμε, πρὶν θανεῖν,	
	ἐκ βαρβάρου γῆς, καὶ μετάστησον θεᾶς	775
	σφαγίων ἐφ' οἷσι ξενοφόνους τιμὰς ἔχω,	
	ἢ σοῖς ἀραία δώμασιν γενήσομαι.'	778
Ορ.	Πυλάδη, τί λέξω; ποῦ ποτ' ὄνθ' ηὑρήμεθα;	777
Ιφ.	τάχ' οὖν ἐρωτῶν σ' εἰς ἄπιστ' ἀφίξεται.	782
	λέγ' οὕνεκ' ἔλαφον ἀντιδοῦσά μου θεὰ	
	Ἄρτεμις ἔσωσέ μ', ἣν ἔθυσ' ἐμὸς πατὴρ	
	δοκῶν ἐς ἡμᾶς ὀξὺ φάσγανον βαλεῖν,	785
	ἐς τήνδε δ' ᾤκισ' αἶαν. αἵδ' ἐπιστολαί,	
	τάδ' ἐστὶ τὰν δέλτοισιν ἐγγεγραμμένα.	
Πυ.	ὦ ῥᾳδίοις ὅρκοισι περιβαλοῦσά με·	
	κάλλιστα δ' ὀμόσας οὐ πολὺν σχήσω χρόνον,	
	τὸν δ' ὅρκον ὃν κατώμοσ' ἐμπεδώσομεν.	790
	ἰδού, φέρω σοι δέλτον ἀποδίδωμί τε,	
	Ὀρέστα, τῆσδε σῆς κασιγνήτης πάρα.	
Ορ.	δέχομαι· παρεὶς δὲ γραμμάτων διαπτυχάς,	
	τὴν ἡδονὴν πρῶτ' οὐ λόγοις αἱρήσομαι.	
	ὦ φιλτάτη μοι σύγγον', ἐκπεπληγμένος	795
	ὅμως σ' ἀπίστῳ περιβαλὼν βραχίονι	
	ἐς τέρψιν εἶμι, πυθόμενος θαυμάστ' ἐμοί.	
Χο.	ξέν', οὐ δικαίως τῆς θεοῦ τὴν πρόσπολον	
	χραίνεις, ἀθίκτοις περιβαλὼν πέπλοις χέρας.	
Ορ.	ὦ συγκασιγνήτη τε κἀκ ταὐτοῦ πατρὸς	800
	Ἀγαμέμνονος γεγῶσα, μή μ' ἀποστρέφου,	
	ἔχουσ' ἀδελφὸν οὐ δοκοῦσ' ἕξειν ποτέ.	

780, 781, 779 after 769, Jackson   780 ὦ θεοί: Πυ. Tr (om. L)   779 Πυ. ⟨L⟩P, del. Tr.
773 λόγων Seidler (λόγου δ' Markland)   λόγοις L   777 after 778, Parker
782 Ιφ. Markland Πυ. (with 781) L   ἀφίξεται Burges ἀφίξομαι L   786 ᾤκισ' ρ ᾤκησ' L
787 ταῦτ' Plut. *Mor.* 182e   ἐστὶ τὰν Plut. ἐστιν ἐν L   789 ὀμόσας Lˢˡ ὀμόσασ' L
796 σ' ἀπίστῳ Markland ἀπιστῶ L   798–99 Ιφ. Monk   799 χέρας Herwerden χέρα L
800 συγκασιγνήτη Lᵖᶜor Tr, P κασιγ- Lᵃᶜ

102

Iphigenia in Tauris

Iph. Report to Orestes, son of Agamemnon –

Pyl. O gods – *Iph.* Why call on the gods when I am speaking?[780]

Pyl. No reason, carry on – I wandered off somewhere else.

Iph. 'Orestes' (you'll learn the name by hearing it twice over), 'She who was slain at Aulis sends you this message,[770] Iphigenia who lives, though to them no longer living.'

Pyl. But where is she? Has she come back from the dead?

Iph. Right here, you're looking at her; don't distract me from what I'm saying! *(Continuing the message)* 'Bring me to Argos, my brother, from this barbarous land before I die; release me from the goddess's[775] sacrifices where I officiate in the slaughter of strangers, or I shall call down a curse upon your house.'

Or. Pylades, what shall I say? Wherever do we find ourselves?

Iph. *(continuing her instructions)* Now perhaps when he questions you he'll find things hard to believe. Tell him that the goddess Artemis rescued me, giving a deer in my place which my father sacrificed, thinking it was me he struck with the sharp sword,[785] and settled me in this land. That is my message; that is what is written in the tablets.

Pyl. The oaths you bound me with are easy indeed! And having sworn a most fair oath I'll not delay long but now will make the oath I swore secure.[790] *(Carrying the letter from Iphigenia to Orestes)* Look, I bring you a letter and deliver it to you, Orestes – it's from your sister here.

Or. I accept it; but putting aside the written tablets I'll first take this pleasure in no mere words. *(He approaches Iphigenia.)* O dearest sister of mine, I am astonished,[795] yet I'll embrace you with unbelieving arm and go into raptures, for I've learned things that astound me!

Cho. Stranger, you're wrongfully defiling the goddess's servant, throwing your arms about her untouchable robes!

Or. My very own sister, child of the same father,[800] Agamemnon, don't turn away from me when you're holding the brother you thought you would never hold!

Euripides

Ιφ. ἐγώ σ' ἀδελφὸν τὸν ἐμόν; οὐ παύσῃ λέγων;
τὸ τ' Ἄργος αὐτοῦ μεστὸν ἥ τε Ναυπλία.

Ορ. οὐκ ἔστ' ἐκεῖ σός, ὦ τάλαινα, σύγγονος. 805

Ιφ. ἀλλ' ἡ Λάκαινα Τυνδαρίς σ' ἐγείνατο;

Ορ. Πέλοπός γε παιδὶ παιδός, οὗ 'κπέφυκ' ἐγώ.

Ιφ. τί φής; ἔχεις τι τῶνδέ μοι τεκμήριον;

Ορ. ἔχω· πατρῴων ἐκ δόμων τι πυνθάνου.

Ιφ. οὔκουν λέγειν μὲν χρὴ σέ, μανθάνειν δ' ἐμέ; 810

Ορ. λέγοιμ' ἂν ἀκοῇ πρῶτον Ἠλέκτρας τάδε·
Ἀτρέως Θυέστου τ' οἶσθα γενομένην ἔριν;

Ιφ. ἤκουσα· χρυσῆς ἀρνὸς ἦν νείκη πέρι.

Ορ. ταῦτ' οὖν ὑφήνασ' οἶσθ' ἐν εὐπήνοις ὑφαῖς;

Ιφ. ὦ φίλτατ', ἐγγὺς τῶν ἐμῶν χρίμπτῃ φρενῶν. 815

Ορ. εἰκώ τ' ἐν ἱστοῖς ἡλίου μετάστασιν;

Ιφ. ὕφηνα καὶ τόδ' εἶδος εὐμίτοις πλοκαῖς.

Ορ. καὶ λούτρ' ἐς Αὖλιν μητρὸς ἀδέξω πάρα;

Ιφ. οἶδ'· οὐ γὰρ ὁ γάμος ἐσθλὸς ὤν μ' ἀφείλετο.

Ορ. τί γάρ; κόμας σὰς μητρὶ δοῦσα σῇ φέρειν; 820

Ιφ. μνημεῖά γ' ἀντὶ σώματος τοὐμοῦ τάφῳ.

Ορ. ἃ δ' εἶδον αὐτός, τάδε φράσω τεκμήρια·
Πέλοπος παλαιὰν ἐν δόμοις λόγχην πατρός,
ἣν χερσὶ πάλλων παρθένον Πισάτιδα
ἐκτήσαθ' Ἱπποδάμειαν, Οἰνόμαον κτανών, 825
ἐν παρθενῶσι τοῖσι σοῖς κεκρυμμένην.

Ιφ. ὦ φίλτατ' – οὐδὲν ἄλλο, φίλτατος γὰρ εἶ –
ἔχω σ', Ὀρέστα, τηλύγετον [χθονὸς] ἀπὸ πατρίδος
Ἀργόθεν, ὦ φίλος. 830

Ορ. κἀγὼ σέ, τὴν θανοῦσαν ὡς δοξάζεται.

Ιφ. κατὰ δὲ δάκρυα κατὰ δὲ γόος ἅμα χαρᾷ
τοὐμὸν νοτίζει βλέφαρον· Ορ. ὡσαύτως δ' ἐμόν.

Ιφ. σὲ δ' ἔτι βρέφος ἔλιπον ἀγκάλαι-
σι νεαρὸν τροφοῦ, νεαρὸν ἐν δόμοις. 835

---

804 τ' Bothe δ' L   807 γε Elmsley τε L   οὗ 'κπέφυκ' Elmsley (οὗ πέφυκ' Seidler)
ἐκπέφυκ' L   811 ἀκοῇ Reiske ἄκουε L   812 οἶσθα ed. Brubach. οἶδα L   813 ἦν νείκη
Mekler, Radermacher ἡνίκ' ἦν L   815 χρίμπτη Wecklein κάμπτη (i.e. -ῃ) L   818 ἀδέξω
Kirchhoff ἀνεδέξω L   829 χθονὸς del. Murray   832–33 thus Lee, 831–33 Ορ. L, 832–33
Ιφ. Bauer   832 δάκρυα Bothe δάκρυ L   833 τοὐμὸν Lee τὸ σὸν L   834 σὲ δ' ἔτι
Collard τό δέ τι L (τὸ P) ὃν ἔτι Diggle

104

Iphigenia in Tauris

Iph. You my brother? Won't you stop that talk? Argos is his haunt, and Nauplia.

Or. Foolish woman, that's not where your brother is![805]

Iph. But was it Tyndareus's daughter from Sparta who bore you?

Or. Yes, to Pelops' grandson, whose son I am.

Iph. What are you saying? Do you have some proof of this for me?

Or. I do. Ask me something about our ancestral home.

Iph. Well, shouldn't it be you that tells, and me that learns?[810]

Or. I'll tell you this first, then, something I've heard from Electra. You know there was strife between Atreus and Thyestes?

Iph. So I've heard; there were quarrels about a golden lamb.

Or. Well, you remember weaving it in a piece of fine weaving?

Iph. O dearest one, you are grazing close to my memory![815]

Or. And wove on the loom a picture of the sun's shifting?

Iph. I wove that picture too on fine-meshed cloth.

Or. And the lustral water you took from your mother to Aulis?

Iph. I remember; the wedding was not so happy as to take away the memory.

Or. And what of the locks you gave to be brought to your mother?[820]

Iph. Yes, tokens for the tomb in place of my body.

Or. And now I'll tell you this evidence that I've seen myself: the ancient spear of Pelops in my father's house, which he wielded when he won the Pisatan maid Hippodameia, killing Oenomaus.[825] That spear was stored away in your maidens' apartment.

Iphigenia accepts Orestes' embrace and breaks into song; Orestes speaks in response.

Iph. O dearest one – nothing else, for you are my dearest –
I hold you, Orestes, far away from your homeland
of Argos, O dear one![830]

Or. And I hold you, who are supposed to have died!

Iph. A tear, a sob mingled with joy
bedews my face – *Or.* and mine as well!

Iph. I left you an infant newborn in the arms
of your nurse, newborn in the house.[835]

105

Euripides

　　ὦ κρεῖσσον ἢ λόγοισιν εὐτυχοῦσ' ἐμὰ
　　ψυχά, τί φῶ;
　　θαυμάτων πέρα καὶ λόγου πρόσω τάδ' ἀπέβα.　　840

Ορ.　τὸ λοιπὸν εὐτυχοῖμεν ἀλλήλων μέτα.

Ιφ.　ἄτοπον ἡδονὰν ἔλαβον, ὦ φίλαι·
　　δέδοικα δ' ἐκ χερῶν με μὴ πρὸς αἰθέρα
　　ἀμπταμένα φύγῃ.
　　ἰὼ Κυκλωπὶς ἑστία,　　845
　　ἰὼ πατρὶς Μυκήνα φίλα,
　　χάριν ἔχω ζόας, χάριν ἔχω τροφᾶς,
　　ὅτι μοι συνομαίμονα τόνδε δόμοις
　　ἐξεθρέψω φάος.

Ορ.　γένει μὲν εὐτυχοῦμεν, ἐς δὲ συμφοράς,　　850
　　ὦ σύγγον', ἡμῶν δυστυχὴς ἔφυ βίος.

Ιφ.　ἐγᾦδ' ἁ μέλεος, οἶδ' ὅτε φάσγανον
　　δέρᾳ 'φῆκέ μοι μελεόφρων πατήρ.

Ορ.　οἴμοι· δοκῶ γὰρ οὐ παρών σ' ὁρᾶν ἐκεῖ.　　855

Ιφ.　ἀνυμέναιος, ⟨ὦ⟩ σύγγον', Ἀχιλλέως
　　ἐς κλισίαν λέκτρων δόλιον ἀγόμαν·
　　παρὰ δὲ βωμὸν ἦν δάκρυα καὶ γόοι.　　860
　　φεῦ φεῦ χερνίβων ἐκεί⟨νων· οἴμοι⟩.

Ορ.　ᾤμωξα κἀγὼ τόλμαν ἣν ἔτλη πατήρ.

Ιφ.　ἀπάτορ' ἀπάτορα πότμον ἔλαχον.
　　ἄλλα δ' ἐξ ἄλλων κυρεῖ　　865
　　δαίμονος τύχᾳ τινός.　　867

Ορ.　εἰ σόν γ' ἀδελφόν, ὦ τάλαιν', ἀπώλεσας.　　866

Ιφ.　ὦ μελέα δεινᾶς τόλμας· δείν' ἔτλαν,
　　ὤμοι, δείν' ἔτλαν, σύγγονε, παρὰ δ' ὀλίγον　　870
　　ἀπέφυγες ὄλεθρον ἀνόσιον ἐξ ἐμᾶν δαϊχθεὶς χερῶν.

836–37 εὐτυχοῦσ' ἐμὰ ψυχά Markland (εὐτυχουσά μου Wecklein, μοι Collard)　εὐτυχὼν ἐμοῦ ψυχᾷ L (ψυχά P, εὐτυχῶν p)　840 ἀπέβα Reiske ἐπ- L　844 ἀμπταμένα Seidler (ἀμπτομένα Markland) ἀμπτάμενος L　845 Κυκλωπὶς ἑστία Hermann Κυκλωπίδες ἑστίαι L　852 ἐγᾦδ' ἁ Bruhn (ἐγὼ δ' ἁ Seidler) ἐγὼ L　854 'φῆκέ Elmsley θῆκε L　856 ⟨ὦ⟩ Bothe (* L)　859 δόλιον Dindorf δολίαν ὅτ' L　861–64 speakers Tyrwhitt 861 Ορ., 862–64 Ιφ. L　861 ἐκεί⟨νων· οἴμοι⟩ Jackson ἐκεῖ L　865–69 speakers Seidler, 867 before 866 Monk　ἄλλα...τόλμας Ορ., then δείν' ἔτλαν etc. Ιφ. L　870 ὤμοι, δείν' ἔτλαν Willink δείν' ἔτλαν, ὤμοι L　871 ἀπέφυγες Musgrave ἀμφ- L

106

Iphigenia in Tauris

O my soul, more fortunate than words can express,
what shall I say?
Beyond marvels, past account has this turned out![840]

Or.   From now on may we be fortunate together!

Iph.   I have found a miraculous joy, O friends;
I fear it may escape me, flying out of my hands
up to the sky!
Hail, Cyclopean hearth;[845]
hail, Mycenae, dear homeland!
I thank you for his life, I thank you for his nurture,
that you reared this brother of mine
as a light for our house!

Or.   In birth we are fortunate, but in experiences,[850] sister, our lives
have been unfortunate.

Iph.   I remember, unhappy as I am, I remember when
my unhappy father thrust the sword at my throat.

Or.   *Oimoi*, I seem to see you there, though I was not present.[855]

Iph.   Unsung by wedding songs, O brother, I was brought
to the snare of Achilles' marriage-bed.
At the altar were tears and wailing.[860]
Alas, those lustrations, *oimoi*!

Or.   I too bemoan our father's remorseless deed!

Iph.   Unfatherly, unfatherly was the fate I was allotted.
And other things are following from others,[865]
through some daimon's stroke of fortune.[867]

Or.   Suppose, poor woman, you had slain your brother![866]

Iph.   How unhappy I was in my dreadful resolution! Dread
things I dared,
I dared dread things, *oimoi*, my brother. Barely[870]
did you escape an unholy death, laid low by my hands.

Euripides

†ἁ δ' ἐπ' αὐτοῖσι† τίς τελευτά;
τίς τύχα μοι συγκυρήσει; 875
τίνα σοι ⟨τίνα σοι⟩ πόρον εὑρομένα
πάλιν ἀπὸ πόλεως ἀπὸ φόνου πέμψω
πατρίδ' ἐς Ἀργείαν
πρὶν ἐπὶ ξίφος αἵματι σῷ πελάσαι; 880
τόδε τόδε σόν, ὦ μελέα ψυχά,
χρέος ἀνευρίσκειν.
πότερον κατὰ χέρσον, οὐχὶ ναΐ,
ἀλλὰ ποδῶν ῥιπᾷ; 885
θανάτῳ πελάσεις ἄρα βάρβαρα φῦλα
καὶ δι' ὁδοὺς ἀνόδους στείχων· διὰ κυανέας μὰν
στενοπόρου πέτρας μακρὰ κέλευθα να- 890
ΐοισιν δρασμοῖς.
τάλαινα τάλαινα·
†τίς ἂν οὖν τάδ' ἂν† ἢ θεὸς ἢ βροτὸς ἢ 895
τί τῶν ἀδοκήτων
ἀπόρων πόρον ἐξανύσας
δυοῖν τοῖν μόνοιν Ἀτρείδαιν †φανεῖ†
κακῶν ἔκλυσιν;

Χο. ἐν τοῖσι θαυμαστοῖσι καὶ μύθων πέρα 900
τάδ' εἶδον αὐτὴ κοὐ κλυοῦσ' ἀπ' ἀγγέλων.

Πυ. τὸ μὲν φίλους ἐλθόντας εἰς ὄψιν φίλων,
Ὀρέστα, χειρῶν περιβολὰς εἰκὸς λαβεῖν·
λήξαντα δ' οἴκτων κἀπ' ἐκεῖν' ἐλθεῖν χρεών,
ὅπως τὸ κλεινὸν ὄνομα τῆς σωτηρίας 905
λαβόντες ἐκ γῆς βησόμεσθα βαρβάρου.
σοφῶν γὰρ ἀνδρῶν τοῦτο, μὴ 'κβάντας τύχης,
καιρὸν λαβόντας ἡδονὰς ἄλλας λαβεῖν.

Ορ. καλῶς ἔλεξας· τῇ τύχῃ δ' οἶμαι μέλειν
τοῦδε ξὺν ἡμῖν. ἢν δέ τις πρόθυμος ᾖ, 910
σθένειν τὸ θεῖον μᾶλλον εἰκότως ἔχει.

874 τὰ δ' ἐπὶ τούτοις Platnauer τἀπὶ τούτοις or ἁ δ' ἐπ' ἄθλοις Diggle   875 συγκυρήσει
Bothe συγχωρ- L   876 ⟨τίνα σοι⟩ Diggle   889 δι' ὁδοὺς Barnes διόδους L   894 τάλαιν'
⟨ἐγὼ⟩ τάλαινα Diggle   895 τίς ἂν οὖν, τίς ἂν Reiske (τίς ἄρ' οὖν Markland)   897 ἀπόρων
πόρον Hermann πόρον ἄπορον L   898 φανεῖ Tr (in margin before κακῶν ἔκλυσιν) and
probably L (erased after Ἀτρείδαιν), om. P   φαίνοι Murray   901 κοὐ Bothe καὶ L
ἀπ' ἀγγέλων Hermann ἀπαγγελῶ L   902 Πυ. Heath, Musgrave (om. L)   905 ὄμμα Paris.
2887   907 τοῦτο Barrett ταῦτα L

108

Iphigenia in Tauris

†*And*† what †*the*† ending †*upon them*†?
What fortune will come upon me?[875]
What path, ⟨*what path*⟩ shall I find to send you
back from this community, from a bloody death,
to our Argive homeland
before the blade comes close to your blood?[880]
This, this, my poor soul,
it is now your task to discover.
Should it be on land, not by ship
but with rushing of feet?[885]
You'll come close to death, then, going through
barbarous tribes and impassable paths; yet long is the way
for ship-borne flight through the Dark Rocks' narrow passage.[891]
Wretched, wretched am I!
What god †...*then*...† or[895] mortal or
what unexpected event
will make us a path from this impasse
and show these two lone descendants of Atreus
deliverance from their troubles?

Iphigenia's song ends.

Cho. These things are marvellous and beyond mere story[900] – and
I've seen them myself, not heard them from reports.

Pyl. *(intervening)* When loved ones come face to face with loved
ones, Orestes, it's natural they should enjoy each other's em-
braces. But now you must stop your sorrowing and face the
problem: how shall we attain salvation's glorious title[905] and
make our exit from this barbarous land? This is the way of
the wise, not to let go of fortune but seize the moment and so
get further joys.

Or. Well said; and I reckon this is fortune's business as well as our
own. When someone is determined,[910] it's likely the divine
power will have more strength.

Euripides

Ιφ. οὐ μή μ᾽ ἐπίσχῃς οὐδ᾽ ἀποστήσεις λόγου,
   πρῶτον πυθέσθαι τίνα ποτ᾽ Ἠλέκτρα πότμον
   εἴληχε βιότου· φίλα γάρ ἐστι ταῦτ᾽ ἐμοί.
Ορ. τῷδε ξυνοικεῖ, βίον ἔχουσ᾽ εὐδαίμονα. 915
Ιφ. οὗτος δὲ ποδαπὸς καὶ τίνος πέφυκε παῖς;
Ορ. Στροφίος ὁ Φωκεὺς τοῦδε κλῄζεται πατήρ.
Ιφ. ὁ δ᾽ ἐστί γ᾽ Ἀτρέως θυγατρός, ὁμογενὴς ἐμός;
Ορ. ἀνεψιός γε, μόνος ἐμοὶ σαφὴς φίλος.
Ιφ. οὐκ ἦν τόθ᾽ οὗτος, ὅτε πατὴρ ἔκτεινέ με; 920
Ορ. οὐκ ἦν· χρόνον γὰρ Στρόφιος ἦν ἄπαις τινά.
Ιφ. χαῖρ᾽, ὦ πόσις μοι τῆς ἐμῆς ὁμοσπόρου.
Ορ. κἀμός γε σωτήρ, οὐχὶ συγγενὴς μόνον.
Ιφ. τὰ δεινὰ δ᾽ ἔργα πῶς ἔτλης μητρὸς πέρι;
Ορ. σιγῶμεν αὐτά· πατρὶ τιμωρῶν ἐμῷ. 925
Ιφ. ἡ δ᾽ αἰτία τίς ἀνθ᾽ ὅτου κτείνει πόσιν;
Ορ. ἔα τὰ μητρός· οὐδὲ σοὶ κλύειν καλόν.
Ιφ. σιγῶ· τὸ δ᾽ Ἄργος πρὸς σὲ νῦν ἀποβλέπει;
Ορ. Μενέλαος ἄρχει· φυγάδες ἐσμὲν ἐκ πάτρας.
Ιφ. οὔ που νοσοῦντας θεῖος ὕβρισεν δόμους; 930
Ορ. οὔκ, ἀλλ᾽ Ἐρινύων δεῖμά μ᾽ ἐκβάλλει χθονός.
Ιφ. ταῦτ᾽ ἄρ᾽ ἐπ᾽ ἀκταῖς κἀνθάδ᾽ ἠγγέλθης μανείς;
Ορ. ὤφθημεν οὐ νῦν πρῶτον ὄντες ἄθλιοι.
Ιφ. ἔγνωκα· μητρός ⟨σ᾽⟩ οὔνεκ᾽ ἠλάστρουν θεαί.
Ορ. ὥσθ᾽ αἱματηρὰ στόμι᾽ ἐπεμβαλεῖν ἐμοί. 935
Ιφ. τί γάρ ποτ᾽ ἐς γῆν τήνδ᾽ ἐπόρθμευσας πόδα;
Ορ. Φοίβου κελευσθεὶς θεσφάτοις ἀφικόμην.
Ιφ. τί χρῆμα δρᾶσαι; ῥητὸν ἢ σιγώμενον;
Ορ. λέγοιμ᾽ ἄν· ἀρχαὶ δ᾽ αἵδε μοι πολλῶν πόνων.
   ἐπεὶ τὰ μητρὸς ταῦθ᾽ ἃ σιγῶμεν κακὰ 940
   ἐς χεῖρας ἦλθε, μεταδρομαῖς Ἐρινύων
   ἠλαυνόμεσθα φυγάδες †ἔνθεν μοι† πόδα
   ἐς τὰς Ἀθήνας †δή γ᾽† ἔπεμψε Λοξίας
   δίκην παρασχεῖν ταῖς ἀνωνύμοις θεαῖς.
   ἔστιν γὰρ ὁσία ψῆφος ἣν Ἄρει ποτὲ 945
   Ζεὺς εἶσατ᾽ ἔκ του δὴ χερῶν μιάσματος.

912 οὐ μή (Elmsley) μ᾽ ἐπίσχῃς οὐδ᾽ ἀποστήσεις Monk οὐδέν μ᾽ ἐπίσχῃ γ᾽ οὐδ᾽ ἀποστήσῃ
(i.e. -σχῃ...-στήσῃ) L 914 ἐστι ταῦτ᾽ Markland ἔσται πάντ᾽ L 918 ὁ δ᾽ ἐστί L. Dindorf
ὅδ᾽ ἔστι L 934 ⟨σ᾽⟩ Markland 938 δρᾶσαι Elmsley δράσειν L

110

Iphigenia in Tauris

Iph. *(interrupting)* You'll not restrain me nor shift me from my subject of asking first what lot in life has fallen to Electra. That topic is dear to my heart.

Or. She is married to Pylades here and leads a happy life.[915]

Iph. But where does he come from, and whose son is he?

Or. Strophius of Phocis is called his father.

Iph. And he is a son of Atreus's daughter, my kinsman?

Or. Yes, cousin to you, and the only true friend I have.

Iph. He was not living when my father put me to death?[920]

Or. No, Strophius was childless for some time.

Iph. Greetings to you, husband of my own dear sister!

Or. And my protector as well, not just my kinsman.

Iph. But how did you dare those dreadful deeds concerning our mother?

Or. Let us not speak of them; I was avenging our father.[925]

Iph. And what was the cause for which she killed her husband?

Or. Leave our mother's actions aside; it's not decent for you to hear of it.

Iph. I'll be quiet, then. But does Argos give you its allegiance?

Or. Menelaus rules there. I'm an exile from our homeland.

Iph. Our uncle has not perhaps abused our ailing house?[930]

Or. No, it's fear of the Erinyes that has thrown me out of the land.

Iph. So that was your reported madness on the shore here too?

Or. That wasn't the first time people have seen me suffer.

Iph. I see; the goddesses were driving you because of our mother.

Or. And forcing their bloody bit into my mouth.[935]

Iph. Then why did you make the journey to this land?

Or. I came commanded by the divine words of Phoebus.

Iph. To do what – something mentionable, or unspoken?

Or. Very well, I'll tell you; these were the beginnings of my many ordeals. When this terrible business with my mother which I do not mention[940] had come into my hands, I was driven, a fugitive, by the Erinyes' pursuit †*whence/thence*† Loxias guided my course †*now indeed*† to Athens, to render justice to the unnamed goddesses. For there is a holy court there, which Zeus once established for Ares because of some pollution on his hands.[946]

Euripides

ἐλθὼν δ' ἐκεῖσε, πρῶτα μέν μ' οὐδεὶς ξένων
ἑκὼν ἐδέξαθ', ὡς θεοῖς στυγούμενον·
οἳ δ' ἔσχον αἰδῶ ξένια μονοτράπεζά μοι
παρέσχον, οἴκων ὄντες ἐν ταὐτῷ στέγει,   950
σιγῇ δ' ἐτεκτήναντ' ἀπρόσφθεγκτόν μ', ὅπως
δαιτός τ' ὀναίμην πώματός τ' αὐτῶν δίχα·
ἐς δ' ἄγγος ἴδιον ἴσον ἅπασι Βακχίου
μέτρημα πληρώσαντες εἶχον ἡδονήν.
κἀγὼ 'ξελέγξαι μὲν ξένους οὐκ ἠξίουν,   955
ἤλγουν δὲ σιγῇ κἀδόκουν οὐκ εἰδέναι
μέγα στενάζων οὕνεκ' ἦ μητρὸς φονεύς.
κλύω δ' Ἀθηναίοισι τἀμὰ δυστυχῆ
τελετὴν γενέσθαι, κἄτι τὸν νόμον μένειν
χοῆρες ἄγγος Παλλάδος τιμᾶν λεών.   960
ὡς δ' εἰς Ἄρειον ὄχθον ἧκον, ἐς δίκην
ἔστην, ἐγὼ μὲν θάτερον λαβὼν βάθρον,
τὸ δ' ἄλλο πρέσβειρ' ἥπερ ἦν Ἐρινύων.
εἰπὼν ⟨δ'⟩ ἀκούσας θ' αἵματος μητρὸς πέρι,
Φοῖβός μ' ἔσωσε μαρτυρῶν, ἴσας δέ μοι   965
ψήφους διηρίθμησε Παλλὰς ὠλένῃ·
νικῶν δ' ἀπῆρα φόνια πειρατήρια.
ὅσαι μὲν οὖν ἕζοντο πεισθεῖσαι δίκῃ
ψῆφον παρ' αὐτὴν ἱερὸν ὡρίσαντ' ἔχειν·
ὅσαι δ' Ἐρινύων οὐκ ἐπείσθησαν νόμῳ   970
δρόμοις ἀνιδρύτοισιν ἠλάστρουν μ' ἀεί,
ἕως ἐς ἁγνὸν ἦλθον αὖ Φοίβου πέδον
καὶ πρόσθεν ἀδύτων ἐκταθείς, νῆστις βορᾶς,
ἐπώμοσ' αὐτοῦ βίον ἀπορρήξειν θανών,
εἰ μή με σώσει Φοῖβος, ὅς μ' ἀπώλεσεν.   975
ἐντεῦθεν αὐδὴν τρίποδος ἐκ χρυσοῦ λακὼν
Φοῖβός μ' ἔπεμψε δεῦρο διοπετὲς λαβεῖν
ἄγαλμ' Ἀθηνῶν τ' ἐγκαθιδρῦσαι χθονί.
ἀλλ' ἥνπερ ἡμῖν ὥρισεν σωτηρίαν
σύμπραξον· ἢν γὰρ θεᾶς κατάσχωμεν βρέτας,   980
μανιῶν τε λήξω καὶ σὲ πολυκώπῳ σκάφει
στείλας Μυκήναις ἐγκαταστήσω πάλιν.

947 μέν μ' Π⁴ (conj. Scaliger) μὲν L 950 στέγει ed. Aldin. τέγει L 951 ἀπρόσφθεγκτ-όν Hermann ἀπόφθ- L 952 τ' ὀναίμην Housman γενοίμην L αὐτῶν Scaliger -οῦ L
961 δίκην Bothe δίκην | τ' L 964 ⟨δ'⟩ Elmsley 976 λακὼν Scaliger λαβ- L

Iphigenia in Tauris

Now when I went there, at first not one of my guest-friends was willing to receive me, a man detested by the gods; but those who felt compunction provided me with guest-fare at a table on my own, though under the same roof.[950] They contrived for me to be unaddressed, in silence, so I could enjoy the feasting and drinking apart from them. Each filled a private pitcher with an equal measure of Bacchus, and took his pleasure. I for my part did not presume to challenge them,[955] but suffered in silence and pretended to ignore it, groaning loudly because I was my mother's murderer. I hear that my misfortunes have become a ritual for the Athenians, and that it remains the custom for Pallas's people to honour the three-quart pitcher.[960]

When I came to Ares' hill, I stood my trial, I taking one platform, the senior Fury the other. We exchanged speeches about my mother's murder, and Phoebus saved me with his testimony. Pallas counted out equal votes for me with her arm,[966] and I left victorious in my murder trial.

Now those who settled there, persuaded by the judgment, had a sanctuary marked out for their possession right by the court. But those of the Erinyes who were not persuaded by the law[970] drove me continually in a ceaseless pursuit, until I came again to Phoebus's hallowed ground and laid myself before his sanctuary, starving myself of food, and swore I would die and end my life right there if Phoebus would not save me, he who had ruined me.[975] Then making his voice heard from the golden tripod, Phoebus sent me here to take the sky-fallen image and set it up in the land of Athens.

Come then, and help me achieve the salvation he has set for us. If we can get our hands on the goddess's image,[980] my seizures will end and I will give you passage on our many-oared craft, and settle you once more in Mycenae. Come, O

Euripides

ἀλλ', ὦ φιληθεῖσ', ὦ κασίγνητον κάρα,
σῶσον πατρῷον οἶκον, ἔκσωσον δ' ἐμέ·
ὡς τἄμ' ὄλωλε πάντα καὶ τὰ Πελοπιδῶν,   985
οὐράνιον εἰ μὴ ληψόμεθα θεᾶς βρέτας.

Χο. δεινή τις ὀργὴ δαιμόνων ἐπέζεσεν
προς Ταντάλειον σπέρμα διὰ πόνων τ' ἄγει.

Ιφ. τὸ μὲν πρόθυμον πρίν σε δεῦρ' ἐλθεῖν ἔχω
Ἄργει γενέσθαι καὶ σέ, σύγγον', εἰσιδεῖν.   990
θέλω δ' ἅπερ σύ, σέ τε μεταστῆσαι πόνων
νοσοῦντά τ' οἶκον, οὐχὶ τῷ κτανόντι με
θυμουμένη, πατρῷον ὀρθῶσαι πάλιν.
σφαγῆς τε γὰρ σῆς χεῖρ' ἀπαλλάξαιμεν ἄν,
σώσαιμί τ' οἴκους. τὴν θεὸν δ' ὅπως λάθω   995
δέδοικα καὶ τύραννον, ἡνίκ' ἂν κενὰς
κρηπῖδας εὕρῃ λαΐνας ἀγάλματος.
πῶς οὐ θανοῦμαι; τίς δ' ἔνεστί μοι λόγος;
ἀλλ' εἰ μὲν ἕν τι τοῦθ' ὁμοῦ γενήσεται,
ἄγαλμά τ' οἴσεις κἄμ' ἐπ' εὐπρύμνου νεὼς   1000
ἄξεις, τὸ κινδύνευμα γίγνεται καλόν.
τούτου δὲ χωρισθεῖσ', ἐγὼ μὲν ὄλλυμαι,
σὺ δ' ἂν τὸ σαυτοῦ θέμενος εὖ νόστου τύχοις.
οὐ μήν τι φεύγω γ', οὐδέ σ' εἰ θανεῖν χρεὼν
σώσασαν· οὐ γὰρ ἀλλ' ἀνὴρ μὲν ἐκ δόμων   1005
θανὼν ποθεινός, τὰ δὲ γυναικὸς ἀσθενῆ.

Ορ. οὐκ ἂν γενοίμην σοῦ τε καὶ μητρὸς φονεύς·
ἅλις τὸ κείνης αἷμα, κοινόφρων δὲ σοὶ
καὶ ζῶν θέλοιμ' ἂν καὶ θανὼν λαχεῖν ἴσον.
ἄξω δέ σ' ἥνπερ καὐτὸς ἐντεῦθεν περῶ   1010
προς οἶκον, ἢ σοῦ κατθανὼν μενῶ μέτα.
γνώμης δ' ἄκουσον· εἰ πρόσαντες ἦν τόδε
Ἀρτέμιδι, πῶς ἂν Λοξίας ἐθέσπισεν
κομίσαι μ' ἄγαλμα θεᾶς πόλισμ' ἐς Παλλάδος
καὶ σὸν πρόσωπον εἰσιδεῖν; ἅπαντα γὰρ   1015
συνθεὶς τάδ' εἰς ἕν νόστον ἐλπίζω λαβεῖν.

988 προς Page τὸ L   ἄγει Canter ἀεί L   991 σέ Canter σοί L   πόνων Paris. 2887
πόνον L   992 κτανόντι Heath κτανοῦντί L   993 πάλιν Markland θέλω L   995 τ' Markland δ' L   998 πῶς Bothe πῶς δ' L   1004–5 σ'...σώσασαν Kirchhoff μ'...σώσασά σ' L
1006 γυναικὸς P -ῶν L   1009 ζῶν Musgrave ζῆν L   1010 ἄξω δέ σ' Canter ἤξω δέ γ' L
ἐντεῦθεν περῶ Seidler ἐνταυθοῖ πέσω L   1011 ἢ L^sl εἴ L   lacuna before 1015, Köchly

114

Iphigenia in Tauris

beloved one, O my very own sister, save our ancestral house and rescue me. All is lost for me and Pelops' descendants[985] if we do not take the goddess's heaven-sent image.

Chr. Some dire divine wrath has seethed up against the seed of Tantalus and drags it through ordeals.

Iph. I have been eager since before you came here to get to Argos and set my eyes on you, brother.[990] I want what you want, to release you from your troubles and raise up our ailing ancestral house again, for I feel no rancour at the man who killed me. Thus I would free my hand from your sacrifice and save our family as well. But I fear for how I can escape the goddess's notice,[995] and the king's when he discovers the stone base stripped of its image. How will I escape death, how justify myself? But if this one thing can come about as well, and you can carry off the image *and* bring me on board your stout-sterned ship,[1000] my risk becomes a fair one. If I am deprived of that, though, I am finished, but you may still see your project through and get home. No, shrink from this I will not, even if I must die in saving you. The truth is, when a man is lost[1005] to his house he is sorely missed, while a woman is a feeble resource.

Or. I'll not become your killer as well as my mother's. Her blood is enough; I want to be your partner and share your fate in both life and death. I'll bring you home if I get home from here myself,[1010] or else I'll die with you and stay with you here. But listen to my opinion: if this were offensive to Artemis, how could it be that Loxias instructed me to fetch her image to Pallas's city and see you face to face? When I put all this[1015] together, it gives me hope of achieving our return.

Euripides

Ιφ. πῶς οὖν γένοιτ' ἂν ὥστε μήθ' ἡμᾶς θανεῖν
λαβεῖν θ' ἃ βουλόμεσθα; τῇδε γὰρ νοσεῖ
νόστος πρὸς οἴκους· ἥδε βούλευσις πάρα.
Ορ. ἆρ' ἂν τύραννον διολέσαι δυναίμεθ' ἄν;   1020
Ιφ. δεινὸν τόδ' εἶπας, ξενοφονεῖν ἐπήλυδας.
Ορ. ἀλλ' εἴ σε σώσει κἀμέ, κινδυνευτέον.
Ιφ. οὐκ ἂν δυναίμην· τὸ δὲ πρόθυμον ᾔνεσα.
Ορ. τί δ' εἴ με ναῷ τῷδε κρύψειας λάθρᾳ;
[Ιφ. ὡς δὴ σκότον λαβόντες ἐκσωθεῖμεν ἄν;   1025
Ορ. κλεπτῶν γὰρ ἡ νύξ, τῆς δ' ἀληθείας τὸ φῶς.]
Ιφ. εἶσ' ἔνδον ἱεροῦ φύλακες, οὓς οὐ λήσομεν.
Ορ. οἴμοι, διεφθάρμεσθα· πῶς σωθεῖμεν ἄν;
Ιφ. ἔχειν δοκῶ μοι καινὸν ἐξεύρημά τι.
Ορ. ποῖόν τι; δόξης μετάδος, ὡς κἀγὼ μάθω.   1030
Ιφ. ταῖς σαῖς ἀνίαις χρήσομαι σοφίσματι.
[Ορ. δειναὶ γὰρ αἱ γυναῖκες εὑρίσκειν τέχνας.
Ιφ. φονέα σε φήσω μητρὸς ἐξ Ἄργους μολεῖν.]
Ορ. χρῆσαι κακοῖσι τοῖς ἐμοῖς, εἰ κερδανεῖς.
Ιφ. ὡς οὐ θέμις σε λέξομεν θύειν θεᾷ.   1035
Ορ. τίν' αἰτίαν ἔχουσ'; ὑποπτεύω τι γάρ.
Ιφ. οὐ καθαρὸν ὄντα· τὸ δ' ὅσιον δώσω φόνῳ.
Ορ. τί δῆτα μᾶλλον θεᾶς ἄγαλμ' ἁλίσκεται;
Ιφ. πόντου σε πηγαῖς ἁγνίσαι βουλήσομαι.
Ορ. ἔτ' ἐν δόμοισι βρέτας ἐφ' ᾧ πεπλεύκαμεν.   1040
Ιφ. κἀκεῖνο νίψειν, σοῦ θιγόντος ὥς, ἐρῶ.
Ορ. ποῖ δῆτα πόντου νοτερὸν εἶ παρ' ἔκβολον;
Ιφ. οὗ ναῦς χαλινοῖς λινοδέτοις ὁρμεῖ σέθεν.
Ορ. σὺ δ' ἢ τις ἄλλος ἐν χεροῖν οἴσει βρέτας;
Ιφ. ἐγώ· θιγεῖν γὰρ ὅσιόν ἐστ' ἐμοὶ μόνῃ.   1045
Ορ. Πυλάδης δ' ὅδ' ἡμῖν ποῦ τετάξεται πόνου;
Ιφ. ταὐτὸν χεροῖν σοὶ λέξεται μίασμ' ἔχων.
Ορ. λάθρᾳ δ' ἄνακτος ἢ εἰδότος δράσεις τάδε;

1018 νοσεῖ Markland νόει L   1019 ἥδε (M. Crusius) βούλευσις Markland ἡ δὲ βούλησις L
1025–26 del. Markland   1025 σκότον Dindorf -ος L   ἐκσωθεῖμεν Brodaeus ἔξω θεῖμεν L
1027 ἱεροῦ Dobree -οὶ L   1031 σοφίσματι West -σιν L   1032–33 del. Parker   1035 σε
Reiske γε L   1037 φόνῳ ed. Aldin. φόβῳ L   1040 νίψειν Madvig νίψαι L   1042 εἶ παρ'
Reiske εἶπας L   1046 πόνου Brodaeus φόνου L

116

Iphigenia in Tauris

Iph. So how can it come about that we escape death and get what
we want as well? This is where our return home is ailing; this
is what we must plan for.

Or. Might we perhaps be able to kill the ruler?[1020]

Iph. A dreadful suggestion, for incomers to murder a host!

Or. But if it will save you and me, it's worth the risk.

Iph. I could not do it – but I commend your resolve.

Or. Then suppose you hid me secretly here in the temple?

[*Iph. As if we could get out safely if we had darkness?*[1025]

Or. Yes, night belongs to thieves, daylight to openness.]

Iph. There are guards inside the sanctuary; we could not evade them.

Or. Alas, we are ruined! How can we get away safely?

Iph. I think I may have an ingenious new contrivance.

Or. What sort? Share your thought, so I can learn it as well.[1030]

Iph. I'll use your torments as a clever device.

[*Or. Yes, women are awfully clever at inventing schemes.*

Iph. I'll say you had killed your mother when you came from Argos.]

Or. Make use of my troubles if you'll profit by it.

Iph. I'll say it's not lawful to sacrifice you to the goddess.[1035]

Or. What reason will you give (I think I can guess)?

Iph. Because you are unclean. I'll be making the sacrifice holy.

Or. So how does this help us capture the goddess's image?

Iph. I'll say I intend to purify you with sea-water.

Or. That leaves the image we've sailed for still in the temple.[1040]

Iph. I'll say I'm going to wash it too, because you've touched it.

Or. So where will you go to along the sea's damp shore?

Iph. To where your ship is moored with flax-woven cables.

Or. Will you or someone else bear the image in your arms?

Iph. I will. It's untouchable for all but me.[1045]

Or. And Pylades here, what role will he have in our task?

Iph. I'll say he has the same pollution on his hands as you.

Or. You'll do this in secret from the king, or with his knowledge?

Euripides

Ιφ. πείσασα μύθοις· οὐ γὰρ ἂν λάθοιμί γε. 1049
σοὶ δὴ μέλειν χρὴ τἄλλ' ὅπως ἕξει καλῶς. 1051
Ορ. καὶ μὴν νεώς γε πίτυλος εὐήρης πάρα. 1050
ἑνὸς μόνου δεῖ, τάσδε συγκρύψαι τάδε. 1052
ἀλλ' ἀντίαζε καὶ λόγους πειστηρίους
εὕρισκ'· ἔχει τοι δύναμιν εἰς οἶκτον γυνή.
τὰ δ' ἄλλ' ἴσως ἂν πάντα συμβαίη καλῶς. 1055
Ιφ. ὦ φίλταται γυναῖκες, εἰς ὑμᾶς βλέπω,
καὶ τἄμ' ἐν ὑμῖν ἐστιν ἢ καλῶς ἔχειν
ἢ μηδὲν εἶναι καὶ στερηθῆναι πάτρας
φίλου τ' ἀδελφοῦ φιλτάτης τε συγγόνου.
καὶ πρῶτα μέν μοι τοῦ λόγου τάδ' ἀρχέτω· 1060
γυναῖκές ἐσμεν, φιλόφρον ἀλλήλαις γένος,
σῴζειν τε κοινὰ πράγματ' ἀσφαλέσταται.
σιγήσαθ' ἡμῖν καὶ συνεκπονήσατε
φυγάς· καλόν τοι γλῶσσ' ὅτῳ πιστὴ παρῇ.
ὁρᾶτε δ' ὡς τρεῖς μία τύχη τοὺς φιλτάτους, 1065
ἢ γῆς πατρῴας νόστος ἢ θανεῖν, ἔχει.
σωθεῖσα δ', ὡς ἂν καὶ σὺ κοινωνῇς τύχης,
σώσω σ' ἐς Ἑλλάδ'. ἀλλὰ πρός σε δεξιᾶς
σὲ καὶ σ' ἱκνοῦμαι, σὲ δὲ φίλης παρηίδος
γονάτων τε καὶ τῶν ἐν δόμοισι φιλτάτων 1070
[μητρὸς πατρός τε καὶ τέκνων ὅτῳ κυρεῖ].
τί φάτε; τίς ὑμῶν φησιν ἢ τίς οὐ θέλειν,
φθέγξασθε, ταῦτα; μὴ γὰρ αἰνουσῶν λόγους,
ὄλωλα κἀγὼ καὶ κασίγνητος τάλας.
Χο. θάρσει, φίλη δέσποινα, καὶ σῴζου μόνον· 1075
ὡς ἔκ γ' ἐμοῦ σοι πάντα σιγηθήσεται,
ἴστω μέγας Ζεύς, ὧν ἐπισκήπτεις πέρι.
Ιφ. ὄναισθε μύθων καὶ γένοισθ' εὐδαίμονες.
σὸν ἔργον ἤδη καὶ σὸν εἰσβαίνειν δόμους·
ὡς αὐτίχ' ἥξει τῆσδε κοίρανος χθονός, 1080
θυσίαν ἐλέγχων εἰ κατείργασται ξένων.

1049–52 thus A. MacDonald 1049 Ιφ., 1050 Ορ., 1051 Ιφ., 1052ff. Ορ. L 1055 ἂν πάντα Markland ἅπαντα L 1056 εἰς Hermann ὡς L 1059 φιλτάτης Livineius, Bothe -ου L 1064 πιστὴ Bothe πίστις L 1066 νόστος Valckenaer -ov L 1044 σὺ δ' ἤ τις Jacobs σοὶ δὴ τίς L 1071 del. Dindorf 1072 θέλειν Musgrave -ει L

118

Iphigenia in Tauris

Iph. I'll persuade him with talk. I could not hide it from him.[1049]
Then it's up to you to see the rest goes well.[1051]

Or. And indeed our fine-oared ship is standing by.[1050] Just one
more thing is needed: these women must help hide our plans.
Appeal to them, then, and find some persuasive arguments;
a woman has the power to arouse compassion. And all the rest
perhaps may turn out right.[1055]

Iph. *(to the Chorus)* O dearest women, I look towards you now; my
future is in your hands, either to prosper or to come to nothing
and be deprived of my homeland and my dear brother and
dearest sister. And let this first of all be a basis for my plea:[1060]
we are all women, a group concerned for each other, most firm
in looking after our common welfare. Be silent for us and help
us make our escape. A loyal tongue is a credit to its possessor.
See how a single fortune holds us three dearest comrades,[1065]
either a homecoming to our native land or death. And if I survive, so you may share our fortune I'll bring you safely to
Hellas. Come, by your right hand I beseech you, and you, and
you by your dear cheek and your knees and those dearest to
you at home[1070] [*your mother and father, and your children,
those that have them*]. What do you say? Which of you will
agree to this, or which refuse it? Speak out: if you reject my
plea, I and my poor brother too are lost.

Cho. Have courage, dear mistress, and just save yourself.[1075] For my
part everything you're instructing me about will be kept quiet,
may great Zeus witness this!

Iph. May you profit from those words and enjoy good fortune!
(To Orestes and Pylades) It's up to you now, and you, to enter
the temple. The ruler of this land will be here right away,[1080]
checking if the sacrifice of the strangers has been completed.

(They proceed into the temple. Iphigenia prays to Artemis.)

Euripides

ὦ πότνι᾿, ἥπερ μ᾿ Αὐλίδος κατὰ πτυχὰς
δεινῆς ἔσωσας ἐκ τεκνοκτόνου χερός,
σῶσόν με καὶ νῦν τούσδε τ᾿, ἢ τὸ Λοξίου
οὐκέτι βροτοῖσι διὰ σ᾿ ἐτήτυμον στόμα.   1085
ἀλλ᾿ εὐμενὴς ἔκβηθι βαρβάρου χθονὸς
ἐς τὰς Ἀθήνας· καὶ γὰρ ἐνθάδ᾿ οὐ πρέπει
ναίειν, παρόν σοι πόλιν ἔχειν εὐδαίμονα.

Χο.   ὄρνις ἃ παρὰ πετρίνας   *[στρ. α*
πόντου δειράδας ἀλκυὼν   1090
ἔλεγον οἶτον ἀείδεις,
εὐξύνετον ξυνετοῖς βοάν,
ὅτι πόσιν κελαδεῖς ἀεὶ μολπαῖς,
ἐγώ σοι παραβάλλομαι
θρηνοῦσ᾿, ἄπτερος ὄρνις,   1095
ποθοῦσ᾿ Ἑλλάνων ἀγόρους,
ποθοῦσ᾿ Ἄρτεμιν λοχίαν,
ἃ παρὰ Κύνθιον ὄχθον οἰ-
κεῖ φοίνικά θ᾿ ἁβροκόμαν
δάφναν τ᾿ εὐερνέα καὶ   1100
γλαυκᾶς θαλλὸν ἱερὸν ἐλαί-
ας, Λατοῦς ὠδῖνι φίλον,
λίμναν θ᾿ εἰλίσσουσαν ὕδωρ
κύκλιον, ἔνθα κύκνος μελῳ-
δὸς Μούσας θεραπεύει.   1105

ὦ πολλαὶ δακρύων λιβάδες,   *[ἀντ. α*
αἳ παρηΐδας εἰς ἐμὰς
ἔπεσον ἁνίκα πύργων
ὀλομένων ἐν ναυσὶν ἔβαν
πολεμίων ἐρετμοῖσι καὶ λόγχαις·   1110
ζαχρύσου δὲ δι᾿ ἐμπολᾶς
νόστον βάρβαρον ἦλθον,
ἔνθα τᾶς ἐλαφοκτόνου
θεᾶς ἀμφίπολον κόραν

1082 κατὰ πτυχὰς Elmsley καταπτύχας L   1083 τεκνοκτόνου Herwerden πατρο- L
1092 εὐξύνετον L^sl ἀξύν- L   1095 θρηνοῦσ᾿ Reiske θρήνους L -οις Stephanus
1101 θάλλον ed. Brubach. -ος L   1102 ὠδῖνι Portus -να L   φίλον Markland -αν L
1104 κύκλιον Seidler κύκνειον L

120

Iphigenia in Tauris

O mistress, you who in the vales of Aulis saved me from a terrible child-killing hand, save me now too, and these, or because of you the word of Loxias will no longer be true for mortals.[1085] Be kind and leave this barbarous land for Athens. It is not proper for you to be be living here when you can possess a city that has good fortune.

Iphigenia follows Orestes and Pylades into the temple. The Chorus, left alone, sings.

Chor.   Halcyon bird,   *[Strophe 1*
       who by the sea's rocky cliffs[1090]
       sadly sing your fate,
       a cry well understood for those with understanding,
       that you sing those songs incessantly for your mate,
       I match myself with you as I lament,
       an unwinged bird,[1095]
       pining for Hellenes' gatherings,
       pining for Artemis bringer of births,
       who dwells by the Cynthian hill
          and the fine-haired palm,
       and the burgeoning bay[1100]
          and the grey olive's sacred branch
          that is dear to Leto's offspring,
       and the lake that whirls around
       its circling water where the melodious swan
          gives service to the Muses.[1105]

       O, those abundant streams of tears   *[Antistrophe 1*
       that fell upon my cheeks
       when with my city's defences destroyed
       I was shipped away
       by enemies' oars and spears![1110]
       Through gold-rich barter
       I reached this barbarous home
       where I attend the deer-slaying
       goddess's virgin servant,

Euripides

παῖδ' Ἀγαμεμνονίαν λατρεύ- 1115
ω βωμούς τ' οὐ μηλοθύτας,
ζηλοῦσα τὸν διὰ παν-
τὸς δυσδαίμον'· ἐν γὰρ ἀνάγ-
καις οὐ κάμνει, σύντροφος ὤν.
μεταβάλλει δ' εὐδαιμονία, 1120
τὸ δὲ μετ' εὐτυχίαν κακοῦ-
σθαι θνατοῖς βαρὺς αἰών.

καὶ σὲ μέν, πότνι', Ἀργεία [στρ. β
πεντηκόντερος οἶκον ἄξει·
συρίζων θ' ὁ κηρόδετος 1125
Πανὸς οὐρείου κάλαμος
κώπαις ἐπιθωΰξει.
ὁ Φοῖβός θ' ὁ μάντις ἔχων
κέλαδον ἑπτατόνου λύρας
ἀείδων ἄξει λιπαρὰν 1130
εὖ σ' Ἀθηναίων ἐπὶ γᾶν·
ἐμὲ δ' αὐτοῦ ῥοθίοις
βήσῃ λιποῦσα πλάταις,
†ἀέρι δ' ἱστία πρότονοι κατὰ πρῷραν ὑπὲρ στόλον
ἐκπετάσουσιν πόδα† 1135
ναὸς ὠκυπόμπου.

λαμπροὺς ἱπποδρόμους βαίην, [ἀντ. β
ἔνθ' εὐάλιον ἔρχεται πῦρ·
οἰκείων δ' ὑπὲρ θαλάμων 1140
ἐν νώτοις ἀμοῖς πτέρυγας
λήξαιμι θοάζουσα·
χοροῖς δ' ἐνσταίην ὅθι καὶ
παρθένος εὐδοκίμων δόμων
†παρὰ πόδ' εἰλίσσουσα φίλας 1145
ματέρος ἡλίκων θιάσους†

1116 τ' οὐ Musgrave (τε Tr) τοὺς L   1117 ζηλοῦσα τὸν Greverus (-σαν τὸν Bothe 1803, -σα τὰν Bothe 1824) ζηλοῦσ' ἄταν L   1119 κάμνει Livineius, Milton -εις L   1120 δ' εὐδαιμονία Markland δυσδαιμονία L   1121 εὐτυχίαν Scaliger -ας L   1125 θ' Elmsley δ' L κηρόδετος Porson κηροδέτας L   1126 Πανὸς οὐρείου κάλαμος Diggle κάλαμος οὐρείου Πανὸς L   1131 εὖ σ' Bothe ἐς L (εἴς Tr)   1132–33 ῥοθίοις βήσῃ λιποῦσα Dale λιποῦσα βήσῃ ῥοθίοις L   1135 ἐκπετάσουσι Tr   1141 ἐν νώτοις ἀμοῖς πτέρυγας Fritzsche πτέρυγας ἐν νώτοις ἀμοῖς L   1143 δ' ἐνσταίην Platnauer δὲ σταίην L   1144 δόμων Köchly γάμων L

122

Iphigenia in Tauris

Agamemnon's child,[1115]
  at altars where sheep are not slain.
I envy one who is constantly
  ill-starred; he does not languish
  in hardships, being raised with them.
But good fortune changes,[1120]
and affliction after prosperity makes
  a heavy life for mortals.

And now, mistress, an Argive penteconter   *[Strophe 2*
  is going to bring you home.
With its shrill voice the wax-bound reed[1125]
of mountain-roaming Pan
will urge the oarsmen on;
and Phoebus the seer, holding
the seven-stringed lyre's voice,
will bring you, singing,[1130]
safely to the Athenians' bright land;
but me you will leave here
as you go on surging oars
†*and with air the forestays will spread out the sail*
  along the prow, over the bow†[1135]
of the fast-conveying ship.

O that I might travel the radiant chariot-road   *[Antistrophe 2*
where the Sun's fine fire goes,
and pause above the chambers of my home,[1140]
staying the motion of
the wings upon my back;
and might take my place in choruses where once,
a maid of illustrious family,
†*whirling my foot beside my dear*[1145]
mother's age-mates' companies†,

123

Euripides

ἐς ἁμίλλας χαρίτων
ἁβροπλούτου τε χλιδᾶς
εἰς ἔριν ὀρνυμένα πολυποίκιλα   1150
φάρεα καὶ πλοκάμους περιβαλλομένα
γένυας ἐσκίαζον.

ΘΟΑΣ

ποῦ 'σθ' ἡ πυλωρὸς τῶνδε δωμάτων γυνὴ
Ἑλληνίς; ἤδη τῶν ξένων κατήρξατο;
[ἀδύτοις ἐν ἁγνοῖς σῶμα λάμπονται πυρί;]   1155
Χο. ἥδ' ἐστίν ἥ σοι πάντ', ἄναξ, ἐρεῖ σαφῶς.
Θο. ἔα·
    τί τόδε μεταίρεις ἐξ ἀκινήτων βάθρων,
    Ἀγαμέμνονος παῖ, θεᾶς ἄγαλμ' ἐν ὠλέναις;
Ιφ. ἄναξ, ἔχ' αὐτοῦ πόδα σὸν ἐν παραστάσιν.
Θο. τί δ' ἔστιν, Ἰφιγένεια, καινὸν ἐν δόμοις;   1160
Ιφ. ἀπέπτυσ'· Ὁσίᾳ γὰρ δίδωμ' ἔπος τόδε.
Θο. τί φροιμιάζῃ νεοχμόν; ἐξαύδα σαφῶς.
Ιφ. οὐ καθαρά μοι τὰ θύματ' ἠγρεύσασθ', ἄναξ·
Θο. τί τοὐκδιδάξαν τοῦτό σ', ἢ δόξαν λέγεις;
Ιφ. βρέτας τὸ τῆς θεοῦ πάλιν ἕδρας ἀπεστράφη.   1165
Θο. αὐτόματον, ἤ νιν σεισμὸς ἔστρεψε χθονός;
Ιφ. αὐτόματον, ὄψιν δ' ὀμμάτων ξυνήρμοσεν.
Θο. ἡ δ' αἰτία τίς; ἢ τὸ τῶν ξένων μύσος;
Ιφ. ἥδ', οὐδὲν ἄλλο· δεινὰ γὰρ δεδράκατον.
Θο. ἀλλ' ἦ τιν' ἔκανον βαρβάρων ἀκτῆς ἔπι;   1170
Ιφ. οἰκεῖον ἦλθον τὸν φόνον κεκτημένοι.
Θο. τίν'; εἰς ἔρον γὰρ τοῦ μαθεῖν πεπτώκαμεν.
Ιφ. μητέρα κατηργάσαντο κοινωνῷ ξίφει.
Θο. Ἄπολλον· οὐδ' ἐν βαρβάροις ἔτλη τις ἄν.
Ιφ. πάσης διωγμοῖς ἠλάθησαν Ἑλλάδος.   1175
Θο. ἦ τῶνδ' ἕκατι δῆτ' ἄγαλμ' ἔξω φέρεις;
Ιφ. σεμνόν γ' ὑπ' αἰθέρ', ὡς μεταστήσω φόνου.
Θο. μίασμα δ' ἔγνως τοῖν ξένοιν ποίῳ τρόπῳ;
Ιφ. ἤλεγχον, ὡς θεᾶς βρέτας ἀπεστράφη πάλιν.
Θο. σοφήν σ' ἔθρεψεν Ἑλλάς, ὡς ᾔσθου καλῶς.   1180

1149 ἁβροπλούτου τε χλιδᾶς England (χλιδᾶς Markland) ἁβροπλούτοιο χαίτας L   1150
εἰς ἔριν del. Cropp   1152 γένυας Markland γένυσιν L   1154 ἤδη Reiske ἦ δὴ L
1155 del. Page   1174 ἔτλη Gaisford τόδ' ἔτλη L

Iphigenia in Tauris

in rivalry of graces
and luxurious finery,
rousing myself for the contest I threw about me
    richly worked robes and tresses,[1150]
darkening my cheeks.

Thoas enters with some servants by Side-entrance B and confronts the Chorus.

THOAS

Where is the Hellene woman who keeps the doors of this
temple? Has she by now consecrated the strangers? [*Are their
bodies glowing with flame in the holy shrine?*][1155]

Iphigenia emerges from the temple holding the image of Artemis.

Cho. Here she is, my lord. She'll tell you all plainly herself.
Tho. Hey! Why are you lifting the goddess's image in your arms,
daughter of Agamemnon, from its immovable base?
Iph. My lord, hold still right there in the doorway!
Tho. What's happened in the temple, Iphigenia?[1160]
Iph. I spit it away (I say that for Holiness's sake).
Tho. What strange new report are you beginning? Speak out plainly!
Iph. The victims you caught for me are unclean, my lord.
Tho. What told you that was so, or are you just guessing?
Iph. The goddess's image turned away in its place.[1165]
Tho. Of its own accord, or did an earth-tremor turn it?
Iph. Of its own accord, and it closed its eyes as well.
Tho. What's the cause of this? Is it the strangers' pollution?
Iph. That's it, nothing else. They have done terrible things.
Tho. Why, did they kill some barbarian on the shore?[1170]
Iph. It's family blood they were tainted with when they came here.
Tho. What blood? I feel a strong a desire to learn this.
Iph. They did away with their mother, sharing the sword.
Tho. Apollo! Not even a barbarian would have dared that!
Iph. They were pursued and driven out of all of Hellas.[1175]
Tho. So that's the reason you're bringing the image outside?
Iph. Yes, into the pure open air, to distance it from the blood.
Tho. And how did you recognize the strangers' pollution?
Iph. I questioned them when the image turned around.
Tho. Hellas raised you wise, for you showed good perception.[1180]

Euripides

Ιφ.	καὶ μὴν καθεῖσαν δέλεαρ ἡδύ μοι φρενῶν.
Θο.	τῶν Ἀργόθεν τι φίλτρον ἀγγέλλοντέ σοι;
Ιφ.	τὸν μόνον Ὀρέστην ἐμὸν ἀδελφὸν εὐτυχεῖν.
Θο.	ὡς δή σφε σώσαις ἡδοναῖς ἀγγελμάτων.
Ιφ.	καὶ πατέρα γε ζῆν καὶ καλῶς πράσσειν ἐμόν. 1185
Θο.	σὺ δ' εἰς τὸ τῆς θεοῦ γ' ἐξένευσας εἰκότως.
Ιφ.	πᾶσαν γε μισοῦσ' Ἑλλάδ', ἥ μ' ἀπώλεσεν.
Θο.	τί δῆτα δρῶμεν, φράζε, τοῖν ξένοιν πέρι;
Ιφ.	τὸν νόμον ἀνάγκη τὸν προκείμενον σέβειν.
Θο.	οὔκουν ἐν ἔργῳ χέρνιβες ξίφος τε σόν; 1190
Ιφ.	ἁγνοῖς καθαρμοῖς πρῶτα νιν νίψαι θέλω.
Θο.	πηγαῖσιν ὑδάτων ἢ θαλασσίᾳ δρόσῳ;
Ιφ.	θάλασσα κλύζει πάντα τἀνθρώπων κακά.
Θο.	ὁσιώτεροι γοῦν τῇ θεῷ πέσοιεν ἄν.
Ιφ.	καὶ τἀμά γ' οὕτω μᾶλλον ἂν καλῶς ἔχοι. 1195
Θο.	οὔκουν πρὸς αὐτὸν ναὸν ἐκπίπτει κλύδων;
Ιφ.	ἐρημίας δεῖ· καὶ γὰρ ἄλλα δράσομεν.
Θο.	ἄγ' ἔνθα χρήζεις· οὐ φιλῶ τἄρρηθ' ὁρᾶν.
Ιφ.	ἁγνιστέον μοι καὶ τὸ τῆς θεοῦ βρέτας.
Θο.	εἴπερ γε κηλὶς ἔβαλέ νιν μητροκτόνος. 1200
Ιφ.	οὐ γάρ ποτ' ἄν νιν ἡράμην βάθρων ἄπο.
Θο.	δίκαιος ηὐσέβεια καὶ προμηθία.
Ιφ.	οἶσθά νυν ἅ μοι γενέσθω; Θο. σὸν τὸ σημαίνειν τόδε.
Ιφ.	δεσμὰ τοῖς ξένοισι πρόσθες. Θο. ποῖ δέ σ' ἐκφύγοιεν ἄν;
Ιφ.	πιστὸν Ἑλλὰς οἶδεν οὐδέν. Θο. ἴτ' ἐπὶ δεσμά, πρόσπολοι. 1205
Ιφ.	κἀκκομιζόντων δὲ δεῦρο τοὺς ξένους. Θο. ἔσται τάδε.
Ιφ.	κρᾶτα κρύψαντες πέπλοισιν. Θο. ἡλίου πρόσθεν φλογός.
Ιφ.	σῶν τέ μοι σύμπεμπ' ὀπαδῶν· Θο. οἵδ' ὁμαρτήσουσί σοι.
Ιφ.	καὶ πόλει πέμψον τιν' ὅστις σημανεῖ... Θο. ποίας τύχας;
Ιφ.	ἐν δόμοις μίμνειν ἅπαντας. Θο. μὴ συναντῶσιν φόνῳ; 1210

1181 μὴν Monk νῦν L   1194 ὁσιώτεροι Tournier -ον L   1201 ἡράμην Musgrave ἀνηράμην L   1207 κρᾶτα κρύψαντες Musgrave κατακρύψαντες L   Θο. Markland (om. L) 1208 Ιφ. Markland (om. L, Θο. P reversing speakers throughout 1208–13)   1210 συναντῶσιν Elmsley -ῷεν L

126

Iphigenia in Tauris

Iph. And they dropped a tempting bait for my mind as well.
Tho. By charming you with some news of those in Argos?
Iph. That my only brother, Orestes, is faring well.
Tho. So you'd spare them, of course, in gladness at their news.
Iph. And that my father lives and is prospering.[1185]
Tho. But you took the side of the goddess, naturally.
Iph. Yes, for I hate all Hellas, which destroyed me.
Tho. Tell me, then: what shall we do about the strangers?
Iph. We are obliged to respect the established law.
Tho. So aren't your lustrations and sword already in action?[1190]
Iph. First I need to cleanse them with ritual purifications.
Tho. With stream water, or with salt water from the sea?
Iph. The sea washes every human evil away.
Tho. Yes, then they'd be more acceptable to the goddess.
Iph. And things would be better that way for me as well.[1195]
Tho. So doesn't the sea break right by the temple here?
Iph. We need a deserted place. We have other things to do.
Tho. Take them where you need to; I'm not eager to see secret rites.
Iph. And I must cleanse the image of the goddess as well.
Tho. Indeed, if the stain of matricide has touched it.[1200]
Iph. If not, I'd never have lifted it from its base.
Tho. Your piety and forethought are quite proper.
Iph. You know what I'd like done, then? *Tho.* That's for you to
    indicate.
Iph. Bind the strangers' hands together.
               Tho. Where could they escape to, though?
Iph. Hellas never can be trusted.
             Tho. Go, servants, see that they are bound.[1205]

(Some of the servants begin to enter the temple)

Iph. And let them bring the strangers here outside…
                  Tho. It shall be so.
Iph. Covering their heads with garments.
           Tho. Before the brightness of the sun.
Iph. And send some of your attendants with me.
           Tho. These ones will accompany you.
Iph. And someone who will announce to our community…
              Tho. What happenings?
Iph. That all must stay inside their homes.
        Tho. So that they won't encounter blood?[1210]

Euripides

Ιφ. μυσαρὰ γὰρ τὰ τοιάδ' ἐστί. Θο. στεῖχε καὶ σήμαινε σύ...
Ιφ. ...μηδέν' εἰς ὄψιν πελάζειν. Θο. εὖ γε κηδεύεις πόλιν.
Ιφ. καὶ φίλων γ' οὓς δεῖ μάλιστα. Θο. τοῦτ' ἔλεξας εἰς ἐμέ.
⟨Ιφ. – ᷉ – ⟩ Θο. ὡς εἰκότως σε πᾶσα θαυμάζει πόλις.
Ιφ. σὺ δὲ μένων αὐτοῦ πρὸ ναῶν τῇ θεῷ... Θο. τί χρῆμα δρῶ; 1215
Ιφ. ἅγνισον πυρσῷ μέλαθρον. Θο. καθαρὸν ὡς μόλῃς πάλιν.
Ιφ. ἡνίκ' ἂν δ' ἔξω περῶσιν οἱ ξένοι... Θο. τί χρή με δρᾶν;
Ιφ. πέπλον ὀμμάτων προθέσθαι. Θο. μὴ †παλαμναῖον λάβω†.
Ιφ. ἢν δ' ἄγαν δοκῶ χρονίζειν... Θο. τοῦδ' ὅρος τίς ἐστί μοι;
Ιφ. θαυμάσῃς μηδέν. Θο. τὰ τῆς θεοῦ πρᾶσσ' ἐπὶ σχολῆς καλῶς. 1220
Ιφ. εἰ γὰρ ὡς θέλω καθαρμὸς ὅδε πέσοι. Θο. συνεύχομαι.
Ιφ. τούσδ' ἄρ' ἐκβαίνοντας ἤδη δωμάτων ὁρῶ ξένους
καὶ θεᾶς κόσμους νεογνούς τ' ἄρνας, ὡς φόνῳ φόνον
μυσαρὸν ἐκνίψω, σέλας τε λαμπάδων τά τ' ἄλλ' ὅσα
προυθέμην ἐγὼ ξένοισι καὶ θεᾷ καθάρσια. 1225
ἐκποδὼν δ' αὐδῶ πολίταις τοῦδ' ἔχειν μιάσματος,
εἴ τις ἢ ναῶν πυλωρὸς χεῖρας ἁγνεύει θεοῖς
ἢ γάμον στείχει συνάψων ἢ τόκοις βαρύνεται·
φεύγετ', ἐξίστασθε, μή τῳ προσπέσῃ μύσος τόδε.
ὦ Διὸς Λητοῦς τ' ἄνασσα παρθέν', ἢν νίψω φόνον 1230
τῶνδε καὶ θύσωμεν οὗ χρή, καθαρὸν οἰκήσεις δόμον,

1212 Ιφ. Markland (om. L, Θο. P) 1213 Ιφ. Markland (paragr. erased in L, Θο. P)
οὓς δεῖ Badham οὐδεὶς L 1214 lacuna Hermann Θο. P (om. L) 1216 πυρσῷ
Reiske χρυσῷ (i.e. -ῷ) L 1219 Ιφ., Θο. TrP (om. L) 1220 σχολῆς Schaefer
σχολῇ (i.e. -ῇ) L 1223 ἄρνας Pierson ἄρσενας L

128

Iphigenia in Tauris

Iph. Yes, for such things are polluting.
　　　　　Tho. (to a servant) You, get going and announce...
Iph. ...that none must come into their sight.
　　　　　Tho. You care for our community well.
　　(The servant leaves)
Iph. And for the friends I most should care for.
　　　　　Tho. There you're talking about me.
⟨*Iph.*　　　　　⟩
　　　　　Tho. No wonder our whole community admires you.
Iph. You, stay here before the temple and . . .
　　　　　Tho. What then am I to do?[1215]
Iph. Cleanse the goddess's chamber with torch-fire.
　　　　　Tho. So it's pure when you return.
Iph. And as the strangers make their way outside...
　　　　　Tho. What must I do?
Iph. Put your garment before your eyes.
　　　　　Tho. So I'll not †*get a guilty one*†.
Iph. And if I seem to be delaying too long...
　　　　　Tho. What limit should I put on this?
Iph. Don't be at all surprised.
　　　　　Tho. Take your time, do the goddess's business right.[1220]
Iph. May this purification turn out the way I want!
　　　　　Tho. I share your prayer.

Orestes and Pylades come out of the temple with hands bound and heads veiled, escorted by Thoas's men. Temple servants follow carrying lambs and other equipment for the purifications. Thoas veils his head and keeps silent.

Iph. Now I see the strangers here emerging from the temple, and the goddess's adornments, and newborn lambs so I can wash off tainted blood with blood, and flaring torches and all the other things that I've prescribed for purifying the strangers and the goddess.[1225] *(Proclaiming)* I call upon the citizens to stay clear of this pollution, any temple-door attendant who is keeping clean hands for the gods, or anyone about to tie the marriage-knot or burdened with childbearing: get away and keep your distance, lest this foulness fall on any of you.
　　(Praying) O maiden mistress, child of Zeus and Leto, if I can wash the blood[1230] from these men and we can sacrifice where we should, your dwelling will be pure and we shall

Euripides

εὐτυχεῖς δ' ἡμεῖς ἐσόμεθα, τἄλλα δ' οὐ λέγουσ' ὅμως
τοῖς τὰ πλείον' εἰδόσιν θεοῖς σοί τε σημαίνω, θεά.

Χο. εὔπαις ὁ Λατοῦς γόνος,   *[στρ.*
      ὅν ποτε Δηλιάσιν καρποφόροις γυάλοις   1235
      ⟨ἔτικτε⟩ χρυσοκόμαν,
      ἐν κιθάρᾳ σοφόν, ὅστ' ἐπὶ τόξων
      εὐστοχίᾳ γάνυται· φέρε δ' ἶνιν
      ἀπὸ δειράδος εἰναλίας,   1240
      λοχεῖα κλεινὰ λιποῦσα, τὰν
      ματέρ' ἀστάκτων ὑδάτων
      ⟨συμ⟩βακχεύουσαν Διονύ-
      σῳ, Παρνάσιον κορυφάν,
      ὅθι ποικιλόνωτος οἰνωπὸς δράκων   1245
      σκιερὸν κάτεχ' ἄλσος εὐφύλλῳ δάφνᾳ,
      γᾶς πελώριον τέρας, †ἄμφεπει μαντεῖον χθόνιον†.
      ἔτι νιν ἔτι βρέφος ἔτι φίλας   1250
      ἐπὶ ματέρος ἀγκάλαισι θρῴσκων
      ἔκανες, ὦ Φοῖβε, μαντείων δ' ἐπέβας ζαθέων,
      τρίποδί τ' ἐν χρυσέῳ θάσσεις, ἐν ἀψευδεῖ θρόνῳ
      μαντείας βροτοῖς θεσφάτων νέμων   1255
      ἀδύτων ὕπο, Κασταλίας ῥεέθρων γείτων μέσον
      γᾶς ἔχων μέλαθρον.

      Θέμιν δ' ἐπεὶ Γαῖαν   *[ἀντ.*
      παῖδ' ἀπενάσσατο ⟨– – ⌣⟩ ἀπὸ ζαθέων   1260
      χρηστηρίων, νύχια
      Χθὼν ἐτεκνώσατο φάσματ' ὀ⟨νείρων⟩,
      οἳ πόλεσιν μερόπων τά τε πρῶτα
      τά τ' ἔπειθ' ἅ τ' ἔμελλε τυχεῖν   1265

1235 Δηλιάσιν Burges   δηλιὰς ἐν L (δηλίας TrP)   1236 ⟨ἔτικτε⟩ Paley   χρυσοκόμαν
Musgrave   χρυσοκόμαν φοῖβον L   1237 ὅστ' Burges   ἅ τ' L   1239 φέρε δ' ἶνιν Kirchhoff
φέρει νιν L   1241–42 τὰν ματέρ' ἀστάκτων ὑδάτων Sansone (ματέρ' Jacobs)   ἀστάκτων
μάτηρ ὑδάτων τὰν L   μάτηρ τὰν ἀστάκτων ὑδάτων Diggle   1243 ⟨συμ⟩βακχεύουσαν
Diggle   1246 σκιερὸν…εὐφύλλῳ δάφνᾳ Cropp (εὔφυλλον δάφνᾳ σκιερᾷ κάτεχ' ἄλσος
Burges, then σκιερᾷ…εὔφυλλον δάφνᾳ edd.)   σκιερᾷ κατάχαλκος εὐφύλλῳ δάφνᾳ L
1249 ἄμφεπε Seidler   1255 βροτοῖς Seidler   βροτοῖς ἀναφαίνων L   νέμων Musgrave
ἐμῶν L   1256 ὕπο Seidler   ὕπερ L   1259 ἐπεὶ Scaliger, Canter   ἐπὶ L   Γαῖαν Bruhn   γᾶς
ἰὼν L   1263 ὀ⟨νείρων⟩ Tr   ὁ L   1264 πόλεσι L?P πολέσιν Tr? (see Comm.)   1265 ἅ τ'
Seidler   ὅσα τ' L   ὅσ' Burges

Iphigenia in Tauris

enjoy good fortune. As for the rest, I do not say it, but signal it
to the gods and to you, who have more knowledge, goddess.

*Iphigenia leaves with the procession by Side-entrance B. Thoas goes
into the temple with his remaining attendants. The Chorus, left alone,
sings in praise of Apollo:*

Cho. A noble son is Leto's child,   *[Strophe*
whom once in Delos's fertile dell[1235]
she brought to birth, the gold-haired god,
skilled with the lyre, who takes delight
in his bow's straight aim. She brought her offspring
from the sea-bound crag,[1240]
leaving her famed place of labour,
  to that mother of pouring waters
  who dances with Dionysus,
  Parnassus's crowning height,
where a mottle-backed dark-eyed serpent,[1245]
possessed the grove, shady with verdant laurel,
a prodigious earth-monster, †*haunts the chthonic oracle*†.
An infant still, still frolicking[1250]
on your dear mother's arms,
you killed it, Phoebus, and stepped onto the holy oracular site;
and on the golden tripod you sit, on an undeceiving throne
dispensing to mortals pronouncements of divine decrees[1255]
from within the shrine, possessing earth's midmost mansion
  beside Castalia's streams.

But when he had displaced   *[Antistrophe*
the Earth-child Themis ⟨   ⟩
from her holy oracle,[1260]
Earth spawned nocturnal dream-apparitions
which told to communities of mortals the first things
and things that followed and things to come,[1265]

Euripides

ὕπνῳ κατὰ δνοφερὰς χαμεύ-
νας ἔφραζον· Γαῖα δὲ τὰν
μαντείων ἀφείλετο τιμ-
ὰν Φοῖβον φθόνῳ θυγατρός.
ταχύπους δ᾽ ἐς Ὄλυμπον ὁρμαθεὶς ἄναξ   1270
χέρα παιδνὸν ἕλιξεν ἐκ Διὸς θρόνων,
Πυθίων δόμων χθονίαν ἀφελεῖν μῆνιν θεᾶς.
γέλασε δ᾽ ὅτι τέκος ἄφαρ ἔβα
πολύχρυσα θέλων λατρεύματα σχεῖν·   1275
ἐπὶ δ᾽ ἔσεισεν κόμαν παῦσαι νυχίους ἐνοπάς,
ὑπὸ δ᾽ ἀλαθοσύναν νυκτωπὸν ἐξεῖλεν βροτῶν,
καὶ τιμὰς πάλιν θῆκε Λοξίᾳ   1280
πολυάνορι τ᾽ ἐν ξενόεντι θρόνῳ θάρση βροτοῖς
θεσφάτων ἀοιδαῖς.

ΑΓΓΕΛΟΣ
   ὦ ναοφύλακες βώμιοί τ᾽ ἐπιστάται,
   Θόας ἄναξ γῆς τῆσδε ποῦ κυρεῖ βεβώς;   1285
   καλεῖτ᾽ ἀναπτύξαντες εὐγόμφους πύλας
   ἔξω μελάθρων τῶνδε κοίρανον χθονός.
Χο.   τί δ᾽ ἔστιν, εἰ χρὴ μὴ κελευσθεῖσαν λέγειν;
Αγ.   βεβᾶσι φροῦδοι δίπτυχοι νεανίαι,
   Ἀγαμεμνονείας παιδὸς ἐκ βουλευμάτων   1290
   φεύγοντες ἐκ γῆς τῆσδε καὶ σεμνὸν βρέτας
   λαβόντες ἐν κόλποισιν Ἑλλάδος νεώς.
Χο.   ἄπιστον εἶπας μῦθον· ὃν δ᾽ ἰδεῖν θέλεις
   ἄνακτα χώρας φροῦδος ἐκ ναοῦ συθείς.
Αγ.   ποῖ; δεῖ γὰρ αὐτὸν εἰδέναι τὰ δρώμενα.   1295
Χο.   οὐκ ἴσμεν· ἀλλὰ στεῖχε καὶ δίωκέ νιν
   ὅπου κυρήσας τοῦσδ᾽ ἀπαγγελεῖς λόγους.
Αγ.   ὁρᾶτ᾽ ἄπιστον ὡς γυναικεῖον γένος·
   μέτεστι χὺμῖν τῶν πεπραγμένων μέρος.

1266 ὕπνῳ Markland -ου L   δνοφερὰς Musgrave -ᾶς L   χαμεύνας Linder γᾶς εὐνὰς L
1268 μαντείων Seidler μαντεῖον L   1272 μῆνιν θεᾶς Wilamowitz θεᾶς μῆνιν νυχίους τ᾽
ἐνοπὰς L (νυχίους τ᾽ ἐνοπὰς del. Seidler)   1276 ἐπὶ δ᾽ ἔσεισεν...παῦσαι Badham ἐπεὶ δ᾽
ἔσεισε...παῦσε L   ἐνοπάς Burges ὀνείρους L   1279 ὑπὸ Wecklein ἀπὸ L   δ᾽ ἀλαθοσύναν Nauck δὲ λαθοσύναν L   1281 τ᾽ Bergk δ᾽ L   1299 χὺμῖν Markland θ᾽ ὑμῖν L

Iphigenia in Tauris

as they slept in darkness on the ground.
  So Gaia purloined
  the oracular office from Phoebus,
  in jealousy for her daughter.
Then lord Apollo sped swift-footed to Olympus,[1270]
and coiled his youngster's arm around Zeus's throne,
begging him to remove the earth-goddess's wrath from his
  Pythian home.
Zeus laughed, that his son had come so quick
in his eagerness to own the gold-rich offerings.[1275]
He shook his hair to end the nocturnal declarations,
and stole away from mortals the night-figures' candour,
restoring to Loxias once again his honours[1280]
and confidence for mortals at his crowded guest-
  frequented throne
  in the chantings of his decrees.

*As the Chorus ends its hymn, one of the servants who escorted the
procession to the shore rushes in by Side-entrance B and up to the
temple door.*

MESSENGER
  You temple-minders and altar-supervisors, where is Thoas the
  lord of our land to be found?[1285] Throw open these fine-riveted
  doors and call our country's ruler out of the temple here.
Cho. What is it, if I may speak without being told to?
Mess. They are off and on their way, that pair of young fellows;
  they have fled this land through the scheming of Agamemn-
  on's daughter, and taken the sacred image[1290] in the hold of the
  Hellene ship.
Cho That's an incredible story! But the one you want to see, the
  lord of the land, has left the temple in a hurry.
Mess. Where to? He must be told what is going on.[1295]
Cho. We do not know. But go, run after him to where you can find
  him and report your news.
Mess. See how treacherous is womankind! You too have a part in
  what has been going on.

133

Euripides

Χο. μαίνῃ· τί δ’ ἡμῖν τῶν ξένων δρασμοῦ μέτα; 1300
οὐκ εἰ κρατούντων πρὸς πύλας ὅσον τάχος;

Αγ. οὔ, πρίν γ’ ἂν εἴπῃ τοὔπος ἑρμηνεὺς τόδε,
εἴτ’ ἔνδον εἴτ’ οὐκ ἔνδον ἀρχηγὸς χθονός.
ὠή, χαλᾶτε κλῇθρα – τοῖς ἔνδον λέγω –
καὶ δεσπότῃ σημήναθ’ οὕνεκ’ ἐν πύλαις 1305
πάρειμι καινῶν φόρτον ἀγγέλλων κακῶν.

Θο. τίς ἀμφὶ δῶμα θεᾶς τόδ’ ἵστησιν βοήν,
πύλας ἀράξας καὶ ψόφον πέμψας ἔσω;

Αγ. †ψευδῶς ἔλεγον αἴδε, καί† μ’ ἀπήλαυνον δόμων,
ὡς ἐκτὸς εἴης· σὺ δὲ κατ’ οἶκον ἦσθ’ ἄρα. 1310

Θο. τί προσδοκῶσαι κέρδος ἢ θηρώμεναι;

Αγ. αὖθις τὰ τῶνδε σημανῶ· τὰ δ’ ἐν ποσὶν
παρόντ’ ἄκουσον· ἡ νεᾶνις ἡ ’νθάδε
βωμοῖς παρίστατ’, Ἰφιγένει’, ἔξω χθονὸς
σὺν τοῖς ξένοισιν οἴχεται, σεμνὸν θεᾶς 1315
ἄγαλμ’ ἔχουσα· δόλια δ’ ἦν καθάρματα.

Θο. πῶς φῄς; τί πνεῦμα συμφορᾶς κεκτημένη;

Αγ. σῴζουσ’ Ὀρέστην· τοῦτο γὰρ σὺ θαυμάσῃ.

Θο. τὸν ποῖον; ἆρ’ ὃν Τυνδαρὶς τίκτει κόρη;

Αγ. ὃν τοῖσδε βωμοῖς θεᾷ καθωσιώσατο. 1320

Θο. ὦ θαῦμα· πῶς σε μεῖζον ὀνομάσας τύχω;

Αγ. μὴ ’νταῦθα τρέψῃς σὴν φρέν’, ἀλλ’ ἄκουέ μου·
σαφῶς δ’ ἀθρήσας καὶ κλυὼν ἐκφρόντισον
διωγμὸν ὅστις τοὺς ξένους θηράσεται.

Θο. λέγ’, εὖ γὰρ εἶπας· οὐ γὰρ ἀγχίπλουν πόρον 1325
φεύγουσιν ὥστε διαφυγεῖν τοὐμὸν δόρυ.

Αγ. ἐπεὶ πρὸς ἀκτὰς ἤλθομεν θαλασσίας,
οὗ ναῦς Ὀρέστου κρύφιος ἦν ὡρμισμένη,
ἡμᾶς μέν, οὓς σὺ δεσμὰ συμπέμπεις ξένων
ἔχοντας, ἐξένευσ’ ἀποστῆναι πρόσω 1330
Ἀγαμέμνονος παῖς, ὡς ἀπόρρητον φλόγα
θύουσα καὶ καθαρμὸν ὃν μετῴχετο·
αὐτὴ δ’ ὄπισθε δέσμ’ ἔχουσα τοῖν ξένοιν
ἔστειχε χερσί. καὶ τάδ’ ἦν ὕποπτα μέν,

1300–1 Χο., 1302–6 Αγ. Heath et al. 1300 Χο., 1301 Αγ., 1302–3 Χο., 1304–6 Αγ. L
1310 εἴης Canter ἦς L 1320 θεᾷ ed. Aldin. θεὰ L 1324 διωγμὸν Hermann -ὸς L
1329 οὓς TrP οὗ L 1334 χερσί Tr χεροῖν L

134

Iphigenia in Tauris

Cho. You're crazy! What have we to do with the strangers' escape?[1300] Won't you go on to the king's palace as fast as you can?

Mess. Not before I hear it stated plainly whether our country's ruler is inside or not. *(Hammering on the door)* Hey there, release the latches – I'm talking to you inside – and make it known to the master I'm at the door,[1305] reporting a load of new troubles.

Thoas emerges from the temple with some of his men.

Tho. Who's raising a clamour around the goddess's home here, battering the doors and sending noise inside?

Mess. †*These women were saying falsely and*† driving me away from the temple, that you were abroad, while you were in there all along![1310]

Tho. What profit were they expecting or chasing after?

Mess. I'll explain their part in this later. Now you must hear what matters right now. The young woman Iphigenia, who attended here at the altar, has gone off out of the country with those foreigners, carrying the goddess's[1315] holy image. The purification was a trick!

Tho. What do you mean? What breeze of fortune did she catch?

Mess. She's rescuing Orestes, you'll be amazed to hear.

Tho. What Orestes? Not the one Tyndareus' daughter bore?

Mess. The man she dedicated to the goddess for her altar here.[1320]

Tho. O marvel – how can I find you a greater name?

Mess. Don't distract yourself with that, but listen to me, and when you've carefully examined and heard, then plan a pursuit to track down those intruders.

Tho. Tell me, then; your advice is good. The route they're fleeing on[1325] is no short voyage; they'll not escape my armed pursuit.

Mess. When we had made our way towards the sea-shore, where Orestes' vessel was secretly moored, Agamemnon's daughter nodded to us, the ones you sent keeping hold of the strangers' bonds, to stand away some distance off,[1330] hinting that the fire she was burning and the purification she intended were secret. Then she herself took hold of the strangers' bonds and walked behind them. This was of course suspicious, but still we your

135

Euripides

ἤρεσκε μέντοι σοῖσι προσπόλοις, ἄναξ. 1335
χρόνῳ δ', ἵν' ἡμῖν δρᾶν τι δὴ δοκοῖ πλέον,
ἀνωλόλυξε καὶ κατῇδε βάρβαρα
μέλη μαγεύουσ', ὡς φόνον νίζουσα δή.
ἐπεὶ δὲ δαρὸν ἦμεν ἥμενοι χρόνον,
ἐσῆλθεν ἡμᾶς μὴ λυθέντες οἱ ξένοι 1340
κτάνοιεν αὐτὴν δραπέται τ' οἰχοίατο.
φόβῳ δ' ἃ μὴ χρῆν εἰσορᾶν καθήμεθα
σιγῇ· τέλος δὲ πᾶσιν ἦν αὐτὸς λόγος,
στείχειν ἵν' ἦσαν καίπερ οὐκ ἐωμένοις.
κἀνταῦθ' ὁρῶμεν Ἑλλάδος νεὼς σκάφος 1345
ταρσῷ κατήρει πίτυλον ἐπτερωμένον,
ναύτας τε πεντήκοντ' ἐπὶ σκαλμῶν πλάτας
ἔχοντας, ἐκ δεσμῶν δὲ τοὺς νεανίας
ἐλευθέρους ⟨
                    ⟩ πρύμνηθεν ἑστῶτες νεὼς 1349
σπεύδοντες ἦγον διὰ χερῶν πρυμνήσια 1352
⟨   ⟩
κοντοῖς δὲ πρῷραν εἶχον, οἱ δ' ἐπωτίδων 1350
ἄγκυραν ἐξανῆπτον, οἱ δὲ κλίμακας 1351
πόντῳ διδόντες τοῖν ξένοιν καθίεσαν. 1353
    ἡμεῖς δ' ἀφειδήσαντες, ὡς ἐσείδομεν
δόλια τεχνήματ', εἰχόμεσθα τῆς ξένης 1355
πρυμνησίων τε, καὶ δι' εὐθυντηρίας
οἴακας ἐξηροῦμεν εὐπρύμνου νεώς.
λόγοι δ' ἐχώρουν· 'Τίνι λόγῳ πορθμεύετε
κλέπτοντες ἐκ γῆς ξόανα καὶ θυηπόλους;
τίνος τίς ὢν ⟨σὺ⟩ τήνδ' ἀπεμπολᾷς χθονός;' 1360
ὁ δ' εἶπ'· 'Ὀρέστης, τῆσδ' ὅμαιμος, ὡς μάθῃς,
Ἀγαμέμνονος παῖς· τὴν δ' ἐμὴν κομίζομαι
λαβὼν ἀδελφήν, ἣν ἀπώλεσ' ἐκ δόμων.'
    ἀλλ' οὐδὲν ἧσσον εἰχόμεσθα τῆς ξένης,
καὶ πρὸς σ' ἕπεσθαι διεβιαζόμεσθά νιν, 1365
ὅθεν τὰ δεινὰ πλήγματ' ἦν γενειάδων.

1336 δοκοῖ Matthiae δο** Lᵃᶜ δοκῇ (i.e. -ῇ) Lᵖᶜ or Tr, P 1338 μαγεύουσ' Reiske ματεύ- L 1343 αὐτὸς Valckenaer αὑτὸς L 1349, 1352 thus Köchly ἑστῶτας L νεώς ed. Aldin. νεῶν L lacuna before 1350, Cropp 1351 ἄγκυραν Scaliger ἀγκύρας L 1353 διδόντες Kirchhoff δὲ δόντες L τοῖν ξένοιν Seidler τὴν ξένην L (τὴν ξένοιν P) τῇ ξένη Musgrave 1359 ξόανα Reiske -ον L θυηπόλους Musgrave -ον L 1360 ⟨σὺ⟩ Markland

136

Iphigenia in Tauris

servants accepted it, my lord.[1335] And in time – to give an impression, of course, of doing something – she raised an ululation and set about reciting barbarian chants, playing the magus, as if she was washing off the bloodguilt.

Now when we had been sitting for quite a time, it came to us that the foreigners once released[1340] might kill her and be gone, making their escape. But since we feared to set eyes on what we should not, we sat on in silence. Finally, though, we all reached the same conclusion, to go to where they were, even though we were forbidden. And then we saw the Hellene vessel lying there,[1345] with oars spread out like wings in trim array, and fifty sailors holding blades ready on the thole-pins, and the young men, free from their bonds...*(one or more lines lost)*...were standing on the ship's afterdeck[1349] and hurriedly drawing the stern-cables through their hands[1352]...*(probably one line lost)*...and were holding the prow steady with poles, and some were lashing[1350] the anchor to the cat-heads, while others[1351] were lowering a ladder into the sea for the two strangers.[1353]

Now that we had seen her trickery we no longer held back. We caught hold of the foreign woman[1355] and the stern-cables, and set about pulling out through their sockets the steering-oars of the stout-sterned ship. Now words began to fly, 'What reason do you have for stealing and transporting carved images and priestesses from this land? Who are you, and whose son, to be trafficking this woman away from our country?'[1360] Then he replied, 'I'm Orestes, her own brother, if you want to know, Agamemnon's son! I'm fetching away my sister, whom I had lost from our home.'

Still none the less we kept our hold on her, and tried to force her to come along with us to you –[1365] and that's how we got those terrible blows on our jaws! They had no iron to

Euripides

κεῖνοί τε γὰρ σίδηρον οὐκ εἶχον χεροῖν
ἡμεῖς τε, πυγμαὶ δ' ἦσαν ἐγκροτούμεναι
καὶ κῶλ' ἀπ' ἀμφοῖν τοῖν νεανίαιν ἅμα
ἐς πλευρὰ καὶ πρὸς ἧπαρ ἠκοντίζετο,   1370
ὥστε ξυναλγεῖν καὶ ξυναποκαμεῖν μέλη.
δεινοῖς δὲ σημάντροισιν ἐσφραγισμένοι
ἐφεύγομεν πρὸς κρημνόν, οἱ μὲν ἐν κάρᾳ
κάθαιμ' ἔχοντες τραύμαθ', οἱ δ' ἐν ὄμμασιν.
ὄχθοις δ' ἐπισταθέντες εὐλαβεστέρως   1375
ἐμαρνάμεσθα, καὶ πέτροις ἐβάλλομεν.
ἀλλ' εἶργον ἡμᾶς τοξόται πρύμνης ἔπι
σταθέντες ἰοῖς, ὥστ' ἀναστεῖλαι πρόσω.
κἀν τῷδε, δεινὸς γὰρ κλύδων ὤκειλε ναῦν
πρὸς γῆν, φόβος δ' ἦν ⟨παρθένῳ⟩ τέγξαι πόδα,   1380
λαβὼν Ὀρέστης ὦμον εἰς ἀριστερόν,
βὰς ἐς θάλασσαν κἀπὶ κλίμακος θορών,
ἔθηκ' ἀδελφήν ἐντὸς εὐσέλμου νεὼς
τό τ' οὐρανοῦ πέσημα, τῆς Διὸς κόρης
ἄγαλμα. ναὸς ⟨δ'⟩ ἐκ μέσης ἐφθέγξατο   1385
βοή τις· Ὦ γῆς Ἑλλάδος ναῦται λεώς,
λάβεσθε κώπης ῥόθιά τ' ἐκλευκαίνετε·
ἔχομεν γὰρ ὦνπερ οὕνεκ' ἄξενον πόρον
Συμπληγάδων ἔσωθεν εἰσεπλεύσαμεν.'
οἱ δὲ στεναγμὸν ἡδὺν ἐκβρυχώμενοι   1390
ἔπαισαν ἅλμην. ναῦς δ', ἕως μὲν ἐντὸς ἦν
λιμένος ἐχώρει, στόμια διαπερῶσα δὲ
λάβρῳ κλύδωνι συμπεσοῦσ' ἠπείγετο·
δεινὸς γὰρ ἐλθὼν ἄνεμος ἐξαίφνης νεὼς
ὠθεῖ †πάλιν πρυμνῆσι'†. οἱ δ' ἐκαρτέρουν   1395
πρὸς κῦμα λακτίζοντες· ἐς δὲ γῆν πάλιν
κλύδων παλίρρους ἦγε ναῦν. σταθεῖσα δὲ

1368 δ' ed. Aldin.   τ' L   1371 ξυναλγεῖν Hermann   ξυνάπτειν L   1376 πέτροις Paley
-ους L   1380 ⟨παρθένῳ⟩ Badham (blank space in L, cf. 1404) ⟨ὥστε μὴ⟩ Tr   1383 εὐσέλμου Paris. 2817 second hand, Pierson εὐσήμου L   1384–85 τό τ'...⟨δ'⟩ ἐκ Paris. 2887
second hand, Markland   τὸ δ'...ἐκ L   1386 ναύτης λεώς F. W. Schmidt   ναῦται νεώς L
1387 κώπης Reiske -αις L   τ' ἐκλευκαίνετε Scaliger τε λευκ- L   1388 ἄξενον Markland
εὔξεινον L   1392 thus Barnes et al.   ἐχώρει στόμια· διαπερῶσα δὲ L   1395 ὠθεῖ Kirchhoff ὤθει L   παλιμπρυμνηδόν Hermann (placing 1346 before 1395), Paley (with 1394
σκάφος for νεώς) παλίμπρυμν' ἰστί' Mekler

138

Iphigenia in Tauris

hand, and neither did we, but fists were being thumped and legs launched from both youths together into our ribs and at our livers,[1370] so that our limbs ached and seized up altogether. Stamped with the terrible marks of our encounter we fled towards the cliff, bearing bloody wounds, some on our heads and others on our faces. Then taking a stand on the slopes we battled on with greater caution[1375] and pelted them with rocks. But archers standing on the afterdeck kept us off with arrows and forced us further away.

Meanwhile a terrible wave had run the ship towards the land, but the maiden was afraid of wetting her foot.[1380] So Orestes took her onto his left shoulder, stepped into the sea and jumped up onto a ladder, and placed his sister within the fine-decked ship, with that bolt from the sky, Zeus's daughter's image. And from mid-ship[1385] a voice cried out: 'O you sailor folk from Hellas land, seize each your oar, stir up a whitening surf! We have what we sailed for past the Symplêgades and into the Unwelcoming passage!'

And so they bellowed out a cheerful roar[1390] and struck the brine. The ship, so long as it was within the harbour, made way, but as it crossed the mouth it collided with a violent wave and was hard pressed, as a sudden terrible wind came and pushed the ship's †*stern-cables back*†. They persevered[1395] and kicked against the wave, but back to the land the inrushing flood drove the ship. Then Agamemnon's daughter

Euripides

Ἀγαμέμνονος παῖς ηὔξατ'· 'Ὦ Λητοῦς κόρη,
σῶσόν με τὴν σὴν ἱερέαν πρὸς Ἑλλάδα
ἐκ βαρβάρου γῆς, καὶ κλοπαῖς σύγγνωθ' ἐμαῖς.   1400
φιλεῖς δὲ καὶ σὺ σὸν κασίγνητον, θεά·
φιλεῖν δὲ κἀμὲ τοὺς ὁμαίμονας δόκει.'
  ναῦται δ' ἐπηυφήμησαν εὐχαῖσιν κόρης
παιᾶνα, γυμνὰς ἐκ ⟨πέπλων⟩ ἐπωμίδας
κώπῃ προσαρμόσαντες ἐκ κελεύματος.   1405
μᾶλλον δὲ μᾶλλον πρὸς πέτρας ᾖει σκάφος·
χὠ μέν τις ἐς θάλασσαν ὡρμήθη ποσίν,
ἄλλος δὲ πλεκτὰς ἐξανῆπτεν ἀγκύλας.
κἀγὼ μὲν εὐθὺς πρὸς σὲ δεῦρ' ἀπεστάλην,
σοὶ τὰς ἐκεῖθεν σημανῶν, ἄναξ, τύχας.   1410
  ἀλλ' ἕρπε, δεσμὰ καὶ βρόχους λαβὼν χεροῖν·
εἰ μὴ γὰρ οἶδμα νήνεμον γενήσεται,
οὐκ ἔστιν ἐλπὶς τοῖς ξένοις σωτηρίας.
πόντου δ' ἀνάκτωρ Ἴλιον τ' ἐπεσκόπει
σεμνὸς Ποσειδῶν, Πελοπίδαις ἐναντίος,   1415
καὶ νῦν παρέξει τὸν Ἀγαμέμνονος γόνον
σοὶ καὶ πολίταις, ὡς ἔοικεν, ἐν χεροῖν
λαβεῖν ἀδελφήν θ' ἢ φόνου τοῦ 'ν Αὐλίδι
ἀμνημόνευτος θεὰν προδοῦσ' ἁλίσκεται.

Χο. ὦ τλῆμον Ἰφιγένεια, συγγόνου μέτα   1420
θανῇ πάλιν μολοῦσα δεσποτῶν χέρας.

Θο. ὦ πάντες ἀστοὶ τῆσδε βαρβάρου χθονός,
οὐχ εἶα πώλοις ἐμβαλόντες ἡνίας
παράκτιοι δραμεῖσθε, κἀκβολὰς νεὼς
Ἑλληνίδος δέξεσθε, σὺν δὲ τῇ θεῷ   1425
σπεύδοντες ἄνδρας δυσσεβεῖς θηράσετε,
οἱ δ' ὠκυπόμπους ἕλξετ' ἐς πόντον πλάτας,
ὡς ἐκ θαλάσσης ἔκ τε γῆς ἱππεύμασιν
λαβόντες αὐτοὺς ἢ κατὰ στύφλου πέτρας
ῥίψωμεν ἢ σκόλοψι πήξωμεν δέμας;   1430

1404 ⟨πέπλων⟩ Markland ἐκ(βαλόντες) Tr 1406 ᾖει TrP εἴη L 1408 ἐξανῆπτεν L^pc or
Tr -ον L^acP 1414 ἐπεσκόπει Matthiae ἐπισκοπεῖ L 1415 Πελοπίδαις Bothe Πελοπίδαις
δ' L 1418 ἀδελφήν θ' Musgrave τ' ἀδελφήν L 1418–19 φόνου τοῦ 'ν Αὐλίδι…θεὰν
Badham φόνου τὸν Αὐλίδι…θεᾶ (i.e. θεᾷ) L 1419 ἀμνημόνευτος Markland -ον L

Iphigenia in Tauris

stood and prayed: 'O daughter of Leto, bring me, your priest-ess, safe to Hellas out of this barbarous land, and forgive my thieving.[1400] You too feel love for your own brother, goddess. You should expect that I too love my kin.'

The sailors followed up the maiden's prayers with an auspicious paean, and at the command applied their shoulders, stripped of clothing, to the oar.[1405] The boat came closer and closer to the rocks. Then one of us ran forward into the sea, and another set about tying looped cables on the ship. And I was despatched straight here to you, my lord, to inform you of what has been happening there.[1410]

Go then, and carry cords and halters with you. Unless the swelling sea becomes calm again, there is no hope of safety for the intruders. The ocean's ruler was watching over Troy, august Poseidon, opposed to Pelops' descendants;[1415] and now, it seems, he'll give Agamemnon's son to you and your people to take in your hands, along with his sister who is guilty of forgetting the sacrifice at Aulis and betraying the goddess.

Cho. O wretched Iphigenia, you are going to die with your brother, falling again into our master's hands![1421]

Tho. Ho, all you people of this barbarian country! Come on now, put reins on horses, race along the shore and find the wreckage of the Hellene ship, then with the goddess's help[1425] speedily hunt down those impious men; and others drag swift vessels into the sea, so that we can ride them down on sea and land, and catch them and hurl them down some rough rockface, or skewer their bodies on stakes![1430]

141

Euripides

ὑμᾶς δὲ τὰς τῶνδ' ἵστορας βουλευμάτων,
γυναῖκες, αὖθις ἡνίκ' ἂν σχολὴν λάβω
ποινασόμεσθα· νῦν δὲ τὴν προκειμένην
σπουδὴν ἔχοντες οὐ μενοῦμεν ἥσυχοι.

ΑΘΗΝΑ

ποῖ, ποῖ διωγμὸν τόνδε πορθμεύεις, ἄναξ   1435
Θόας; ἄκουσον τῆσδ' Ἀθηναίας λόγους.
παῦσαι διώκων ῥεῦμά τ' ἐξορμῶν στρατοῦ.
πεπρωμένον γὰρ θεσφάτοισι Λοξίου
δεῦρ' ἦλθ' Ὀρέστης, τόν τ' Ἐρινύων χόλον
φεύγων ἀδελφῆς τ' Ἄργος ἐσπέμψων δέμας   1440
ἄγαλμά θ' ἱερὸν εἰς ἐμὴν ἄξων χθόνα,   1441
τῶν νῦν παρόντων πημάτων ἀναψυχάς.   1441b
    πρὸς μὲν σ' ὅδ' ἡμῖν μῦθος· ὃν δ' ἀποκτενεῖν   1442
δοκεῖς Ὀρέστην ποντίῳ λαβὼν σάλῳ,
ἤδη Ποσειδῶν χάριν ἐμὴν ἀκύμονα
πόντου τίθησι νῶτα πορθμεύειν πλάτῃ.   1445
μαθὼν δ', Ὀρέστα, τὰς ἐμὰς ἐπιστολάς
(κλύεις γὰρ αὐδὴν καίπερ οὐ παρὼν θεᾶς),
χώρει λαβὼν ἄγαλμα σύγγονόν τε σήν.
ὅταν δ' Ἀθήνας τὰς θεοδμήτους μόλῃς,
χῶρός τις ἔστιν Ἀτθίδος πρὸς ἐσχάτοις   1450
ὅροισι, γείτων δειράδος Καρυστίας,
ἱερός· Ἁλάς νιν οὑμὸς ὀνομάζει λεώς.
ἐνταῦθα τεύξας ναὸν ἵδρυσαι βρέτας,
ἐπώνυμον γῆς Ταυρικῆς πόνων τε σῶν,
οὓς ἐξεμόχθεις περιπολῶν καθ' Ἑλλάδα   1455
οἴστροις Ἐρινύων. Ἄρτεμιν δέ νιν βροτοὶ
τὸ λοιπὸν ὑμνήσουσι Ταυροπόλον θεάν.
νόμον τε θὲς τόνδ'· ὅταν ἑορτάζῃ λεώς,
τῆς σῆς σφαγῆς ἄποιν' ἐπισχέτω ξίφος
δέρῃ πρὸς ἀνδρὸς αἷμά τ' ἐξανιέτω   1460
ὁσίας ἕκατι θεά θ' ὅπως τιμὰς ἔχῃ.

1432 γυναῖκες Markland -ας L   1438 πεπρωμένον Monk -οις L   1441b om. P
1445 πορθμεύειν Tyrwhitt -ων L   πορθμεύειν πλάτην Diggle (πλάτην Badham)
1453 τεύξας Pierson τάξας L   1454 γῆς Hermann τῆς L   1455 see on 84   1458 θὲς
Bothe, Porson θέσθε L   1460 ἐξανιέτω Heath ἐξ ἀννέτω L   1461 θεά θ' Markland
θεᾶς L

142

Iphigenia in Tauris

As for you witnesses of these intrigues, you women, I'll make you pay your penalty later, when I get the leisure. Now with this business before me, I'll not linger here in idleness.

Before Thoas can dispatch the pursuit, the goddess Athena flies into view and alights on the temple-roof.

ATHENA

Where, where are you carrying this pursuit, lord[1435] Thoas? Listen to what I, Athena, have to say. Cease your pursuing, stop launching the flood of your forces. It was destined that Orestes should come here through Loxias's oracles, fleeing the Erinyes' wrath, to convey his sister's person back to Argos[1440] and bring the sacred image into my country, achieving respite from his present troubles.

That is my proclamation to you. As for Orestes, whom you expect to catch and kill on the storm-tossed sea, already Poseidon at my request is making the ocean's surface calm for his voyage.[1445] *(Speaking into the distance)* And you, Orestes, learning my instructions (you can hear my goddess's voice, though you are not here), take the image and your sister and go on your way. And when you reach god-built Athens, there is a place near the furthest borders of Attica,[1450] neighbouring the crags of Carystos,[1451] a sacred place called Halai by my people. There build a temple and set the image in it, named for the Tauric land and your ordeals through which you struggled, roaming over Hellas[1455] in Fury-goaded frenzy. People in future time will hymn Artemis, the Tauropolian goddess. And make this a rule: when the people keep her festival, as recompense for your slaughter let a sword be held to a man's throat and blood be drawn,[1460] for the sake of holiness and so that the goddess may keep her honours.

Euripides

σὲ δ' ἀμφὶ σεμνάς, Ἰφιγένεια, λείμακας
Βραυρωνίας δεῖ τῇδε κληδουχεῖν θεᾷ,
οὗ καὶ τεθάψῃ κατθανοῦσα, καὶ πέπλων
ἄγαλμά σοι θήσουσιν εὐπήνους ὑφάς,   1465
ἃς ἂν γυναῖκες ἐν τόκοις ψυχορραγεῖς
λείπωσ' ἐν οἴκοις. τάσδε δ' ἐκπέμπειν χθονὸς
Ἑλληνίδας γυναῖκας ἐξεφίεμαι
γνώμης δικαίας οὕνεκ' ⟨
        at least two half-lines lost
                    ⟩ ἐκσώσασά σε
καὶ πρίν γ', Ἀρείοις ἐν πάγοις ψήφους ἴσας   1470
κρίνασ', Ὀρέστα· καὶ νόμισμ' ἔσται τόδε,
νικᾶν ἰσήρεις ὅστις ἂν ψήφους λάβῃ.
ἀλλ' ἐκκομίζου σὴν κασιγνήτην χθονός,
Ἀγαμέμνονος παῖ· καὶ σὺ μὴ θυμοῦ, Θόας.

Θο. ἄνασσ' Ἀθάνα, τοῖσι τῶν θεῶν λόγοις   1475
ὅστις κλυὼν ἄπιστος οὐκ ὀρθῶς φρονεῖ.
ἐγὼ δ' Ὀρέστῃ τ', εἰ φέρων βρέτας θεᾶς
βέβηκ', ἀδελφῇ τ' οὐχὶ θυμοῦμαι· τί γὰρ
πρὸς τοὺς σθένοντας θεοὺς ἁμιλλᾶσθαι καλόν;
ἴτωσαν ἐς σὴν σὺν θεᾶς ἀγάλματι   1480
γαῖαν, καθιδρύσαιντό τ' εὐτυχῶς βρέτας.
πέμψω δὲ καὶ τάσδ' Ἑλλάδ' εἰς εὐδαίμονα
γυναῖκας, ὥσπερ σὸν κέλευμ' ἐφίεται.
παύσω δὲ λόγχην ἣν ἐπαίρομαι ξένοις
νεῶν τ' ἐρετμά, σοὶ τάδ' ὡς δοκεῖ, θεά.   1485

Αθ. αἰνῶ· τὸ γὰρ χρεὼν σοῦ τε καὶ θεῶν κρατεῖ.
ἴτ', ὦ πνοαί, ναυσθλοῦτε τὸν Ἀγαμέμνονος
παῖδ' εἰς Ἀθήνας· συμπορεύσομαι δ' ἐγώ,
σῴζουσ' ἀδελφῆς τῆς ἐμῆς σεμνὸν βρέτας.

1462 λείμακας Pierson   κλίμακας L   1463 τῇδε...θεᾷ Markland   τῆσδε...θεᾶς L
1469 lacuna Reiske (after 1468 Brodaeus)   1469–70 ἐξέσωσα δὲ καὶ πρίν σ' Schol.ᴿⱽ Ar.
Frogs 685 (καὶ om. Schol.ⱽ)   1471 ἔσται (Dupuy) τόδε Markland   εἰς ταυτό γε L
1473 κασιγνήτην Elmsley -ον L   1478 τί γάρ; Reiske   1479 del. Diggle   1485 θεά ed.
Aldin. θεᾶ (i.e. θεᾷ) L   1486 Αθ. Tr or a later hand in L (om. L)   1487–89 Αθ. ed. Aldin.
Ἀπολλών L   ναυσθλοῦτε Canter -σθε L

144

Iphigenia in Tauris

You, Iphigenia, are to serve the goddess as key-keeper in the holy meadows of Brauron. There you will also lie buried when you die, and people will dedicate to you the fine-textured woven clothes[1465] which women who have given up their lives in childbirth leave in their homes. *(Indicating the Chorus)* And I give instruction to send these Hellene women out of this country because of their righteous judgment... *(at least two half-lines lost)*...having rescued you[1469b] also before when I judged the votes equal on Ares' hill,[1470] Orestes. And this too will be a rule, that he who gets equally balanced votes shall prevail.

Come then, convey your sister out of this country, son of Agamemnon; and Thoas, restrain your anger.

Tho. Queen Athena, the man who hears the gods' words and disobeys them is not in his right mind.[1476] I feel no anger at Orestes if he has gone with the goddess's image, nor at his sister. Where is the credit in struggling against the gods, who have the power? Let them go to your land with the image of the goddess,[1480] and may they establish it there with all good fortune! I'll send these women too to happy Hellas, as your instruction demands. I'll calm the spear I'm raising against the intruders, and my ships' oars, as that is your wish, goddess.[1485]

Ath. I commend you. What must be controls you and the gods. Go, winds, give passage for Agamemnon's son to Athens; And I will go with them and keep my sister's holy image safe.

Athena flies away towards the shore. The Chorus chants a farewell, then addresses Athena:

Euripides

Xo. ἴτ' ἐπ' εὐτυχίᾳ, τῆς σῳζομένης   1490
μοίρας εὐδαίμονες ὄντες.
ἀλλ', ὦ σεμνὴ παρά τ' ἀθανάτοις
καὶ παρὰ θνητοῖς, Παλλὰς Ἀθάνα,
δράσομεν οὕτως ὡς σὺ κελεύεις.
μάλα γὰρ τερπνὴν κἀνέλπιστον   1495
φήμην ἀκοαῖσι δέδεγμαι.

[ὦ μέγα σεμνὴ Νίκη, τὸν ἐμὸν
βίοτον κατέχοις
καὶ μὴ λήγοις στεφανοῦσα.]

1490–99 Xo. Seidler 1490–91 ΑΘ., 1492–99 Xo. L or Tr 1491 εὐδαίμονες ed. Aldin. -
ος L 1495 τερπνὴν L. Dindorf -ὸν L 1497–9 del. Blomfield

146

Iphigenia in Tauris

Chor. Go on your way in good fortune,
   happy in attaining your salvation.[1491]

   O lady revered amongst immortals
   and amongst mortals, Pallas Athena,
   we will do as you command us.
   Welcome and unexpected indeed[1495]
   is the declaration that I have heard.

   [Venerable Victory,
   may you keep hold of my life
   and not cease crowning me.]

*The women leave for the shore by Side-entrance B, accompanied by
Thoas and his men.*

COMMENTARY

For abbreviations see pp. 273f. »» means 'for fuller information and references see...' Square brackets enclose the more technical discussions of text and language.

1–235. Introductory scenes

1–66 Prologue speech (Iphigenia) – *67–122* Scene (Orestes and Pylades) – *123–235* Parodos (*amoibaion* or sung dialogue of Chorus and Iphigenia). This sequence sets the basis for the action of the play, introducing the main characters, explaining their situation and history, and establishing mood. Euripides' plays always begin with a solo prologue speech and usually add at least one dramatic scene before moving into lyric mode with the Chorus's arrival. Iphigenia's withdrawal at the end of her speech allows Orestes to be introduced (65–66 n.). Scene and setting are discussed in the Introduction, pp. 34–37.

1–66. Prologue speech: Iphigenia explains her situation

Iphigenia comes out from the temple to air her dream and meet with the women of the Chorus who will assist with her libations. Her speech, like all Euripides' prologue speeches, is addressed to the audience but is not merely informational; the emotional dimensions of her past and her present predicament are also conveyed. A brief summary of her genealogy (1–5) leads directly into an evocative recollection of her sacrifice at Aulis (6–9). A detailed narrative of the sacrifice and her rescue (10–33) emphasizes the grandeur and ambition of the Trojan expedition and picks out the individuals she associates with her suffering (Agamemnon, Menelaus, Calchas, Odysseus, Achilles); her attitude to each will be important at later points in the play. Calchas's proclamation of the will of Artemis is dramatized through direct speech, and a pathetically simple narrative leads up to the critical moment when Iphigenia faced her sacrificial slaughter. Her own repellent duties at the Taurian temple are rapidly sketched (34–39), then in troubling detail she tells the dream which has linked her former and present lives so disturbingly (42–60) and led to her ritual preparations (61–66). All of this narrative's emotional dimensions will be explored more fully in the lyrics of the Parodos.

1–5. Pelops son of Tantalus etc.: introductory genealogies are a mannerism, increasingly elaborated, in later plays of Euripides (*Heracles, Ion, Phoenician Women, Orestes, Wise Melanippe,* cf. *IA* 49ff.). In Aristophanes, *Frogs* 1119–1248 Euripides claims the merits of clarity and accuracy for his openings by contrast with Aeschylus, while Aeschylus parodies Euripides' mannerism by capping seven of his opening sentences, including this one, with the famous ληκύθιον

150 COMMENTARY

ἀπώλεσεν (*Frogs* 1232f., 'Pelops son of Tantalus went to Pisa with his swift mares and *lost his little oil-jar*'). In fact this genealogy is carefully phrased, culminating with Iphigenia and balanced with the account of her sacrifice (6–9). It also draws attention to the family's history at the very beginning of the play. Pelops was supposed to have won the hand of Hippodameia in a chariot race with her father Oenomaus, who challenged suitors to carry off his daughter and killed them if they failed to outrun him. The story is attested from the sixth century onwards in many versions (»» Gantz 540–45, Fowler 2013, 428–31, 720–22) including an elaborate narrative in Pindar's *Olympian* 1. That Pelops cheated by bribing Myrtilus to sabotage Oenomaus's chariot is a variant first attested in the fifth-century mythographer Pherecydes (fr. 37 Jacoby/Fowler), but here **with his swift mares** implies a genuine victory (in Pindar's account Poseidon supplied Pelops with 'untiring winged horses', cf. 191–93 n.). The story of Pelops' victory, highlighted at the outset and again as Iphigenia and Orestes are reunited (823–25 n.), perhaps foreshadows the escape of Orestes (his great-grandson) with Iphigenia from their barbaric pursuers at the end of the play (»» Sansone 1975, 290; O'Brien 1988a).

1. son of Tantalus: Tantalus is mentioned only in passing since Iphigenia is summarizing the story of the dynasty after Pelops established it by marrying Hippodameia (in *Iliad* 2.100–8 the dynasty begins with Zeus's gift of a sceptre to Pelops). Tantalus will be mentioned again simply as the doomed family's ancestor (199–201, 987f.) or as the subject of the story that he served Pelops's flesh to the gods, which Iphigenia rejects (386–91 n.). [Τανταλείος, 'Tantaleian' stands for the genitive form of the name in epic style (»» Breitenbach 205; such forms were regular patronymics in Aeolic dialect). Cf. 988 Ταντάλειος again, 5 Τυνδάρειος, 170, 1115, 1290 Ἀγαμεμνόν(ε)ιος), 1259 Γάϊος and perhaps 1260 Λατῷος (see note there).]

2. wedded: γαμεῖ is a historic present tense (*CGCG* §33.54–56; Rijksbaron 22–25), 'often used to mark significant events in the course of a person's life' (Rijksbaron 23f.).

3. Atreus: see 193–94 n. [Ἀτρέως δ' ἄπο is Badham's correction of L's Ἀτρέως δὲ παῖς, where παῖς may have been copied by mistake from the end of line 5. L's reading gives 'and Atreus's son was (or 'from Atreus sprang') Menelaus and Agamemnon'. This is accepted by Diggle 1981, 75, but in our context a simple listing ('from Hippodameia…and from Atreus…and from him (Agamemnon)…' is more likely (»» Parker 55).]

5. Tyndareus's daughter: 'the Tyndareian daughter' (cf. 1 n.), i.e. Clytemnestra, sister of Helen.

6–7. By the eddies which Euripus etc.: a carefully structured sentence builds up to ἔσφαξεν **slaughtered** at the start of line 8. **Euripus:** the channel between Euboea and the mainland, 35 m wide and 8.5 m deep at its narrowest, hence the **eddies, dense breezes** and **dark swell**. Tidal currents flow through it at up to 12

COMMENTARY
151

km per hour, reversing course three or four times a day and at times forming whirlpools. Aulis is on the mainland. **dark:** κυάνεος describes turbid sea-water at 392, *Hel.* 1502 (differently 179), Bacchyl. 13.124.

8. slaughtered me – so it is believed: general ignorance of Iphigenia's escape is emphasized again at 176f. 'slaughtered as people believe' (δοκήμασι), 771 'though to them no longer living', 831 'you who are supposed to have died' (ὡς δοξάζεται). All versions of the story have Agamemnon's expedition delayed by winds or a calm which the seer Calchas attributes to a demand of Artemis (variously motivated) for the sacrifice of Agamemnon's daughter. The sacrifice proceeds but in most versions Iphigenia is spared at the last moment and an animal victim substituted for her: see Introduction, pp. 17–22 and notes below on details. The verb σφάζω refers literally to the cutting of a victim's throat, then more broadly to sacrificial killing or any brutal murder. Iphigenia uses it repeatedly in recalling her sacrifice at her father's hands (20, 177, 360, 563, 770). Lines 784f. and 852f. make it clear that in this telling as in Aeschylus's *Oresteia* and in *IA* Agamemnon himself wielded the sword. For σφάζω see also 552 (Orestes recalling the murder of Agamemnon), 598 (Orestes anticipating his own sacrificial death), 685 (συσφαγῆναι, Pylades wanting to share it). Cognate words denote the process (σφάγια 20 n., [40], 776; σφαγή 339 n., 726, 994, 1459), victim(s) (σφάγιον 211, 280, 337, πρόσφαγμα 243 n., 458), the officiant who cuts the victim's throat (σφαγεύς, 623) and the bowl into which the blood is drained (σφαγεῖον, 335).»» Casabona 1966, 155–96; van Straten 103–14; *ThesCRA* I.116–18; Henrichs 2000, 180 and 2013, 126f. See also *ThesCRA* I.129f. and Bremmer 2013, 2019b and 2019c, 352–57 on human sacrifice in *Iph.Taur.*, *Iph.Aul.* and *Hecuba* (Polyxena).

10. a thousand ships: 1,186 in the *Iliad*'s Catalogue of Ships (*Il.* 2.494–759), but the round number is standard in Euripides (141, *Andr.* 106, *El.* 2, *Or.* 351, *IA* 174, 355); cf. A. *Ag.* 45.

12–13. wanting to get for the Achaeans the glorious crown of victory: cf. *Supp.* 315 πόλει...στέφανον εὐκλείας λαβεῖν, 'to get for your city a crown of glory', and (though corrupt and inauthentic) *IA* 1528–31. Such crowns are figurative but reflect the actual crowning of individual military victors or those associated with them (e.g. *El.* 163f., *Pho.* 854–56). The victory is not 'assimilated to a victory in the games' as Parker suggests.

14. and avenge: μετελθεῖν, 'to go after', refers to pursuit or prosecution by an injured party (LSJ μετέρχομαι IV.2; again for pursuit of Helen, *Cyc.* 280f.). The image of the Atreidae as prosecutors derives from Aeschylus (»» Fraenkel on *Ag.* 41). **for Menelaus's satisfaction:** χάριν φέρων, 'bringing gratification', implies both revenge and sexual repossession of Helen. In A. *Ag.* 416–22 the chorus describes Menelaus's frustration in her absence: 'The beauty (χάρις) of shapely statues is hateful to the husband...sad dream-borne apparitions visit him bringing empty gratification (φέρουσαι χάριν ματαίαν)'.

152   COMMENTARY

15. when the voyage was terribly delayed: 'in a terrible non-sailing'. ἄπλοια
denotes weather conditions that prevent sailing (cf. *IA* 88, Hdt. 2.119.2, Thuc.
2.85.6, 4.4.1 etc.). **and he did not get winds for it:** this makes the delay due to a
dead calm as in S. *El.* 564 and probably *IA* 10 and 88 rather than adverse winds as
in the *Cypria* (Introduction, p. 19, A. *Ag.* 147–50, 192–204. On the alternative
accounts in these and later sources see Bury 1941–45; Diggle 2007, 147–50).
[πνευμάτων τ' οὐ τυγχάνων, 'and not getting winds', is Rauchenstein's correction. δεινῆς τ' ἀπλοίας etc. gives 'not getting a terrible non-sailing and winds'.
»» Diggle 1994, 52f.]

16. he resorted to burnt offerings: i.e. divination from the entrails of a
sacrificed animal, the way in which certain parts burned on the altar, and the
flames (»» Mastronarde on *Pho.* 1255–58, *ThesCRA* III.6–8). This kind of
divination was used at every stage of a military campaign (»» Pritchett 1979, 74–
78; Jameson 1991, 205; Wilkins on *Hcld.* 399–409; *ThesCRA* III.42f.). **Calchas
made this pronouncement:** λέγει is a historic present tense (2 n.) stressing this
crucial moment.

20. till Artemis receives your daughter…slaughtered: Iphigenia's death
will appease the deity's hostility: '*Sphagia* is used in a number of situations such
as oath-taking, some types of purification, certain rites for the dead or for heroes,
and the assuaging of winds (e.g. Xen. *An.* 4.5.4), as well as the crossing of rivers
by an army and the final rite in front of the battle-lines' (Jameson 1991, 201 adding sea-crossings, 202f. For the battle-line rite see Wilkins (16 n.); R. Parker
2000; Dillon 2008.

20–21. you vowed etc.: the myths of Iphigenia, like other myths of human
sacrifice, often explain the sacrifice as paying for an offence against a deity
(Agamemnon killed a stag sacred to Artemis and/or boasted of surpassing her as a
hunter). Euripides applies to this myth, perhaps for the first time, the motif of the
incautious vow as in the stories of Idomeneus and Jephthah; this makes
Agamemnon's situation less culpable and more tragic (»» Gantz 582–88; Lloyd-
Jones 1983, 101f.; on the motif in Greek myth and elsewhere, Davies 2010).[1] The
influence of the seer's perhaps fallible judgment (it is Calchas who declares
Iphigenia the year's **fairest product**) is also stressed at A. *Ag.* 186. Tension
between generals and seers was not unusual in real situations (»» Pritchett 1979,
47–49; R. Parker 2000, 304–307). The beauty of mythical victims of human
sacrifice is regularly emphasized, matching the requirement for victims of animal

---

[1] Sourvinou-Inwood (2003, 32, 33, 35f.) says that it makes Agamemnon fully
culpable since the sparing of Iphigenia makes it clear that Artemis did not explicitly require the sacrifice and he could have chosen to abandon the expedition
rather than perform it. But that would have left the vow unfulfilled, at least
according to Calchas's advice. We might think that a smarter Agamemnon would
have devised a different way of fulfilling his vow, but the implication in this play
as in Aeschylus's (*Ag.* 192–217) is that he was trapped by Calchas's demand.

COMMENTARY 153

sacrifice to be unblemished (»» Bonnechere 2013, 25–27). **the light-bearing goddess:** i.e. Artemis Phosphoros who like her counterpart Hecatê was worshipped as a bringer of light (φῶς) and especially salvation for communities in crisis (»» Suk Fong Jim 2022, 57–59, 126, 145–47). She was often depicted carrying two torches which symbolized this function and were reflected in torch-bearing rituals promoting it (»» Graf 1985, 228–36; *LIMC* II 'Artemis', esp. pp. 744, 749). Sourvinou-Inwood 2003, 32 with n. 68 notes that the torch-bearing Artemis was prominent in the iconography of Brauron and Mounychia.[2]

22–23. has a child: τίκτει, 'bears' (picking up τέκοι, 20) is a 'registering' or 'resultative' present tense denoting an action with its continuing effect (*CGCG* §33.18, Rijksbaron 9 n. 1). **thus he awarded etc.:** a bitterly ironic comment, Iphigenia blames Calchas and Odysseus in particular for instigating her sacrifice (cf. 531–35).

24–25. through Odysseus's trickery etc.: Odysseus devised and enforced the plot which brought Iphigenia to Aulis for sacrifice on the pretence of marrying Achilles: cf. *IA* 524–33, 1361–63, Soph. F 305 (from his undated *Iphigenia*). The cunning and ruthless hero is also seen as the prime mover of the murder of Astyanax (the epic *Sack of Troy* in Proclus's summary (*GEF* p. 147), E. *Tro.* 721–23 etc.) and the sacrifice of Polyxena (E. *Hec.* 218ff., Gantz 658f.). The scheme was a traditional part of the story as in the *Cypria* (Introduction, p. 19) and A. *Ag.* 239ff. (»» Armstrong–Ratchford 1985, 6–8). Iphigenia dwells bitterly on her betrayal in *IT* 214–17, 364–77, 537–39, 818–21, 856–59.

26–27. I was lifted high etc.: cf. 359–68, 783–85, 852–61, E. *El.* 1021f.; A. *Ag.* 231–34, 'After the prayer her father told the servants to raise with a will like a kid, high above the altar, neck forward...' In a typical Greek sacrifice (*thysia*), animal victims of a manageable size were lifted over the altar, the throat cut, and the blood partly scattered on the altar for the god and partly caught in a blood-bowl (*sphageion*) for use in human consumption (»» van Straten 103–13 with Ekroth 2005; on the *sphageion*, Ekroth 14–19). In A. *Ag.* 231ff. Agamemnon ordered his attendants to lift Iphigenia over the altar 'like a kid'. The lifting is memorably depicted in a wall-painting from the House of the Tragic Poet in Pompeii (*LIMC* V, 'Iphigeneia' no. 38) which may reflect the influential 4th C painting by Timanthes (*LIMC* no. 4). It probably does not appear in extant vase-paintings but is seen in some early images of the sacrifice of Polyxena.[3] **ready**

---

[2] Bremmer 2013, 89 sees a suggestion that Agamemnon had made his incautious vow to save his community in a moment of crisis, but the hint would be hardly noticeable.

[3] »» Mylonopoulos 2013, 74–78 with Plates IV–VI, Henrichs 2013, 128–31. The well-known Tyrrhenian amphora in the British Museum (Mylonopoulos Pl. V) is *LIMC* VII, 'Polyxena' no. 26. The fragment of a proto-Attic crater in which Mylonopoulos sees the sacrifice of Polyxena (his Pl. IV) has been connected by

154 COMMENTARY

for the sword: ἐκαινόμην ξίφει, 'I was being slain with sword'; imperfect tense as the process was interrupted by Artemis's intervention. Bremmer (2013, 91) notes that the weapon is a sword (ξίφος; φάσγανον, 758, 853) as in pre-battle *sphagia* rather than the butcher's knife (μάχαιρα) used for ordinary animal sacrifices (»» *ThesCRA* V.308–12); similarly *IA* 1429, [1578] (Iphigenia), *Hec.* 436, 543 (Polyxena) and the iconography of both these sacrifices, also *Pho.* 1091 (Menoeceus's sacrificial suicide). The Taurians likewise use a sword (621, 880, 1190), as will the ritual at Halai commemorating Orestes' near-sacrifice (1459). In tragedy the sword is often an instrument of murders and suicides, and often with sacrificial connotations.

28–30. Artemis stole me away etc.: see Introduction, pp. 17–19 on the traditions concerning Iphigenia's reprieve, the animal substitution and her settlement with the Taurians. **a deer in my place**: a suitable victim for Artemis. There is some scattered evidence, archaeological and iconographic, for real sacrifices of deer to Artemis in the ancient Greek world, and more abundant evidence for some non-Greek areas (»» Larson 2017).

29. through the radiant sky: λαμπρός is a favourite Euripidean epithet for the *aether* or sky (and not only its upper levels which are the domain of the gods), e.g. *Med.* 829, *Hipp.* 178, *Or.* 1087. Divinely aided disappearances usually involve transport by a wind and/or a cloud (»» Collard–Cropp–Lee 1995, 268 on *Wise Melanippe* F 481.18) and often involve immortalization (»» Larson 1995, 16). Euripides' Helen was wrapped in a cloud and carried through the *aether* to Egypt by Hermes (*Hel.* 43–45) while her image made by Hera from the stuff of the *aether* went to Troy (*Hel.* 33–35, 583–86).

30. the Taurians' land: see Introduction, pp. 22–27.

32–33. who running with wing-swift speed of foot etc.: 'who puts a swift foot equal to wings'. The name Thoas suggests swiftness (θέω 'run', θοός 'swift'). Similar etymologies on names in Euripides are listed by Wecklein and Platnauer noting the parody of this one in Aristophanes, *Women of Lemnos* F 373 *PCG*, 'Thoas, who is slowest amongst men in running'. The name belonged to several legendary figures including the king of Lemnos (*Iliad* 14.230, 23.745) who was Hypsipyle's father. Euripides seems to have invented Thoas king of the Taurians for this play. πόδας ὠκύς, 'swift-footed' was a formulaic epithet of Achilles who still practices his running not far away (436–37 n.).

34. placed me as priestess: τίθησι is another 'registering' present tense (22–23 n.); Iphigenia now is the priestess in Artemis's temple.

35–37. by the laws of the festival which please the goddess: Iphigenia begins to describe her duties but cannot express her distaste for them without risk of offending the goddess, so she expresses it indirectly (**whose name alone is fair**). Α ἑορτή (etymology unknown) is a festival with ritual regulations (*nomoi*)

others with Iphigenia (*LIMC* V, 'Iphigeneia' no. 2). The magnificent 'Polyxena sarcophagus' (late 6th C; Mylonopoulos Pl. VI) was discovered only in 1994.

COMMENTARY   155

featuring sacrifice(s) and communal activities (singing, dancing, feasting etc.: »» Mikalson 1982). For Iphigenia the Taurians' ἑορτή is far from festive because it involves human sacrifices which are ritually correct (*hosioi*: 130–32 n.) for them but not for Greeks (as the Chorus says explicitly, 463–66). Artemis's attitude remains ambiguous: Iphigenia says here that the human sacrifices please the goddess, and this must be true at least insofar as they honour her and she accepts them; but she also doubts whether they are what the goddess really wants, or should want (381–91, 1086–88, 1230–33). The story will end with Artemis honoured more humanely with token human bloodshed at an Athenian ἑορτή, the Tauropolia (1458–61). Comparisons of this passage with *Eumenides* 186–92, where Athena sarcastically calls the Erinyes' tortures and mutilations of their victims their kind of ἑορτή, are a litle misleading. The Taurians' ἑορτή is respectable in their eyes, though in Iphigenia's opinion misconceived. [Some understand 'Artemis...whose name alone is fair', with reference to the cult-name Καλή or Καλλίστη, 'Fair' or 'Fairest', but the reference would be abstruse and the focus here is on the dark side of the rituals. The sentence beginning with line 35 is incomplete because Iphigenia interrupts her comment on the nature of the festival. Placing 37 after 41 (Markland) or after 40 with 38–39 and 41 deleted (Stinton 1977, 150–52) gives a lame conclusion: see next note.]

38–41. by the law etc.: the text is uncertain at several points and various deletions have been proposed. Sansone and Erbse retain the whole passage. I think lines 40–41 are an editorial interpolation like 59–60, spelling out information which is not needed at this point (similarly Barrett 2007, 474–79). The wording of line 41 seems derived from line 66. Lines 38–39 are needed because the fact that Iphigenia sacrifices Hellenes needs to be stated now in preparation for the narrative at 53–58. On the other hand, lines 40–41 are not properly connected with what precedes, and the fact that the victims are slaughtered by priests inside the temple and not by Iphigenia herself will be explained only at 620–24; until then her sacrificial duties are stated either ambiguously (38, 58) or with a suggestion that she sometimes kills victims herself (53, 442–45, 585f.). Thus it seems possible that she will kill her brother just as her father 'killed' her; and even after the recognition she still talks as if she might have done so (870–72, 994). '[T]echnically Iphigeneia may perhaps not have killed prisoners, she clearly came very close' (Bremmer 2013, 92). For the sparse evidence of priestesses killing sacrificial victims see Bremmer *ibid.,* Connelly 2007, 182f.

[Murray deleted 38–39 and made κατάρχομαι intransitive ('I perform the initial rites'), but that leaves the nature of the sacrifices only vaguely hinted at. Diggle deletes 38–39 and 41 and makes κατάρχομαι govern ἑορτῆς ('And so by the laws in which the goddess Artemis delights...I initiate the festival etc.'); similarly Stinton placing 37 after 40. But κατάρχομαι would be strangely used for initiating the festival and should refer to a specific ritual procedure, surely the one described in 53f. and denoted by κατηρξάμην in 56 (cf. 244f., 617–24). For

156 COMMENTARY

further discussion see Parker, who prefers the text recommended by Stinton (35–36, [38–39], 40, [41], 37) but makes κατάρχομαι intransitive as Murray.]

38. for this community: πόλει as in LSJ 'πόλις' III.1. The Taurians are a *polis*, i.e. organized like a Greek *polis*, also in 464, 595, 877(?), 1209, 1212, 1214. In these references 'πόλις designates primarily the community of the Taurian people but it also indicates this community's political and urban structures' (Kyriakou on 595f.). In 1209 Iphigenia wants an announcement made 'to the *polis*', which implies an urban population.

42–66. Iphigenia has come outside to relieve the grief caused by a dream, and to pour funeral libations for her brother who she now thinks is dead. In her dream she has seen the royal palace at Argos destroyed by an earthquake and a single undamaged column taking on human form, which as priestess she prepared for sacrifice with a purifying lustration. From this she has inferred that her family (the palace) is now extinct and that Orestes, its sole surviving heir (the column), is dead. Dream interpretation was common in ancient near eastern culture, and dreams and their (mis)interpretation are an ancient narrative motif allowing foreshadowing, suspense etc. They occur frequently in Homer and Herodotus, for example, as well as in tragedy (note A. *Pers.* 176ff., [A.] *PV* 645ff. in addition to those mentioned below).

Iphigenia's dream belongs to the symbolic type, in which the dreamer witnesses a scene that must be interpreted on waking (rather than receiving a direct message from a dream-figure). Her account of it, starting with **I seemed in my sleep** (44) is typical of ancient dream records (»» Hanson 1980). It unfolds in a series of quasi-cinematic scenes which are reflected in the narrative's frequent present-tense verbs: Iphigenia sleeps, then flees from the palace as the earthquake strikes, then watches it collapsing, observes the column standing and speaking, and performs her lustration. For the content Euripides adapts a motif from earlier versions of the Orestes legend. In Stesichorus's *Oresteia* Clytemnestra dreamed of Agamemnon as a snake with a bloodied head from which his successor arose (fr. 180 Davies–Finglass). In Aeschylus's *Choephori* she dreams of giving birth to a snake which bites her breast, and sends Electra with libations to Agamemnon's tomb; Electra finds Orestes' offering there and is reunited with him. In Sophocles' *Electra* Clytemnestra has seen a portent of Orestes' return and sends Chrysothemis to the tomb; she sees Orestes' offering but cannot persuade Electra that he is alive. In Euripides' *Electra* the dream is eliminated, the libations are transformed into Electra's water-carrying (*El.* 54ff., 112ff. with a lament similar to Iphigenia's) and Electra again refuses to believe the evidence of Orestes' offering at the tomb (*El.* 508ff.). Iphigenia's ignorance of Orestes' presence recalls Electra's ignorance in the earlier plays and compounds the irony of her believing that he is dead when in fact he is alive and close by.

Iphigenia misinterprets the dream and the truth it conveys, and the dream consequently has a more complex dynamic function in the play's plot than those

COMMENTARY   157

in the earlier plays. It does indeed symbolize the downfall of her house and her separation from it, and the column does represent Orestes, but that need not imply that he is dead and the family permanently ruined. Since the column speaks, a likelier interpretation is that Orestes is alive and that she will confront him and purify him with a lustration – but how that will happen and what will follow from it remains unclear. As Trieschnigg (2008) points out, Euripides probably expected his audience to recognize this and to expect that the dream would prove to be true, thus setting a puzzle as to how that would come about in a way which would lead to the redemption of both Orestes and Iphigenia. The truth of the dream will in fact emerge gradually and tantalizingly in the course of the play. First Orestes, while refusing to identify himself, informs her that her brother is alive (and she jumps to the conclusion that the dream was false, 567–69). Next she plans to send Orestes, still unidentified, back to Argos with her letter (which would actually make the dream false), only for Orestes to insist that she sacrifice him while Pylades takes the letter (so the dream might after all have predicted correctly that she would sacrifice him). Finally Orestes is identified when Pylades recites the letter including his name, and the likelihood that his sister will sacrifice him recedes, but the dream will nevertheless be fulfilled paradoxically when Iphigenia pretends to prepare the captives for sacrifice and performs her mock lustration at the seashore (1316 n.).

42–43. Now I will tell to the sky etc.: relating a troubling dream to the sun or sky is an apotropaic act meant to repel the evil implied in the dream: cf. S. *El.* 424f. (Clytemnestra) and for Babylonian/Assyrian parallels West 1997, 54. On the sources and associations of dreams see 1261–62 n. **the strange new apparitions:** καινός here refers to something new and disturbing as also in 1160 (something happening in the temple) and 1306 (the news from the shore); elsewhere things new and unexpected (239, the discovery and capture of Orestes and Pylades) or new and ingenious (1029, Iphigenia's escape plan). **if this be any remedy:** Iphigenia doubts the effectiveness of telling her dream to the elements, but doing so conveniently allows her to explain her troubles to the audience as other women do in S. *El.* 86ff., E. *El.* 54ff., *Med.* 56–58, *Andr.* 91–95.

45. the maidens' apartment: the *parthenón* is the part of the house in which girls led their segregated lives (cf. 826; in [A.] *PV* 645f. the apparitions troubling Io came 'to my apartment'). Iphigenia's regression in her dream to the innocent girlhood state which preceded the onset of her troubles and anxieties is a realistic touch, subtly exploited for dramatic purposes (Devereux 1976, 294–99). It recurs in the Chorus's wistful imaginings (452–55, 1138–52).

47–49. I saw the cornice of the palace falling etc.: the earthquake shattering the palace symbolizes the ruin of the royal family as at *HF* 904–9, *Ba.* 585–603, *Erechtheus* F 370.45–54. The 2nd C AD dream-analyst Artemidorus says (4.60) that in such dreams homeland implies parents: 'for example, someone saw his homeland shaken by an earthquake, and his father was convicted on a capital

158   COMMENTARY

charge and put to death'. For the architectural details (θριγκός 'cornice', σταθμοί 'columns') see Stieber 2011, 39f., 48–52, and for the word σταθμός Chadwick 1996, 253–61. **thrown in ruins:** the adjective ἐρείψιμον (< ἐρείπω) is seen uniquely here; cf. *Iliad* 14.15 ἐρέριπτο δὲ τεῖχος Ἀχαιῶν ('the Achaeans' wall lay in ruins') and aorist ἤριπε describing falling warriors some 24x in the *Iliad*, e.g. 4.462 ἤριπε δ' ὡς ὅτε πύργος, 'he fell as when a tower (falls)'.

50–52. One column alone was left etc.: the column is not distinctly identified with Orestes except in Iphigenia's waking inference at 56, so the dream's ambiguity is maximized. There is also a recollection of A. *Ag.* 897f. where Clytemnestra hypocritically welcomes the returning Agamemnon as 'the grounded column of a high roof, an only-born child to a father'. **from its capital:** plural ἐπικράνων is perhaps used for resonance with δόμων πατρῴων or perhaps evokes the capital's ornate design (Stieber 2011, 41). The word ἐπίκρανον ('head-piece') denotes an architectural capital in Pindar, frs. 6b.4 and 33d.7 Snell–Maehler, and a human head-covering in E. *Hipp.* 201 (there are no other instances in classical poetry). **auburn hair (κόμας ξανθάς):** several Homeric heroes have blonde or auburn hair, especially Menelaus (ξανθὸς Μενέλαος). Euripides attributes it to him (*Or.* 1532, *IA* 175) and to others of the Mycenean royal family (Orestes here and *El.* 515, Iphigenia herself *IT* 174, *IA* 681 etc.; also Clytemnestra *El.* 1071, Helen *Hel.* 1224). The likeness of the siblings' hair will be seen by the audience when they meet, adding to the poignancy of their not recognizing each other, especially as hair was featured in the recognitions in Aeschylus's *Choephori* and Euripides' *Electra*.

54. sprinkling it with water: lustral water (χέρνιψ, χέρνιβες, 'handwashing(s)') brought in a metal bowl (χερνιβεῖον) was used in sacrificial ceremonies to purify the sacred area and participants and consecrate the victim (e.g. *El.* 791ff.). »» *ThesCRA* V.167–70, van Straten 32–43 (including a probable example in one of the Iphigenia vase-paintings, *LIMC* no. 19 = Taplin 2007 no. 48).

57. male children are the pillars of their houses: the stability and integrity of the *oikos* rest on the son and heir. For the image cf. Pind. *Ol.* 2.81f. (Hector), A. *Ag.* 897f. (see 50–52 n.), *Anth.Pal.* 7.441, 7.648. This verse became proverbial, cf. Artemidorus 2.10.32 (quoting it as an example of dream-interpretation), Stobaeus 4.24.36, Menand. *Monost.* 720, Suda ε 3691.

[59–60]. *Neither can I connect etc.*: anticlimactic lines, and pointless since only Agamemnon's son could support Agamemnon's palace. The lines refer to Pylades, son of Strophius of Phocis and a sister of Agamemnon (498 n.), but in this context Iphigenia has no reason to wonder if she might have a cousin who could be the subject of her dream. The lines were inserted to allow for her not recognizing Pylades' name when she hears it at 249. That he was born after her sacrifice will be explained in due course (920f.).

62. absent one to absent one (ἀποῦσ' ἀπόντι): Iphigenia thinks of Orestes as buried far away in Argos. In fact he is very close to her, as the audience will learn

COMMENTARY 159

almost immediately. [L's παροῦσα παντί, 'present to everyone' is nonsense. Canter's παροῦσ' ἀπόντι 'present one to absent one' was probably transmitted at an intermediate stage but would have less point here than in other plays on 'present/absent' (*Hipp.* 184, *El.* 245, 263, 331, *Ion* 385, *Hel.* 861).]

64. Hellene women: see Introduction, pp. 37–39 on the identity of the Chorus and their role in the play.

65–66. I'll go inside: the Chorus's delay and Iphigenia's withdrawal allow rather artificially for Orestes and Pylades to arrive and play their scene without being observed, and with a frisson of suspense as the Chorus might arrive at any moment. **this dwelling (δόμων)...the temple (ἀνακτόρων):** both words seem to refer to the temple, so Iphigenia apparently resides within it rather than nearby and is associated with the goddess unusually closely, like Ion who sleeps in Apollo's temple whenever he wishes (*Ion* 314f.).

67–122. Orestes and Pylades reach the temple

Orestes and Pylades enter surreptitiously, conversing as they check to see that the coast is clear (67–76). As Pylades continues to check, Orestes explains their mission in a speech of complaint to Apollo, stressing his obedience to the god, the tribulations he has suffered, and their present danger (77–94). As if despairing of help from Apollo, he turns to Pylades for advice on how to get an entry into the temple; or is the task so hard that they should give up and return home before it's too late (94–103)? Pylades reminds him that they must obey the god and show courage, and suggests waiting till nightfall to attempt an entry (104–17). Orestes agrees: the god will help them if they persist in helping themselves (118–22). Orestes' uncertainty and near-despair in this scene imply not a defective character but rather the extremity of his situation and of the burden he must bear despite his youth and inexperience and the remoteness and ambivalence of Apollo's guidance. He responds positively to Pylades' call for courage. His doubts will be renewed when he is captured and facing death (570f., 691f., 711–15, 723), but the recognition will restore his confidence (909–11, 1012–16).

67–68. Look out etc.: Orestes' opening line and Pylades' reply are rhymed and exactly matched in phrasing; perhaps their movements were coordinated too. There is a similar furtive entrance for Polynices (alone) in *Pho.* 261ff. The entry of two characters in urgent dialogue is dramatically striking: in tragedy cf. *IA* 302ff., S. *Phil.* 1222ff., [E.] *Rhes.* 565ff.

72. and this the altar: a monumental altar in front of the temple (Introduction, p. 35). Later we will hear that Orestes' body is to be burned on another altar inside the temple (626). **that Hellene blood drips down on:** the human victims would be lifted and held over the altar as their throats were cut (26–27 n.).

73. Its copings...are brown with bloodstains: 'It has copings brown from bloodshed'. γοῦν, **at any rate** is a qualified 'yes' (Denniston 451); this is not necessarily human blood. If θριγκώματα is correct, these copings are distinct

160 COMMENTARY

from the **θριγκοί** in the next line which must be the copings of the temple. Vase-paintings and other images often show a layer of stone overlapping the top of an altar, sometimes more elaborately carved and with a raised edge. [**θριγκώματα**, Ruhnken's conjecture for L's τριχώματα ('growths of hair', < τριχόω), is adopted by most editors. Some (e.g. Murray, Sansone, Parker, Amiech) retain τριχώματα and understand it as congealed, hair-like trickles of blood, perhaps evoking the auburn hair of the column which Iphigenia consecrated in her dream and identified with Orestes (51f.; thus Hourmouziades 1965, 52f., Sansone 1979, 158 n. 7, Torrance 2009, Parker).[4] The allusion is however rather pointless and there is no reason for Pylades to describe what he sees with a fanciful metaphor.][5]

74. And beneath the copings themselves (θριγκοῖς δ' ὑπ' αὐτοῖς): these must be the copings of the temple front (cf. 129), a natural place for exhibiting **spoils (σκῦλα)** stripped from enemies and dedicated to the gods (e.g. *El.* 6f., »» Pritchett 1991, 133–47). The shift from the copings of the altar to the copings of the temple is perhaps marked by **αὐτοῖς** and could be made clear to an audience by the actors' gestures. [For this interpretation see Stieber 2011, 51. The trophies can hardly be hung on the altar as supposed by e.g. Kovacs, Cropp 2000, Kyriakou.]

75. choice pickings: ἀκροθίνια are 'top-of-heap things' selected for the gods from spoils of war, harvests etc. Pylades sardonically notes that in this case they are the heads of human victims decorating the Taurians' temple as the Greeks decorated their temples with the skulls of sacrificed oxen (*boukrania*). The identification of human heads here has been doubted (e.g. Wright 2005, 185), but since Pylades mentions them as further evidence of human sacrifices it is hard to see what else they might be. Herodotus says that the Taurians impaled their victims' heads (4.103, see Introduction, pp. 19f.), and a 4th C vase-painting of the escape from the temple (*LIMC* V, 'Iphigeneia' no. 29; Taplin 2007, no. 50) shows a severed head fixed to a pole attached to the temple-front, apparently combining Euripides with Herodotus. Ammianus Marcellinus (22.8.33) says they fixed them

---

[4] Torrance rejects **θριγκώματα** mainly because 'There are no instances in Greek literature...where the word θριγκός or θρίγκωμα is used to describe an altar', but that is hardly surprising as altars are rarely described in detail. Torrance's suggestion that τριχώματα could mean 'veins' (metaphorically) like τρίχες (literally) in medical texts is implausible as Parker notes.

[5] Parker calls τριχώματα 'rare' and unlikely to be a corruption of θριγκώματα. In fact the latter is the rarity and more open to corruption: τρίχωμα 140+ instances in the *TLG*, θρίγκωμα (later θρίγγωμα) only in Plut. *Mor.* 685b (a metaphor) and 13x in late Byzantine authors. In Josephus, *AJ* 15.11.3 mss. τριχώμασι is probably a corruption of θριγκώμασι. Alternative forms τριγχός/-όω/-ίον for θριγκός etc. are attested from the first century AD, which may explain the corruptions in our passage (as Grégoire noted) and in Josephus.

COMMENTARY

161

to the temple walls. A display of heads was probably staged in Sophocles' *Oenomaus*, and perhaps in Euripides' *Oenomaus* as well.

76. I must look all around etc.: Pylades' exploration keeps him busy during the first part of Orestes' speech. Ms. L makes this the first line of Orestes' speech ('You must look...'), but that blunts the impact of his outburst against Apollo.

77–92. Orestes' opening question turns into an agitated summary of his earlier wanderings, culminating in his return to Delphi and plea to Apollo for further guidance. Then a second long period (85–92) summarizes Apollo's instructions promising 'respite from your tribulations'. Orestes' experiences between the matricide and his last appeal to Apollo will be related after the reunion (940–78).

77. what is this net etc.: Orestes likens himself to an animal driven into a hunter's net laid across his path. The Erinyes are often imaged as hunting-hounds, e.g. A. *Cho.* 924, *Eum.* 111 (Orestes escapes them 'like a fawn from the net'), E. *El.* 1342–44 (»» Cropp on *El.* 1252).

81–83. many rounding laps: now Orestes is driven by the Erinyes like a chariot-horse (cf. 934f., *El.* 1253, *Or.* 36f.). The 'yoke of madness' image is common (»» Garvie on A. *Cho.* 1021–25). καμπίμους, **rounding** refers to the καμπαί, 'turning-posts' which marked each end of a race-course. The adjective is attested only here (the form κάμπιος much later). **my wheeling madness** continues the metaphor (τροχηλάτου, 'wheel-driving').

[84]. The line is repetitious and anticlimactic, and almost identical with 1455 where περιπολῶν **wandering** is essential to the etymology of *Ταυρο-πόλος* (1453–57 n.).

85–92. you said I must go etc.: here and in his later response (976–78) Apollo himself addresses Orestes (as he does in Aeschylus, *Eumenides* 64–93). In historical times the god 'spoke' through the voice of the Pythia, but these are mythical times when gods interacted freely with mortals.

87–88. the goddess's image which they say fell here: cf. 977f., 986, 1384f. A few ancient images of the gods in Greece, as well as sacred stones such as the Omphalos at Delphi (1254–58 n.), were supposed to have fallen from the sky, e.g. the mythical Palladion of Troy, the Athena Polias at Athens and the Dionysos Kadmeios at Thebes (»» Burkert 1985, 91 with n. 84, Lo Monaco 2018, 466f., Zgoll 2021, 242 n. 91). The idea of a tradition in which the image emerged from the underworld is due to a misunderstanding of the text of Apollodorus, *epit.* 6.26.[6] The Taurian Artemis is pictured at about half human height in several vase-

---

[6] Apollodorus, *epit.* 6.26: τοὺς ξένους φονεύουσι καὶ εἰς τὸ ἱερὸν ⟨πῦρ⟩ ῥίπτουσι. τοῦτο ἦν ἐν τῷ τεμένει διά τινος πέτρας ἀναφερόμενον ἐξ Ἅιδου: 'they murder strangers and throw them into the sacred fire. This was in the sanctuary, carried up out of Hades through a certain rock'. Without the supplement ⟨πῦρ⟩ ('the sacred fire' rather than 'the sanctuary') 'this' appears to be the image (ξόανον) mentioned in the previous sentence.

162 COMMENTARY

paintings related to the play. It was probably thought of as wooden, the typical form of early Greek cult-images,[7] and hence easily portable. Our text usually calls it an ἄγαλμα ('ornament', the commonest Greek word for a statue) or βρέτας (an imported word of uncertain origin). The term ξόανον is used once (1359 n., cf. 111 n.). For its form and iconography see Hall 2013, 20–26, Lo Monaco 2018, 447–73.

89. either by craft etc.: this foreshadows the later course of the drama in which the lucky reunion of Orestes and Iphigenia leads to their escape through both craft (the *mêchanêma*) and several more lucky breaks (which are not necessarily independent of divine agency: cf. 909–11 n.). The τέχνη/τύχη ('craft/luck') contrast was something of a cliché, e.g. Agathon F 6, F 8.

91. of what would come after etc: the ultimate purpose of Orestes' mission will only be revealed by Athena at the end of the play (1449–61). In the meantime his uncertainty creates suspense and emotional tension as he wavers between suspicion and confidence about the god's real motives (67–122 n.).

92. respite from my ordeals: the same promise is made to Orestes by Apollo when he sends him from Delphi to Athens in A. *Eum.* 83, and at *El.* 1291 when Castor instructs him about his purification. We know that this respite means restoration, although the phrase is in itself ambiguous (for Sophocles' Heracles a similar promise meant death: S. *Trach.* 76–81, 166–72, 824–26, 1169–73).

96. enclosing walls: 'enclosures (consisting) of walls', i.e. the walls of the temple itself. ἀμφίβληστρα has the same sense as ἀμφιβλήματα in *Hel.* 70. Both words more often refer to casting-nets or garments.

97–98. a scaling-ladder: κλιμάκων προσαμβάσεις probably means a single ladder as in *Pho.* 1173 (κλίμακος προσαμβάσεις) and probably *Ba.* 1213 rather than plural as in *Pho.* 489. It seems unlikely that Orestes would think of needing more than one ladder. For κλίμακες 'ladder' (singular) see also 1351 n. Slightly different are A. *Sept.* 466 κλίμακος προσαμβάσεις 'ladder-scalings' and E. *Pho.* 744 τειχέων προσαμβάσεις 'wall-scalings'. [L has δωμάτων πρὸς ἀμβάσεις ἐκβησόμεσθα, 'Shall we go out to the ascents (steps?) of the temple', with ἐκ- altered from either εἰσ- 'into' or ἐμ- 'onto'. The confusion is compounded by L's μάθοιμεν 'learn' replacing λάθοιμεν **avoid being seen.**]

99. the bronze-made doors: i.e. the main doors of the temple which are often pictured in the vase-paintings and would normally be released from the outside by Iphigenia's key (130–32 n.). κλῆθρα are probably barred **doors** as often in Euripides rather than 'bars' or 'bolts' for which bronze is an unlikely material; cf. Barrett on *Hipp.* 577–81, 808–10 and e.g. *HF* 332, *Or.* 1571 (μοχλοῖς ἄραρε κλῆθρα, 'the doors are fixed with bars'), *Phaethon* 223.

---

[7] See the exhaustive study of Pritchett 1998, 204–94, 1999, 172–82. The image at Brauron seen by Pausanias and probably referred to in an Athenian inscription of 416/5 BC (*IG* I³ 403.13) was an ἀρχαῖον ξόανον (Paus. 1.23.7: »» Pritchett 1998, 256–60).

COMMENTARY 163

100. †*of which we know nothing*†: the text must have included a future-tense verb. [Badham's ὧδ' οὐδὸν ἔσιμεν, 'shall we thus enter the threshold' is plausible except that 'threshold' is not quite apt and the form of the word in tragedy is ὀδός (S. *OC* 57, 1590, Astydamas F 9). Suggested alternatives include ἱερὸν 'sanctuary' (Köchly), οἶκον 'temple (Maehly), ἄδυτον 'inner precinct' (Wecklein).]

105. we must not dishonour the god's instruction: Pylades' response recalls his only words in Aeschylus's *Choephori*, spoken as Orestes hesitates to kill his mother, 'Where, then, are the oracles of Loxias...?' (*Cho.* 900–2). [ἀτιστέον is the verbal noun from ἀτίζω, not seen elsewhere but inferred here by Valckenaer. L's οὐ κακιστέον means 'we must not worsen' or 'we must not reproach', but Pylades is talking about actions not words.]

110. the face of murky night: i.e. the darkness of night; similarly A. *Pers.* 428 νυκτὸς ὄμμα, E. *Pho.* 543 νυκτὸς βλέφαρον, and of dawn E. *El.* 102 (ὄμμα), 730 (πρόσωπον). Sun or Moon themselves may also be 'eyes' (193–94 n.)

111. the carved image: i.e. a *xoanon* (87–88 n., 1359 n.). ξεστόν is often translated as 'polished', but **carved** is more apt for the primitive image. On Euripides' use of the word see Stieber 2011, 343–45.

113–14. Yet see etc.: Pylades seems to suggest that they should look for a way of lowering themselves into the temple through some opening high up, but L's text is corrupt and perhaps defective. Platnauer suggested that a lost line between 113 and 114 filled out the relative clause. [The whole sentence fits poorly with what precedes and with what follows, and δέ γε, a strong **Yet**, seems out of place here (»» Denniston 155). *inside the triglyphs*: εἴσω τριγλύφων might mean 'inside the frieze' ('triglyphs' means the complete frieze at *Or.* 1372, *Ba.* 1214), and that might imply 'inside the temple' (cf. Willink on *Or.* 1370–72), but even then the exact sense is unclear. The once popular theory of J. J. Winckelmann that it means 'between/through the triglyphs' and shows that Greek temples once had spaces in or between their triglyphs is now discredited. Lastly, ὅποι κενὸν δέμας καθεῖναι is a contorted way of saying *to where there is a space for letting down one's body*. »» Kovacs 2003, 4–6; Parker 78f.; Stieber 2011 66–73 (discussing possibly relevant architectural details).]

114–15. Noble men face up to ordeals: Greek ethics stressed the interdependence of virtue and *ponoi* or *mochthoi* (ordeals, exertions), e.g. *Hcld.* 625, *Archelaus* F 233, F 236–240, Xen. *Mem.* 2.1.28 (Virtue's advice to Heracles), and many other extracts in Stob. 3.29 'On devotion to *ponoi*'. See also 122 n.

116–17. We surely have not sailed etc.: 'Surely not *(a)* we have come a long journey by oar, yet *(b)* are now going to launch a return etc.'; for this rhetorical structure cf. e.g. *Hel.* 575 (»» Denniston 371). 'Oar' is a common synecdoche (part for whole) for 'ship' (or in 140, 'fleet'), e.g. 242, 1427, 1445, *Andr.* 855, *Hel.* 191 (»» Breitenbach 174, lyric examples). [Ms. L makes this the beginning of Orestes' reply, but that clearly begins with line 118 and the point is more suited to Pylades as part of his exhortation. The exhortation ends well enough without it,

164 COMMENTARY

but it is not obviously an interpolation as Dindorf suggested (followed by Page 1934, 77; Cropp 2000).»» Diggle 1981, 76f.; Parker.]

118–22. Yes, your advice is good etc.: Orestes overcomes his doubts and accepts Pylades' advice: they should obey the oracle (105), hide till night (106–109) and accept their exertions nobly (114f.). ἀλλ(ά) in line 118 is 'assentient' (Denniston 16–20).

119. to some nearby place etc.: 'whither within (this) land we shall escape notice hiding (our) body.'

120–21. I for my part will not be responsible etc.: τὸ τοῦδε is 'the (conduct) of this man (i.e. myself)'; for this τό + genitive see e.g. *Alc.* 785 τὸ τῆς τύχης 'the (influence) of fortune'. For ὅδε = 'I/me' cf. S. *Trach.* 305 τῆσδέ γε ζώσης 'at least while I am living', 1013 ἐπὶ τῷδε νοσοῦντι 'upon me as I suffer'.

[This is Weil's reading, adopted by Wecklein, Platnauer and Parker. L's οὐ γὰρ τὸ τοῦ θεοῦ γ' αἴτιον γενήσεται means 'The god for his part will not be responsible', implying that Orestes can rely on Apollo's aid and needs to match it with his own endurance and effort. Renehan 1976, 64f. defends this, but such optimism is uncharacteristic of Orestes at this point and he is responding to Pylades' exhortation in 105. Heath's αἴτιος γενήσομαι ('I shall not be responsible for the god's oracle going unfulfilled') is printed by Diggle, Kovacs and Cropp 2000, but as Weil noted it accounts less well for the emphatic γε.]

122. young men are never excused etc.: 'no exertion bears an excuse for young men'. The young in particular are expected to strive for virtue: cf. 114–15 n. and e.g. *Cretan Women* F 461, *Archelaus* F 237, Pl. *Rep.* 536d3.

123–235. Parodos: the Chorus enters and converses with Iphigenia

The women of the Chorus process from their living quarters to the temple doors singing of their devotion to the goddess and call on Iphigenia to tell them why she has summoned them (123–42). Iphigenia re-enters with some temple servants and laments the supposed death of Orestes and ruin of her family, then pours libations into the ground with a prayer to Orestes, as she would at his tomb (143–77). The women join in her grief, singing a lament for the troubles of the royal family (178–202), and Iphigenia in turn surveys the miseries she was born to suffer: her sacrifice at Aulis and exile with the Taurians, sacrificing human victims instead of the happy devotions of a well-born maiden, and now the loss of Orestes (203–35). On the character and dramatic role of the Chorus see Introduction, pp. 37–39.

The Chorus's arrival song combines with Iphigenia's laments in an 'amoibaic' Parodos. Euripides was famous for introducing solo song (monody) into the Parodos movement, sometimes in the form of lamentation (»» Cropp on *El.* 112–66). Here a relatively formal lament (*thrênos*, 144, 182) with antiphonal singing, ritual language and actions, and a narrative recital of woes develop emotional motifs established in Iphigenia's prologue speech. The scene recalls Electra's libation scene with the Chorus of palace servants in Aeschylus's

COMMENTARY   165

Choephori, of which the Parodos of Euripides' *Electra* is also a transformation, but with the obvious difference that Electra grieves for her cruelly murdered father and still hopes for Orestes' return whereas here the audience knows that Iphigenia's lament for his death and the extinction of their family is mistaken (unless she is destined to kill him herself). The Parodos of *Helen* is very similar in structure and content, except that Helen is already singing as the Chorus arrives and there is strophic responsion.

A sombre mood is established by language (see notes below) and by a metre consisting almost entirely of lyric anapaests, basically ⌣ ⌣ − − ⌣ ⌣ − etc. but varied with dactyls (− ⌣ ⌣) and often spondees (− −) which compound the solemnity. The mood must have been reinforced by processional and then mourning music. There is no responsion and the manuscript tradition is unreliable, so the definition of cola is sometimes doubtful. A few lines (197, 213?, 220, 231f.) seem to use strings of short syllables in varying rhythms for emotional effect. »» Parker lxxxix, 83–87.

123–36. The processional entrance of a Chorus of devotees resembles those of *Bacchae* and *Cretans* (in *Phoenician Women* the Chorus is destined for service at Delphi). Ms. L assigns these lines to Iphigenia, then 137–42 to the Chorus. Lines 126–36 are obviously the Chorus's, and most editors give them 123–25 as well. Taplin tentatively (1977, 194 n. 3) and Diggle (followed by Kyriakou) give 123–25 to Iphigenia so as to avoid a long initial silence on her part, but *Hipp.* 58–60 and *Or.* 140–42 are not similar and she need not enter much before 137 (cf. Parker 82f.). Other choruses demand ritual silence for their own processions: *Ba.* 70 (stating origin and devotion to the god), A. *Eum.* 1035, 1038, F 87, Ar. *Frogs* 354.

123. Be silent: εὐφαμεῖτ(ε), 'speak well', i.e. avoid wrong speech which might damage the ritual process (cf. *Ion* 98–101; Pulleyn 1997, 184).

124–25. the twin converging rocks: the mythical Symplêgades or 'Clashing Rocks', famous from the story of the Argonauts, cf. *Med.* 2, 1263, *Andr.* 793–96. They ceased clashing after the Argo passed safely through them. They were identified with the Kuaneai ('Dark Rocks'), two islets about 4 km apart near the northern entrance to the Thracian Bosporus (e.g. Hdt. 4.85.1, Strabo 1.2.10, 7.6.1). The Rocks make a symbolic frontier between the civilized Greek world and the world beyond, and are here identified by synecdoche with the Black Sea area and its dangers. There is no suggestion that the Taurians live close to them; their remoteness and alienness are stressed repeatedly in the Parodos. For the phrasing here cf. *Med.* 1263f., 'the very inhospitable (ἀξενωτάταν) passage of the dark Symplêgades'. **twin (δισσάς)**: Euripides usually avoids the simple 'two' with poetic pleonasms like δισσοί ('twin youths', 264), δίπτυχοι ('twofold youths', 242, 474, 1289), δίδυμοι ('the two of them', 456), διπλοῖ ('double griefs', 688); see also 323, 407, 655. **[πόντου…ἀξείνου, the Unwelcoming Sea:** L has ἄξε(ι)νος, 'inhospitable' in 218, 253, 341. Here and in 395, 438, 1388 it has almost certainly been displaced by the euphemistic εὔξεινος, 'hospitable', the

166   COMMENTARY

Black Sea's later standard name in Greek. The sense 'Unwelcoming' is always relevant in this play. The epithet originated in Iranian *akshaeina* 'dark' (Moorhouse 1940, 1948; Allen 1947, 1948; Bremmer 2013, 93f.). -ξειν- is metrically necessary in 125, 218, 438 (all lyric), -ξεν- in 341 (dialogue) and 395 (lyric) and usually printed in 253, 1388 (dialogue).]

127. Dictynna: a probably Minoan goddess associated with Mt. Diktê in Kydonia (W. Crete) and like Britomartis associated or identified with Artemis in classical times: see especially Hdt. 3.59.2 (her temple in Kydonia), Ar. *Frogs* 1359f. (as huntress), E. *Hipp.* 145–50 (associated with wildlife), Callim. *Hymn.* 3.189ff. (Dictynna/Britomartis as companion of Artemis). The name suits the wildness of the Taurian goddess. »» *LIMC* III, 'Diktynna'.

128–29. the gilded copings: for gilded temple-exteriors cf. *Ion* 157 χρυσήρεις οἴκους, the Delphic temple (»» Miller 1929–32, 59f.); these and *Ion* 1154 (referring to stars) are the only instances in literature of the adjective χρυσήρης. **of your fine-columned temple:** cf. 403–406 n.; in both places the Greek has the grandiose plural 'temples'. The adjective εὔστυλος is found only here in literature; cf. περίστυλος, *Andr.* 1099 (the 'column-surrounded' temple at Delphi), εὐκίων in *Ion* 185 (εὐκίονες αὐλαὶ θεῶν, 'fine-columned halls of the gods'), *Anth.Pal.* 7.648.7 (Leonidas of Tarentum) and 4x in Byzantine poets. The same phrase appears, perhaps borrowed from *Iphigenia*, in a fragment of a verse epitaph from Vergina (the old Macedonian capital) dated around 400 BC and commemorating a Kallimachos who may have been the famous architect and sculptor of that name (*SEG* 46.830). [It has been suggested that Euripides' word εὔστυλος either has the technical sense 'with columns correctly spaced' known later from Vitruvius 3.3.1 or that both here and in the epitaph it alludes to the ornate Corinthian order which Kallimachos was credited with inventing (»» Stieber 2011, 42–48). Either would be anachronistic and a little incongruous in this context.]

130–32. I walk in this holy maiden-procession: 'I conduct a holy maidenly foot'. Periphrasis with πόδα is common, e.g. 649, 936. Throughout the Parodos the women refer to themselves in the singular as choruses often do while Iphigenia addresses them in the plural (143). The Greek word-order intertwining this phrase with **servant of your holy key-keeper** and placing ὁσίας ὅσιον prominently together is impossible to replicate in translation. **holy** is an approximate translation of the Greek ὅσιος, a complex and culturally conditioned term which can refer to any thing, person or conduct which conforms with the divinely established order of the world and is therefore pleasing to the gods.[8] The concept recurs significantly in the play (cf. 343, 466, 871, 945, 1037, 1045, 1161, 1194, 1320, 1461). Iphigenia and the maidens of the chorus are **holy** in the sense that their lives are pure and they properly fulfil their duties as servants of Artemis.

---

[8] »» Rudhardt 1958, 30–37; Chadwick 1996, 221–26, Peels 2015, 27–67. 'Holy' is of course an equally complex and culturally conditioned term, as the full *Oxford English Dictionary* makes clear.

COMMENTARY   167

key-keeper: as priestess Iphigenia holds the temple key as she will at Brauron (1463). Lycurgus is key-keeper of Zeus's temple at Nemea (*Hyps.* F 752h.28), and Io of his temple at Argos (A. *Suppl.* 291). The key (actually a z-shaped lever which would lift the latch when passed through the door) appears regularly in depictions of Iphigenia as priestess. **133–36. far from the ramparts etc.:** from lines 1106–12 we learn that the women were taken by the captors of their native city and reached the Taurians through the slave trade. As war-captives they are like the chorus of Aeschylus's *Choephori.* Athena will arrange their return to Greece at the end of the play (1465–67, 1482f.). **of horse-rich Hellas:** εὐίππου evokes the 'horse-grazing' (ἱππόβοτος) lands and 'horse-taming' (ἱππόδαμος) heroes of epic, connoting prosperity and an aristocratic way of life: cf. *Pho.* 17, *Ba.* 574, S. *OC* 668; for the idea, [A.] *PV* 465f. **Europe with its lushly wooded pastures** is contrasted with the barrenness of the Taurian land; cf. 219, 399–402. In Hdt. 7.5.3 the Persian Mardonius recommends Europe to king Xerxes for its fine trees. Artemis herself favours lush, well-watered meadows: cf. 1462–63 (Brauron), *IA* 1463, 1544 (Aulis), *Hipp.* 73–78. [χόρτων εὐδένδρων seems to be a descriptive (character-izing) genitive, cf. *Med.* 846f. 'city of/with sacred rivers', *Pho.* 801f. 'grove of/with holy leaves', Soph. F 659.5 'meadow of/with river-borne drinking-waters' (»» Diggle 1994, 417–19). Attached to a proper name (**Εὐρώπαν**) it is unique and perhaps suspect. Barnes changed the name to Εὐρώταν, the Laconian river Eurotas denoting Sparta as in 400. This is favoured by Hall 1987, 430–33 and Diggle 1994, 418 since the Tauric peninsula was properly in Europe, but we hear no more of Sparta (except incidentally at 400) and the Chorus's home city remains anonymous. At 396 the gadfly pursues Io across the Bosporus 'passing to Asian land from Europe' (393–97 n.). »» Cropp 1997, 25f.]

137. I have come etc.: Euripides' choruses often introduce themselves and explain their arrival at the start of the Parodos, e.g. *Andr.* 119–21, *El.* 167–74, *HF* 107–109.

138. brought me, brought me (ἄγαγες ἄγαγες): duplication (*anadiplosis*) is a common figure in Euripides' lyrics (»» Breitenbach 214–21), here expressing the women's anxiety about Iphigenia's summons.

139–42. of him who went etc.: the contrast between the greatness of Agamemnon's expedition to Troy and its sorry consequences is often stressed in Greek poetry (e.g. *Odyssey* 24.24–34, A. *Cho.* 345–71, *Eum.* 455–61, E. *El.* 2–10, 479–81). It is ironically evoked here since Iphigenia and the Chorus are unaware of the expedition's consequences and still focus on its grand departure. The chorus of *Electra* recalls the fleet's joyous departure ('Famous ships, that once went Troyward with those countless oars…') before moving to Achilles, his terrifyingly decorated armour and his death with countless others in the ill-fated war (*El.* 432–86). **with that famous fleet etc.:** 'with famous thousand-ship myriad-equipment oar'. For 'oar' = fleet see 116–17 n. Cf. *Or.* 352 χιλιόναυν

168 COMMENTARY

στρατόν 'thousand-ship force', *IA* 174 ἐλάταις χιλιόναυσιν 'thousand-ship oars (= fleet)', A. *Ag.* 45 στόλον χιλιοναύτην 'thousand-ship expedition'. τεύχεα are the Homeric warrior's armour (LSJ 'τεῦχος' I.1), so **ten thousand armaments** stands for 'ten thousand warriors'. [These comparisons suggest that the two epithets should be dative with κώπᾳ (Barnes) rather than genitive with Agamemnon (Seidler, Diggle), although Xerxes is πολυναύτης 'many-shipped' in A. *Pers.* 84.]

142. †*of the famous sons of Atreus* (Ἀτρειδᾶν τῶν κλεινῶν)†: inept sense and defective metre. Hermann suggested that some words elaborating the description of Agamemnon are missing (see Kovacs's text). Parker concludes that 'What Euripides may have written here we have no idea' and for convenience prints Dindorf's ⟨γένος⟩ Ἀτρειδᾶν etc., translating 'kin of the glorious Atreidae' (but γένος would mean 'offspring', LSJ 'γένος' II.1).

143–77. Iphigenia explains that she has summoned the Chorus to assist in her libation and lament for her brother whose death, revealed to her in a dream, means the extinction of her family. She proceeds to pour the libation.

144–47. how painful the lamentations etc.: 'how do I lie in ill-lamenting laments'. δυσ- in **δυσθρηνήτοις** suggests unnaturalness or distortion, as e.g. Aegisthus δυσθνῄσκων 'dying horribly', *El.* 843. Greek poets often combined a δυσ- or ἀ-compound adjective with a cognate noun or verb in a kind of oxymoron: cf. 201, 203f., 216, 566, 889, 897 (»» Breitenbach 236–38, Fehling 1968). For ἔγκειμαι suggesting helpless subjection to suffering, grief etc. see LSJ 'ἔγκειμαι' I.2 and especially *Andr.* 91f. οἷσπερ ἐγκείμεσθ' ἀεὶ θρήνοισι καὶ γόοισι καὶ δακρύμασιν, 'in what laments and wailings and tears I lie continually'. **lyreless plaints:** the lyre suggests harmony, calm and joy, its absence their opposites. For 'lyreless' music in tragedy cf. A. *Ag.* 990f., *Eum.* 331–33, *Alc.* 447 (commemorating Alcestis), *Hel.* 185 (Helen's lyreless *elegos*), *Pho.* 1028 (the Sphinx's song: see Mastronarde there). For the mournful *elegos* in Euripides see also 1091, *Tro.* 119, *Hyps.* F 752g.9 (with kithara). *Elegos* may have originally denoted any song in elegiac rhythm and developed the special sense 'sung lament' only in the late fifth century (Bowie 1986, 22–27 and in *BNP*; but see the reservations of Aloni 2009, 169). **this unmusical song:** 'this not well-mused song' (*litotês*/ understatement). The drunken songs of the Cyclops (*Cyc.* 426) and Heracles (*Alc.* 760, F 907) are ἄμουσα ('museless'), the Sphinx's songs ἀμουσόταται ('extremely museless'. *Pho.* 807).

148–56. Disasters come upon me etc.: Iphigenia explains what the dream has told her but does not describe it as she has in the prologue, so the Chorus can only assume that she has interpreted it correctly. **Gone is my ancestral house etc.** implies that the Atreid line has expired with the death of its last male heir. It might in fact be continued if Orestes' and Iphigenia's sister Electra had sons (682 n., 695–98 n.), but that calculation is irrelevant in this emotional context.

COMMENTARY   169

157–59. those ordeals at Argos: i.e. the conflicts which now seem to have led to the final destruction of the Pelopid dynasty. These are vaguely imagined as the work of an impersonal **daimon** punishing the dynasty for its past sins. Iphigenia and the Chorus see the daimon as also causing her own and Orestes' sufferings (195–202, 865f., 987f.).

159–66. For him I shall pour these libations etc.: a mixture of milk and honey (*melikraton*) with wine is emptied onto the ground in the libations known as *choai* ('pourings'). Similar libations for the dead are described at *Or.* 115; cf. *Odyssey* 10.519f. (separate pourings of these and water), A. *Pers.* 611–15 (all four ingredients), S. *El.* 895 (milk). **»** Graf 1980, *ThesCRA* I.237–53 (libations for the dead, 245), V.191–204 (equipment), Henrichs 1983 (wineless libations). χοάς... ὑγραίνειν is lit. 'to moisten libations', with χοάς an internal object like e.g. Pind. *Nem.* 10.75 θερμὰ...τέγγων δάκρυα 'soaking warm tears'. **this bowl belonging to the dead:** κρατῆρα refers to the contents as in English 'bowl of milk'; cf. *Ba.* 687, *Iliad* 8.232. The Greek has 'these libations and bowl', with τε used 'appositionally', cf. 169 τεῦχος καὶ λοιβάν, 'vessel with its liquid' (**»** Denniston 502).

[Ms. L's ὑδραίνειν gives 'I shall water these libations'. The metaphor is possible,[9] but the correction is very slight. For defences of ὑδραίνειν see Sansone 1979, 157f.; Cropp 1997, 26f.; and for the correction Diggle 1994, 216–18; Parker.]

163. milk (παγάς, 'springs, jets') **from young mountain-heifers:** all these terms emphasize the milk's natural purity and perfection which the ritual requires; cf. A. *Pers.* 611, 'white milk, good to drink, from a pure cow'. Young heifers unsullied by domestic and agricultural use are also choice sacrificial victims, cf. 359–60 n., *Hec.* 205f., *IA* 1082f.

165. the labour of humming bees: honey for libations is described similarly in 634f., *Erech.* F 370.85f., A. *Pers.* 612f., Soph. F 398.4f. **humming** renders the vague poetic word ξουθός, an 'iconym' used variously to suggest colour, sound or movement (hovering), thus an appropriate epithet for birds, bees etc.; cf. 635 (the bee again), *HF* 487 and F 467.4 ('*xoutho*-winged bee'), *Hel.* 1111 (the trilling nightingale's throat), Chaeremon F 1.7 ('rustling breezes'). Here it probably evokes the sound of the bees' vibrating wings as they collect their nectar; this seems more apt than a colour-word such as 'tawny'. **»** Silk 1983, 317–19; Risch 1992 (noting that Mycenaean *ksouthos* was a colour word describing cattle and that the poetic uses presumably developed later).

166. as comforts for the dead: cf. A. *Pers.* 610 ἅπερ νεκροῖσι μειλικτήρια, '(libations) which are sweeteners for the dead'. The idea of libations for the dead as 'sweeteners' (μειλίγματα, e.g. A. *Cho.* 15, *Eum.* 107), keeping them contented and friendly, was long established (**»** Andronikos 1968, 25f.; Johnston 1999, 46–

---

[9] R. Parker 1983, 35 n. 11: 'Libations to the corpse after burial could be spoken of as a χέρνιψ or λουτρόν, as though the process of purification continued (Soph. *El.* 84, 434 etc.)...'. Cf. A. *Cho.* 129, χέρνιβες poured at Agamemnon's tomb.

170 COMMENTARY

63). **[are poured:** Nauck's χεῖται seems more apt for these χοαί than L's κεῖται ('are laid down, established') and is printed by Diggle and Kovacs. Most editors keep L's reading.]

167–68. Now hand me the vessel: Iphigenia addresses a servant who has been carrying the bowl referred to in 160; cf. E. *El.* 140, *Hel.* 865–72.

170–71. scion of Agamemnon: 'Agamemnonian scion', in epic style (1 n.). Orestes is 'Agamemnonides' at *Odyssey* 1.30, Clytemnestra 'the Agamemnonian wife' *Od.* 3.264. For the word θάλος see Chadwick 1996, 140f.

172–74. I shall bring to your tomb no auburn hair: in the recognition scene of Aeschylus's *Choephori* Orestes places on Agamemnon's tomb a lock of his hair which Electra finds; its similarity to her own hair convinces her that it must be his (*Cho.* 174–76), and he proves it by matching the two (*Cho.* 229f.). This and Aeschylus's other proofs are satirized in the recognition scene of Euripides' *Electra*, but here the reminder of the Aeschylean scene perhaps serves to foreshadow Iphigenia's own reunion with her brother.

175. Far have I been removed from the homeland: τηλόσε...πατρίδος recalls the Homeric formula τηλόθι πάτρης (*Iliad* 1.30 etc.). ἀπενάσθην is from ἀποναίω, epic aorist with causal sense; cf. 1260 ἀπενάσσατο, *Med.* 166 ἀπενάσθην (»» LSJ 'ναίω' II.2, 'ἀποναίω' II, 'καταναίω').

176. as people believe: cf. 8 n.

178–202. The Chorus responds to Iphigenia and laments the decline of the Atreid dynasty, beginning with Thyestes' usurpation of the kingship which led to a series of further crimes (189–98). The avenging daimon which imposed those crimes (157–59 n.) now afflicts Iphigenia with (it seems) the loss of her brother and thus the extinction of her family (199–202). Their reference to the daimon provokes Iphigenia's response (203ff.). [This passage was assigned to the Chorus by Hermann; L gives all of 186–235 to Iphigenia, but 186–202 are the lament which the Chorus have just said they will sing. L's text is more than usually disrupted, especially in lines 187–195. I have adopted Parker's text for the most part, making the most of L's wording while supposing that words have been lost at several points. Uncertainties remain.]

178–81. antiphonal songs: ἀντιψάλμους ('counter-twanging') images the Chorus as a lyre accompanying Iphigenia's songs. The word is found only here and in a similar but fragmentary context, Aesch.(?) F 451e.13; cf. Ar. *Birds* 217–19 τοῖς σοῖς ἐλέγοις ἀντιψάλλων...φόρμιγγα '(Apollo) plucking his lyre in response to your laments'. **barbarian clamour of Asian chants:** i.e. wild cries of the kind featured in A. *Pers.* 935–1077. The description suggests 'alien', 'uncontrolled' and musically 'tense, strident, ornamented' (»» West 1992, 388 on 'Asiatic' features of Greek music), evoking the Greek women's barbarian surroundings. These features were probably represented in the Chorus's music and dance (»» Moutsopoulos 1992), but the language that follows is not distinctly 'barbarian' here or in other Euripidean cases such as *Pho.* 679f., 1302f., *Or.*

COMMENTARY 171

1383–85, *Ba.* 158f. (»» Colvin 1999, 83–85). [Ms. L supported by the papyrus gives 'and an Asian refrain, barbarian clamour'. Bothe's minimal change gives better phrasing, cf. *Tro.* 512f. καινῶν ὕμνων...ᾠδάν, 'a song (consisting) of new chants'.]

182–85. that mournful music for the dead: μοῦσαν, 'muse' stands for music like 'Cypris' for 'love', 'Hades' for 'death'; cf. *Med.* 196, 421, *Hyps.* F 752h.7; »» Breitenbach 176. The second **τὰν** is a relative pronoun as sometimes in tragic lyrics. **distinct from paeans:** paeans usually expressed celebration, relief or positive expectation (cf. 1403–4 n.) and were associated especially with Apollo (with whom the healing god Paion came to be identified). Tragedy often contrasts paeans with laments (e.g. A. *Cho.* 342–44), sometimes in an oxymoron such as 'paean of the dead', *Cho.* 151; cf. A. *Sept.* 866–69, *Ag.* 645, F 161, E. *Alc.* 424, *Tro.* 578, *Hel.* 173–78. »» Käppel 1992, 47–49, 310–15; Rutherford 1995, 121–24; Ford 2006, 294.

187–88. Gone is the glory etc.: φῶς ('light') can denote individuals with emphasis on the glory and/or salvation they bring to their communities (»» Cropp on *El.* 449). The word refers to Orestes at 849, *Or.* 243 and probably A. *Cho.* 131. Diggle (1981, 78f.) and others see a reference to Orestes here too, but at this point the Chorus are focused on the lustre and strength which the dynasty once had. **of its royal power: σκήπτρων** is lit. 'of the sceptre(s)', a frequent 'majestic' plural, e.g. *El.* 11, 321, Stevens on E. *Andr.* 1223. [Burges' σκῆπτρον τ' ('the light and the sceptre') would suggest a more specific reference to Orestes (cf. 235 n.) and is printed by Diggle and Kovacs. The added ⟨ἔρρει⟩ makes 187f. two anapaestic dimeters. Some editors prefer to keep ἔρρει φῶς σκήπτρων, οἴμοι and either delete πατρῴων οἴκων or change it to πατρίων οἴκων (a single dimeter). Parker makes lines 186f. a single sentence ('Alas, gone is the glory of the royal power of the house of the Atreids'), but the string of genitives that this creates seems less likely and the phrasing suggests that τῶν Ἀτρειδᾶν οἴκων depends on οἴμοι.]

189–90. From the prosperous kings etc.: the text again has to be restored since L's τίν' is meaningless and the sentence has no verb. Murray's **ἦν, was** solves both problems. ἀρχά could mean 'the rule', but **the beginning** is consistent with **From** and with what follows.

191–93. trouble surges out of troubles etc.: L's text lacks at least a subject and verb before **δινευούσαις ἵπποις πταναῖς:** perhaps something like 'trouble surges out of troubles, ⟨*since Pelops' sons contended for the kingdom he had won*⟩ with his circuiting ('whirling') winged mares' (cf. 1–5 n.). In *IT* 812–17 and more fully in *El.* 699–746 and *Or.* 807–18 Euripides traces the dynasty's troubles to the conflict of the brothers Atreus and Thyestes for possession of the golden lamb and the kingship of Mycenae. In *Or.* 987–1012 and 1547–49, the lamb is said to have been sent as a punishment for Pelops' murder of Oenomaus's charioteer Myrtilus after the race (»» S. *El.* 504–15 with Finglass's commentary, Gantz 111f., 541–43), but a reference to that here seems unlikely since, as Kyriakou notes, the story

172   COMMENTARY

of Myrtilus is ignored in the play's other recollections of the chariot race (1ff., 822–26). The **winged mares** were included in the depiction of the race on the 6th C Chest of Cypselus at Olympia (Pausanias 5.17.7). According to Pindar, *Ol.* 1.71–88 they were given to Pelops by the god Poseidon so that he could win the race (cf. E. *Or.* 989 ποτανὸν μὲν δίωγμα πώλων, Pelops' 'winged-horse-driving'). [δινευούσαις could have been transitive with an object in the lost preceding lines, the winged horses 'whirling the chariot' around the circuit. Some editors understand the mares as the horses of the sun-god Helios driving his chariot on its daily path across the sky (a common image) and delete δ' in 193 so as to make Helios the subject throughout,[10] but that is oddly phrased and puts all the emphasis on the Sun's change of course while barely alluding to its cause.]

193–94. and Helios shifting etc.: the topic is the change in the Sun's course which Euripides associates with the strife between Atreus and Thyestes also in *El.* 727–36 (the earliest extant account) and *Or.* 1001–1006 as well as in 811–16 below. Ancient accounts vary greatly, including both the occasion for this change and the cosmological details (»» Gantz 547f.; Cropp on *El.* 727–36; Egli 2003, 53–69). In 811–16 Orestes reminds Iphigenia that she once wove a picture of Atreus and Thyestes quarrelling over the lamb along with the change of the sun's course, which in that context is presumably a matter of Zeus affirming Atreus's kingship (as in *El.* 727ff.) rather than a reaction against Atreus's crime. The same may be true here: the troubles of the house began with the sending of the golden lamb and the Sun's change of course affirming Atreus's kingship, and since then woe has followed upon woe. **his eye's sacred brightness:** the Sun is a divine eye seeing all from the heaven: cf. S. *Ant.* 103f. χρυσέας ἁμέρας βλέφαρον 'the eye of golden day', 879f. τόδε λαμπάδος ἱερὸν ὄμμα 'this sacred torch's eye', *Trach.* 102 κρατιστεύων κατ' ὄμμα '(the Sun) powerful in eye', Ar. *Clouds* 285 ὄμμα γὰρ αἰθέρος ἀκάματον σελαγεῖται 'heaven's tireless eye blazes'. Similarly the full moon, Pind. *Ol.* 3.19f., A. *Sept.* 389f. See also 110 n. [Paley's ⟨μετέβασ'⟩, 'transferred' provides a needed verb for this sentence and is probably the correct reading in *El.* 728. One more missing word (– –) would make line 194 an anapaestic dimeter.]

197. †*murder on murder etc.*†: difficult metre and dispensable sense; perhaps to be deleted. Parker notes that the other runs of short syllables in the Parodos express Iphigenia's grief over her separation from the life she should have had, and from her brother (213?, 220, 231f.).

199–201. Thence retribution etc.: simply phrased, ἔνθεν ποινὰ τῶν πρόσθεν δμαθέντων ἐκβαίνει εἰς οἴκους Τανταλιδᾶν. Iphigenia is the latest victim of the

---

[10] Thus Kovacs (≈ Wecklein), μόχθος δ' ἐκ μόχθων ἄσσει, | δινευούσαις ἵπποισιν ⟨ἐπεὶ⟩ | πταναῖς ἀλλάξας ἐξ **ἕδρας** | ἱερὸν ⟨μετέβασ'⟩ ὄμμ' αὐγᾶς | Ἅλιος, 'and trouble surges out of troubles, ⟨*ever since*⟩ with his circuiting winged mares Helios shifted ⟨*and transferred*⟩ from its seat his eye's sacred brightness'. See also Platnauer; Sansone; Kyriakou; O'Brien 1988a, 105 n. 17.

COMMENTARY   173

retribution incurred by her forebears. **ποινά** with the genitive means **retribution for** (»» LSJ ποινή I.1–2), not 'from' as often translated. **those slain before** are the sons of Thyestes murdered by Atreus in the feud provoked by the golden lamb (196). The wording recalls A. *Ag.* 1223 ἐκ τῶνδε ποινάς φημι βουλεύειν τινά, 'from these (the murders of Thyestes' sons) I say that someone (Aegisthus) is planning retribution') and 1338–42 νῦν δ' εἰ προτέρων αἷμ' ἀποτείσῃ | καὶ τοῖσι θανοῦσι θανὼν ἄλλων | ποινὰς θανάτων ἐπικράνῃ, 'but now, if he (Agamemnon) repays the blood of those slain before, and by dying makes retribution to the dead for those other deaths'. Ποιναί could be personified spirits of vengeance, i.e. Erinyes as in A. *Cho.* 947, *Eum.* 323 (cf. E. *Supp.* 490, *HF* 887), and here the **ποινά** which **emerges** to afflict the house is at least close to being personified (thus LSJ 'ποινή' II). [**δμαθέντων** is from the poetic verb δαμάζω 'subdue', frequent in epic for killing or overpowering. I take **Τανταλιδᾶν** with οἴκους (**the house of the Tantalids**) rather than with **τῶν πρόσθεν δμαθέντων** where it seems less apt ('those formerly slain Tantalids').]

201–2. the daimon pursues abhorrent designs: σπεύδει...ἀσπούδαστ(α), 'pursues things not to be pursued', both oxymoron and etymological figure like *Alc.* 242f. ἀβίωτον...χρόνον βιοτεύσει 'he will live an unlivable life'; see also 144–47 n., Breitenbach 229f. For this **daimon** see 157–59 n.   [Line 202 is probably incomplete (Hartung, Parker) and originally a pareomiac (catalectic anapaestic dimeter) bringing the chorus's lament to an end.]

203–35. The Chorus has said that Iphigenia is afflicted by the daimon that persecutes her family. She responds that it has determined her whole life from the moment when she was born and condemned by her father's vow to be sacrificed to Artemis, and recalls the circumstances of her sacrifice in pathetic detail, including her parting from Orestes whom she now must lament.

203–5. the daimon has been baneful for me: δυσδαίμων δαίμων, 'the daimon (has been) ill-daimonic' (144–47 n., 201 n.). **†from my mother's womb†**: ζώνας is lit. 'girdle'; pregnancy is sometimes described as bearing or nurturing beneath or within the girdle, e.g. *Hec.* 762, LSJ 'ζώνη' I.2. The word is often understood here as 'marriage' and **that night** as Clytemnestra's wedding-night when Agamemnon 'loosed her virgin girdle', but the night of Iphigenia's birth when the Fates spun the thread of her life is more relevant. Either way, ζώνας is a unique metonymy. [If the text is complete, the sense is 'from the start..., (from) my mother's womb and that night...', but Diggle may be right in thinking that some words of a less abruptly phrased sentence have been lost. Parker prints a lacuna of two part-lines. Kovacs prints the text with changes proposed by Willink: ⟨ἐκ⟩ τᾶς ματρὸς ζώνας | ⟨λύσεως⟩ καὶ νυκτὸς κείνας ('from the loosing of my mother's girdle and that night'), deleting the second ἐξ ἀρχᾶς.]

207. the divine Moirai: the Moirai are 'Apportioners', primeval goddesses thought to attend births and spin the threads of a mortal's destiny or 'portion' (*moira*). They are known in Homer (*Il.* 24.49, 209; cf. the *Klôthes* or 'Spinners' in

174 COMMENTARY

Od. 7.197, *Aisa* 'Destiny' in *Il.* 20.127f.). Hesiod calls them Klôthô, Lachesis and Atropos, daughters of Night or of Zeus and Themis (*Theog.* 904–6); »» Gantz 7, *LIMC* VI, 'Moirai'. **drew tight a hard childhood:** i.e. drawing tight the threads with which they wove her life (συντείνουσιν is a 'registering' present tense: 22–23 n.). Iphigenia was still virtually a child when she was sacrificed, and Agamemnon's vow had condemned her to death at the time of her birth.

209–13. Leda's ill-used daughter: Clytemnestra was tricked into enduring the sacrifice of her daughter. **victim:** σφάγιον, 'object of slaughter' (8 n., 20 n.), focusing on the violence of the killing. **a joyless sacrifice:** θῦμ' οὐκ εὐγάθητον is an oxymoron. θῦμα is the general term for a sacrificial offering which both gods and mortals should enjoy. At normal animal sacrifices a cheerful women's ululation (*ololugmos*) greeted the victim's death. I see no difficulty in understanding εὐκταίαν as **promised by his vow.**[11] On the vow itself see Introduction, pp. 11f. with n. 26. [†*gave birth to, nurtured*†: Seidler's ἔτεκεν κἄτρεφεν, *bore* ⟨*and*⟩ *nurtured* restores an anapaestic dimeter but spoils the emotive effect of the asyndeton. Parker retains ἔτεκεν ἔτρεφεν as resolved iambic (‿ ⏑⏑ ‿ ⏑⏑). Kovacs rewrites.]

214–17. In a horse-drawn carriage etc.: Iphigenia was brought to Aulis on the pretence that she was to marry Achilles. A carriage was characteristic of aristocratic and mythical weddings (»» Oakley–Sinos 1993, 27–32 with illustrations). Iphigenia's arrival at Aulis in a carriage is staged at *IA* 590–97, as are the doomed Agamemnon's in A. *Ag.* 783–809 and the doomed Clytemnestra's in E. *El.* 988–97. **they set me on the sands:** ἐπέβασαν transitive (LSJ 'ἐπιβαίνω' B.1). **an ill-wedded bride:** for the phrasing cf. 144, 201, 203f. with notes. **Nereus's daughter's son:** i.e. Achilles, son of the Nereid Thetis.

218–19. a guest of the Unwelcoming Sea: ἀξείνου πόντου ξείνα, another oxymoron. **a barren home:** in contrast with the lushness of Greece, cf. 133–36 n. οἴκους has a broad sense as e.g. *HF* 406, S. *El.* 1136.

220. no marriage etc.: 'marriageless, childless, cityless, friendless'. Iphigenia is deprived of all that would normally give her life meaning. Euripides favours this emphatic figure (only here with four adjectives), e.g. *Andr.* 491, *Hel.* 689, *Or.* 310, *Ba.* 995, *Hyps.* F 752h.18 (»» Breitenbach 226f. comparing *Iliad* 9.63). Runs of short syllables heighten the emotion as in 231, 232.

208. I who had suitors: ἁ μναστευθεῖσ(α), 'the one wooed'. **from amongst the Hellenes** implies men from all of Greece and of suitably high status. In *El.* 20–24 Electra was wooed by 'the first men of the land of Greece' before Aegisthus put a stop to it, and in *El.* 312f. she recalls being wooed by her uncle

---

[11] Kyriakou finds it 'unlikely that Iphigenia would think that her sacrifice was necessitated by her father's vow: she was sacrificed because of her father's criminal folly…which led him to believe the seer who misinterpreted the demands of Artemis'; but Iphigenia has not questioned the relevance of the vow (15–21), nor does she ever accuse her father of criminal folly.

COMMENTARY 175

Castor before his deification. Hesiod recorded that 'men from all of Greece' (Παν-έλληνες) wooed the daughters of Proetus (Hes. fr. 130 in Strabo 8.6.6). Cleisthenes of Sicyon invited 'any one of the Hellenes who thought himself worthy of becoming his son-in-law' to join the competition for his daughter's hand (Hdt. 6.126). [The verse makes no sense after 207 (L) and fits much better after 220 than after 207 (where it would have to be altered to refer to Iphigenia), or after 209 (where it would refer to Clytemnestra).]

221. not singing Hera at Argos: as a local princess Iphigenia would have played a leading part in the Heraea, the chief festival of Hera celebrated annually at the Argive Heraion between Argos and Mycenae. Hera was patron goddess of the Argolid and a protector of marriage and married women. The festival is evoked more extensively in the Parodos of *Electra* (»» Cropp on *El.* 167–212).

222–24. nor on the sweet-voiced loom etc.: referring to the sound of the shuttle whisking the thread back and forth through the warp. Elsewhere the shuttle itself is the singer, e.g. E. *Meleager* F 528a (= Ar. *Frogs* 1316: see Dover there), Soph. F 890, Leonidas *Anth.Pal.* 6.288.5. **picking out with my shuttle etc.:** this evokes the preparations for the Panathenaea, Athenian equivalent of the Argive Heraea. Both festivals were in July, soon after the beginning of the new year. Both included the presentation to the goddess of a new robe (*peplos*) woven by aristocratic girls of marriageable age. In Athens the robe was presented to the ancient statue of Athena Polias in the Erechtheum and decorated with scenes from the Gigantomachy, the mythical battle in which Athena helped Zeus destroy the rebellious Giants (here called loosely **Titans**). The weaving of the *peplos* is presented as an ideal maidens' activity as in *Hecuba* 466–74 (again with 'Titans').[12] Iphigenia could never have participated in the Panathenaea but uses the ritual life of Athens, as well as of her own city, to exemplify the kind of life she has lost. Kowalzig 2006, 80 suggests that this anticipates her 'Athenianization' which is confirmed by her integration into Athenian cult at the end of the play; cf. Taddei 2015, 157f. »» Barber 1992 (making of the peplos), Shear 2021, 39–82 (mythology and iconography of the Panathenaea), 157–70 (decoration of the peplos).

225–26. inflicting a bloody fate: 'bloodying a blood-spraying destruction'. Compressed phrases like αἱμόρραντον ἄταν are typical of Euripides' lyrics, e.g. 437 ('fine-staded running-tracks'), 1116 ('non-sheep-sacrificing altars') (»» Breitenbach 207–9). For αἱμάσσουσ' ἄταν, 'bloodying a destruction' cf. *Pho.* 1298f. πέσεα...αἱμάξετον 'they will perform bloody fallings' with 159–61 n. on χοὰς ὑγραίνειν, 'pour moist libations'. **unfit for the lyre:** cf. 144–47 n. [This is L's text except for the change of αἱμορράντων ('on blood-spraying (or 'blood-sprayed') strangers') to αἱμόρραντον ('blood-spraying destruction') and deletion

---

[12] The traditional Titanomachy was a separate battle occurring before Athena's birth, Hes. *Theog.* 629ff. On the occasional conflation of Titans and Giants see Battezzato 2016, 144–50 and on *Hec.* 472.

176 COMMENTARY

of βωμούς (which disturbs the metre and may have been added to explain or simplify the phrasing). Similarly Weil and Platnauer, but there is much uncertainty. Diggle obelizes both lines. Kovacs and Parker adopt more radical changes.]

229. Yet now: καί is 'adversative' as in e.g. *HF* 509, A. *Eum.* 110, S. *Trach.* 1048 (»» Denniston 292 (9), Verdenius 1975). Iphigenia usually pities her victims but now grieves only for her brother. In the next scene she says she will harden her heart against the unrecognized strangers brought to her for sacrifice (344ff.)

230–35. but weep for the brother etc.: strings of short syllables in 231f. (as in 220) and asyndeton in 232 convey Iphigenia's emotion as she recalls her parting from her brother. The description of Orestes in his mother's arms recalls *Hom.Hymn.* 2.187 where Demeter reaches Eleusis and finds the baby Demophon's mother παῖδ' ὑπὸ κόλπῳ ἔχουσα νέον θάλος ('holding her child, young scion, in her lap'). Orestes is here seen as a baby at the time of Iphigenia's sacrifice (cf. 372f., 834–36), whereas in *IA* (1241–48, 1450–52) he is a little boy. Any account must make him still a boy when Agamemnon is murdered ten years later. He returns to Argos to avenge his father a few years later, then spends more than a year being pursued by the Erinyes, tried at Athens, pursued again, returning to Delphi and voyaging to the Taurian land. Iphigenia, aged about fifteen when she was sacrificed, is now around thirty. Electra is aged between Iphigenia and Orestes and by now married to Pylades (695f., 912–23). **[still a tender child:** Parker notes that ἔτι θάλος ('still a scion') only makes sense if θάλος is taken with νέον and the third ἔτι discounted ('present only for the sake of euphony'). The metre in 231f. is best analysed as resolved anapaests: $(- \smile \smile \; | \; \smile \smile \smile \smile \; | \; \smile \smile -\; |$ $\smile \smile \smile \; || \; \smile \smile \smile \; | \; \smile \smile \smile \; | \; \smile \smile \smile)$.]

235. Argos's sceptred ruler: Ἄργει σκηπτοῦχον, 'sceptre-holder in Argos', cf. 187–88 n. The adjective σκηπτοῦχος is often joined with βασιλεύς in the epic formula 'sceptre-holding king' and is here used as a noun as in *Iliad* 14.93, *Odyssey* 8.47, Semonides 7.69 *IEG*. Orestes was heir to the sceptre first given by Zeus to Pelops and held by Agamemnon in *Iliad* 2.100–8. On the allusion here see Xian 2020.

236–391. A herdsman reports the strangers' capture to Iphigenia

The structure is simple: introductory dialogue, Herdsman's speech, Iphigenia's speech reacting to his news. Report scenes with set-piece speeches relating off-stage events to a character in the presence of the Chorus, or to the Chorus alone, were a fundamental and consistently popular feature of Greek tragedies. Euripides' *Bacchae* resembles *Iphigenia* in having two, while *Phoenician Women* (again a late play) has two separate messengers reporting a sequence of offstage events. Aeschylus' *Persians* and *Seven*, as well as the Aeschylean *Prometheus*, likewise have sequences of narrative speeches; Sophocles' *Antigone* has two reports by the Guard followed by a later Messenger-speech. The speeches are epic in language and narrative style, focusing on details of scene and action to achieve

COMMENTARY   177

almost cinematic effects and featuring reported speech. Unlike epic, they focalize
the unfolding events through the experience of an ordinary, uninspired and
sometimes uncomprehending witness such as the Herdsman here or the servant in
1327–1419. As with the Guard in *Antigone*, the low status of the reporters in
Iphigenia leads to humorous contrasts between the characters and their epic-
dramatic roles. Their speeches are related and contrasted with each other in
various ways (see on 1327–1419).

236–37. Brief interjections from the Chorus are usually thought to have been
spoken by the Chorus-leader, but this is not certain and some might well be given
to the whole Chorus (e.g. 576f., 1075–77). I use 'Chorus' without differentiation,
as do the manuscripts.

238–59. In the introductory dialogue the lowly Herdsman addresses Iphigenia
in a rather portentous manner, while she reacts impatiently (240, 254, 256).

239. the strange new announcement (καινῶν κηρυγμάτων): see 42–43 n.

240. what is so amazing: Iphigenia reacts to the Herdsman's demand for her
attention. [This is better than 'What is this distracting us from our present
discourse' (Cropp 2000 with Seidler, Weil and others), since ἐκπλῆσσον has no
object and no discourse is in progress (contrast 773 μὴ λόγων ἔκπλησσε με 'Don't
distract me from what I'm saying'). For the sense of the verb here cf. E. *Ion* 241,
403, *Or.* 549.]

241–42. the dark Symplêgades: see 124–25 n., also for **δίπτυχοι νεανίαι,
a pair of young men.** The same phrase is seen in *Med.* 2 and 1263. **on their
ship: πλάτῃ,**' by oar', cf. 116–17 n.

243. sacrifice and offering: the bodies will be burned on an altar inside the
temple after the sacrificial killing (626). [The prefix in **πρό-σφαγμα** need not
imply a preliminary sacrifice. The word is normally used of blood-offerings to the
dead and suits the grisly nature of the sacrifice envisaged here: »» Cropp on *El.*
1174; Casabona 1966, 170–74.]

244–45. you cannot be too soon etc.: οὐκ ἂν φθάνοις ἂν, 'you could not be
beforehand', is colloquial (LSJ 'φθάνω' IV.2, Collard 2018, 63). Like any Taurian
the Herdsman is keen on human sacrifices (cf. 279f., 336f.). **lustrations
(χέρνιβας):** cf. 54 n. **consecrations (κατάργματα):** cf. 38–41 n. The victim's
head be scattered with barley-grains and hairs cut from the head with
a knife as a preliminary offering. Both barley-grains and knife were brought in
a special basket (κανοῦν, cf. *El.* 810–12). »» Burkert 1983, 3–7 and 1985, 55–57;
van Straten 38f.; *ThesCRA* I.116, V.269–74.

246. What country's look: σχῆμα is a general word for appearance or form,
here suggesting clothing, physical features and bearing. For recognition by clothes
cf. A. *Supp.* 234–37, E. *Hcld.* 130, *Hec.* 734f., *Hyps.* F 752h.11–14. [L's ὄνομ(α)
barely makes sense: 'what country's name…'.]

248–51. You've not heard…the strangers' names etc.: the Herdsman has
heard Pylades' name during the fight that he goes on to describe (321), but

178 COMMENTARY

Iphigenia does not recognize it or connect it with her own family since Pylades was born after her sacrifice ([59–60] n., 920 n.). The question of Orestes' name draws attention to his continued anonymity, which will be repeatedly exploited in the recognition sequence (342, 350, 468–75 etc.).

253. right at the breakers' edge: here and in 255 the Herdsman's language takes on a poetic colouring, as often in his upcoming speech. ἐπὶ ῥηγμῖνι θαλάσσης, 'upon the sea's breaking', is an epic formula, e.g. *Iliad* 1.437.

255. with briny water (δρόσῳ): δρόσος is properly 'dew' but often used poetically for pure or cleansing water (LSJ 'δρόσος' I.2). Iphigenia will get Orestes and Pylades to their ship by pretending that she must purify them with sea water (θαλασσίᾳ δρόσῳ, 1192–94 n.). See also 442–445 n.

256. [**ποῦ, where** is Bothe's alteration of L's πῶς, 'how'. The repetition 'how…and in what way' is possible, but **Get back to telling me** implies that Iphigenia returns to the question she asked in line 252. Parker retains πῶς, arguing that the Herdsman has already answered the question 'where?' in 253; yet he proceeds to describe the location in 260–63.]

[**258–59**]. *These men are late in coming* etc.: the lines are best deleted as a melodramatic interpolation (so recently Diggle, Kyriakou, Parker). If **οὐδέ πω** implies that Greeks have never been sacrificed before, the statement is untrue (cf. 38f., 344–47, 584–87). If it implies that these prisoners have not yet been duly sacrificed, it makes Iphigenia unexpectedly eager to kill them. [Seidler's change of οὐδέ πω to οἵδ' ἐπεί (favoured by Erbse 1984, 202–204; Cropp 2000, 192) gives 'These men have come late-in-time since the goddess's altar was (last) crimsoned etc.' (ἐπεί as in *Med.* 26, *Or.* 78; LSJ 'ἐπεί' A.I.2). This could be understood as explaining Iphigenia's curiosity, but that does not account for her referring to the sacrifices in such lurid terms.][13]

260–339. The Herdsman's speech is organized in three parts with Euripidean precision, 'meanwhile' introducing the second and third parts (281, 301). Each part focuses on a narrative-descriptive set-piece: *260–80*, scene-setting and discovery of Orestes and Pylades (the narrative sequence of mysterious discovery, debate and fateful decision is like that of the Guard's speech in *Antigone* 249ff. and the herdsman's in *Bacchae* 677ff.); *281–300*, Orestes' madness; *301–35*, 'epic' description of the battle and capture of Orestes. Humorous or mock-epic moments include the debate on the possible divinity of the strangers (267ff.),

---

[13] Other suggestions: (1) understand Iphigenia's sudden hostility to Greeks as due to her grief for Orestes (cf. 344–50: Sansone 1978, 42–47); (2) read οἵδ' ἐπεί and place 258f. after 245 in the mouth of the Herdsman (Wecklein); but she cannot ask where the prisoners come from if the Herdsman has just said that they are Greek, and the lines do not follow 245 in the relevant piece of the Hellenistic papyrus P. Hibeh 24 (which unfortunately ends with line 255); (3) place 258f. after 335 at the end of the Herdsman's narrative (Most 2000; but they are not needed there and a transposition over some eighty lines is unlikely).

COMMENTARY 179

Orestes' assault on the cattle (296–330), the gathering and arming of the peasants and their inferiority to the noble youths (301ff., 323ff.). Against this are set the serious features of these events: Orestes' madness (the only presentation in this play of his affliction by the Erinyes), Pylades' loyal defence of him and their noble resistance, and the divine protection they receive (328ff.). Orestes' final humiliation in madness and capture is also the beginning of his liberation.

260–64. As we were driving etc.: ἐπεί etc. is a common opening for tragic report speeches, e.g. 1327, *El.* 774, *Ion* 1122. **our woodland-grazing (ὑλοφορβ-ούς) cattle:** the adjective is unique here, but cf. Hes. *Works* 591 βοὸς ὑλοφάγοιο, 'a woodland-feeding cow'. **there was a hollow-fronted cleft etc.:** content and phrasing are typical of epic scene-setting, e.g. *Iliad* 22.147–57 (Scamander's springs), *Odyssey* 5.55–75 (Calypso's dwelling), 6.85–88 (the Ogygian shore): »» de Jong 1991, 148–60 on scenery in Euripides' report speeches. **a purple-fishers' shelter:** purple dye was collected from the shellfish *murex* trapped in wicker pots and sun-dried (»» Pollux 1.47–49; Thompson 1947, 209–19). A purple-fisher is the speaker of Euripides' *Stheneboea* F 670.

266. navigating his way: πορθμεύων ἴχνος, 'ferrying/conveying footstep'. The verb is used similarly with an internal object at 936 and 1435, and with a direct object at 371, 735, 1358 (see also 1444–45 n.), otherwise only 5x in Euripides (πορθμεύς, *Alc.* 253) and rarely elsewhere in tragedy (A. *Cho.* 685, S. *Trach.* 802, [E.] *Rhes.* 429; πόρθμευμα, A. *Ag.* 1558;). The fine crafting of the line is amusingly incongruous when it describes the herdsman tiptoeing fearfully away (perhaps backwards as England suggests).

268–74. Then one of us, a god-fearing man etc.: the pious man thinks the two youthful 'deities' may be either the Dioscuri (Castor and Pollux) or sons of a Nereid, and prays for protection in case they become angry with the intruding mortals. Parker says that he calls 'at random on all the marine deities that come into his head', not knowing whether the figures are male or female since he 'has not yet seen Orestes and Pylades' and 'has only heard that δαίμονές τινες are present'. In fact it is clear that all of the herdsmen can see the two male figures. One has got a bit closer and drawn them to the attention of the others (**Don't you see,** 267). The pious man now looks at them (εἰσιδών, 269) and guesses at their identity. The irreverent man must be able to see them as well when he identifies them as shipwrecked sailors.

270–71. son of sea-goddess Leucothea etc.: the pious man prays to Palaemon for protection from the two mysterious figures. Leucothea ('White Goddess') and her dolphin-riding son were worshipped especially on the Isthmus of Corinth and around the Peloponnese. In *Odyssey* 5.333–53 she helps the shipwrecked Odysseus by lending him her veil, taking the form of a shearwater. Elsewhere she is said to have once been Ino, daughter of Cadmus and a nurse of Dionysus, who leapt into the Saronic Gulf with one of their sons (Melicertes/Palaemon) after her husband Athamas went mad and killed the other son. The mythology is

180   COMMENTARY

complicated and varied, e.g. Hyginus, *Fab.* 2 and 4 (the latter claiming to be
based on Euripides' *Ino*), E. *Med.* 1282–89, Pind. *Ol.* 2.28–30, *Pyth.* 11.1f., Ov.
Met. 4.416–542, *Fast.* 6.485–550, Apollod. 3.4.3 (»» Gantz 176–80, 478; *LIMC*
V, 'Ino'; *LIMC* VI, 'Melikertes'; Larson 1995, 123–25; Pache 2004, 135–80).

272. Zeus's twins are the Dioscuri, the demigods Castor and Pollux, sons of
Zeus and Leda, brothers of Helen and Clytemnestra.

273–74. prides (ἀγάλματα) of Nereus: i.e. sons of **Nereids**, the fifty
daughters of Nereus and Doris catalogued in Hesiod's *Theogony* 240–64, famous
for their round-dancing as a **chorus** (a favourite theme of Greek poetry and art),
riding the waves and escorting ships (cf. 427–29, *El.* 434 with Cropp's note,
»» Barringer 1995). Three grandsons of Nereus are named in *Theog.* 930–33 and
1003–07: Triton son of Amphitrite, Phocus son of Psamathe and Achilles son of
Thetis. For children as ἀγάλματα of parents or families see LSJ 'ἄγαλμα' 1,
Wilamowitz on E. *HF* 49, Fraenkel on A. *Ag.* 208. Kyriakou notes that no such
pair of grandsons of Nereus is known from myth, so 'this reference must count as
an otherwise unattested piece of Greek lore'; but the pious man is only speculat-
ing. Barrett (2007, 361) and Parker maintain implausibly that he is not necessarily
referring to relatives of Nereus.

275–78. bold in irreverence (ἀνομίᾳ): ἀνομία is rejection of accepted beliefs
and practices (*nomoi*), as e.g. *Ba.* 387, 995, 997. Some commentators think this is
ironic since the 'foolish' man is right in denying that Orestes and Pylades are divine, but Euripides' humour is more even-handed than that. The man is also wrong
in assuming that they are shipwrecked and cowering in fear and has no idea that
they are noble youths on a divinely sponsored mission. The Herdsman will get
nearer the truth (304, 314, 328f.) in light of what happens next.

280. our country's customary victims: ἐπιχώρια is 'local', the kind that
Taurians regularly seek out.

281–300. The description of Orestes' madness and vision of the Erinyes is a
poetic construct, not a clinical account, though Euripides does introduce 'realistic'
elements of clinical observation such as his trembling, bellowing and frothing at
the mouth (»» Parker 116f.). The descriptions here and in Aeschylus's *Choephori*
(1048–62) and Euripides' *Electra* (1342–46) and *Orestes* (253–76), and of
Heracles' madness in *Heracles* (867–71, 931–1001), have many features in
common (see the notes below). Orestes' paranoid attack on the cattle recalls
Ajax's attack on the livestock (mistaking them for the Greek leaders) in
Sophocles' *Ajax* (*Aj.* 51–65, 296–300). The Erinyes were underworld demons
embodying retribution, said in Hesiod's *Theogony* (185) to have been born from
the severed genitals of Ouranos/Sky (»» Burkert 1985, index 'Erinyes, Erinys';
Gantz 13–15; *BNP* 'Erinys'; *LIMC* III, 'Erinys'). Like the madness-scene in
Orestes, this narrative allows them to be understood either as real or as the
product of Orestes' guilt-racked imagination. They are real enough in Orestes'

COMMENTARY   181

later account of their pursuit and his trial at Athens (939–44, 961–71), but that
does not cancel the suggestion of their imaginariness here.

282–84. and tossed his head (κάρα...διετίναξ(ε)): like the maddened
Heracles in *HF* 867 (τινάσσει κρᾶτα). **his hands shaking: ὠλένας τρέμων
ἄκρας,** 'trembling in extreme (i.e. the ends of his) arms'. **and cried out like a
hunter: βοᾷ** is a historic present tense (2 n.) highlighting crucial points in the
narrative here and at 298 **παίει,** 307 **πίπτει.** [The comparison has been questioned
since Orestes is actually the prey (or imagines he is) rather than the hunter; hence
the conjectures recorded by Diggle who himself obelizes **κυναγὸς ὥς** (see his
apparatus with Kyriakou's discussion). But the Herdsman says only that Orestes
sounded like a hunter alerting his fellow-hunters to the prey, and as Parker says,
that is not implausible.]

285–91. Orestes in his madness sees three Erinyes as he does in *Or.* 408 (see
Willink there). Two are described in lines 285–87, a third in 288–91.

285–87. this she-dragon (δράκαιναν): the Erinyes are dragon-like in A. *Eum.*
128 (δεινῆς δρακαίνης μένος 'the terrible she-dragon's strength'), E. *Or.* 256 (αἱμ-
ατωποὺς καὶ δρακοντώδεις κόρας 'blood-eyed dragon-like females'). **brandishing terrible snakes: δειναῖς ἐχίδναις...ἐστομωμένη,** 'sharpened with terrible
snakes'; the Erinys presumably brandishes the snakes as weapons against Orestes.
Erinyes were often pictured with snakes entwined in their hair and around their
arms (cf. Garvie on A. *Cho.* 1049f.). [Most editors interpret **ἐστομωμένη** as
'sharpened': cf. LSJ 'στομόω' III–IV with 'στόμα' III.1, 'στόμωμα' II; »»
Collard–Cropp–Lee 1995, 77 on *Cretans* F 472e.44 (the only other known use of
the simple verb by Euripides). Other options fit less well with **against me** (e.g.
'fringed', Kovacs; 'mouthed', i.e. with gaping snakes for hair, Paley, cf. Parker).]

288. breathing flame...†*from her garments* (ἐκ χιτώνων):†: an unsolved
problem. Dark garments are ascribed to the Erinyes in A. *Cho.* 1049 (φαιοχίτωνες
'dark-garmented) and *Eum.* 370f. (μελανείμοσιν ὀρχησμοῖς 'with black-robed
dancing'). Some words elaborating the description of this third Erinys may have
dropped out between **χιτώνων** and **πῦρ** (Wecklein) or between **ἐκ** and **χιτώνων.**
[Jackson's ἡ 'κ γειτόνων δὲ (1955, 146–48) is unconvincing though printed by
Diggle (cf. Diggle 1981, 79) and Kovacs. ἐκ γειτόνων 'from the neighbours' is
idiomatic for 'next door', 'in the vicinity' (cf. Austin on Menand. *Aspis* 122) and
not appropriate here.]

289–90. beats (ἐρέσσει, 'rows') **the air with her wings:** the Erinyes were
often depicted as winged. **my mother, a rocky mass:** this Erinys, it seems,
hovers threateningly and holds a stone image of Clytemnestra, something like the
Gorgon's head used by Perseus to turn his enemies to stone, a proverbial source of
horror (»» Cropp on *El.* 855–57), or the boulder which eternally threatens to fall
on Tantalus (386–91 n.: »» O'Brien 1988b, 43f. on its relevance here). I do not
know of any depiction of an Erinys armed in this way. [Heimsoeth's ὄγκον is the
likeliest correction of L's ὄχθον which hardly makes sense ('hill', 'outcrop',

182   COMMENTARY

'tomb-mound'?). Diggle printed Bothe's ἄχθος, 'weight' (cf. [A.] *PV* 350 ἄχθος οὐκ εὐάγκαλον, Atlas's 'burden not easy on the arms').]

291–92. to our vision there were no such figures: only Orestes can see the Erinyes, but their imaginariness is not played on here as it is in *Orestes* (cf. 281–300 n.). **figures: μορφῆς σχήματ(α)** are 'form-shapes' as in *Ion* 992; cf. *Pho* 162 μορφῆς τύπωμα 'form-print', 'silhouette'.

292. [†ἠλλάσσετο†: middle ἀλλάσσομαι should mean 'change' (e.g. 'change our path', *El.* 103) or 'give/take something in exchange'. Neither sense fits comfortably here and renderings such as 'mistook', 'misinterpreted' or 'confused' are unjustified. Kyriakou and Parker reject 'was answered by' (Cropp 2000).]

[294]. *sounds that they say etc.*: a lame interpolation explaining to inattentive readers that Orestes must have thought that the lowing and yelping of the herdsmen's cows and dogs were coming from the Erinyes. This disrupts Euripides' portrayal of the Herdsman, who in fact knows nothing about Orestes and does not understand what is going on (later he misinterprets the youths' apparent invulnerability, 328f.). The Erinyes were often imaged as hunting-dogs (e.g. A. *Cho.* 924, 1054, *Eum.* 131f. etc., E. *El.* 1342, *Or.* 260; »» Sansone 1988 on possible Mycenean examples), but never as cows, so the interpolator may have written ἃ φᾶσ' (Brodeau's conjecture) referring only to the dogs' barking (**κυνῶν ὑλάγματα**).

[Line 299 is a related interpolation (see note there and West 1981, 62). De Jong 1991, 164f. explains both lines as an example of the role of the messenger as 'exegetical' medium: 'making use of the information provided by the stranger's speech…[the Messenger] explains it in terms of the Erinyes delusion…'. But Orestes has not identified the Erinyes and the Taurian herdsman is in no position to do so; he can only say that he and his party could see **no such figures**. The lines are nevertheless retained by most editors, some with adjustments to 'improve' the sense of 294. Parker prefers to obelize 294 since 'interpolators do not write complete nonsense', but that is not what this is.]

295–96. Now we had drawn together etc.: καθήμεθα is the unaugmented imperfect, **were sitting**. In 1342f. Thoas's men 'sat on in silence' (καθήμεθα σιγῇ) after sitting for a long time. Here the tense is 'immediative', describing the men's activity (or lack of it) directly after drawing together (»» *CGCG* §33.52, Rijksbaron 17f.); similarly 302 ἐξωπλίζετο, 309 εἶχεν πόνον, 324 ἐξεπίμπλαμεν, 1337 κατῇδε. Why they sat down remains unclear because of the textual uncertainty in 295. **καθήμεθα** could mean 'stayed put' as in *Andr.* 670, F 709, *Pho.*752, Soph. F 479.3, but in those cases the looser sense is obvious.

[ὡς †θανούμενοι†: L's reading hardly makes sense (there is no reason why the herdsmen should expect to die, nor why that should cause them to sit down) but is not easily corrected (its alternative θαμβούμενοι, 'as being amazed', is an implausible attempt to do so). Wilamowitz's θανουμένου (Diggle, Kovacs, Cropp 2000) gives 'as with him (i.e. expecting him) to die', a genitive absolute with unexpressed subject (KG 2.81, *CGCG* §52.32 n. 1), but while the herdsmen might

COMMENTARY 183

think Orestes' seizures are life-threatening (cf. 285–91), why should this cause them to draw together and sit in silence? Parker prints Heimsoeth's θεώμενοι, 'watching': 'they sit down together in silence, because they think of themselves as spectators' – an unlikely way of getting a good view in this situation.]

296–98. But he unsheathed his sword etc.: Orestes sees the cattle as Erinyes, as Ajax thinks the sheep he slaughters are the Greek leaders (S. *Aj.* 91–100, 295– 300) and as Heracles kills his own sons thinking they are Eurystheus's (*HF* 967– 1000). In *Orestes* 264–76 Orestes first sees Electra as an Erinys and then calls for a bow with which to shoot down the winged Erinyes who he thinks are attacking him.   **leapt like a lion etc.**: a frequent simile for Homeric warriors applied incongruously to the rampaging Orestes; in *Iliad* 15.630–37 Hector is like a lion attacking a herd of cows guarded by an inexperienced herdsman, and in *Il.* 20.164–75 Achilles rouses himself like a wounded lion hunted by a band of rustics (»» Kyriakou on 296b–99, Jiménez Justicia 2017). The simile is already recalled humorously in *Odyssey* 6.130–38 where the naked Odysseus advances like a ravening lion towards Nausicaa and her maids.   **thrusting at flanks and ribs**: ἐς applies 'in common' to both λαγόνας and πλευράς, a poetic asymmetry as in 886f., *El.* 163, *Hec.* 144: »» KG 1.550, Breitenbach 211f., Wilamowitz on *HF* 237 (*sic*, for 238).

[**299**]. Another explanatory interpolation like line 294, disrupting the sequence from 298 to 300. Diggle, Kovacs and Parker all keep the verse. According to Parker, 'Attic dramatists...are very little inhibited by consideration of what a character might, or might not, say in real life. Euripides' over-riding concern here is likely to have been that the audience should understand the reason why Orestes behaves as he does'. But the reason is obvious without this.

300. sea-swell: πέλαγος...ἁλός and similar pleonasms are derived from epic, e.g. *Odyssey* 5.335 (»» Diggle 1981, 79f.).   **bloomed with a blood-red foam**: αἱματηρὸν...ἐξανθεῖν, 'bloomed/foamed out blood-red'. ἄνθος is the sea's foam at Alcman fr. 26.3 *PMGF*, Hdt. 2.12.1 etc. A. *Ag.* 659 exploits the metaphor, the sea 'blooming' with the drowned corpses of the returning Greek army (»» Borthwick 1976, 5–7).

301–35. The description of the battle has both epic and mock-epic elements as the heroic youths are contrasted with the inferior herdsmen in terms of numbers, weapons, fighting techniques and spirit. Similar elements are found in the battle at the shore (1354–74) and at varying levels of seriousness in the report speeches of *Andromache* (1118–55, Neoptolemus against the Delphians), *Captive Melanippe* (F 495, Aeolus and Boeotus against the huntsmen) and *Helen* (1600–11, Greeks against Egyptians). They are transformed in the description of the rampaging Maenads of *Bacchae* 731–64, and parodied in the Phrygian's description of the fight between Orestes and Pylades and the Phrygian slaves, *Orestes* 1474–88b.

303. conchs: i.e. shells of the purple-bearing murex (260–64 n.). After the suggestion of heroic combat (**every one was arming himself**) the herdsmen's

184   COMMENTARY

weapons turn out to be rocks (310, 318f. etc.: »» Hall 1989b, 122; cf. West 1992, 121 on shell-horns in Greek literature and art).

307. the stranger fell: like Heracles felled by Athena's rock in *HF* 1004–7 or Orestes debilitated in *Or.* 227f., 277. **the assault of madness:** the basic sense of πίτυλος (etymology unknown) seems to be 'oar-stroke' (cf. 1050, 1346, *Tro.* 1123, *Hyps.* F 752g.11, Aristophanes F 86 *PCG*), but Euripides uses the word for a variety of 'strokes' or attacks both literal and metaphorical (madness *HF* 1187, fear *HF* 816, weeping *Hipp.* 1464): »» Beekes 'πίτυλος'; Silk 1983, 325f. Barrett on *Hipp.* 1464 reviews a range of usages (but with unneeded emphasis on *repeated* strokes, cf. Parker here and on *Alc.* 796–98).

308. dripping foam: an epileptic's symptom as for the maddened Heracles in *HF* 934 and Orestes in *Or.* 219f. where Electra wipes off the foam as Pylades does here.

310. pelting and pounding: βάλλων ἀράσσων also describes Neoptolemus's attackers (*Andr.* 1154) and the blinded Polymestor pursuing his tormentors (*Hec.* 1175).

312. shielded him with his well-woven cloak: the phrasing recalls *Iliad* 5.315 where Aphrodite folded her arms about her son Aeneas and 'put in front of him as a covering the fold of her shining robe' (πρόσθε δέ οἱ πέπλοιο φαεινοῦ πτύγμ᾽ ἐκάλυψεν). πέπλων...εὐπήνους ὑφάς ('clothing's well-threaded weavings') recurs in 1465; cf. 814 ὑφήνασ(α)...ἐν εὐπήνοις ὑφαῖς. Plural πέπλοι for 'clothing' is common in Euripides, its sense imprecise (»» Dodds on *Ba.* 821f.).

313. watching out for the wounds etc.: Pylades acts as a true *philos*, protecting his comrade with a stoical disregard for his own safety.

316. a wave of foes: cf. *Supp.* 474f., *Pho.* 859f. κλύδων δορός ('a wave of spearmen'), *Ion* 60 πολέμιος κλύδων ('a wave of conflict').

[317]. and the calamity etc.: a pedestrian explanation of 316, deleted by Bothe (cf. West 1981, 77 n. 7, Kovacs), retained by most editors.

320. at that point: δή indicates a critical moment in the narrative like e.g. *IA* 97 (οὗ δὴ: »» Denniston 219f.), *Captive Melanippe* F 495.5.

321–22. let us make sure we die in the noblest way: a commonplace, e.g. *Iliad* 22.304f. (Hector), E. *Hec.* 346–48 (Polyxena), *IA* 1375f. (Iphigenia), *Cyc.* 201 (Odysseus), Ar. *Knights* 80f. (a slave!). Orestes exhorts Electra similarly after their condemnation by the people of Argos, *Or.* 1060f.

323. two brandished swords: δίπαλτα...ξίφη, 'double-brandished swords', cf. 124–25 n.

324. we fled: at *Captive Melanippe* F 495.32–37 the unheroic attackers flee from the heroes Aeolus and Boeotus into bushes, trees and ravines. **and crowded into the rocky gullies:** ἐξεπίμπλαμεν, 'we were filling', is another 'immediative' imperfect tense (295–96 n.). More follow in 325–29 describing the continuing action.

COMMENTARY

185

325–27. when any fled (εἰ φύγοι τις)…when they repelled (εἰ δὲ… ὠσαίατο): εἰ with Optative here is equivalent to 'whenever' (Goodwin §462f., *CGCG* §49.13 and 16, Rijksbaron 72f.). ὠσαίατο has the Ionic/Epic 3rd plural middle ending (Smyth §465f), suiting both metre and the speech's epic style. **those** ('that (group)')…**just then retreating:** ὑπεῖκον is a present participle with imperfect meaning. The plural verb ἤρασσον with collective singular subject (τὸ ὑπεῖκον) is not unusual (*CGCG* §27.6).

328–29. Yet here was a wonder: once again the human witness's insight into divine influence is limited (cf. 275–78 n., 291–93). The Herdsman thinks the youths were miraculously protected by Artemis so as to be unblemished sacrificial victims. They are indeed divinely protected, but for a different reason. In 1414–19 the Messenger similarly misinterprets Poseidon's activity during the escape. In *Captive Melanippe* F 495.27 a messenger reports the miraculous protection of Melanippe's sons from enemy weapons but does not try to identify the divine agent (presumably their father Poseidon, who probably explained this at the end of the play). Euripides often uses the restricted knowledge of his 'messengers' effectively (»» de Jong 1991, 14–19).

330–33. we subdued them etc.: 'we subdue them not by valour, but surrounding them in a circle we knocked etc.' χειρούμεθα is a historic present tense (2 n.) bringing us to the next stage of the narrative (*CGCG* §33.55; Rijksbaron 24f.).

333–35. Then we brought them to the ruler etc.: κομίζομεν is likewise a historic present. **and sent them:** ἔπεμπε imperfect as the sending is still in effect (the prisoners and their escort are on their way: *CGCG* §33.51, Rijksbaron 18f.). **for consecration and slaughter:** 'to lustrations (54 n.) and blood-bowls (26– 27 n.)'; the Herdsman returns to his opening announcement (244f.).

336–39. Pray, young lady etc.: report speeches usually end with a moralising or evaluative comment (e.g. *Hec.* 580–82, *Supp.* 726–30, *Captive Melanippe* F 495.40–43). The Herdsman means that these are just the kind of victims (noble young Greek men) that Iphigenia should pray for so as to get her revenge on Hellas, just as Hippolytus asserting his own virtue says to Theseus, 'Pray to get legitimate sons like this (illegitimate) one', *Hipp.* 1455. For the instruction εὔχου, **Pray** see also e.g. *El.* 563–65, *Ion* 423. ὦ νεᾶνι, **young lady:** the word νεᾶνις is distinctly poetic and found 29 times in Euripides including *IT* 619 (ὦ νεᾶνι), 660 and 1313 for Iphigenia. She must be around thirty years old (373–75 n.), but this helps to make her a sympathetic character. Parker notes that she will have been masked accordingly. **strangers like these for victims:** τοιάδ(ε)…ξένων σφάγια, 'such victims (consisting) of strangers'. **If you kill etc.** explains the outcome if the prayer is granted, as often in prayers, e.g. *Odyssey* 7.332f. ἀναλίσκης is a strong word implying total destruction (»» LSJ 'ἀναλίσκω' II, Kyriakou; also A. *Sept.* 815, E. *HF* 1423). **your slaughter at Aulis:** like Iphigenia herself (8 n.). the Herdsman speaks of her sacrifice as a virtual killing. His comments prepare

186 COMMENTARY

for her revelation that she will harden her heart towards the captives, and also for the fooling of Thoas and the Taurians later. They cannot imagine that she will want to spare her Greek captives or escape herself (cf. 1181–87), but in fact her only expression of resentment against Greeks in general for their part in her sacrifice comes as she hardens heart in this scene. There is also a dramatic irony: she should indeed be welcoming the arrival of these captives, but as rescuers not victims. [In line 336 Mekler's imperfect ηὔχου, 'you were praying' would make this the only passage suggesting that Iphigenia has previously been eager to kill Greeks (contrast especially 344–47), but even if she had been the Herdsman would hardly be aware of the content of her prayers. »» Cropp 1997, 27–29; Parker. Kyriakou offers a tortuous rationale for preferring ηὔχου.]

340–41. It's amazing etc.: 'You have told amazing things of the one who went mad, whoever has come etc.' [τὸν μανένθ' is a correction of L's τὸν φανένθ', 'the one who has appeared'. With φανένθ' the comment might possibly hint at Orestes' arrival as a rescuer for Iphigenia (Cropp 1997, 29f.), but his madness is the more obvious topic and the singular participle puts the focus on him alone whereas both he and Pylades have 'appeared'. The same error is seen in L's text of the hypothesis.]

342–43. Very well etc.: this covers the Herdsman's exit, leaving Iphigenia alone with the Chorus. **bring the strangers with you:** there is no further trace of the Herdsman, although he might possibly return with the captives at 456, now played by an extra while the actor who has played his part returns as either Pylades or Orestes (Introduction, p. 34). **we will attend:** presumably Iphigenia and the Chorus rather than a dignified 'I'. **our holy duties:** τὰ ὅσια are 'the things required by divine law' which Iphigenia manages as priestess (»» 130–32 n., Chadwick 1996, 225f.).

344–91. Iphigenia's speech is virtually a soliloquy in the presence of the Chorus, signalled by the opening address to her heart (344) and expressing her confused feelings on being confronted with Greek captives now that she 'knows' Orestes is dead. Although she briefly turns to the now absent captives (348–50), to the dead Orestes (379–80), and to the Chorus (351–53), this does not alter the essentially inward character of the whole speech. It is rhetorically articulated in three parts: reactions to the opportunity to avenge her suffering at Aulis as the Herdsman has suggested (344–60, cf. 336–39), recollections of her experience there and thoughts of her lost family, especially Orestes and their father's disastrous ambitions (361–79), and reflection on Artemis's responsibility for the sacrifice and the conflict between the goddess's demands for purity and her demands for human blood (380–91). Is Artemis an unworthy daughter of Zeus and Leto, or not their daughter at all? Or are high moral standards not to be expected from the gods? Or does Artemis not really require human sacrifices? Iphigenia insists that no deity can be bad, so the demand for human sacrifices must come not from the goddess but from misguided humans, and stories which justify it by telling of gods

COMMENTARY   187

enjoying human flesh are not to be believed (380–91 n.). Thus the vengefulness
she has espoused at the beginning of her speech is undermined by the memories of
own suffering, her grief for Orestes, and her natural inclination to sympathy, and
the tone is set for her dealings with the prisoners in the following scenes.

344–50. O my long-suffering heart: self-addresses of this kind originate in
epic (e.g. *Odyssey* 20.13–21) and were often used by Euripides, e.g. *Alc.* 837,
Or. 466, *Cresphontes* F 448a.85; parodied in Ar. *Ach.* 485.

[349]. Probably another explanatory interpolation like lines 294 and 299,
deleted or at least suspected by all recent editors.

350. whoever you are etc.: not imagining that one of them might be her own
brother. The irony will be exploited repeatedly in the scenes leading to the recognition (456–826 n.).

352–53. seeing others more unfortunate (τοῖσι δυστυχεστέροις): people
suffering misfortunes might be expected to sympathize with others whose misfortunes are greater than their own, but in fact our own misfortunes make us indiffer-
ent to theirs.[14] [This is Wecklein's correction of L's τοῖσιν εὐτυχεστέροις, 'others
more fortunate'. One might question why unfortunate people should lack sympathy only for those more unfortunate than themselves, but Iphigenia is thinking
about the captives before her, who are indeed more unfortunate than she is.
Kirchhoff (following Reiske) wrote τοῖσιν εὐτυχεστέροις αὐτοῖς κακῶς πράξασιν
('those more fortunate who (now) have fared badly themselves'), but Iphigenia
knows nothing about the captives' previous fortunes. F. W. Schmidt's deletion of
351–53, accepted by Diggle, Kovacs and on balance Kyriakou, seems extreme
although the thought flows well enough from 350 ('whoever you are who have
come here') to 354ff. ('It should have been Helen and Menelaus'). The papyrus's
πράσσοντες, faring is better than L's πράξαντες, 'having fared'; her misery is
longstanding and is now increased by the loss of her brother.]

354–58. But to this day etc.: Iphigenia thinks of Helen and Menelaus as
proper victims of her revenge since it was because of them that the Trojan war
was fought and she herself was sacrificed (cf. 13f.). Similarly Hecuba argues that
Helen, not Polyxena, should be sacrificed to the dead Achilles (*Hec.* 265–70).
Vilification of Helen (ψόγος Ἑλένης) is a commonplace in poetry about the
Trojan War and its aftermath (cf. Cropp on *El.* 213f. and especially the choral
wishes for her death in *Hec.* 944–51, *Tro.* 1100–17 and below, 439–46). The topic
is paradoxically treated in the prologue scene of *Helen* where Teucer meets the
real (innocent) Helen. In Ptolemy Chennos's eccentric *New History* (1st C AD,
summarized in Photius, *Bibl.* 190) Helen and Menelaus were indeed brought to
Iphigenia and sacrificed by her.

---

[14] 'There was not one of them but would have passed a blind man begging in the
street, not one that felt moved to pity by a tale of misfortune, not one who did not
see in death the solution of the all-absorbing problem of misery which left them
cold to the most terrible anguish in others.' Balzac, *Père Goriot* (tr. E. Marriage).

188 COMMENTARY

354–55. no wind…no vessel: the sequence οὔτε ('neither')…οὐ ('not') heightens the emotional effect; similarly 373f. (as emended), *Med.* 1348f., *Or.* 41 (»» Denniston 510f.).

357. so I could make them pay: ἀντετιμωρησάμην is aorist indicative as normally for the unfulfilled consequence of a hypothetical event (»» KG 2.388f., Goodwin §333, cf. Rijksbaron 62 n. 4).

358. setting the Aulis here against that Aulis: matching or balancing the sacrifice of Helen against her own sacrifice (LSJ 'ἀντιτίθημι' I.1.b rather than II).

359–60. like a heifer: Iphigenia is often imaged as a heifer or a young goat in tragic references to her sacrifice, e.g. A. *Ag.* 232 (see 26–27 n.), E. *IA* 1083; also Heracles' daughter in *Hcld.* 489, Polyxena in *Hec.* 206, 526. An animal sacrifice usually initiated the wedding process, and here the imageries of wedding ceremony and sacrifice are merged as throughout *IA* (433, 718–21 etc.): cf. Oakley–Sinos 1993, 11, Seaford 1987, 108–10, Rehm 1995. Mossman 1995, 147–51 discusses the varied connotations of such animal imagery in different contexts. A nubile heifer is, like Iphigenia herself, an apt victim for Artemis (Osborne 2016, 242f.). **manhandled me for slaughter:** 'manhandling me were slaughtering me'. The men controlled Iphigenia's struggles as they lifted her over the altar, cf. 26–27 n. **the sacrificer was the father who begot me:** A. *Ag.* 224f. ἔτλα δ' οὖν θυτὴρ γενέσθαι θυγατρός, 'and so he dared to become his daughter's sacrificer'; E. *IA* 1177f. (Clytemnestra), 'The father who begot you (ὁ φυτεύσας πατήρ) has destroyed you, my daughter, no other, with no other hand'.

362. how many times did I cast my hands: ὅσας…χεῖρας ἐξηκόντισα, 'how many hands did I cast'. In Callimachus, *Hymn.* 3.26–28 Artemis 'stretched many hands' (πολλὰς…ἐτανύσσατο χεῖρας) towards Zeus's cheek. The verb (ἐξ)ακοντίζω applies to javelin-throwing and is used by Euripides also for martial-arts moves (1369f.), the flashing limbs of maenads (*Ba.* 665), prayers penetrating the earth (*Or.* 1241), the sun's rays (*Ion* 1155).

[363]. and at the knees etc: probably an interpolation adding pathos but distorting the picture of Iphigenia vainly reaching out to touch her father's cheek in supplication. She might cast a hand towards his cheek while clinging to his knees, but that is not quite what the Greek says. [Diggle retains the verse, Kovacs deletes it. Parker retains it but rejects ἐξαρτωμένη as perhaps 'an early emendator's… replacement for some word, or words, which had been lost, or become illegible'.]

364–65. you are making me the bride etc.: 'I am being wedded an ugly wedding by you'.

366–68. the women of Argos are singing etc.: wedding celebrations typically included songs and aulos-music for dancing (e.g. *IA* 437–39) at the home of bride or groom (Oakley–Sinos 1993, 22–30). **are singing wedding songs for me:** 'are hymning me with hymenaeals', another emotive word-resonance. **pipe music fills our palace:** αὐλεῖται…πᾶν μέλαθρον, 'the whole hall is being piped', a passive construction like *Hel.* 1433–34 'the whole land must be shouted (βοᾶσθαι)

COMMENTARY 189

with hymnodies of blessing', *El.* 691 'the whole house will be ululated (ὀλολύξ-εται)', cf. *Hcld.* 401, *Ion* 463, S. *OT* 1092.

369. Achilles, then, was Hades: her bridegroom was not after all the famous hero but the god of the Underworld. 'Marriage with Hades' is a common figure for the premature deaths of girls whose lives should have been fulfilled in marriage, e.g. Iphigenia herself in *IA* 461 ('Hades will wed her'), 946 (Achilles 'born not from Peleus but from an avenging spirit'); cf. Seaford 1987, 106f. In *Iliad* 16.33–35 Patroclus stresses Achilles' ruthlessness by calling him the son of sea and rocks, not Peleus and Thetis.

370. in a carriage: ἐν ἁρμάτων...ὄχοις, 'in a conveyance (consisting) of a carriage', a pleonasm typical of high poetry, e.g. 410, 742, 858f., 1345; »» Breitenbach 197f. This one appears also at *Hipp.* 1166, *Supp.* 662, *Pho.* 1190 and here is compounded by grandiose plural forms. For the carriage in weddings see 214–17 n.

372–75. Hiding my face behind a delicate veil etc.: 'keeping my face through delicate veilings'. A bride's face would be veiled from her leaving her family's house to her unveiling before the groom (»» Oakley–Sinos 1993, Index 'veil' with illustrations; Reeder 1995, 127; Llewellyn-Jones 2003, 219–26). Iphigenia speaks emotively as if she was already dressed for the wedding when she left Argos. The *aidôs* which prevented her from kissing her brother and sister **(shame forbade me)** is the inhibition (fear, embarrassment, uncertainty) of a bride leaving her sheltered virginal life for a public wedding, sexual initiation, and the control of an unknown husband in an alien home.[15] For the association of veiling with *aidôs* see Cairns 1996, 153–56; Llewellyn-Jones 155–80.

373–75. I had not lifted my brother...in my arms: Orestes was still a babe in arms (230–35 n.). **not shared a kiss:** emotional phrasing (354–55 n.).

378–79. what a fine and enviable heritage etc.: 'from what fine things and enviable things of your father's are you gone'. She thinks of Orestes as heir of a great and successful king (cf. 543, 850 n.), not yet knowing about the family's recent history and overlooking its murky past and her own part in it (186–213).

380–91. From bitter reflection on her father's role in her suffering Iphigenia moves to bitter reflection on Artemis's demand for her sacrifice, and then to the thought that this may not have been the goddess's wish: 'I deplore the goddess's hypocritical acceptance of human sacrifices. Such ignorance is hardly possible in a daughter of Zeus and Leto – nor can I believe the story of Tantalus' feast with its implication that gods could relish human flesh. The Taurians must be projecting their own murderousness onto the goddess, for I cannot ascribe badness to any divinity.' The idea that stories attributing unworthy qualities and actions to

---

[15] None of this suggests that 'she covered herself in her bridal veil as soon as she heard news of her forthcoming marriage' and 'was so excited...at the prospect of her wedding that she refused to lift her veil even to kiss farewell to her baby brother or little sister before she rushed off to Aulis' (Llewellyn-Jones 224).

190 COMMENTARY

the gods should be rejected as mere human inventions (poets' fictions, myths etc.) justifying human weaknesses or crimes appears in Xenophanes (c. 570–c. 478 BC) B1.21–24 and B 11–16 DK. Socrates and Plato promoted it at Athens: cf. Pl. *Euthyphro* 5e–6 (which suggests it was not widely accepted in 399 BC), *Republic* 377f., *Laws* 941b. Aristophanes mocks the disreputable use of such stories in *Clouds* 901–6, 1079–82, unfairly accusing Socrates of teaching it. Euripides' characters express the idea also in *Heracles* 1340–46 (Heracles rejects myths of adultery and conflict amongst the gods) and *Trojan Women* 969–82 (Hecuba rejects the idea of goddesses participating in a beauty contest). Elsewhere his characters criticize unworthy actions of gods (*Hipp.* 120, *Andr.* 1161–65, *HF* 339–47, 1303–10, *Ion* 436–51, *Ba.* 1348; cf. *Bellerophon* F 286b.7) or appeal to them in a way which invites criticism (*Hipp.* 451–58). To reject some myths is not to reject all myths or conventional religion; indeed, the inevitable falsity of some myths is already recognized in Hesiod's *Theogony* (26–28, cf. Solon fr. 29 *IEG*). In raising these issues in his plays Euripides reflects a moralistic tendency in contemporary thinking about the gods and does so with serious though undogmatic intent. The characters who raise them, whether unjustly suffering heroes such as Heracles or gods' protégés such as Ion, Iphigenia or Theonoe, invite sympathy for the 'higher' conception of divinity on which they insist, and which in the case of Iphigenia is validated by the development and outcome of the play. In its immediate context Iphigenia's speculation illustrates how she must cope with a predicament she does not fully understand and suggests that acceptance rather than resentment will sway her dealings with Orestes. By the end of her speech she has at least partially excused both her father and the goddess. Artemis, it seems, shares Iphigenia's need for redemption – and will find it in the purer environment of Attica (1012–15, 1086–88, 1230–33). »» R. Parker 2005, 143–47; Mastronarde 2010, 161–74; Rutherford 2012, 374–82.

381–83. bloodshed...childbirth...corpse: three powerful sources of pollution requiring separation of the polluted person from normal religious processes and contact with the divine (itself threatened by pollution) until ritual purification was achieved: cf. e.g. *Alc.* 22f., *Hipp.* 1437–39 (death), *El.* 652–54, 1124–26 (childbirth), *Cretans* F 472.16–18 (both). Plutarch, *Mor.* 170b criticizes superstitions about Artemis's horror of pollution and cites anonymous verses illustrating it: 'If you're hurrying from a hanging, if you've been in touch with childbirth, if you've come from a corpse laid out...'. Iphigenia will exploit the superstition in tricking the Taurians (1035–41, 1163–1200). »» Burkert 1985, 75–84; R. Parker 1983, chs 2 and 4.

385–86. In no way could...Leto have given birth to such great ignorance: *amathia* 'unlearnedness' and its opposite *sophia* 'wisdom' often have a moral dimension. They recur in discussions of possibly unworthy divine behaviour, e.g.

COMMENTARY 191

Tro. 972, 981f., *Hipp.* 120, *Andr.* 1165, *HF* 347; cf. 570–71 n. [ἂν ἔτεκεν is a simple metrical correction of L's ἔτεκεν ἄν.][16]

386–91. I for my part do not believe etc.: Tantalus was one of the great sinners of Greek myth, and Iphigenia's great-great-grandfather (which adds relevance to her rejection of his story). Stories of both his crime and his punishment vary (»» Gantz 531–36) but always have to do with violations of the gods' favour and hospitality. The *Odyssey* (11.582–92) places him in the Underworld, eternally and fittingly tantalized by food and drink which he cannot reach. Some other archaic sources mention a proverbial 'rock of Tantalus' eternally threatening to fall on him and apparently designed to stop him enjoying divine pleasures which he had improperly gained or abused (cf. Eur. *Orestes* 4–10, 982–86; O'Brien 1988b). The explanation that he returned the hospitality of the gods by serving them the flesh of his son Pelops at a banquet, so that Demeter ate some of the flesh and the gods had to reconstitute Pelops, is spelled out by late sources (Schol. Pind. *Ol.* 1.40, Hyginus, *Fab.* 83) but was current earlier. Pindar in *Olympian* 1.36–63 rejects it as a malicious neighbours' rumour which arose when Pelops was taken to Olympus by a love-struck Poseidon ('Impossible for me to say that any of the gods is greedy-gutted'. »» Gerber 1982, xi–xiii, 53–104; Hubbard 1987; Slater 1989; Nagy 1990, 116–35). Is Iphigenia saying that the feast never occurred, or that it occurred but Tantalus did not serve Pelops' flesh, or that he served Pelops' flesh but the gods did not enjoy eating it? Sansone 1975, 288f. argues for the third possibility, but the second is more naturally inferred and echoes Pindar (cf. O'Brien 1988a, 105 n. 19). In any case, Iphigenia's point is that this story is no precedent for human sacrifices because it is probably not true. Again this is not a categorical denial. On the possible nuances of such expressions of disbelief about mythical stories see especially Stinton 1976.

After her speech Iphigenia probably remains on stage during the following choral ode. Some editors assume that she exits into the temple and re-enters as the prisoners arrive in 456–66, but there is no indication of this in the text (in 343, **we will attend to our holy duties**, 'we' may refer either to Iphigenia herself or to Iphigenia and the Chorus, rather than to Iphigenia and servants in the temple).

392–455. First Stasimon: reflections on the strangers' arrival

Strophe 1: The Chorus addresses the waters of the Bosporus through which the new arrivals have sailed. What kind of men can they be to have braved the voyage

---

[16] With L's order the three syllables of ἔτεκεν occupy the third foot of the verse. This is paralleled in tragedy only in *IA* 630 and S. *El.* 1361 (both πατέρα): »» Cropp–Fick 1985, 49, Type 6.3. Parker prefers Porson's ἔτικτεν ('It's not possible that Leto gave birth') since 'the past potential...does not combine well with οὐκ ἔστιν ὅπως..., and I find no parallel quoted'. But Iphigenia is questioning the proposition, not categorically denying it. For parallels see Isocrates 12.250, 15.206, [Pl.] Alcibiades I.106d7–9.

192   COMMENTARY

and sought out the barbarous Taurians? *Antistrophe 1:* Perhaps merchants sailing for profit, a common but misguided motive. *Strophe 2:* How hard their journey must have been as they voyaged into this remoteness. *Antistrophe 2:* And how slim the Chorus's hopes of seeing Helen punished, or of being rescued and restored to the homes where they belong.

The song, full of motion and impressionistic geographical detail, is neatly constructed. Each strophe is a movement in itself, intricately phrased; all but the third are clearly subdivided into two parts. The opening rhetorical device of an address to the Bosporus sustains the mood of question and comment throughout. Themes from the play's first segment are restated as it reaches its close: the Taurians' foreignness to their Hellenic visitors, the enormity of their human sacrifices, the difficulty of Orestes' task, the women's suffering in exile and their need for restoration to a happiness whose value their suffering has taught them to recognize. This theme of nostalgia and hoped-for restoration is fundamental to the play as a whole. Kannicht 1956 studies the ode's themes and argument in detail.

The metre is largely aeolo-choriambic (almost entirely so in the second pair), with cola of varying length built around a choriambic nucleus (– ⏑ ⏑ – : »» Dale 1968, 131–56, West 1982, 30, 115–20, Parker xcii–xciv). Exceptions are lines 395–410, 399–414 and 425–442 (lyric iambic trimeters), 400–415 and 404–419 (iambic–spondaic) and 402–417 ('archilochean' combining double-short and single-short lengths: ⏑ – ⏑ ⏑ – ⏑ ⏑ – × | – ⏑ – ⏑ – –). Each strophe and antistrophe closes with a pherecratean (– – – ⏑ ⏑ – –), a common clausular rhythm, as does the first section of the first pair (397–412). »» Parker 144–48.

392–406. *(Strophe 1)* The address to the Bosporus, symbolic passage from Hellas to the beyond, stresses the difficulty of Orestes' voyage and introduces thematic comparisons and contrasts between Io's persecution and exile (394f.) and those of Orestes and Iphigenia, and between the comforts of Hellas (399–401) and the hostility which awaits those who visit the Taurians (402–6).

392. Dark, dark confluences of sea: i.e. the mouth of the Bosporus where water flows in from the Black Sea at more than 3 km per hour (there is also a subsurface counter-current). For κυάνεαι, **dark** see 6–7 n. The song begins with an address introducing a vivid evocation of a sea voyage: cf. 1089–93 below and especially *Hec.* 444–46 αὔρα, ποντιὰς αὔρα, ἅτε ποντοπόρους κομίζεις θοὰς ἀκάτους ἐπ' οἶδμα λίμνας ('Breeze, sea-breeze, you who carry swift barks over the sea-swell'); also *El.* 432–41 and *Tro.* 122–28 (the ships that brought the Greek army to Troy). Emotive repetition (*anadiplosis*) is a feature of Euripides' lyric style, mocked by Aristophanes in his parody of a Euripidean monody, *Frogs* 1331–63 (esp. 1352–55): »» Breitenbach 214–21. Cf. 402 below, also 138 (chorus), 835f., 869f., 881, 894 (all Iphigenia in the recognition duet).

393–97. the gadfly flying from Argos: the Chorus recalls the story of Io, memorably presented and developed in A. *Supp.* 291–315, 538–89, [A.] *PV* 561–886; cf. Bacchyl. 19.15–51, S. *Inachos* F 269a–295; Apollod. 2.1.3 cites other

COMMENTARY 193

early sources. Io was transformed into a cow to facilitate or conceal Zeus's passion for her, then maddened by a gadfly sent by the jealous Hera which drove her from Argos through Europe and Asia to Egypt. There she gave birth to Zeus's son Epaphus (the bull-god Apis), whose great-grandson Danaus migrated back to Argos. Io was an ancient figure of Argive religious and genealogical myth, probably once a goddess herself but assimilated to the Olympian Hera. The myth made her, like Iphigenia, priestess and temple-keeper of a goddess who subjected her to wanderings which led to a divinely ordained destiny.»» Gantz 199–203, *LIMC* V, 'Io I'. The name 'Bosporus' (mis-etymologized as 'Ox-ford') was supposed to commemorate Io's fleeing across the Thracian Bosporus ([A.] *PV* 729–35 changes the locale to the Cimmerian Bosporus east of the Crimea, which was normally regarded as separating Asia from Europe, cf. 133–36 n.). In this ode (393–97, 422–26) the Thracian Bosporus and the Clashing or 'Dark' Rocks make a barrier between Hellenic and non-Hellenic realms. **passing to Asian land from Europe:** 'exchanging Asian land for Europe'. [**flying: ποτώμενος** rather than L's πετόμενος (same sense) gives exact responsion with 409 -πì πόντια; cf. *Hipp.* 1272f. ποτᾶται...ἐπì πόντον, '(Eros) flies over the sea', Alcman fr. 26 *PMGF* ὅς τ' ἐπì κύματος ἄνθος...ποτᾶται, '(a seabird) which flies over the foam'. **ἄξενον, Unwelcoming:** see 124–25 n.]

399–402. Who then are these men etc.: what kind of men have undertaken this dangerous adventure, and why? The 'why' is developed in the antistrophe. **Eurotas...Dirce:** rivers which make Sparta and Thebes lush and pleasant by contrast with the **unwelcoming land** of the Taurians (cf. 133–36 n.). Euripides avoids making the Chorus think of Argos or Athens, the cities with which Orestes and Iphigenia are and will be connected. Sparta is imaged by the Eurotas and its **reeds** at *Hel.* 209, 349, 493, *IA* 179; cf. Theognis 785. **venerable streams (ῥεύματα σεμνά):** σεμνός, like ἁγνός, ἱερός, emphasizes the purity and sanctity of streams (e.g. *Med.* 69, *Tro.* 206) and other natural features associated with the divine, as well as religious sanctuaries.

403–6. for Zeus's daughter: κούρᾳ Δίᾳ, 'for the Jovian girl', like 'Jovian son' (Heracles) in *Ion* 200; cf. 1 n. The original sense of δῖος, 'heavenly, divine' is less apt here. **columned: περικίονας,** 'columned-around'; the elaborate temple (cf. 128–29 n.) is contrasted with its crude function. The word περικίων is found only here and in *Erechtheus* F 369 (Ἀθάνας περικίοσιν...θαλάμοις, 'Athena's columned halls'), later noted in Pollux 1.77 and repeated in Philostratus, *Life of Apollonius* 2.20; cf. S. *Ant.* 285 ἀμφικίονας ναούς, 'columned temples', E. *Ion* 185 εὐκίονες αὐλαì θεῶν, 'fine-columned courts of the gods'.

407–21. *(Antistrophe 1)* Guessing that the search for wealth has motivated these sailors, the Chorus reflects on the uncertainties of wealth-seeking (416–18 n.), the proverbial capacity of hope to mislead (414 n.), and the need to recognize the *kairos* (proper measure) and limit one's desires accordingly. Underlying these thoughts is their recognition that something more than wealth (*olbos* in a limited

194 COMMENTARY

sense) is needed for true happiness (*olbos* in a broader sense, *eudaimonia*), and that happiness for them lies in a return to normal life (»» Kannicht 1956, 104–108). The classic statement of the variety of men's wealth-seeking endeavours and their unpredictable outcomes is Solon fr. 13.43–76 *IEG* where trade by sea and its dangers come first in the list; cf. Hesiod, *Works* 618–94, Sophocles F 555.

407. with double-pounding surges of pinewood oar (ῥοθίοις εἰλατίνας δικρότοισι κώπας): the oars create tracks of surf on either side of the ship; cf. *El.* 775 δίκροτον…ἁμάξιτον, 'double-grooved cart-track (δίκροτος was also a technical term for a bireme). **surges:** ῥοθ- is onomatopoeic for the sound of oar-stirred surf (cf. 426, 1132, 1387; »» Kannicht on *Hel.* 1269, Diggle on *Pha.* 80, Morrison–Williams 1968, 203, 311). [Reiske's conjecture gives two epic-style noun-epithet combinations (ῥοθίοις δικρότοισι, εἰλατίνας κώπας) interwoven in a manner typical of Euripides' narrative-descriptive lyrics, e.g. *Med.* 842 (Breitenbach 260, §10); this is better than L's four datives, 'with splashing pinewood double-pounding oars' (cf. 1132f. ῥοθίοις…πλάταις). For εἰλατίνας κώπας cf. *Hyps.* F 752g.14 εἰλατίνας πλάτας.]

409–10. their naval vessel: νάϊον ὄχημα is another elevated pleonasm like 'carriage-conveyance' etc. (370 n.), *Med.* 1122f. μήτε ναῖαν…ἀπήνην μήτ' ὄχον πεδοστιβῆ 'neither naval wagon nor land-going carriage', S. *Trach.* 656 πολύκωπον ὄχημα ναός 'many-oared ship-conveyance'. **over the sea's waves (ἐπὶ πόντια κύματα):** epic phrasing like *Iliad* 7.88 ἐπὶ οἴνοπα πόντον 'over the wine-dark sea', 13.27 ἐπὶ κύματα; cf. A. *Sept.* 210 ποντίῳ σὺν κύματι, [A.] *PV* 89 ποντίων… κυμάτων, E. *Hipp.* 735f. ἐπὶ πόντιον κῦμα, 753f. διὰ πόντιον κῦμα, also 393–97 n. [L's ἔπλευσαν is wrong since πλέω is never transitive as in English 'sail a ship'. ἔστειλαν is the best of many conjectures.]

411. in ever more urgent quest of riches: φιλόπλουτον ἅμιλλαν αὔξοντες, 'increasing (their) wealth-loving striving'. In *Med.* 557 ἅμιλλαν πολύτεκνον, 'multi-child striving' is 'striving to have many children'.

414. Cherished hope etc.: men cannot know when their hopes and ambitions are leading them to disaster: cf. Hes. *Works* 498–501, Solon fr. 13.33–70 *IEG*, Theognis 637–40, S. *Ant.* 616f., Thuc. 5.102ff., West on Hes. *Works* 96.

[†*becomes, to the affliction of mortals*†: L's metre is defective and the simple change of γένετ' to ἐγένετ' leaves awkward rhythm and inexact responsion. The repetition βροτῶν…ἀνθρώποις, *mortals…men* is also suspect though accepted by Kannicht 1956, 115 n. 5. For conjectures see Parker 147.]

416–18 a weight of wealth (ὄλβου βάρος): wealth more often has 'depth' (βάθος *El.* 1287, S. *Aj.* 130, βαθύπλουτος Aesch. F 451g.3, *Supp.* 554, Eur. F 453. 15, Bacchyl. 3.82), but here 'The men pursue something excessive, a burden threatening to destroy them' (Kyriakou).

419. in common expectation (κοινᾷ δόξᾳ): all alike have expectations of wealth, though only some understand its proper nature and limits (420f.).

COMMENTARY   195

[L's κοιναὶ δόξαι (nominative) is less fluent, 'Their expectations (are) common'
(cf. Pind. *Nem.* 1.32f.).]
  420. misses the measure of wealth: ἄκαιρος ὄλβου, '(is) *kairos*-less' of
wealth', i.e. their judgment fails to recognize a proper mark or amount for the
seeking of wealth, whereas for others **it finds a proper moderation (ἐς μέσον
ἥκει** 'it comes to the middle'). For the idea of a proper amount (*kairos*) of wealth
cf. e.g. Pind. *Nem.* 7.58 ἐοικότα καιρὸν ὄλβου, 'a fitting measure of prosperity'.
For recommendations to avoid excess by observing it e.g. Hes. *Works* 694 (μέτρα
φυλάσσεσθαι, καιρὸς δ' ἐπὶ πᾶσιν ἄριστος, 'observe due measure; a proper
amount is best in everything'), Theognis 335f. (πάντων μέσ' ἄριστα 'the median
of everything is best'), 401f., Pind. *Ol.* 13.47f. For those who judge it rightly, true
olbos is more than endlessly increased wealth.»» Kannicht 1956, 106–108,
Trédé-Boulmer 2015, 65. [**οἷς** is demonstrative (LSJ 'ὅς, ἥ, ὅ' A.II.4; Gildersleeve §522). For the phrase **ἄκαιρος ὄλβου** (rather than γνώμα ὄλβου, 'judgment
of wealth') see Kannicht 106f., and for **ἐς μέσον,** 'to the middle' Kannicht 107
(cf. Theognis 335 above, Pind. *Pyth.* 11.52). Tucker's ἐς μέτρον, 'to the (right)
measure' could be right and is preferred by Parker since ε(ἰ)ς μέσον normally
means 'into the midst', 'in the open' etc. Hesiod's μέτρα φυλάσσεσθαι etc.
(above) caps his long account of the perils of seafaring.)]

422–38. *(Strophe 2)* One sweeping lyric sentence pictures the ship's progress
through the Thracian Bosporus and along the dangerous southwest coast of the
Black Sea to Leuke, the White Island, modern Snake Island (Greek Phidonisi,
Ukrainian Ostriv Zmiinyi), an area of just 17 hectares about 35 km east of the
Danube delta, strategically important in recent times. The distance from the
Bosporus is some 770 km for a coasting ship. For later descriptions see e.g. Strabo
7.6.1, Arrian, *Periplous* 24f. The Salmydessian coast is the first 135 km from the
Bosporus, 'barren, rocky, harbourless, much exposed to north winds' (Strabo; cf.
[A.] *PV* 726f., Xen. *Anab.* 7.5.12; Silberman on Arr. *Peripl.* 25, n. 262). On Greek
navigation in this area see Introduction, p. 24.; on the early Greek presence there,
S. West 2003 and 2019. For the White Island see below on lines 435–37.
  422. the converging rocks: see 124–25 n.
  423–24. the unsleeping shores of Phineus's sons: ἄϋπνους, unsleeping
presumably means 'never calm', 'constantly windswept' (see 422–38 n.). Phineus
was the mythical blind prophet-king of Salmydessus (or sometimes Bithynia),
harassed by the Harpies until the Argonauts Zetes and Calais, sons of Boreas the
North Wind, drove them off or killed them. He was a popular subject for tragedy
and the mythical tradition is complicated and variable (»» Gantz 212, 349–56). In
the story told allusively in Sophocles' *Antigone* 966–87 his young sons were
blinded and imprisoned by their stepmother while their own mother Cleopatra
(daughter of Boreas and the Athenian princess Oreithuia) was herself imprisoned.
  [**Φινεΐδᾶν** (genitive plural) is a correction of L's Φινηΐδᾶς (adjusted by
Triclinius to Φινεΐδᾶς), accusative plural of an otherwise unknown adjective

196 COMMENTARY

Φινεῖς, 'Phineid', like χθὼν Θησῇς 'Thesean land' in A. *Eum.* 1025f.), but neither spelling gives the rhythm – ˘ ˘ – needed to match the metre of line 440, Λήδας Ἑλένα φίλα (– – ˘ ˘ – – ˘ –).]

425–26. on Amphitrite's surf: for ῥοθίῳ, surf see 407 n. Amphitrite was a Nereid (273–74 n.) who became Poseidon's wife and Triton's mother (Hes. *Theog.* 930–33). Epic language associated her with waves (*Odyssey* 3.91, 12.60) and sea-monsters (*Od.* 5.422, 12.97).

427–29. choruses of fifty Nereid maidens: fifty is the standard number for for many real choruses such as Athenian 'dithyrambic' ones. Tragic choruses often create effects by capturing in their own words and movements the joyous dancing of an imagined chorus, or of themselves in another context (»» Henrichs 1996). Here the Nereids' freedom is implicitly contrasted with the Greek women's captivity. The Second Stasimon will develop these effects more fully. The topic of the Nereids also leads towards the topic of Achilles since one of them, Thetis, was his mother. [**circle and sing:** μέλπουσιν ἐγκύκλιοι, 'sing circled', i.e. as a circular chorus (κύκλιος χορός). The missing word will be an object for 'sing', e.g. West's ἁβρά 'delicate (songs)' which Parker prints. L's dative ἐγκυκλίοις gives 'sing with/in circular ⟨...⟩,' but μέλπω 'sing' nearly always has some kind of object in Euripides (not, though, in A. *Ag.* 245).]

430–32. in sail-swelling gusts etc.: πλησ-ίστιος is an epic word (*Odyssey* 11.7 = 12.149). **the embedded steering-oars:** εὐναίων (< εὐνή, 'bed') probably refers to the secure fit of the steering oars in their socket (εὐθυντηρία, 1356). Alternatively, 'the steering oars were housed, i.e. secured with the blades feathered in the water. Thus they could be said to sleep, since they do no work' (Morrison–Williams 1968, 199: but why house the steering-oars when running before a brisk wind?). For the technicalities see Morrison–Williams 291f.; Casson 1971, 224–28. **sing at the stern:** συριζόντων ('piping, whistling, hissing') probably refers to the hissing of the steering-oars cutting through the water (Wilamowitz 1921, 567f.; Morrison–Williams 1968, 199).

433–34. on southerly breezes or Zephyr's breaths: Zephyros is the west wind, fair for sailing from Greece to Troy in *Telephus* F 727c.1 (with the southerly Notos), A. *Ag.* 691f. (below), Pind. *Nem.* 7.28–30. For the phrasing cf. *Odyssey* 14.253 ἐπλέομεν Βορέῃ ἀνέμῳ 'we sailed with the North wind', A. *Ag.* 691f. ἔπλευσεν Ζεφύρου...αὔρᾳ 'she sailed with Zephyr's breeze', S. *Ant.* 335f., 587–89.

435–36. the bird-thronged land, the white shore: Leuke, the White Island, was named either for its white rocks or for the flocks of nesting sea-birds associated with the sanctuary of Achilles there (Arrian, *Periplous* 21–23, Pausanias 3.19. 11–13). Achilles was worshipped by the Greeks who colonized the northern Black Sea area from Asia Minor from the late 7th C on (literary and archaeological evidence for the cult dates from as early as the mid-6th C). Achilles' spirit was said to have been taken from his pyre to the island by his mother Thetis (the

COMMENTARY   197

epic *Aethiopis* in Proclus's summary, p. 112 *GEF*; cf. Pind. *Nem.* 4.49f.; E. *Andr.* 1260–62). Legends proliferated, and Achilles was also said to have reached the island in pursuit of the abducted Iphigenia (Schol. Pind. *Nem.* 4.49; Lycophron, *Alexandra* 186–201) who was one of several heroines (Helen, Polyxena, Penthesilea, Medea et al.) said to have become the god Achilles' consort (Hommel 27ff.). »» (cult and sources) Hommel 1980; Hedreen 1991; S. West 2003, 162–65; Dana 2007, 177–82; Burgess 2009, 98–131; (archaeology) Rusyaeva 2003; Okhotnikov–Ostroverkhov 2007; (later literary constructions) Zeitlin 2019, 457–69.

436–37. Achilles' fair running-ground: δρόμους καλλισταδίους, 'finestade running-tracks', a poetic pleonasm like 1234 εὔπαις γόνος 'fine-child offspring', 1325f. ἀγχίπλουν πόρον 'near-voyage route' (»» Breitenbach 188f.). A stade (185 metres) was the standard length of a track for footraces. Achilles could be imagined exercising at his home on the White Island, but this phrase suggests the location known as Ἀχιλλέως δρόμος ('Achilles' running-track', Hdt. 4.55, 4.76.4 etc.), i.e. the long Tendra sandspit (Tendrovskaya Kosa) lying off the Ukrainian coast NW of the Crimea (Strabo 7.3.19; cf. Parroni on Pomponius Mela 2.5). Euripides' poetic description conflates the two mythic locations.

438. The description of the voyage is cut off at this striking point in a manner familiar from Pindar's lyric narratives.

439–55. *(Antistrophe 2)* The Chorus's thoughts move finally from the captives' voyage to their own and Iphigenia's exile and isolation. Their feelings are summed up in the hopeless wish for Helen's punishment, for news from home, for restoration to the happiness of their earlier lives there.

439–46. If only etc.: the women echo Iphigenia's longing (354–58 n., 521–26).

442–45. hair ringed with a bloody dew: 'ringed (with) a bloody dew around (her) hair'; **δρόσον** is a retained accusative, equivalent to the object of an active verb (»» Diggle 1981, 80f.; KG 1.125 n. 7). The **bloody dew** is the lustral water poured from a container in a circular motion on the victim's head to initiate the sacrifice (cf. 53f., 622, 645, and on δρόσος 255 n.). Its bloodiness here is metaphorical, indicating the association between the lustration and death, but the phrasing seems to evoke Clytemnestra's lurid celebration of her revenge on Agamemnon, A. *Ag.* 1389f.: 'Breathing out a sharp spew of blood he strikes me with a dark shower of gory dew (φοινίας δρόσου)'. **by my mistress's stroke upon her throat:** 'by (my) mistress's throat-cutting hand'; on such phrasing see 225–26 n. [**so that…she might die: θάνῃ** is a vivid subjunctive after the optative main verb: »» Diggle (above), Goodwin §181, *CGCG* §45.3.]

450–51. to end these pains of slavery: 'pain-ending of the slavery of wretched me'. The invented word **παυσίπονος** appears in a parody of Euripides' lyric style at Ar. *Frogs* 1321 ('the grape-bunch's pain-ending curl') and a few times in later texts.

198   COMMENTARY

452–55. Even in dreams etc.: dreams of home would comfort the women even if they cannot be rescued. Even illusions can console, e.g. *Tro.* 681–83, *Or.* 235f. The women will again imagine returning to their homes in 1137–52. The two phrases in 454f. are 'in apposition to the sentence', like 1441b ἀναψυχάς, 1459 ἄποινα (»» KG 1.284f., Smyth §994, *CGCG* §27.14). The text is however uncertain at several points. [⟨κἀν⟩ γὰρ ὀνείροισι συνείην is a plausible correction of L's defective and unmetrical γὰρ ὀνείρασι συμβαίην. συνείην, **might I be joined with** is more apt than συμβαίην ('might I meet with'), although σύνειμι in this sense normally refers to being/living with people or with conditions such as sickness or troubles. In 454 L's ὕμνων would refer to hymns that the women would dream of singing at home, but a sudden focus on this one feature of their dreams is unlikely and ὕπνων is a simple correction. Either way, τερπνάν ('pleasant boon of slumbers') may be preferable to L's τερπνῶν (**boon of pleasant slumbers**). In 455 L's ὄλβα is meaningless. Some editors accept Dupuy's ὄλβου, 'of bliss', but the sense of the phrase remains obscure. »» Kannicht 1956, 111f. (accepting ὕμνων and ὄλβου), Parker on 452–55.]

456–826. Scenes leading to the recognition

The central part of the play has two main dramatic sequences featuring recognition (456–826) and escape planning (902–1088); Iphigenia's song celebrating the reunion (827–899) separates these sequences like a choral ode. The recognition sequence is long, elaborate and circuitous, especially in the negotiations over the carrying of the letter and the choice of carrier. Iphigenia questions Orestes (467–577), then proposes to release one of the prisoners with a letter to Argos and, after Orestes has chosen to stay and be sacrificed, exits to fetch the letter (578–643). A brief choral song provides dramatic punctuation (644–56), then Orestes and Pylades show their nobility and devotion as each offers to die for the other (657–724). Iphigenia re-enters with the letter, and in negotiating its safe transport to Argos is led to recite it and so reveal her identity (725–92). Finally Orestes claims her and must overcome her scepticism her with proofs that he is indeed her brother (793–826).

Elaborated recognitions of this kind have their roots in epic (especially the *Odyssey*) and had become a stock element in tragedy. Notable amongst the extant plays are Aeschylus's *Choephori*, Sophocles' *Oedipus* and *Electra* and Euripides' *Electra*, *Ion* and *Helen* (»» Cropp on Eur. *El.* 487–698). This recognition has special associations with Electra's recognitions of Orestes in *Choephori*, Euripides' *Electra* and Sophocles' *Electra* (in Sophocles' play Electra, like Iphigenia, is sure he is dead). The fragmentary *Cresphontes* had Cresphontes recognized by his mother just as she was about to kill him, and in *Alexandros* Paris was almost killed by his brothers before their family relationship was revealed. *Iphigenia* goes one better insofar as neither party knows the identity of the other and Iphigenia, though less sceptical than the Euripidean Electra, has to be convinced of Orestes'

COMMENTARY   199

identity (see below on 798–810, 811–26). The elaboration of this extremely artificial situation maximizes the suspense and emotional effect of the recognition process.[17] Dramatic ironies abound as the dialogue plays with names, identifications and the history of the royal family, the family relationships which brother and sister unwittingly share, the possibility that sister will kill and bury brother and consciousness of unpredictable outcomes contrasted with Orestes' despair and resentment against Apollo. Orestes' refusal to reveal himself is well motivated through shame (see 500–1 n.). Iphigenia's reserve, competing with her involuntary emotional reactions to what Orestes tells her, can be understood similarly: shame inhibits her from identifying herself to strangers as the victim of the sacrifice and her father's cruelty, and with the family she now thinks ruined.

456–66. The Chorus's anapaests provide a transition from the song to the next scene as the prisoners arrive escorted by some of the Taurian herdsmen who had brought them to the king and were told to bring them to the temple (333–35). These might include the one who reported their capture, now played by an extra (342–43 n.). They will be dismissed into the temple at 468–71 and then forgotten. The temple servants who assisted Iphigenia with her libations are probably still present and will be available to guard the prisoners while Iphigenia fetches her letter (638 n.). This scene is represented in vase-paintings and in wall-paintings from Pompeii (*LIMC* V, 'Iphigenia' nos 14–16, 52–53).

    456–57. with hands tied tight together: χέρας συνερεισθέντες, 'pressed-together their hands'; χέρας is another retained accusative, cf. 442–45 n. with KG 1.125 §8 and 1.316(b), Xen. *Hell.* 3.3.11 δεδεμένος καὶ τὼ χεῖρε καὶ τὸν τράχηλον ἐν κλοιῷ, 'bounds hands and neck in a collar'. **the pair of them (δίδυμοι):** see 124–25 n.

    458. a new sacrifice (πρόσφαγμα): see 243 n. **Be silent, friends:** see 123 n.

    459–62. Truly the choicest pickings etc.: for ἀκροθίνια see 75 n. δή draws attention to the fine looks and bearing of the captives which confirm the Herdsman's report. Their physique and bearing, and the nobility they have shown in the battle, increase their value as victims for sacrifice (»» Bonnechere 2013, 25–32).

    463–66. O Mistress, if it is pleasing to you etc.: the prayer is in ritual form (invocation, justification, request) and carefully phrased, allowing that the human sacrifices are holy (ὅσιαι) for the Taurians (πόλις ἥδε: 38 n) and so perhaps pleasing to Artemis even though they are **unholy (οὐχ ὁσίας)** according to Greek religious law (cf. 130–32 n.). In dramatic term this leaves Artemis's attitude open and suggests that these sacrifices might somehow be averted. [L's text adds 'in giving them to Hellenes', probably derived from a note explaining 'us' as Bergk suggested.]

---

[17] Hall 2013, 74f. discusses the various emotional effects generated by this and other extended recogntions.

200 COMMENTARY

467–91. Iphigenia and Orestes face each other for the first time. Her first reaction after attending to her duties confirms that she cannot exercise the ruthlessness she promised in 348ff. In fact, she instinctively puts herself in the place of Orestes' sister. Orestes' response is indignant, truculent and high-spirited, rejecting Iphigenia's sympathy and revealing his reserve which will prolong the recognition.

467–69. first I must make sure etc.: as in 342f., Iphigenia shows her conscientiousness in sacred matters before reflecting on her own reactions to the situation. Victims must be in good condition when sacrificed (20–21 n.) and must seem unconstrained, hence **no longer tied up** (»» Burkert 1985, 56).

472–73. Who...can be the mother etc.: Iphigenia guesses that Orestes and Pylades are brothers but will soon learn that they are only 'brothers in affection' (497f.). Like Creusa unknowingly meeting her son (*Ion* 308, 324), and Hypsipyle her two sons (*Hyps.* F 752d.5), she thinks first of the mother who bore these fine young men. Here dramatic ironies are compounded: Orestes has murdered his mother to avenge his murdered father, and she is a sister who will lose him when he is sacrificed. [L's text and punctuation give 'Who...can be the mother that bore you, and your father, and your sister if you have one?', but strangers are not normally asked to identify their parents *and* any sister they might happen to have. Markland's adjustment avoids this oddity and makes the sister a distinct topic.]

474–75. what a pair of young brothers etc.: 'Deprived of what a pair of young men will she be brotherless'.

475–78. Who can know etc.: a fundamental element in traditional Greek belief, e.g. Solon fr. 13.33–70 *IEG*, Hdt. 1.32, E. *Hipp.* 1108–10, F 152, others in Stobaeus 4.41. Here once again a dramatic irony: she is indeed unaware of where this meeting will lead.

477. no one knows anything for sure (σαφές): cf. *HF* 62 'Nothing in the gods' designs is sure (σαφές) for humans', *Bellerophon* F 304.1 'Where is sureness (τὸ σαφές) in man's life?', S. *OT* 977f. (Jocasta, misguidedly) 'Fortune prevails (in human affairs) and men have no sure (σαφής) foreknowledge of anything'. [L's κακόν gives 'no one knows anything bad'. Parker prefers Weil's τέλος ('end', 'outcome'), but one would expect 'no one knows the end of anything' rather than 'no one knows any end' (Martin 2020, 198).]

479. wretched strangers: as in other recognition sequences, the characters repeatedly address each other as strangers (ξένοι) with dramatic irony: cf. 509, 547 (Iphigenia to Orestes), 579, 728 (to Orestes and Pylades), 597 (Orestes to Iphigenia); 'whoever you are' 483, 628.

482–83. why...vex yourself: σὲ is reflexive (KG 1.559, *CGCG* §29.16–17). L's simple λυπεῖς would mean mean 'vex (others)', and μέλλουσι 'our imminent troubles'. **lady** is perhaps the best approximation to γύναι, avoiding the condescending nuance of English 'woman'; Parker suggests the slightly antiquated 'madam'. Dickey 1996, 87 notes that in Menander and Aristophanes γύναι 'sometimes occurs from men to unrelated women, in contexts ranging from

COMMENTARY   201

respectful to scornful' (her study does not include tragedy). Here and in 496, 498, 542, 546 the context suggests that Orestes' tone is coldly polite. That he is addressing his sister is a further dramatic irony.

484–85. I find it foolish: οὗτοι…σοφόν, 'not wise' with a suggestion of moral ignorance or gaucheness (385–86 n.). **if someone who is going to kill etc.:** Orestes despises both the executioner who commiserates with his/her victim as Iphigenia has just done and the victim who laments his own fate (486–89). [L's θανεῖν ('someone who is about to die') misses the distinction.][18]

486–89. and foolish too etc.: if executioners should not express pity, neither should their victims disgrace themselves by demanding it; cf. *HF* 282f., 'I consider someone who holds out against the inevitable (i.e. being killed by a ruthless enemy) to be stupid (σκαιός)'. **showing foolishness: μωρίαν τ' ὀφλισκάνει,** 'he owes (is chargeable with) foolishness', still with a moral overtone. **one should let fortune have its way:** *HF* 307–11, 'Face death with us, which awaits you in any case…The man who tries to fight off godsent fortunes is resolute, but his resolution is crazy.'

492–575. The dialogue proceeds in a lengthy stichomythia (stylized line-for-line dialogue used mainly for questioning, persuading, plotting and agitated argument: »» Seidensticker 1971; Collard 1980; Rutherford 2012, 170–79). *Iphigenia* shares with Euripides' other later plays (after 420) an extensive use of stichomythia, here also 617–27 (questioning), 734–54 (exchange of oaths), 805–21 (recognition proofs), 915–39 (questioning), 1020–49 (escape planning), 1159–1222 (deception of Thoas). Four of these passages (492–569, 805–21, 1020–49, 1159–1221) make a sequence which is common to the 'recognition and intrigue' plays: opening dialogue, recognition, planning, deception. The form is ideally suited to cryptic expressions, which contribute to the scene's suspense and dramatic irony. Iphigenia is nearly always the questioner and Orestes the reluctant answerer, but at 528f., 540f. and 550f. he briefly seizes the role of questioner and the possibility of Iphigenia's identifying herself is suggested, only to be passed over. At other moments (516, 526, 570f.) Orestes' truculence and preoccupation with his own plight prevent him from reacting to hints about Iphigenia's background. »» Schwinge 1968, 270–92.

492. †*named here*†: ἐνθάδ' ὠνομασμένος hardly makes sense and is obelized by Diggle, Kovacs and Parker. [It can hardly mean 'named by Orestes at the sea-shore as reported by the Herdsman' (or 'named by the Herdsman here in my presence') as supposed by earlier editors. To Parker's objections add that these would require an aorist participle ὀνομασθείς; the perfect ὠνομασμένος means 'bearing the name'.]

---

[18] Some editors print the future infinitive κτενεῖν, but the aorist infinitive with μέλλω is quite possible (see LSJ 'μέλλω' II, Finglass on *OT* 967). Nothing suggests that Seidler thought κτανεῖν was a future infintive as Parker alleges.

202 COMMENTARY

495. Of what Hellenic land: ποίας...πατρίδος is lit. 'of what kind of land', but ποῖος is often a slightly vague 'which' or 'what' (LSJ 'ποῖος' IV); similarly in 499, 511, 549, 1188, 1199, 1319 (n.).

496, 498. lady (γύναι): see 482–83 n.

498. Brothers in affection: Pylades' brotherly loyalty to Orestes was proverbial, e.g. *Or.* 882, 1014f., cf. Introduction, p. 10. He was actually Orestes' cousin (son of Agamemnon's sister married to Strophius of Phocis), but they were raised together after the child Orestes was sent to safety in Phocis either before or after his father's murder (»» Gantz 683). [Köchly's conjecture γένει ('not siblings by birth') for the repeated γύναι is plausible and printed by Sansone and Kovacs.]

500–1. I should be called Unfortunate (Δυστυχής): cf. *Hec.* 785f., 'What woman was ever so unfortunate as I?', 'None, unless you mentioned Fortune herself.' For misfortune implied in names see e.g. *Ba.* 367, 508, Chaeremon F 4 (all Pentheus/πένθος, 'grief'), S. *Aj.* 430f. (Aias/αἰαῖ, 'alas') with Garvie's note; cf. Aristot. *Rhet.* 1400b17–25 citing Soph. F 658.2 (Sidero/σίδηρος, 'Iron'), E. *Tro.* 990 (Aphrodite/ἀφροσύνη, 'Madness') etc. Orestes conceals his real name through shame (*aidôs*) at his past actions and present predicament, and a desire to avoid further humiliation (502). Iphigenia dismisses the concealment with a pun (τοῦτο...δὸς τῇ τύχῃ, **credit that to fortune**, i.e. blame fortune for making you Unfortunate).

504, 503, 502: reordered by Barthold. Only 502 answers 503, and 503 could hardly be asked after 502.

504. my body...not my name: Orestes uses the sophistic distinction between word (*logos*, *onoma*) and substance (*ergon*, *pragma*, *sôma*) which Euripides played with frequently, especially in *Helen* (42f., 66f., 588, 1100 etc.; »» Kannicht 1969, I.57–60).

502. By dying unnamed I shall remain unmocked: i.e. his enemies will not be able to gloat over it. For this fear of mockery after death cf. *HF* 284–86 (with Bond's commentary), 'Since we have to die, we should avoid dying roasted by fire, allowing our enemies to mock us, which to me is a greater evil than death'.

506–8. your question offers me no profit: answering can do him no good since he will soon be dead. This prompts Iphigenia's next response, asking him to answer her **as a favour**, i.e. not for any benefit to himself. By generously (and proudly) naming Argos Orestes sets in motion the recognition that will lead to rescue for himself, Pylades and Iphigenia.

510. Yes, from Mycenae: Euripides occasionally refers to Argos/Argives as Mycenae/Mycenaeans, sometimes with no significant distinction (thus *IT* 532, 592, 982) but sometimes evoking the city's legendary wealth and prestige (thus here and in 845f.). In the *Iliad* Mycenae is Agamemnon's capital and controls a large territory, but in Euripides' time it was derelict following its destruction by Argos in the 460s. On Argos/Mycenae as imagined in tragedy see Said 1993.

COMMENTARY 203

once...prosperous suggests the desolation of the city after the loss of its rightful rulers, cf. 189f.

515–16. Platnauer placed the lines here so that the topic of Orestes' home city is completed before Iphigenia asks about his exile (511–12) and about Troy (513–14, 517ff.). **your arrival is longed for:** ποθεινός...ἦλθες, 'longed-for have you come'. More dramatic irony: this stranger is much more longed for than she knows. Orestes' offhand reply both compounds the irony and cancels the possibility that he will now identify himself.

511. You left...as an exile: ἀπῆρας intransitive as in 967 (LSJ 'ἀπαίρω' II.2 with LSJ Supp.).

512. both unwilling and willing (οὐχ ἑκὼν ἑκών): his mission is voluntary but hardly welcome; cf. *Iliad* 4.43 ἑκὼν ἀέκοντί γε θυμῷ 'voluntarily though with unwilling spirit'. Other such oxymorons: *Alc.* 521 'dead and not dead', *Or.* 904 'Argive and not Argive'(»» Breitenbach 238 with lyric examples). Words for 'willing' and 'unwilling' are often strikingly paired in other ways, e.g. *Iliad* 7.197, *Od.* 3.272, *E. Hcld.* 531, *Hipp.* 319, *Andr.* 357.

514. Very well, as an aside etc.: up to this point Iphigenia has asked about Orestes and Pylades (472–96) and more particularly about Orestes and his background (497–512). Now Orestes agrees to talk about something else which he assumes will be incidental. He is then surprised to be questioned about the outcome of the Trojan War and the fates of the Greek leaders.

520. it is no idle report: οὐδ' ἄκραντ' ἠκούσατε, 'nor have you heard things unfulfilled'.

521–22. Has Helen returned etc.: Iphigenia turns first to those responsible for her own sacrifice, especially Helen (354–58 n., 439–46). **an evil return for one of my family:** i.e. for Agamemnon, killed by Clytemnestra when he returned from Troy with Helen.

523. She has long owed me payment etc.: 'she pre-owes a wrong to me also', a cryptic allusion to her sacrifice which in dramatic terms avoids hinting at her identity prematurely.

525–26. Hateful creature etc.: Iphigenia reacts angrily at the thought of Helen living comfortably at Sparta with the husband she betrayed (as in Book 4 of the *Odyssey*) but deflects attention from her own grievance by adding that all Greeks have reason to hate her. Orestes' response is allusive and ironic.

528. How you pull everything together etc.: 'How you collect and question me (about) everything at once'.

531–36. Calchas and **Laertes' son** Odysseus were the ringleaders in Iphigenia's sacrifice, cf. 15–27 with 24–25 n. The usual story about Calchas (understandably ignored here) is that he died of frustration after losing a prophetic contest with Apollo's son Mopsus at Colophon or some other oracular site of Apollo in Asia Minor (»» Gantz 702). **O Mistress:** i.e. Artemis, who was often addressed by this title and is Iphigenia's patroness. **And what:** τί γάρ with 'progressive'

204 COMMENTARY

γάρ as in 820, 936 (Denniston 82–85). **He has not yet reached home etc.:** Odysseus is reported missing but alive throughout the *Odyssey*, e.g. 4.551–60. **May he perish etc.:** cf. the Cyclops' curse on Odysseus, *Odyssey* 9.530f. **all his affairs are ailing (νοσεῖ):** a common metaphor, cf. 680, 693 (with added sense of pollution), 930, 992, 1018. Odysseus's return was harassed by Poseidon, his ships and crew lost, his house and wife besieged by suitors.

537–39. Thetis's son: Achilles, cf. 24–25 n., 214–17, 364–71. **a vain marriage he made:** it was of course not completed, but Orestes' mention of it prompts Iphigenia's bitterly ambiguous comment in 539. By **those who have suffered from it** she means herself, but that is unclear to Orestes since οἱ πεπονθότες is not only plural but masculine, as often when singular female subjects refer to themselves in the plural, e.g. E. *El.* 1010 (»» KG 1.83).

541. I am from there: Iphigenia does not name her home city, but for dramatic reasons Orestes follows this up only at 657ff. **I was lost:** ἀπωλόμην is meaningfully ambiguous, either 'I went missing' or 'I perished'.

542, 548. lady (γύναι): see 482–83 n.

543. the general they call fortunate: i.e. Agamemnon, fortunate as leader of the great campaign against Troy (139–42, *Hec.* 753). Similarly Menelaus, *Hel.* 457, *Or.* 351–55.

548. and destroyed someone else as well: a veiled reference to himself, like Haemon's veiled prediction of his own suicide at S. *Ant.* 751. For πρός 'in addition', 'as well' see LSJ 'πρός' D.

550. He surely was nothing to you: more play with the possibility that Iphigenia will identify her family.

552. slaughtered: Agamemnon's murder is likened to a sacrificial slaughter (σφαγή, 8 n.) in e.g. *El.* 123. So is Clytemnestra's in *El.* 961, 1243 (cf. 1221–23), *Or.* 39, 291.

553. O lamentable – she who killed etc.: Iphigenia is unusual in expressing sympathy for Clytemnestra's role in the murder of her husband, perhaps guessing that she was driven to it by anger at the sacrifice of her daughter as Clytemnestra herself claims in A. *Ag.* 1401–20, S. *El.* 525–51, E. *El.* 1018–45.

559. a righteous wrong (κακὸν δίκαιον): the justice of punishing Clytemnestra was tainted by the injustice of a son killing his mother, cf. *El.* 1244, *Or.* 538f., Aristot. *Rhet.* 1401a36–b3.

560. But gets no good fortune from the gods: οὐ τὰ πρὸς θεῶν εὐτυχεῖ, 'does not fare well as to things from the gods'. **though he acted justly:** Orestes' constant claim, e.g. A. *Cho.*1027 κτανεῖν τέ φημι μητέρ' οὐκ ἄνευ δίκης, 'I affirm that I killed my mother not without justice'.

562. Electra: she is by now married to Pylades, cf. 230–35 n.

565. unhappy the father: again sympathy, now for the father who 'killed' her. This again avoids any indication of her identity, which will only be revealed in the wording of the letter which brings about the recognition (769–87).

COMMENTARY   205

566. for the thankless sake: χάριν ἄχαριν, 'as a non-*charis charis*'. Iphigenia was sacrificed for the sake of Helen (and as a *charis* to Menelaus, 14 n.), but the *charis* brought harm rather than good in return. For this kind of oxymoron see 144–47 n. and cf. A. *Ag.* 1545 ἄχαριν χάριν, *Cho.* 44, E. *Pho.* 1757 χάριν ἀχάριτον, [A.] *PV* 545 πῶς χάρις ἀ χάρις, 'how is that *charis* a *charis*?'

567–68. The dead king's son etc.: at last Iphigenia asks about her brother, and Orestes' prevaricating answer once again postpones the recognition. He describes himself as a wretched fugitive (**nowhere and everywhere,** i.e. always on the move, cf. *El.* 234), but Iphigenia hears only that he is alive and assumes that he is in Argos and will receive her letter there (582–90, 735f.).

569. Deceptive dreams, farewell: more dramatic irony, as Iphigenia fails to realise that it is her own misinterpretation of her dream that has misled her.

570–71. Nor indeed are the gods etc.: Orestes again shows no curiosity about Iphigenia and turns her joyful comment into a bitter reflection on the deceptiveness of oracles, alluding to the advice of Apollo which he thinks has led him to his death. He puts this cryptically so that Iphigenia will not perceive his identity, nor how his complaint is relevant to his own situation. He will repeat the complaint more explicitly to Pylades (711–15, 'Phoebus the seer (μάντις) deceived me etc.'; cf. 77–94), and Pylades will encourage him not to give up hope (719f., 'the god's pronouncement (μάντευμα) has not yet destroyed you'). The Third Stasimon will explore (ambivalently) Apollo's oracular powers, 'on an undeceiving throne dispensing to mortals pronouncements (μαντείας) of divine decrees'. **the gods who are called wise (σοφοί):** cf. 385–86 n., 484–85 n., *El.* 972 'But where Apollo is foolish, who are wise (*sophoi*)?', 1246 'Wise though he is, he gave you unwise bidding'. **more undeceiving (ἀψευδέστεροι):** Aeschylus's Orestes had relied on Apollo as 'an undeceiving seer' (μάντις ἀψευδής, *Cho* 559, cf. *Cho.* 297, 900f., 1030, *Eum.* 169, 593–96, 615 (Apollo: μάντις ὢν οὐ ψεύσομαι, 'As a seer I shall not speak falsely'). In the happy ending of *Orestes* the hero retracts his condemnation (*Or.* 1666f., 'O seer-god (μαντεῖε) Loxias, so you were no false seer (οὐ ψευδόμαντις)'). In an unidentified play of Aeschylus (F 350) Thetis complains that she expected 'Phoebus's divine mouth, pregnant with mantic skill' to be 'undeceiving (ἀψευδές)', yet after promising her son Achilles a long life he has now killed him.

[572–75]. These lines seem out of place and are, I think, best deleted (cf. Cropp 1997, 30f., Kovacs 2003, 7f.). If they are genuine, Orestes follows up his oblique comment on Apollo's deceptiveness with an even more oblique reflection which has no bearing on what Iphigenia has just said. Kyriakou and Parker suggest that more than two lines are needed to conclude the stichomythia, but that is not a compelling point (*Helen* 594–96 ends a long stichomythia; Orestes has so far alluded to his own situation quite curtly). Parker adds that the additional lines are needed 'to give the audience the feeling that Iphigenia has had time to think up her plan', but she planned to send the letter long ago and now has

206   COMMENTARY

only to decide that this is the time to use it (cf. 638 n.). The lines might have originated in a marginal comparison or as an interpolation made for emotional effect and modelled on Orestes' similarly worded complaint in 711–15. Without them the Chorus's enquiry about their families follows closely and naturally on the discussion of Iphigenia's family.

[Two specific difficulties: (1) ἓν δὲ λυπεῖται μόνον, *he feels grief at one thing only* either refers cryptically to Orestes himself or is corrupt (and has not been convincingly emended: Diggle and Parker obelize it). (2) μάντεων πεισθεὶς λόγοις, *persuaded by seers' pronouncements* cannot refer to human seers interpreting Apollo's words since Orestes consistently says that he was instructed by Apollo himself (cf. 85–92 n.), while an allusion to Apollo as deceptive *mantis* (cf. 570–71 n.) is unlikely when Orestes has just alluded to him as a deceptive god. The statement sounds more like a routine condemnation of seers (e.g. *Iliad* 1.106–8, Soph. *OT* 390–98, 707–25, E. *El.* 399f., *Hel.* 744–60, *IA* 520, 956–58, F 795) whose advice has led to someone's destruction.]

576–77. The Chorus's question provides a pause before Iphigenia introduces the scheme which the news of Orestes' survival has suggested to her. It also reminds us of the Chorus's personality and helps to prepare their role in the later dramatic action.

578–96. The plot again links a moment of despair with an unrecognized step towards salvation. Orestes' declaration of no confidence in Apollo is followed immediately, and quite unexpectedly, by the proposal from Iphigenia which will lead to the recognition. The letter itself is ultimately of no practical importance since the recognition comes when she recites her message verbally, but it increases the dramatic possibilities of the recognition scene by giving the means of recognition and salvation a material form and allows the crowning moment in which Pylades hands the letter to Orestes after a journey of a few metres. The fact that she prepared the letter long before adds a dimension to the sympathetic portrayal of Iphigenia (she has never despaired of rescue, her former prisoner bore her no resentment), and her going to fetch it allows the noble scene of self-denial and farewells between Orestes and Pylades. There is also suspense as we wait for the letter's addressee to be named before Pylades can go on his way. See further 725–68 n., 769–97 n., Burnett 1971, 52–56.

Writing is virtually unknown, at least by convention, in the world of epic (the fateful 'signs' carried by Bellerophon to Lycia in *Iliad* 6.168f. are an exception), but letters were a well-worn device in tragedy by the time Euripides produced *Iphigenia*. It is noticeable that Iphigenia has not written her own letter, but that is a dramatic convenience which does not need to be explained and does not imply that upper-class women were illiterate in Euripides' time. Phaedra has no difficulty in writing her suicide note when the plot of *Hippolytus* requires it. On women's literacy at Athens in the classical period (no doubt confined to a small

COMMENTARY 207

minority) see Harris 1989, 96, 102f., 106–10, and on letter-writing in Euripides' plays (*Hippolytus, Stheneboea, Palamedes, IT, IA*) Ceccarelli 2013, 218–35.

579. pursuing both your advantage...and mine: dramatic irony. Iphigenia does not yet know the full benefit of her scheme; similarly 639–42.

580. this is the best basis etc.: 'the good comes about most of all thus'.

583. to my loved ones there is almost enough to show that she is from Argos, but vague language (also in 589–92) allows Orestes to continue missing the point (cf. 541 n.).

584. a letter: a δέλτον ('tablet') was a light wooden plaque containing a thin layer of wax as a writing surface. On the format of Iphigenia's letter see 727 n.

585–87. not reckoning my hand guilty etc.: the prisoner recognized that he was dying by virtue of the Taurian law (τοῦ νόμου ὕπο) and that his sacrifice was therefore legitimate (δίκαια). Iphigenia says repeatedly that she follows the Taurian law (35, 38, 470f., 1189), and the chorus-women recognize that Taurian law allows what Greek law does not (463–66). That law (*nomos*) determines what is just and unjust is a commonplace, e.g. E. *Hec.* 800f., Lysias 2.19, Aeschines 3.199, Aristot. *Eth. Nic.* 1129b12ff.

[τὰ τῆς θεοῦ τάδε δίκαι' ἡγούμενος is Hermann's text. L has θνῄσκειν γε τῆς θεοῦ ταῦτα δίκαι' ἡγουμένης ('to be dying by virtue of the law since the goddess considers these things legitimate'), but γε is redundant (and contradicted by the Hibeh papyrus), ταῦτα is metrically impossible and ἡγουμένης is inappropriate (Iphigenia is explaining the prisoner's opinion). Hermann's text has been criticized for two reasons: (1) Platnauer (repeated by Kyriakou) translated 'thinking this the lawful action of the goddess' and objected that 'the direct object τάδε coming in the middle of the predicative phrase τὰ τῆς θεοῦ δίκαια is very doubtful'; but the object of **ἡγούμενος** is **τὰ τῆς θεοῦ τάδε, these rites of the goddess**. (2) According to Parker, 'it is surely too much to imagine a Greek *himself* thinking it lawful to sacrifice strangers'; but that is what this Greek did think about the Taurian law.]

590. to one of my loved ones: she means Orestes, of course, and seems to imagine an idealized brother living safely in Argos (639f., 774–76, 804) even though she has virtually been told that he has killed his mother and is in exile (556, 567f.). She also seems to assume that she can get away with releasing one of the captives and that the ship will be able to leave undetected.

592. those I love: her *philoi* as in 583, 590, 639f.   [φιλῶ is Musgrave's correction of L's θέλω, 'those whom I want (to send the letter to)'.]

595. the community (πόλις) requires these things: cf. 38 with note.

597–642. Orestes' insistence on claiming the role of victim introduces the motif of self-sacrifice in friendship which will be developed in the next scene. He will not escape by leaving a comrade to face what should be his own fate (598–602), nor incur the the disgrace of betraying a friend, especially so close a friend as Pylades (605–8). Euripides also plays with the possibility that Iphigenia will

208 COMMENTARY

sacrifice her own brother. Orestes' self-denial revives her thoughts of him just as that begins to seem certain, and she is moved to treat the unknown stranger as she would her brother, offering him the funeral rites that she cannot offer to Orestes himself. This paradox is explored with great pathos in the dialogue that follows.

598. a great weight: Orestes responds to Iphigenia's remark about the lightness of her message (594).

605–7. It brings great disgrace etc.: αἴσχιστον ὅστις…, 'It's most disgraceful, whoever…' (»» KG 2.441f.). This is not just a matter of moral principle. Orestes would have to live with the disgrace of having saved himself by betraying his friend. **friends:** τὰ τῶν φίλων, 'the affairs of his friends', a vague generalization; cf. 1006 τὰ γυναικός ('a woman'), *Hel.* 276 τὰ βαρβάρων ('barbarians'), *Melanippe* F 497.2 τὰ γυναικῶν ('women'), Gildersleeve §581.

608. whose life I value etc.: 'whom I want no less than myself to see the light'.

609–10. what a noble root etc.: that noble behaviour stems from noble birth is a commonplace in archaic (especially epinician) poetry, sometimes echoed in tragedy, though questioning it is also common (»» Denniston on *El.* 253; Collard–Cropp–Gibert 2004, 76f. on *Alexandros* F 61b). **what proper friendship you show:** 'how properly are you a friend to friends', phrased like S. *Ant.* 99, E. *Andr.* 376f. Orestes and Pylades fulfil Greek aristocratic ideals of friendship (*philia*) in an exemplary way, cf. e.g. Theognis 101–4, 113–16, 398f., 529f.

612–13. I too…am not without a brother: acute dramatic irony, especially when she then agrees to reward Orestes' nobility by killing him.

618. this is the fortune etc.: συμφοράν has its basic neutral sense as in 850, 1317, *El.* 238 'in what state of fortune (συμφορᾶς) you are'), *Hel.* 643 'the god is driving you towards a fortune (συμφοράν) better than this one'. An implied 'misfortune' (as in 549, 599) would offend the goddess and make Orestes' response pointless. [συμφοράν is the reading of the Hibeh papyrus, which also has τήνδε. L's προστροπήν would mean 'invocation' or more specifically 'supplication' of the goddess; it cannot mean 'duty' or 'task'.]

620. I am under ('am placed into') **compulsion:** the language may evoke her own sacrifice, when Agamemnon 'went under the yoke of compulsion' to kill Iphigenia (A. *Ag.* 218).

621. female killing male: killings at Greek animal sacrifices were normally done by a male specialist, supervised by whoever was responsible for the sacrifice (»» van Straten 168–70; Osborne 1993). The idea of a woman killing a victim, especially a male victim, might shock a Greek audience (cf. Osborne 400f.), but these words may also allude to Cassandra's prophetic warning in A. *Ag.* 1231, 'The female (Clytemnestra) is slayer of the male'. [P. Hibeh's κτείνουσα (**Killing me with the sword**) is more appropriate than L's θύουσα ('sacrificing me with the sword') and makes the allusion to *Ag.* 1231 clearer. θύουσα would refer to the whole sacrificial process, which Iphigenia actually will conduct (617f.).]

COMMENTARY   209

622. I'll sprinkle holy water around your head: cf. 54 n., 442–45 n. The detail reminds us of Iphigenia's dream in which she saw herself lustrating the column which represented her brother. This pre-sacrifice lustration might then seem to be what the dream foretold (42–66 n.).

625–35. what kind of burial etc.: Orestes' body will be taken into the temple from the altar outside (72 n.), Iphigenia will dress and adorn it, anointing it with oil, and the body will then be cremated on an altar inside the temple while she pours libations of honey into the flames. Finally, the ashes and bones will be taken away and dropped into a chasm nearby. No mention is made of beheading or exhibition of the head on the temple front (74 n.), presumably because Euripides is sentimentalizing this parting exchange between Iphigenia and her brother. The description also departs purposefully from that of Herodotus who describes the Taurians as impaling their sacrificial victims' heads and either burying the bodies or pushing them off a cliff (Hdt. 4.103.2, cited pp. 19f. above).

626. A sacred fire inside: cf. 72 n.; altars inside temples were not rare (»» Corbett 1970, 150, 152). **a broad chasm in the rock:** chasms typically give access to the underworld, e.g. *El.* 1271 for the Erinyes, *Ion* 281 for Erechtheus, *Supp.* 501 for Amphiaraus, cf. S. *OC* 1661f. This one would be separated from the sanctuary and not the source of the fire. Diodorus 20.14 cites this passage reading χάσμα χθονός ('a broad chasm in the earth') and misunderstands it as referring to a fiery pit as in Carthaginian infant sacrifices (see also 87–88 n. with n. 6 on Apollodorus *epit.* 6.26).

627. if only my sister's hand etc.: the phrasing with πῶς ἄν, 'how might', is often used in tragedy for an urgent or unattainable wish, e.g. *Med.* 97, 173–75, *Hipp.* 208–11. Orestes thinks of Electra rather than Iphigenia, the sister who will actually tend his body. Normally the women of the family (especially the older women, but there are none such for Orestes) would wash, oil and dress the body for laying out in the home (*prothesis*) and later carrying out (*ekphora*) to the grave. The verb περιστέλλω often denotes the preparation, e.g. *Alc.* 664, *Med.* 1034. »» Kurtz–Boardman 1971, 142–61; Garland 2001, 23–34.

630–31. Yet: for οὐ μὴν...ἀλλά, 'not but what' see Denniston 28f.; *CGCG* §59.75. **I too will not neglect etc.:** ὧν γε δυνατὸν οὐδ᾽ ἐγὼ 'λλείψω χάριν, 'Neither will I neglect the favour of those things, at least, of which it is possible (not to neglect the favour)'; i.e., she will do all she can to provide the care which Electra cannot provide. [This interpretation suits the context and phrasing (οὐδ᾽ ἐγὼ...) better than taking οὐδέ as a strong negative, 'I will certainly not...' (Parker; cf. Denniston 197f.; Slings on Pl. *Clitophon* 409e2). 'λλείψω = ἐν-λείψω. L's λείψω means simply 'leave'.]

632–35. I'll give you much adornment etc.: Iphigenia presumably envisages dressing, adorning and anointing Orestes after he is killed and before his body is burned on an altar inside the temple. The process is suitable for an epic hero. In *Odyssey* 24.58–68 the ghost of Achilles hears how after the *prothesis* his body

210 COMMENTARY

was clothed in fine robes brought by Thetis and the Nereids and after seventeen days of mourning was anointed with oil and honey and then cremated. In classical Athens the adornment of a body for burial included flowers, wreaths, ribbons and jewellery, and it was wrapped in a shroud (Kurtz–Boardman 1971, 144). Little is known of the use of honey for funerals in this period (Kurtz–Boardman 191).[19] **and †*quench*† your body with yellow olive-oil:** we need something like 'anoint', but no suitable verb has been found (»» Kyriakou). **the flower-dripped dew of the humming mountain-bee:** see 165 n.

637. lest you hold this hostility against me: μή μούγκαλῇς = μὴ μοι ἐγκαλῇς, 'lest you bring as a charge against me'. [Jackson 1955, 175 corrected L's μὴ μου λάβῃς ('don't take my hostility'). Parker prints **μὴ μούγκαλῇς** with a stop ('don't hold my hostility against me'), but a negative command with present subjunctive verb is unparalleled in pre-Hellenistic Greek.]

638. servants, guard them here etc.: the prisoners must remain **unbound** as sacred property of the goddess (467–69). These servants are probably those who assisted Iphigenia with her libations, have remained with her since then and will be sent back into the temple when she re-enters from it at 725 (»» Bain 1981, 37–39). Parker prefers to assume that temple servants come and go unobtrusively as needed (they might, for example, have re-entered the temple at the end of the parodos and emerged again as the captives arrive). Kyriakou (pp. 39, 213–15) argues that no Taurians should be present in the ensuing scene and that the *prospoloi* addressed here must be the Chorus (as in 63), but this assumes that Iphigenia's plan to release Pylades with the letter must be kept secret. In fact she has had the letter ready for some time and has only been waiting for the right person to carry it (582–96); the opportunity arises now because these prisoners can be relied on and are acquainted with Argos. There are also two of them, and apparently one sacrifice will satisfy the community (595f.). Iphigenia expects Thoas to allow Pylades' release (741f.) and even thinks that she too will eventually be allowed to return to Argos (751f.). All of this is a different matter from the later plan which involves the theft of the divine image and the escape of both prisoners and herself. If no servants are present in the ensuing scene, some will have to return with Iphigenia only to be dismissed immediately (725f.). For the prisoners' arrival and the ensuing conversation in visual art see *LIMC* V, 'Iphigeneia' nos. 14–18, 52–55.

639–42. Perhaps it's unexpected news: Iphigenia speaks guardedly, not identifying the 'loved ones' she plans to send the letter to and thus avoiding overconfidence and the possibility that some divine power will be tempted to thwart her hopes. This makes yet another dramatic irony: she does not know just how unexpected and incredible the delivery of the news will be. Incredulity and joy are constant motifs in recognition scenes, cf. 782, 793–97, 832, 837–42.

---

[19] The use of honey to preserve the bodies of Spartan kings is a special case with heroic connotations.

COMMENTARY 211

643–57. The Chorus's brief song punctuates the action and catches the balance of emotions: commiseration for Orestes' death, consolation in Pylades' escape. Paradoxically, Orestes welcomes his death and Pylades regrets his escape, anticipating his offer to stay and die with Orestes in the next scene. The women address the prisoners in excited dochmiac metre, and they reply in spoken trimeters (»» Parker xc–xci, 192f.). Lines 643–45 and 647–49 are probably each four dochmiacs (see notes below), so that the addresses to Orestes and Pylades are symmetrical and lines 651–57 addressed to both are like an epode.

645. destined: μελόμενον, 'being a concern (to)'; cf. *Hel.* 196f., 'the ruins of Ilium are a concern (μέλουσι) to destructive fire', *Hel.* 1161, *Andr.* 850. **lustral water's bloody shower:** cf. 442–45 n. **[⟨*wretched one*⟩: ⟨μέλεον⟩** makes the verse two regular dochmiacs. Repeated μελ- words often express sorrow or anxiety in tragedy, e.g. 853f., *Supp.* 598, *Ion* 900, *Hel.* 173. The adjective αἱμακτός (< αἱμάσσω, 'stain with blood') is seen only here.]

646. Be happy: χαίρετε also means 'farewell', but its literal sense is played on here as in line 708.

649. you will set foot (πόδ' ἐμβάσῃ): for the idiom with πόδα see 130–32 n. [L's ποτ' ἐπεμβάσῃ gives 'you will at some time enter upon your native land', with awkward phrasing and metre.]

652–54. †*Ah, Ah, you are perishing etc.*†: L's text is almost meaningless. [Bothe's ⟨δύο⟩ διολλῦσαι '(dispatchings) destroying two' (i.e. both prisoners) is printed by Diggle, Kovacs and Parker. According to Parker it 'gives excellent sense following 650: the sending home of Pylades destroys both men'. But the Chorus has just congratulated Pylades on his release (648f.), and while he refuses to rejoice (650) and they then grieve for him too (655f.), there is no reason for anyone to think his return home will destroy him. Musgrave's διόλλυσαι... πότερος ὁ μᾶλλον, 'you are perishing...which one the more?' (Sansone, Cropp 2000 and earlier editors with some variations) is open to the same objection; only Orestes is going to perish.]

655. My mind still wavers etc.: 'My mind still intends ambivalent twin things'; cf. 124–25 n., *Iliad* 16.435 διχθὰ δέ μοι κραδίη μέμονε φρέσιν ὁρμαίνοντι, 'My heart intends divergently as I deliberate in my mind'.

658–724. Orestes finally pursues the question of the priestess's identity and her connection with Argos, only for Pylades to take the discussion in a different direction with his noble demand to die with Orestes. Like Orestes, Pylades speaks of his fear of disgrace (674, 683), but again that is not his only motive, nor an ignoble one (see 605–607 n.). Orestes' replies with a speech constructed in three parts, each neatly subdivided: 687–98 arguments against Pylades giving up his own life (an additional disgrace for Orestes, Pylades not doomed to misfortune like Orestes, he can rescue Orestes' name and family); 699–707 injunctions to Pylades (survive and prosper, commemorate Orestes, protect Electra); 708–15 Coda (Fare well, Pylades' loyalty commended, Apollo's disloyalty rebuked).

212 COMMENTARY

Pylades responds accordingly, promising to fulfil Orestes' wishes, reaffirming his own *philia* and suggesting that Apollo may yet be vindicated (716–22).

662. Calchas wise in bird-signs: in the *Iliad* Calchas is 'best of all bird-seers' (1.69), 'prophetic bird-teller' (13.70).

663. and famed Achilles: Ἀχιλλέως...ὄνομα, 'the name of Achilles'. Such periphrases originate in epic diction (e.g. 'might of Heracles' or 'Heraclean might' for 'mighty Heracles') and proliferate in lyric and tragic poetry (»» KG 1.280, Breitenbach 201f.). Cf. 905–6 n.

665–66. This stranger is an Argive etc.: at last Euripides allows Orestes to see this.

670–71. the sufferings of kings: such as those of the leaders at Troy whom Iphigenia has asked about. Pylades wants to change the subject and suggests that anyone could ask about such well-known men. **everyone who gives them any thought:** 'all from whom there is any attention'. For the generalizing subjunctive ᾗ without ἄν see Goodwin §540, *CGCG* 50.21 n. 1).

675. I shared the voyage etc.: 'having sailed together, it's binding on me to die together as well'. Pylades argues similarly in *Or.* 1074. The shift from πλεύσας (nom.) to δεῖ με (acc.) is not unusual (anacoluthon, cf. 695–98(?), 947f., 964f.; »» KG 2.108). [L's κοινῇ τ᾿ ἔπλευσα is slightly illogical ('I both sailed with you, I should also share your death').]

678. The people at large etc.: 'I shall seem to the many (for the many are bad [or 'the bad are many'])'. Pylades distinguishes his inferiors (κακοί) from noble men of good breeding (ἀγαθοί), as often in early Greek ethical poetry (Theognis, Pindar etc.; for the fourth century see Dover 1974, 41–45). Nobles fear being criticized by inferiors, e.g. *Iliad* 22.104–10, *Od.* 6.275–88, 21.320–29. Admetus fears his enemies will blame him for having let his wife die in his place, *Alc.* 954–60.

679. that I got home safely myself: the concentration of σ-sounds in προδοὺς σεσῶσθαι σ᾿ αὐτός etc. is an example of the 'sigmatism' for which Euripides was apparently notorious (»» Mastronarde on *Med.* 476); cf. 757, 762f., 765 again involving forms of σῴζω. [L's σώζεσθ(αι) gives a very unlikely elision of the infinitive ending, and the perfect σεσῶσθαι makes better sense. Accented σ(ὲ) should probably be understood as in 656, contrasting **you** with **myself.**]

682. seeing that I'm married etc.: ὡς δὴ...γαμῶν, 'as indeed marrying' (a 'registering' present tense, 22–23 n.). δή stresses that this is what the πολλοί would unjustly think (»» Denniston 230). **heiress** in a limited sense: here and in *Hipp.* 1011 the word ἔγκληρος is equivalent to the technical term ἐπίκληρος denoting a woman in whom her father's estate (κλῆρος) was vested if her father had died without a male heir. In Athenian law Electra would become ἐπίκληρος to Agamemnon's estate once Orestes was dead, and her sons by Pylades would inherit it at their maturity. Pylades would manage the property in the meantime. »» Kyriakou on 680–82.

COMMENTARY 213

684–85. and it's surely right: 'and there isn't (any way) how it's not right'. **burned with you:** understand συν-πυρωθῆναι from the preceding infinitives (KG 2.568).

687–88. Don't say such things: εὔφημα φώνει, 'voice propitious things' (cf. 123 n.), here implying not just 'be quiet' but 'stop this talk of death, or it might come true'. **I must bear my own troubles:** Orestes refuses to allow Pylades to share the pain of his misfortune and so multiply his own pain. Aristotle discussing friendship points out that for this reason we ought to allow our friends to share in our troubles as little as possible, hence the saying ἅλις ἐγὼ δυστυχῶν, 'It's enough that I suffer misfortune' (*Eth.Nic.* 1171b4–18, noted by Lloyd 2002, 152; cf. Isaeus 2.8 ἱκανὸς…αὐτὸς ἀτυχῶν). Thus Admetus explains why he concealed his wife's death from Heracles ('It was enough that I lament my own trouble', *Alc.* 1041), Oedipus reacts to Antigone's wish to share his exile and death ('Stay here and prosper; I'll take care of my own troubles', *Pho.* 1685).

691–92. For my part: τὸ…εἰς ἐμέ is adverbial as in *HF* 171. **it's no bad thing etc.:** a conventional response to extreme misfortune, e.g. *Hcld.* 595f. (Heracles' daughter), *HF* 1255–1302 (Heracles), *Tro.* 637 (Andromache), S. *Aj.* 430–80 (Ajax), *Ant.* 461–7 (Antigone), Bacchyl. 3.37–47 (Croesus), Hdt. 7.46.3f. On such rhetoric see Fowler 1987, and on shame as a motive in such conclusions Dover 1974, 236–42.[20]

695–98. If you are saved etc.: (You) once saved, having acquired sons from my sister…my name can come to be…'. The optatives γένοιτ' ἄν and ἐξαλειφ–θείη ἄν make cautious predictions (cf. 673, 1055; *CGCG* §34.13); Orestes does not know that Pylades will get home safely. He wants his name remembered and his *oikos* perpetuated through sons born to Electra and Pylades. He therefore tells Pylades to prepare a cenotaph bearing a memorial where he will be mourned (702–5), and not to abandon Electra and leave his father's *oikos* without heirs (706–8). Pylades responds accordingly (716–18). The cenotaph is essential for preserving Orestes' name, a commonplace in funeral epigrams such as *Anth.Pal.* 7.271, 272 (= Callimachus, *epigr.* 17, 18 Pfeiffer), 274, 291, *IEryth.* 305. Preservation of name and fame compensate for loss of life, Theognis 237–52; Tyrtaeus fr. 12.27–32 *IEG* adds mourning and honoured descendants. In *Odyssey* 24.80–94 Achilles' ghost learns that the Achaeans piled up a great barrow in which his bones were buried, mixed with those of Patroclus and beside those of Antilochus: 'thus you did not lose your name (ὄνομα) even in death, but always amongst all men you will have fair fame' (24.93f.). Orestes dies without glory but still wants

---

[20] According to Kyriakou, 'Orestes' point is not that his life is generally not worth living or that it is preferable for him to die than live in this situation…[he] does not choose to die because of his plight but in order to save his helper, friend and brother-in-law whose survival is important to him for various reasons'. Nevertheless, what he says here is that he is better off dying than living, given his godsent afflictions; and Pylades responds to this (719–22).

214 COMMENTARY

his name preserved and honoured. **you will get sons from my sister:** in this play Electra has been married to Pylades after the matricide (cf. 716f., 912–15), as at the end of Euripides' *Electra* and *Orestes*. Hellanicus, *FGrH* 4 F 155 (in Pausanias 2.16.7) named Medon and Strophius as their sons (»» Fowler 2013, 560f.).

[The anacoluthon σωθείς...ὄνομά τ' ἐμοῦ γένοιτ' ἄν is easily understood (cf. 675 n.), but the sequence τε...οὐδέ is very rare (»» Denniston 514; Diggle suggests that a line may gave been lost before 697, and Kovacs supplies e.g. ⟨σύ τ' ἄν τὸ λοιπὸν βίον ἔχοις εὐδαίμονα⟩, '⟨you could live henceforth a happy life,⟩ and my name...'). The phrasing ὄνομα...ἐμοῦ γένοιτ' ἄν ('my name would come to be') is also odd. Sansone compares Pl. *Prot.* 335a7 οὐδ' ἄν ἐγένετο Πρωταγόρου ὄνομα ἐν τοῖς Ἕλλησιν ('nor would the name of Protagoras have come to be amongst the Hellenes'), but that includes a predicate (cf. LSJ 'γίγνομαι' II.2–3) and, as Kyriakou notes, it refers to Protagoras's name *becoming* known; similarly E. *Hel.* 588 τοὔνομα γένοιτ' ἄν πολλαχοῦ, τὸ σῶμα δ' οὔ ('one's name can come to be in many places, one's body not').]

699. dwell in your father's house: δόμους...πατρός is often rendered as '*my* father's house', but Orestes is talking about Pylades living a normal life as his father's heir, as he himself cannot.

700. horse-rearing Argos: cf. 133–36 n.

701. by this right hand of yours I charge you: Orestes grasps Pylades' right hand in a gesture of supplication; cf. 1068 (Iphigenia grasps the right hands, cheeks or knees of chorus-members as she begs for their silence), *Hipp.* 325f., 605, *IA* 909. The formula is parodied in Ar. *Thesm.* 936f. Here the gesture is also a request for Pylades to affirm the promise through the clasping of right hands (*dexiôsis*: S. *Trach.* 1181f., *Phil.* 813, *OC* 1632; »» Torrance in Sommerstein–Torrance 2014, 144–47).

702–5. pile up a barrow etc.: Orestes speaks his own epitaph. His requests for a cenotaph, tomb offerings and a report to his family of the sad manner of his death are typical of funerary epigrams, especially for those dying abroad or at sea: »» Lattimore 1962, 126–36, 199f., Tarán 1979, 132–49. In *Iliad* 7.86–91 Hector imagines future voyagers to Troy viewing Ajax's tomb and remembering how he killed him. Kyriakou notes that Orestes 'does not explicitly mention the Taurians or any other unpleasant or demeaning aspect of his sacrifice'. **tokens of remembrance (μνημεῖα):** i.e. things that will cause him to be remembered. Iphigenia recalls sending locks to her mother from Aulis as μνημεῖα for her own tomb (821). **at the hands of an Argive woman etc.:** Iphigenia will initiate and supervise the sacrifice, although she has explained that she will not strike the death blow herself (621–24; cf. 38–41 n.). **let my sister offer tears and hair:** Orestes' request may recall the famous offering of a lock of his own hair at Agamemnon's tomb which preceded his reunion with the mourning Electra (A. *Cho.* 7, 168ff., S. *El.* 52, 900f., E. *El.* 91, 508ff.). Iphigenia laments being unable to offer a lock of her hair at Orestes' tomb (171f.). For other examples see

COMMENTARY 215

Cropp on *El.* 91, and for tomb offerings in general Kurtz–Boardman 1971, 75–89, 99–102; Johnston 1999, 41–43.

706–7. never forsake my sister etc.: more dramatic irony as Orestes' thoughts move from the sister preparing to kill him to the sister he knows. She will be all the more reliant on her husband's goodwill when the loss of its male heir has left Agamemnon's *oikos* destitute and Pylades' alliance with it therefore worthless.

708. fare well: the parting formula χαῖρε has its literal sense here, as Kyriakou notes. In this final instruction Orestes wishes Pylades the happiness he deserves because of his unfailing loyalty and support.

711–15. Phoebus, seer though he is etc.: Orestes compares Pylades' loyalty with Apollo's apparent betrayal, ending his speech on a note of despair which will once again be answered by Pylades' optimism. On Apollo as seer (*mantis*) and Orestes' complaint see 570–71 n.

713. in shame: the god feels *aidôs* (shame, embarrassment) at his poor treatment of a mortal and wishes to avoid being criticized for it. Cf. *Ion* 1555–59 (Apollo and Creusa), *Hel.* 884–86 (Aphrodite and the phantom Helen). »» Cairns 1993, 302 n. 135.

715. I perish in my turn: the verb ἀνταπόλλυμαι puns on the god's name, emphasizing his responsibility for Orestes' ruin: cf. *Phaethon* 225f.

716–18. You shall have a tomb etc.: i.e. a cenotaph. Pylades responds exactly to Orestes' requests in 702–7.

720. [though indeed you are standing etc.: recent editors change καίτοι γ' ἐγγὺς to καίτοι κἀγγὺς (= καὶ ἐγγὺς) since the combination καίτοι γε (as opposed to καίτοι...γε) is very rare in poetry (Diggle 1981, 85). It is however common in prose and there is no reason why a poet should not have used it. καίτοι καί is even rarer in poetry.][21]

721–22. yet sure, O sure it is etc.: a common argument against despair, here countering Orestes' argument for it (691–94); e.g. *HF* 101–4, F 100, F 301, Theognis 1143f., S. *Trach.* 124–26, Thuc. 7.77.3f.; cf. Aristot. *Nic.Eth.* 1116a2–4. See also 475–78 n. on unpredictable fortunes. The periphrastic ἔστιν...διδοῦσα (≈ δίδωσι) adds emphasis to Pylades' gnomic statement (»» *CGCG* 52.51, KG I.38–40, Bentein 2016, 216). **on occasion: ὅταν τύχῃ**, 'when it happens'. Kyriakou prefers 'when the time comes' suggesting 'that a reversal is bound to occur sooner or later', but Pylades has no grounds for such confidence and simply means that they should hope for the best. Kyriakou compares *Hipp.* 428–30, *El.*

---

[21] καίτοι γε is attested in *Tro.* 1015 (probably wrongly), Ar. *Ach.* 611 and Com. adesp. fr. 1000.10 *PCG* (cf. Austin 1987, 70); in prose a few times in late 5th/early 4th C texts and then some 800 times to around 400 AD. Diggle leaves the prose examples aside, while Kyriakou and Parker seem unaware of them. καίτοι καί in poetry, only S. *Ant.* 949 (conj. Hermann; in [A.] *PV* 642 καί means 'even').

216 COMMENTARY

1169, F 979, but in those cases it is respectively Time, God and Justice that guarantee a reaction. For the alternative senses see Barrett on *Hipp.* 428–30.

723. Phoebus's words are giving me no help: Orestes complains once again that Apollo is not fulfilling the promises that persuaded him to embark on his mission (85–94) – just as Iphigenia arrives to complete the recognition.

725–68. The recognition sequence approaches its climax as Iphigenia returns with her letter. Two further diversions are provided as she requests an oath from Pylades and oaths are exchanged, then Pylades' request for a contingency clause brings her to the point of reciting her message and so at last naming Orestes. The procedure is neatly packaged in stichomythia: oaths proposed 735–42, oaths stated 743–46, guarantor-gods named 747–49, sanctions 750–52 (»» Fletcher 2012, 4–11 and on this scene 194–202; details in the notes below). This scene is represented in a number of South Italian vase-paintings inspired by the play (*LIMC* V, 'Iphigeneia', nos. 19–26; cf. Taplin 2007. nos 48, 49; Hall 2013, 69–83). Mueller 2016, 179–84 discusses its symbolic function.

725–26. Be gone now etc.: the temple servants who have guarded the prisoners since she went to fetch the letter (638 n.) are removed so that the recognition and planning can proceed without Taurians present.

727. the many-leaved letter: δέλτου...πολύθυροι διαπτυχαί, 'the tablet's multi-leaved folds'. This probably refers to a single pair of tablets folded together (cf. 584 δέλτον, 760 ἐν δέλτου πτυχαῖς, similarly *IA* 98, 112); Aristotle cites it as an example of poetic exaggeration, 'making one many' (*Rhet.* 1407b35). The content she recites to Pylades is quite short even in its poetic form (770–78), and the letter is small and slight in the vase-paintings, like the examples from a late 5th-century Athenian tomb described by Pöhlmann–West 2012, 3–5. [L's πολύθρηνοι is unmetrical and means 'much-lamenting'. Aristotle's πολύθυροι is not known elsewhere in this sense, but θύρα could mean '(tablet)-leaf' and δίθυρος 'two-leaved' in Attic usage (Pollux 4.18, 10.57; LSJ 'δίθυρος').]

741–42. And will the king...Yes, I'll persuade him: Iphigenia will in fact persuade the king to let her take both both Pylades and Orestes to the shore, where Orestes will put *her* on board along with the image of Artemis. **I'll put the man on board:** ναὸς ἐσβήσω σκάφος, 'I'll move (him) into the ship's hull'; ἐσβήσω is causative (LSJ 'εἰσβαίνω' II) like ἐπιβαίνω earlier (214–17 n.). For 'ship's hull' cf. 410 n., 1345.

746. I shall see you safely past the Dark Rocks: i.e. back to the civilized Greek world (124–25 n.).

747–49. Which god do you call on etc.: oath-taking required the naming of gods as witnesses who could ensure the punishment of perjurers (»» Sommerstein–Torrance 2014, 132–38). Iphigenia naturally swears by her patroness Artemis. Pylades swears by Zeus, the ultimate guarantor of all oaths. The fact that they are in Artemis's sanctuary adds to the solemnity of both their oaths.

COMMENTARY   217

750–52. And if you abandon your oath etc.: oath-takers pronounce sanctions for perjury in the form of 'conditional self-curses' (»» K. Konstantinidou in Sommerstein–Torrance 2014, 6–47 with 24–29 on this and similar tragic scenes). Here Pylades and Iphigenia deny themselves the return to their homeland for which both are hoping.

753–58. Listen, though etc.: Pylades now realises that he must guard against having sworn to something he might be unable to deliver. This serves the dramatic purpose of causing Iphigenia to recite her message and pronounce Orestes' name. Pylades' request is legalistically phrased (ἐξαίρετον...τόδ(ε), **this exception:** LSJ 'ἐξαιρετός' II.2). His distinction between **χρήματα, the goods** and **σῶμα, my self** ('my body') also has a legalistic tone. The χρήματα/σῶμα distinction is common from the late fifth century onwards, e.g. Democritus B 40, B 280 DK, Thuc. 1.141.5, 2.53.2 etc., Antiphon 5.63, Lysias 19.58, 25.4, 29.11. For the etymological play (**σῶμα...ἐκσώσω, I salvage myself**) cf. 765 and e.g. *Hec.* 301f., *HF* 203, S. *Ant.* 676, Pl. *Cratyl.* 400c.4–10; and for the sigmatism here and in 762f. and 765 see 679 n.

754. share it with us: ἔστω κοινός, 'let it be common', cf. 673.

759. more ways give more chances: 'multiple things hit on multiple things', perhaps a proverbial expression.

760. the folded letter: see 727 n.

765. by saving yourself (τὸ σῶμα σώσας) **etc.:** more etymological play (and more sigmatism) with a further neat contrast between **self** (σῶμα) and **words** (λόγους).

766. for both of us: 'on behalf of your matters (i.e. 'yourself', cf. 605–7 n.) and of me'. [L's τῶν θεῶν gives 'on behalf of the gods and of me'.]

769–97. Iphigenia's recital of her message finally leads her to name her brother and herself. She must in any case tell Pylades where to deliver the message, but the full recital allows a number of novel excitements. Iphigenia tells Pylades what she could very well be telling Orestes directly. His realisation of what is happening is emotionally striking and contrasts with her own continuing unawareness of his identity. Pylades can clinch the recognition by the simple act of 'delivering' the letter to Orestes (cf. 578–96 n.).

780, 781, 779. Pylades is amazed at hearing Orestes' name (**O gods,** 780) but politely does not press Iphigenia to explain this (781). She then repeats the name (779) and names herself as the sender (770–71). Pylades can hardly believe that she is alive, let alone that he is actually speaking to her (772), and she curtly points out that he is doing so (773) and recites her message for Orestes in full (774–76, 778) before Orestes reacts (777). [Jackson placed these lines after 769, supposing that they were omitted accidentally and then added at the foot of the page and re-entered wrongly when the text was recopied. With L's order, Pylades' amazement at hearing Orestes' name (780), his request for Iphigenia to proceed with her message (781) and her appeal to Orestes (779) come improbably after the

218 COMMENTARY

bulk of her message (774–78). »» Jackson 1955, 9–12 with further arguments of Kovacs 2003, 9–11; Parker on 769–81. L's order was defended by Schwinge 1968, 238–43, Bain 1977, 36 n. 1 and retained by Sansone, Diggle, Cropp 2000, Kyriakou. For the placement of 778 before 777 see the note below.]

781. I went off (ἐξέβην): i.e. I left the track (cf. *Med.* 56, S. *Phil.* 896; LSJ 'ἐκβαίνω' II.3).

772. But where is she etc.: Jackson's assignment of this line to Pylades rather than Orestes as in L is surely right, though not adopted by Kovacs or Parker. Iphigenia is talking to Pylades throughout 744–792. Orestes' only intervention is addressed to Pylades (777), and Iphigenia ignores it.

773. Don't distract me etc.: μὴ λόγων ἔκπληοσέ με, 'Don't knock me out of (my) words': cf. 912, *Or.* 549. [L's λόγοις gives 'Don't astound me with (your) words' (cf. 240 n.).]

776. I officiate in strangers' slaughter: 'I have stranger-murdering duties', cf. 53f. ('this stranger-killing art of mine') with 38–41 n.

778, 777. or I shall call down a curse: by not rescuing Iphigenia Orestes will share responsibility for her 'death' at Aulis and she will call down a curse on him and his family, to be enforced by her Erinyes. Parker places Iphigenia's threat before Orestes' aside (777), arguing that an interruption would reduce the impact of her appeal.

782. Now perhaps when he questions you: i.e. Orestes, to whom the message is addressed. The **things hard to believe** are the facts concerning her survival which she has not explained in the letter. τάχ' οὖν is a rhetorical idiom introducing a hypothetical objection requiring a response, e.g. *Supp.* 184 (see Collard's note), *Hec.* 1247, S. *Phil.* 305, Pl. *Apol.* 34c7, Isocr. 5.39, 12.149 (τάχ' οὖν ἄν τινες ἄτοπον εἶναί με φήσειαν, 'Now perhaps some people might say I'm being absurd'). [οὖν is 'progressive' (**Now**) leading to this further step in her instructions (»» Denniston 426). ἀφίξεται must replace L's ἀφίξομαι ('I shall arrive at') if this line is spoken by Iphigenia.]

788–90. The oaths you bound me with etc.: 'O (you) having encircled/ ensnared me with easy oaths', i.e. easy to fulfil and thus release herself from; **oaths** plural because this was a two-way process. For the notion of binding with oaths cf. *Med.* 161f., where Mastronarde compares Hdt. 3.19.2; and for making the oath **secure** Xen. *Anab.* 3.2.10, *Cyrop.* 5.1.22 etc., LSJ 'ἐμπεδόω'. [ὁμόσας, **having sworn** referring to himself is better than ὁμόσασ(α) referring to Iphigenia. Pylades has no need to congratulate Iphigenia on her oath.]

798–810. Orestes has readily accepted the 'incredible' identification of his sister, but Iphigenia remains sceptical and requires proofs of his identity, thus delaying the reunion (rather artificially) one last time. The motif is reminiscent of *Odyssey* 23 where Penelope refuses to recognize Odysseus until he reveals his knowledge of their marital bed, or the recognition scene of Euripides' *Electra* where Electra is finally convinced of Orestes' presence when she is shown his childhood scar,

COMMENTARY   219

but Iphigenia is simply incredulous rather than circumspect or petulant, and the delay is more perfunctory.

798–802. Stranger, you're wrongfully defiling etc.: Orestes begins to embrace Iphigenia, she turns away from him, and the Chorus warns him to treat her respectfully. He then begs her not to shrink from embracing her very own brother, thus getting her attention. The embrace is delayed until she is convinced of his identity (827–30). [Lines 798–99 are assigned to the Chorus in L. Monk assigned them to Iphigenia, arguing that she must react immediately to Orestes' attempt to embrace her. Recent editors have accepted this. Telò (2003) reviews opinions and argues that this formal warning suits the Chorus better, even if this is their only intervention in the scene and other recognition scenes handle such moments differently (Ion rejects Xuthus's embrace, *Ion* 519–24; Menelaus rejects Helen's embrace, *Hel.* 567).]

803. Won't you stop that talk: 'won't you stop talking?', i.e. 'Come off it' (French 'Tu parles!'); cf. Hdt.7.10η.1 παῦσαι λέγων λόγους ματαίους περὶ Ἑλλήνων, 'stop talking rubbish about the Greeks', Ar. *Wasps* 1194 παῦε παῦ', οὐδὲν λέγεις, 'Stop, stop, you're talking nonsense'; Fantuzzi on *Rhesus* 273, Collard 2018, 173.

804. Argos is his haunt: this is what τὸ τ' Ἄργος αὐτοῦ μεστόν ('Argos is full of him') seems to mean, although there is no exact parallel. In Ar. *Frogs* 1021 Aeschylus's *Seven* is a drama Ἄρεως μεστόν, 'full of Ares'. Also loosely comparable is *Alexandros* F 62d.7 πᾶν ἄστυ πληροῖ Τρωϊκὸν γαυρούμενος 'He fills the whole town of Troy exulting in his success.'

805. Foolish woman: foolish in her inability to see the truth, a sympathetic comment rather than a rebuke. For the vocative τάλαινα in such expressions see e.g. *Hipp.* 327, A. *Sept.* 262, S. *El.* 388, 879, and for the various nuances of τάλας, τάλαινα Denniston on *El.* 1171, Schmidt 1968, 36–39, Wilson 1971.

811–26. The proofs offered by Orestes are subtly invented to evoke the three key events which summed up the family's history in the Prologue (1ff.) and Parodos (186ff.): Pelops' race for Hippodameia, the quarrel of Atreus and Thyestes, the sacrifice of Iphigenia. Their recollection now and their reduction to relics seem to consign them to the past and to suggest the opening of a new chapter as the play's turning-point is reached. The tokens which Orestes says he knows only **by hearsay from Electra** (811) – weaving and ritual offerings of water and hair – echo the traditional story of Orestes (in *Choephori* Orestes' hair and Electra's weaving effect the recognition as libations are poured at Agamemnon's tomb) but are transformed into items of Iphigenia's personal history. Pelops' spear (823–25 n.) is newly imported and has several features which give it unique value as a proof: it is very old and long hidden away, it is the only relic which Orestes has seen himself, and being secluded in the **maidens' apartments** (826) it is known to very few people (the recognition tokens in *Ion* 1337–62 have similarly unique features). Moreover, this reminder of Pelops' escape with Hippodameia closes the

220 COMMENTARY

first half of the play with a reference back to its opening (1f.) which may be seen as setting the tone for Orestes' escape with Iphigenia (»» Burnett 1971, 64, O'Brien 1988a, 103, 113f.). All these effects are overlooked by Aristotle in *Poetics* 1454b30–36 where the proofs are criticized as being too artificial by contrast with the 'plausible' revelation of Iphigenia's identity through her wish to send the letter (1455a16–19).

811. I'll tell you this first, then: λέγοιμ' ἄν, 'I would tell', is a tentative or polite alternative to the future indicative (cf. Rijksbaron 41). It may preface a declaration or argument, sometimes (as here) responding to a request or invitation; cf. E. *Supp.* 465, *El.* 1060, *Or.* 640, Soph. *OT* 95 (reluctant assent), Ar. *Lys.* 119. It may also preface a narrative speech (»» 939 n.).

812. strife between Atreus and Thyestes: for the mythical details concerning the golden lamb and the Sun's change of course see notes on 191–202, Cropp on *El.* 699–746.

814. fine weaving: cf. 312 n.

818. And the lustral water etc. : i.e. water from an Argive spring in which Iphigenia would have bathed on the morning of her wedding. The special *loutrophoros* vessel was presumably kept at Argos as a relic. The *loutra* ritual in marriage suggested purification and release at the transition from one stage of life to the next, and promoted fecundity (»» Oakley–Sinos 1993, 15f. with index '*loutrophoros*' and illustrations, Reeder 1995, Catalogue nos 22–27). Those who died before marriage also received *loutra*, and *loutrophoroi* might be dedicated to commemorate them as well as a completed wedding; hence a special resonance here as e.g. at *HF* 482. **you took** ('received') **from your mother to Aulis:** normally the bride's mother would have assisted her daughter in fetching the water and supervised the bath. The mention here recalls Iphigenia's isolation at Aulis (cf. 364–68). [ἀδέξω = ἃ ἐδέξω. L's ἀνεδέξω gives 'And you received lustral water', but λούτρ(α) is better taken as another object of οἶσθ(α) (814) as Iphigenia's reply (οἶδα) shows.]

819. That wedding was not so happy etc: 'For that marriage did not (by) being fortunate deprive me (of remembering it)', cf. *Andr.* 913, LSJ 'ἐσθλός' II.3, 'ἀφαιρέω' II.3. She is compelled to remember the horrors of what should have been a joyful occasion. Some scholars complain pedantically that this implies that she might have forgotten her wedding if it had been a happy one. [The syntax of μ' ἀφείλετο is correctly explained in a note above the line in L, τοῦτο τὸ μὴ εἰδέναι, 'of knowing/remembering this' (mistranslated in Parker's note).]

820–21. And what of the locks etc.: for τί γάρ see on 533 (531–36 n.). Again the gift has a pathetic ambivalence since hair was cut and dedicated by girls preparing for marriage as well as in mourning and as a tomb-offering (Oakley–Sinos 1993, 14). **tokens…instead of my body:** her tomb would be an empty one like the one Orestes expects for himself (702–5 n.).

COMMENTARY   221

823–25. the ancient spear of Pelops: see 1–5 n., 191–93 n., 811–26 n. Pelops was regularly portrayed heroically with a spear, e.g. on the east pediment of the temple of Zeus at Olympia (»» *LIMC* VII, 'Pelops'). **stored away in your maidens' apartment:** the spear was secluded as an heirloom, like Odysseus' bow and other 'laid-away' valuables (κειμήλια) stored in a special room to which Penelope as mistress of the house held the key (*Odyssey* 21.1–60). Ordinary weapons were normally hung in the more public men's rooms (ἀνδρῶνες) where they were more accessible and more liable to damage (cf. *Od.* 16.284–94, 19.1–25, Alcaeus fr. 357 Lobel–Page, Hdt. 1.34.3). Euripides takes a slight liberty in placing Pelops' spear in the **maidens' apartment** rather than simply the women's quarters, but this (besides making it more private) underlines the comparison between Hippodameia (carried away by Pelops long ago) and Iphigenia (now to be carried away by Orestes), and the contrast between Iphigenia's anxious dream set in the maidens' apartment (46) and the joyful outcome now before her. This is an apt resting place for the spear which accompanied **the maid from Pisa** from maidenhood to marriage.

827–99. The reunion celebrated

Iphigenia breaks into song to express her emotions as she and her brother embrace in the climactic moment of a tragic recognition (cf. *El.* 578f., *Ion* 1437–40, *Hel.* 625–30, S. *El.* 1226 and the parodies of Euripides in Ar. *Thesm.* 912–15, *Frogs* 1322). The embrace seems to last until Iphigenia turns to the Chorus at 842 and lightheartedly suggests that her joy might fly off to the sky. Prompted by spoken interjections from a more restrained Orestes, her thoughts move from joy at the recovery of her brother (827–49) to recollection of her own near-death (850–67), then to her near-killing of Orestes (866–72). The sequence becomes a virtual monody for Iphigenia (though still addressed to Orestes) as she anxiously explores their urgent need for an escape plan (873–99), subject of the next scene.

The Reunion celebration, like a choral ode, provides a major break between the dramatic scenes of recognition and planning. Exchanges of song (*amoibaion*) or of song with speech (*epirrhema*) between actor and chorus or between two actors are a standard and probably fundamental element of both tragedy and comedy. Many of Euripides' plays include the type found here, with one actor singing and one speaking, a loose non-strophic structure, and mainly dochmiac rhythms in the sung part. Several are reunion celebrations in other late plays and have much in common with this one: *Ion* 1437–1509 (Creusa and Ion), *Helen* 625–99 (Helen and Menelaus), *Hypsipyle* 1591–1632 (Hypsipyle and her sons); similarly S. *Electra* 1232–87 (Electra and Orestes). Jocasta's monody on her meeting with Polyneices in *Phoenician Women* 301–54 uses similar material in a different form. Common themes are the overflowing of joy and remembered grief, the unexpectedness of the reunion and of fortune's changes, reflections on past

222   COMMENTARY

trials and the uncertain prospects of future happiness. »» Matthiessen 1964, 134–38, Popp 1971, 260–66, Chong-Gossard 2006.

Iphigenia starts with one-and-a-half dialogue-trimeters, then breaks into dochmiacs interspersed (as often) with iambic and cretic measures, all with frequent resolutions heightening the excitement. The rhythm modulates into double-short rhythms at 848, 876, 880, 884–89, 895–97. Some problems are treated in the notes below (»» Parker xc–xci, 227–31; De Poli 2017 (lines 827–36); Willink 2009, 213–17). The mood is also heightened by verbal effects, especially apostrophe (845–49, 881f.), exclamations (861, 869, 894), questions (837–39, 874–80, 884f., 895–99), anaphora and other reduplications (832, 835f., 847, 852, 864, 869f., 874–76, 881, 894).

828–30. far away (τηλύγετον) from your homeland: τηλύγετος is an epic epithet for children (e.g. Orestes in *Il.* 9.143, 285), apparently meaning something like 'cherished', 'tender', 'late-born' or 'only-born'; etymology uncertain (»» Richardson on *Hom.Hymn.* 2.164, Beekes 'τηλύγετος'). Here Euripides seems to have related it artificially to the adverb τῆλε as in the epic phrase τῆλε φίλων καὶ πατρίδος αἴης, 'far from loved ones and homeland' (*Iliad* 11.817, 16.539, *Odyssey* 19.301, 24.290, *Hom.Hymn.* 3.526). [Deleting χθονός (Murray, Parker) makes line 829 a resolved iambic trimeter (⏑ – ⏑ – | ⏑ – ⏑ ⏖ | ⏑ ⏖ ⏑ –): »» Parker 230f., 232.]

832–33. a tear, a sob etc.: the repeated **κατά** belongs with the verb **νοτίζει** (*tmêsis*, as often in Euripides' lyrics, e.g. 880, 1145, 1276, 1279: »» Breitenbach 266, KG 1.534f.). [L gives these lines with 831 to Orestes, but the sung line 832 and the rest of that sentence must belong to Iphigenia. Bauer (1872, 13) gave all of 832–33, with L's τὸ σόν, to Iphigenia ('A tear...bedews your face, and mine as well'; thus Diggle and Parker). For the text printed here (and by Kovacs), with Lee's **τοὐμὸν** replacing τὸ σόν (**my face**) and **ὡσαύτως δ' ἐμόν (and mine as well)** spoken by Orestes see Cropp 1997, 33f. Iphigenia might notice Orestes' tears, but it seems unlikely that she would describe his emotions in some detail and her own in two words.]

836–38. O my soul etc.: addresses to the soul (or θυμός 'spirit', καρδία 'heart') mark moments of high emotion or stress, e.g. 881f., *Ion* 859, *Or.* 466f., F 307a, F 924, S. *Trach.* 1259–62. For **κρεῖσσον ἢ λόγοισιν** ('more strongly than for words') see LSJ 'κρείσσων' II.

843–44. flying...up to the sky: Euripides uses this image for blessings vanished at *Med.* 440, *Andr.* 1219, *HF* 69, 510 (also for escape from troubles, *Ion* 796, *Or.* 1375 etc., cf. Barrett on *Hipp.* 1290–93). [L's ἀμπταμένος would refer to Orestes flying away, but the topic now is Iphigenia's joy.]

845. Cyclopean hearth: i.e. the palace within the fortress of Mycenae (cf. 510 n.). Legend attributed the building of its massive stone walls to the gigantic Cyclopes, brothers of the Titans, also alluded to in *El.* 1158, *HF* 15, 944, *Tro,* 1087f. etc.

COMMENTARY   223

849. a light (φάος) for our house: see 187–88 n.

850. In birth we are fortunate etc.: fortunate as children of a royal family (378–79 n.), unfortunate in suffering from the family's past crimes (186–213).

852–53. I remember etc.: ἐγῷδ' = ἐγὼ οἶδα. [Bruhn adjusted L's ἐγὼ μέλεος ('I, unhappy, remember') to give two dochmiacs in 852 and an emotional repetition of the verb. μελεόφρων ('unhappy-minded') is unique and perhaps invented by Euripides for the resonance with μέλεος (cf. 645 n.), like μελεοπόνος – μελεοπαθής in [A.] *Sept.* 963.]

856–59. Unsung by wedding songs etc.: stressing both the pathos of the girl's untimely death (cf. e.g. *Hec.* 416, S. *Ant.* 813–16, 876f., 917f.) and the cruel deception of Iphigenia over her 'marriage' to Achilles (cf. 366–71, *IA* 693). For the tradition see 24–25 n. [κλισίαν λέκτρων is lit. 'bed-couch', a pleonasm (370 n.) like *Alc.* 925 λέκτρων κοίτας, *Med.* 437 κοίτας (gen.) λέκτρον etc. (LSJ 'λέκτρον' II, Breitenbach 194). λέκτρον is a poetic word, very frequent in Euripides (90+ times compared with 5 in Aeschylus and 6 in Sophocles) and usually plural.]

861–72. L's speaker-assignments were corrected by Tyrwhitt (861–64) and Seidler (865–69) so that Iphigenia sings throughout and Orestes responds with iambic trimeters. Monk reunited 867 with 865.

861. those lustrations: see 54 n., 244. [L's χερνίβων ἐκεῖ ('the lustrations there') is metrically deficient. Orestes' reply, ᾤμωξα κἀγώ ('I too cry οἴμοι'), shows that Iphigenia has just cried οἴμοι.]

865–67. other things are following from others: their present plight is another step in the sufferings of their family stemming from the golden lamb episode (cf. 195–202). For the phrasing cf. *Hec.* 690 ἕτερα δ' ἀφ' ἑτέρων κακὰ κακῶν κυρεῖ, 'other evils are occurring from/after other evils'. **through some daimon's stroke of fortune (τύχᾳ):** this turn of events is divinely motivated, unpredictable from the human point of view but nevertheless caused by a **daimon** intent (it seems) on eliminating the Pelopid dynasty (157–59 n.). For this sense cf. *Hipp.* 371f. τύχα Κυπρίδος, 'Kypris's stroke of fortune', *HF* 1393 Ἥρας μιᾷ πληγέντες...τύχῃ, 'struck by one blow of fortune from Hera' (»» Platnauer here, Bond on *HF* 1393). On τύχη 'fortune' see Introduction, pp. 8f.

866–72. Suppose, poor woman etc.: i.e., 'How close you came to killing me just as your father killed you'. **ὦ τάλαινα** is again sympathetic (though with a different nuance from 805: see note there), but Iphigenia's reply (**τόλμας, ἔτλαν**) picks up on its possible negative sense, 'daring' or 'ruthless'; cf. A. *Ag.* 224f. ἔτλα δ' οὖν θυτὴρ γενέσθαι θυγατρός, 'so he (Agamemnon) dared to become his daughter's sacrificer. **an unholy (ἀνόσιον) death:** i.e. repellent to the gods according to Greek religious law (130–32 n., 463–66 n.).

873–74. †And† what †the† ending †upon them†: inadequate sense. [Suggestions (app. crit.): 'As to what follows on these things, what ending (is

224 COMMENTARY

there?' (Platnauer/Diggle comparing A. *Ag.* 255 τἀπὶ τούτοισιν); 'What (is) the ending for (our) trials?' (Diggle).»» Kyriakou, Parker.]

876–80. What path...shall I find for you etc.: Iphigenia thinks only of saving Orestes. She does not yet know about his need to steal the image of Artemis or think about escaping herself, but will take the lead in planning an escape for all of them after hearing about his mission in the next scene. **from this community, from a bloody death**: if the text is correct, ἀπὸ πόλεως ἀπὸ φόνου is virtually a hendiadys, 'from a bloody death in this community'. For the Taurian *polis*/community see 38 n., and for the emotive repetition (anaphora) cf. 832 and e.g. *Hel.* 695 ἐμὲ δὲ πατρίδος ἀπο⟨πρὸ⟩...ἔβαλε θεὸς ἀπὸ πόλεος ἀπό τε σέθεν (a god cast me away from our homeland, from our city and from you'), *Or.* 170f. οὐκ ἀφ' ἡμῶν, οὐκ ἀπ' οἴκων | πάλιν ἀνὰ πόδα σὸν εἰλίξεις ('Will you not turn your foot back from us, from our house');»» Breitenbach 232f. **before the blade comes close**: ἐπὶ... πελάσαι *tmêsis*, cf. 832–33 n. [**πόλεως** is perhaps out of place here, even if the Taurian community can be called a *polis* (38 n.). Parker prints Köchly's ἀπὸ ξένας, 'from a foreign land' (LSJ 'ξένη' 2). Other suggestions: ἀπὸ πόλεως ἀνδροφόνου, 'from a man-slaying community' (Sansone), ἀποπόλεως ἀπὸ φόνου, 'from slaughter far from your city' (Cropp 1997, 35f.). Diggle's ⟨τίνα σοι⟩ makes this verse an enoplian (dactylic colon: »» Parker xcvi–xcvii) like 848, 880, 886.]

881. my poor soul: see 836–38 n.

886–89. through barbarous tribes etc.: the preposition δι(ά) applies 'in common' to βάρβαρα φῦλα and ὁδοὺς ἀνόδους (cf. 296–98 n.). **impassable** ('pathless') **paths**: the oxymoron stresses the difficulty of the challenge (cf. 144–47 n., 897).

894. Wretched, wretched am I: [The metre is anomalous here and again in 896, and the bare **τάλαινα τάλαινα** is unparalleled in Euripides. An addition such as Diggle's τάλαιν' ⟨ἐγὼ⟩ τάλαινα (cf. *Pho.* 1294, *Phaethon* 270) may be needed.]

895–99. What god...or mortal or what unexpected event ('what from amongst things unexpected'): the last phrase adds a vague third possibility, rather like *Hel.* 1137 and [A.] *PV* 116 ('mortal or immortal or intermediate'), A. *Sept.* 197 ('man, woman or intermediate'). [The shape of the sentence is fairly clear, but ἄν should come with an optative verb, not the future φανεῖ in 898, and **τάδ(ε)** 'these things' does not fit. Similar appeals occur in tragedy with varied phrasing, e.g. A. *Sept.* 93f. τίς ἄρα ῥύσεται, τίς ἄρ' ἐπαρκέσει θεῶν ἢ θεᾶν; ('Who then will rescue, who will protect, of gods or goddesses'), *Hipp.* 675–77 τίς ἂν θεῶν ἀρωγὸς ἢ τίς ἂν βροτῶν πάρεδρος ἢ ξυνεργὸς ἀδίκων ἔργων φανείη; ('What divine defender, or what mortal comrade or helper might appear against these unjust deeds'); also *Pho.* 1515–18 (τίς ἄρα), *Alc.* 213f., *Hyps.* F 752h.6–9, S. *Aj.* 879–87 (all τίς ἂν + optative). Possibly τίς ἂν οὖν, τίς ἂν (Reiske) with φαίνοι (Murray). »» Parker 231, 241.]

COMMENTARY 225

897. a path from this impasse (ἀπόρων πόρον): see 886–89 n. [L's πόρον ἄπορον gives wrong sense ('an impassable path') and metre.]

898. two lone descendants: not strictly true (Electra is a third), but emotionally apt like Antigone's 'me, the sole surviving princess' ignoring Ismene (S. *Ant.* 940f.).

900–1. These things are marvellous etc.: the Chorus's comment echoes Iphigenia (839f.) and marks the end of the lyric celebration.

902–1088. Planning of the escape

Pylades' call to action after the reunion is almost formulaic (e.g. *Odyssey* 21.226–29, A. *Cho.* 510–13, S. *El.* 1288–94, E. *El.* 596f.), but the simple progression to planning is interrupted by Iphigenia's enquiry about Electra, her introduction to Pylades, and her questions to Orestes about the matricide, its consequences, and his current mission (912–38). Orestes' narrative (939–86) then completes his earlier survey of his ordeals (77–92), recounting the experiences at Athens which left him pursued by the unappeased Erinyes and despatched by Apollo on his mission. His trial at Athens is mentioned for the first time in the play, and mythical innovations – the unappeased Erinyes, his threatened suicide at Delphi – link Euripides' account of the rescue of Iphigenia with that tradition. The curious aetiology of the Choes ceremony may be a further piece of virtuoso myth-making (947–60 n.). Orestes ends with an appeal to Iphigenia for her help in their escape, to which she responds willingly, offering her own life if necessary for Orestes' survival (989–1006). Orestes' response, renouncing his own survival if it must be without her, recalls the earlier self-sacrificing exchange between him and Pylades, but with a more optimistic tone (1007–16). The planning emerges slowly in another stichomythia, with full attention to each of its details and difficulties (1017–55). The pattern is similar to those of other recognition and intrigue plays (*El.* 612–70, *Ion* 971–1028, *Hel.* 1032–87). As Orestes' suggestions lead to an impasse, Iphigenia takes charge and devises a plan, like Electra and Helen in their plays (Helen's deception strategy is very like Iphigenia's). The scene ends with her successful appeal to the Chorus for their collaboration (1056–77) and a final instruction to Orestes and Pylades with an appeal to Artemis for their salvation (1078–88).

902–4. When loved ones come face to face etc.: 'For friends coming into the sight of friends, to take encirclements of arms is likely/reasonable; but it's necessary also, ceasing from sorrowings, to go on to that (subject)…'.

905–6 attain salvation's glorious title: the value of salvation (σωτηρία) was emphasized in 593f., cf. 979–86. τὸ κλεινὸν ὄνομα τῆς σωτηρίας seems to be a periphrasis for 'renowned salvation' (cf. 663 n.). [The Paris apograph's ὄμμα 'countenance' (a word often confused with ὄνομα in mss.) is preferred by most recent editors but does not go particularly well with **attain** or **glorious**.]

226   COMMENTARY

907–8. not to let go of fortune etc.: 'not exiting from fortune, seizing the moment, to get other joys', i.e. the joys of escape and homecoming in addition to those of the reunion which fortune has just brought about. Cf. *El.* 596f. (Electra reunited with Orestes), 'I now possess dear greetings' joys (ἡδονάς), and will in time bestow them once again (when we are out of danger)'. [Diggle and Kovacs accept Dindorf's deletion of these lines, but Orestes' reply presupposes them (cf. Platnauer, Parker).]

909–11. this is fortune's business: Orestes perceives that fortune will continue to help them if only they work with it. There is no strong distinction between τύχη **fortune** and τὸ θεῖον, **the divine power** (determiner of human fortunes: cf. 865–67 n.). In *El.* 610 the Old Man advises Orestes that his success will depend on himself and fortune, then at 890–92 credits the gods and fortune for his success. That divine assistance requires human effort is a commonplace, cf. 120–21 n.

912. You'll not restrain me: [L's text suggests 'nothing will restrain me', with two aorist subjunctive verbs which are then ungrammatical. For οὐ μή μ' ἐπίσχῃς (aorist subjunctive) followed by οὐδ' ἀποστήσεις (future indicative) cf. e.g. S. *El.* 42f., *OC* 450–52.]

915. married to Pylades: cf. 695–98 n.

917. Strophius…is called his father: i.e. he has that title, not suggesting that he might not actually be his father. κλῄζεται and κέκληται are both used in this way, e.g. *Andr.* 75, *El.* 366, *Or.* 1402.

918. Atreus's daughter: i.e. Agamemnon's sister (498 n.).

920. He was not living etc.: hence Iphigenia did not recognize Pylades' name earlier (249). This makes Pylades younger than both Orestes and Electra. **when my father put me to death:** Parker makes ἔκτεινε imperfect ('tried to kill me') since the killing was not completed (cf. 27 ἐκαινόμην), but the aorist is more naturally understood in a simple reference to the event (cf. 992).

924–27. how did you dare etc.: Iphigenia takes up her questioning from the point reached in 552–59 before Orestes was identified. She avoids spelling out the **dreadful deeds**, and Orestes shows the same reluctance to discuss the murder as he did in 554, offering the same justification (avenging his father) as in 558. Iphigenia apparently accepts that Orestes was justified in killing his mother, and Orestes never answers her question about Clytemnestra's reasons for killing Agamemnon (926f.). Thus she hears nothing about Clytemnestra's reaction to her own sacrifice, or about Clytemnestra's seduction by Aegisthus, or about Cassandra.

926. for which she killed her husband: κτείνει is a 'registering' present tense (22–23 n.). Clytemnestra is forever her husband's killer.

929. Menelaus rules: i.e. as his nephew's protector. At the end of *Orestes* Menelaus leaves Argos for Sparta so that Orestes can rule in Argos.

931. has thrown me out: ἐκβάλλει, 'throws out', again a 'registering' present tense; Orestes' exile continues.

COMMENTARY 227

932–35. Iphigenia guesses that Orestes' recent mad fit was caused by the Erinyes (932), he explains that this was only the latest attack of many (933), she now understands that he is being persecuted as a matricide (934), and he confirms that this is so (935). [The sequence is well explained by Kyriakou and Parker. Monk had placed lines 934–35 before 932–33 so that the detail of the Erinyes' pursuit precedes the mention of their recent attack (thus Diggle, Kovacs, Cropp 2000).]

932. So that was your reported madness: 'So (it was with) these (fits of madness that) you were reported (as) having been maddened'. This makes ταῦτ(α) an internal object to μανείς, but ταῦτ' ἄρ(α) might be a colloquial 'So that's why' (Collard 2018, 99).

934. the goddesses were driving you: for the chariot image see 81–83 n. [The verb ἐλαστρέω (ἠλάστρουν: root ἐλα-) is rare and used by Euripides only here and at 971. He may have meant to evoke ἀλάστορες, 'avengers'. The word ἀλάστωρ is linked with the root ἐλα- (ἐλάστωρ, 'driver') in some lexica, and in a sacred law from Selinous an ἐλάστερος is similar to an ἀλάστωρ (Jameson et al. 1993, 16f., 116–18, Johnston 1999, 47–49). Zeus Elasteros is named in one or more inscriptions from Paros (»» *SEG* 13.449a).]

935. And forcing their bloody bit etc.: bloody is proleptic for the bleeding caused when the bridle draws the bit sharply into the horse's mouth: cf. A. *Ag.* 1066f. χαλινὸν δ' οὐκ ἐπίσταται φέρειν | πρὶν αἱματηρὸν ἐξαφρίζεσθαι μένος (Cassandra 'does not know how to endure the bridle before foaming out her temper in blood': tr. Collard) with Fraenkel's note.

936. Then why did you make the journey: ἐπόρθμευσας πόδα, 'did you ferry (your) foot' (130–32 n., 266 n.). For for τί γάρ see on 533 (531–36 n.).

939. Very well, I'll tell you: Orestes overcomes his reluctance to answer Iphigenia's questions, like Electra responding to the disguised Orestes' inquiry about her degrading situation in *El.* 300. For λέγοιμ' ἄν see 811 n.; introducing a narrative, A. *Sept.* 375, E. *Hec.* 1132 etc.

940–41. When this terrible business...had come into my hands: he avoids naming the matricide and his blood-pollution directly.

942–44. I was driven, a fugitive etc.: this account looks similar to *El.* 1250ff. where Orestes is instructed after the matricide to go from Argos to Athens as directly as he can, subject to the Erinyes' pursuit. The text is however slightly incoherent and some important detail may be missing (see below). In *Orestes* 1643–48 Orestes is to spend a year in exile before his acquittal at Athens. In Aeschylus's *Oresteia* he flees from Argos to Delphi where Apollo purifies him but he must wander for a long period, still pursued by the Erinyes, before reaching Athens. **Loxias:** the title always refers to Apollo as an oracular god (cf. 1013, 1084, 1280, 1438) and is commonly associated with the adjective λοξός 'oblique, ambiguous' (»» Beekes 'λοξός'). Allan and Potter (2014) argue for a tragic convention whereby speakers use the names Phoebus ('Bright One') or Loxias

228   COMMENTARY

('Oblique One') according to their confidence or lack of it in the clarity and reliability of oracles. This is difficult to detect in Aeschylus's *Choephori* and *Eumenides* where Apollo is often called Loxias in assertions of his authority, or in several related plays of Euripides (*Electra, Orestes, IT, Helen*) where Allan and Potter suggest that Euripides intentionally violated the convention. In *IT* 1084f. Iphigenia refers to 'the word of Loxias' as typically true, and in 1438–41 Athena confirms that 'Loxias's oracles' guided Orestes' mission in accordance with destiny. **παρασχεῖν, to render:** the infinitive of purpose after πέμπω is mostly poetic (also 977f.: LSJ 'πέμπω' I.3, Smyth §2009, *CGCG* §51.16). **the unnamed goddesses** are the Erinyes, unnamed because of the danger in naming deities with such destructive powers (»» Cropp on *Captive Melanippe* F 494.18, Henrichs 1991, 169–79, 1994, 37–39); yet they are often named as Erinyes (nine times in this play, three of them in this speech).

[If this is a complete and continuous sentence, the meaning will be 'I was driven...to (a place, i.e. Delphi) whence Loxias guided my course to Athens etc.' (for ἔνθεν in this sense see *HF* 260, LSJ 'ἔνθεν' II), but this is implausibly vague and the combination δή γ' is hardly possible in this context (Denniston 247). Weil's ἐμμανῆ πόδα | ἔστ᾽ εἰς Ἀθήνας δή μ' ('I was driven on maddened foot until Loxias sent me to Athens') is printed by Wecklein and Kovacs and favoured by Platnauer but is a substantial rewriting and still does not account well for δή. Parker punctuates before ἔνθεν and leaves δή γ' obelized ('I was driven by the Erinyes' pursuit. Therefore Loxias directed my course to Athens'), but this seems rather abrupt. Possibly some words completing a sentence about Orestes' flight to Delphi have been lost after φυγάδες.]

945–46. there is a holy court etc.: ψῆφος, 'vote' is a synecdoche for 'voting-place' as in 969. **εἶσατ(ο), established** is from ἵζω, aorist middle. The Council of the Areopagus ('Ares-hill') was Athens' highest and most respected court with responsibility, amongst other things, for trying cases of deliberate killing of an Athenian citizen. It was usually supposed to have been established by Zeus when the gods tried Ares for the murder of Poseidon's son Halirrothius, who had raped Ares' daughter Alcippe (»» Cropp on *El.* 1258–63). Aeschylus in *Eumenides* invented a new tradition in which it was established by Athena for the trial of Orestes. Euripides here and in *Electra* accommodates both accounts, with the court already existing before Orestes' trial. The court is ὁσία, **holy** (130–32 n.) because it is sanctioned by the gods and observes their will in reaching its decisions. It was in fact regarded as an incorruptible guarantor of justice and established law, a point stressed repeatedly by Athena as she creates the court in *Eumenides* (*Eum.* 482–84, 674f., 690–710): »» Harris 2017, 405–12, and on Aeschylus's manipulation of the legal realities Sommerstein 2010, Leão 2010.

947–60. This part of Orestes' story links him with the annual rite of the Choes ('Pitchers') which occurred on the second day of the three-day Anthesteria, an ancient Ionian spring festival honouring Dionysus. Its central feature was the

COMMENTARY 229

competitive drinking of the new wine (opened on the first day of the festival) from large pitchers by participants who each had their own wine, jug and table. This was done both in private homes (as by Orestes in 949ff.) and in a public contest. The day of the Choes was rather like Hallowe'en, an 'impure day' when ancestral spirits were thought to be at large[22] and the rituals insisted on separation and avoidance of contact and pollution. Orestes' visit made an apt *aition* (mythical origin) which is repeated and elaborated in later sources, especially the 4th C Atthidographer Phanodemus with additional circumstantial detail (*FGrH* 325 F 11). Aelian fr. 73 Herscher records a different explanation in which the festival began as an atonement when some Aetolian visitors were murdered after introducing wine to Athens with intoxicating effects which were unfortunately misunderstood. The Choes ritual is featured in the closing scenes of Aristophanes' *Acharnians* (959ff.), where its jovial character is emphasized. *»»* Pickard-Cambridge 1988, 1–16 (with sources); Burkert 1983, 213–26 and 1985, 237–40; Hamilton 1992; R. Parker 2005, 293–95, 313; Harder on Callimachus, *Aetia* fr. 178.1–2.

The *aition*, of which this is the earliest record, is unusually presented in the middle of the play and given considerable prominence. It is also anachronistic, as if Orestes' recent experience has already become an Athenian tradition. All this may suggest that Euripides invented it (see recently Scullion 1999–2000, 225f.; Kyriakou 311–13; Torrance 2019, 90–92), but it could be older (e.g. R. Parker 1983, 386; Seaford 2009, 230f.; Fowler 2013, 455 n. 22). Within the drama, the Athenians' acceptance of Orestes at the Choes can be seen as anticipating their acceptance of the once homicidal Taurian Artemis and emphasizing the importance of such carefully negotiated ritual institutions (*»»* Wolff 1992, 325–29; Kyriakou 312).[23]

947–48. when I went there etc.: 'having gone there…none of my guest-friends received me' (anacoluthon, 675 n.). The **guest-friends** are Athenians allied with Orestes and his family in the reciprocal relationship of *xenia* and expected to offer him hospitality and support when called on.

951. to be unaddressed: silence was required from homicides before their purification, and from those associating with them. *»»* Sommerstein on A. *Eum.* 448; R. Parker 1983, 350 (Cyrenean cathartic law), 370f., 390f. (Telephus in Mysia); Henrichs 1994, 44 with n. 80.

952. I might enjoy the feasting (δαιτός…ὀναίμην): Homeric phrasing, cf. *Od.* 19.68 δαιτὸς ὄνησο, 'enjoy the feast!' [L's γενοίμην gives 'I might be separate from their feasting and drinking'.]

---

[22] Photius μ 439, 'μιαρὰ ἡμέρα', R. Parker 2005, 294f.; Johnston 1999, 63–66.

[23] Romano (2012, 139–41) suggests that Orestes cites the *aition* for a rhetorical purpose, to claim special (oracular) knowledge and thus reinforce his demand for help in making his escape. But Orestes says he is reporting hearsay, and he hardly needs special authority in appealing to his own sister.

230   COMMENTARY

953–54. Each filled a private pitcher etc.: 'filling a measure of the Bacchic god equal for all into a private pitcher, they took pleasure'. The god is identified with his gift (Dodds on *Ba.* 284; Seaford on *Cyc.* 519–28). Athenian symposia normally involved shared cups, small at the beginning and increasingly large as the evening progressed (»» Davidson 1997, 61–69).

957. groaning loudly etc.: Herwerden's deletion of this line was favoured by Platnauer (who however misconstrued the syntax) and accepted by Parker because (1) μέγα Orestes has just said that he **suffered in silence**, and (2) he has avoided naming the matricide directly (925, 927, 940) and **my mother's murderer** (μητρὸς φονεύς) seems inconsistent with this. But the point may be that he groaned privately while not complaining to his hosts, and he does later call himself his mother's murderer (1007; cf. 79, 964–67).

958–60. I hear that my misfortunes etc.: see above on 947–60. **the three-quart pitcher:** the Athenian *chous* was roughly 3.2 litres (2.8 imperial quarts, 3.4 US quarts).

962–63. I taking one platform, the senior Fury the other: Pausanias 1.28.5: 'The white stone blocks [in the Areopagus court] on which defendants and prosecutors stand are called The Stone of Hybris [Violence] and The Stone of Anaideia [Ruthlessness].' There are a few 1st–2nd C AD representations of Orestes' trial, perhaps linked with an engraving by Zopyros showing him with one foot raised on a small stone mound in front of him (Pliny, *NH* 33.156; on these and other relevant references see Pritchett 1998, 143). Orestes' description matches the formal exchange of arguments in Aeschylus, *Eumenides* 566–680 where the Chorus-leader presents the Erinyes' case, Orestes responds and Apollo intervenes as witness (576) and co-defendant (579f.).

964–65. We exchanged speeches etc.: 'I speaking and hearing...Phoebus saved me' (anacoluthon, 675 n.). The exchange of speeches shows the fairness and openness of the Athenian legal process, cf. *Hcld.* 181–83 and for the formulaic 'speaking and hearing' Soph. *OC* 190, 1288, Thuc. 4.22.1, [Andocides] *Against Alcibiades* 7.7, Pl. *Symp.* 173b8. For procedures in Athenian homicide cases see MacDowell 1978, 118–20; Todd 1993, 271–76; Phillips 2008, 59–64; sources in Phillips 2013, 44–84. **with his testimony:** in *Eumenides* Apollo asserts Orestes' innocence by declaring that he promulgated the matricide himself with Zeus's authority and that it was justified (*Eum.* 576–80, 614–21 etc.; cf. E. *El.* 1266f.).

965–66. Pallas counted out (διηρίθμησε) equal votes: a simplified version of the actual procedure in Athenian courts as described in the Aristotelian *Constitution of Athens* 69.3 (tr. H. Rackham): 'When all have voted, the attendants take the vessel that is to count and empty it out on to a reckoning-board with as many holes in it as there are pebbles, in order that they may be set out visibly and be easy to count...And those assigned by lot to count the voting-pebbles count them out (διαριθμοῦσιν) on to the reckoning-board, in two sets...'.

COMMENTARY 231

This and lines 1469–72 imply that the Athenian jury voted equally for and against Orestes and that Athena simply counted out the votes and declared the defendant acquitted, thus setting the precedent for the future Athenian rule (the so-called 'Vote of Athena'); similarly *El.* 1265–69. I think this was probably the case in Aeschylus's *Eumenides* as well, but many scholars think that in that play Athena made the votes equal by casting a vote of her own and then made her declaration (»» Sommerstein on *Eum.* 711–53). [ὠλένῃ, **with her arm:** ὠλένη is properly 'forearm', mostly in poetry (cf. epic λευκώλενος ῞Ηρα, 'white-armed Hera') and often in Euripides (23x, cf. 283, 1158). Here it is usually described as a synonym for 'hand' (cf. Bond on *HF* 1381, also Dodds on *Ba.* 1125), but that is not quite true. In *HF* 1381 Heracles holds his weapons in his hands but thinks of his arms bearing and wielding them. Here Athena reached out her arm to pick up and distribute the votes, formally and conspicuously.]

967. I left victorious: ἀπῆρα intransitive (511 n.).

968–71. Now those who settled there etc.: Euripides adapts the ending of *Eumenides* where all of the Erinyes threaten to reject the verdict following the tied vote but are finally persuaded by Athena to accept a home 'close to the house of Erechtheus', i.e. the temple of Athena Polias on the Acropolis, where they will bring continual justice and prosperity to the land. The cave of the Eumenides was actually on the lower slopes of the Areopagus hill, facing the Acropolis (»» Sommerstein on *Eum.* 855). **right by the court:** 'beside the vote itself' (cf. 945–46 n.). **not persuaded by the law (νόμῳ):** i.e. the law established by Athena's ruling for Orestes' acquittal (νόμισμα 1471, νόμος *El.* 1268).

971. drove me: ἠλάστρουν, see 934 n. **in a ceaseless pursuit:** 'in restless runnings; for ἀνιδρύτοισιν see LSJ 'ἀΐδρυτος'.

972. Phoebus's hallowed ground: i.e. Delphi, where Apollo had ordered him to kill his mother. In *Eumenides* he is at Delphi and has been ritually purified by Apollo but is still pursued by the Erinyes before going to Athens for trial.

973–75. and laid myself before his sanctuary etc.: by starving himself Orestes would avoid direct responsibility for his own death (cf. e.g. S. *Ant.* 773–76) while threatening the sanctuary with its pollution, a serious threat against a god (»» 381–83 n.; R. Parker 1983, 33, 37, 65f.). βίον ἀπορρήξειν is lit. 'break off my life' but does not imply suicide. In *Or.* 863f. the condemned Electra asks whether she must 'break off her breath' (πνεῦμ' ἀπορρῆξαί) by stoning or the sword; cf. A. *Pers.* 507 (drowning Persians), E. *Tro.* 756 (Astyanax thrown from the walls of Troy).

976. making his voice heard from the golden tripod: αὐδὴν λακών is 'sounding out a voice' (»» LSJ 'λάσκω' III.2). This is Apollo's own voice (85–92 n.). For the god himself seated on the Delphic tripod see 1254–58 n.

977–78. the sky-fallen image: see 87–88 n. διοπετής (-πετ- as in πίπτω) is a variant on the Homeric διϊπετής first seen here and in Eur. F 971. On the form and various senses of διϊπετής see Fantuzzi on [E.] *Rhes.* 43.

232   COMMENTARY

981–82. I will…settle you once more in Mycenae: in fact Iphigenia will serve Artemis at Brauron (1440 n., 1462–67), but Apollo has not included this final outcome in his guidance to Orestes (91 n.).

983. Come, O beloved one: ὦ φιληθεῖσ(α) makes a slightly weightier address than ὦ φίλη ('O dear one'), like Socrates' ironic ὦ φιλούμενε Ἀγάθων in Pl. *Symp.* 201c8. **O my very own sister:** lit. 'O sibling head'; the address to the head, a tragic idiom, also heightens the personal and emotional nature of the appeal: see LSJ 'κάρα' 3, commentators on Soph. *Ant.* 1.

984–85. save our ancestral house etc.: now that Orestes has found Iphigenia he overlooks the possibility that Pylades could ensure the survival of the *oikos* by getting sons with Electra (695–98 n.). Pylades is irrelevant in the remaining action except as Orestes' accomplice. **Pelops' descendants:** i.e. the house of Atreus (1414–19 n. with note 38).

987–88. some dire divine wrath has seethed up etc.: see 157–59, 199–202 with notes. The plural δαιμόνων ('of daimons') gives added vagueness. For ἄγει, **drags** see LSJ 'ἄγω' I.3.

989–1019. Orestes has begged his sister to help him steal the image of Artemis and escape with him to Athens, thus ending both his and her ordeals and ensuring the survival of their house. Iphigenia replies: 'I am indeed eager to help with all that, but I don't see how I can avoid being punished by Artemis and Thoas when you make off with the image. If you can get it *and* me away, then the risk to myself is well worth taking; if not, I am finished yet you may still be able to complete your mission. Well, I'm willing to take the risk even if I do have to die, for our house can do without me but not without you.' Orestes in turn insists that he will not leave without her but adds that Artemis can hardly be opposed to the theft of her image if Apollo has sent him to do just that and in doing so find his sister. Probably, then, they can both escape safely with the image. Iphigenia agrees; in that case they should start planning a way of doing this successfully.

992. the man who killed me: [Agamemnon did not in fact kill Iphigenia, but the aorist κτανόντι represents the intention more vividly than L's very rare future κτανοῦντι, 'who was going to kill': cf. e.g. *Ion* 1291, 1500, S. *Aj.* 1126 with Finglass's note, KG 1.166f.]

995–96. I fear for how I can escape: an indirect question construction (Goodwin §376).

998. how justify myself: 'what argument is there in me?'

999. if this one thing can ('will') **come about as well:** i.e. the safe escape which she has just said she needs. For the **one thing** needed cf. 1052 ἑνὸς μόνου δεῖ, *Supp.* 594 ἓν δεῖ μόνον μοι, *Or.* 1172 ἑνὸς γὰρ εἰ λάβοιμεν, εὐτυχοῖμεν ἄν, and for ἕν τι, 'one particular thing' *Med.* 381, Xen. *Oecon.* 3.1.7, Pl. *Theaet.* 206c8. ὁμοῦ is 'jointly', 'concomitantly' as e.g. *Pho.* 1435, S. *OT* 1276, *Phil.* 1032. The future γενήσεται implies 'if this is really going to happen' (»» Rijksbaron 68f.), while the present γίγνεται states a definite consequence if it does, cf.

COMMENTARY   233

Alc. 386 ἀπωλόμην ἄρ', εἴ με δὴ λείψεις ('I'm lost if you're going to desert me'), *Hipp.* 501 κρεῖσσον δὲ τοὖργον, εἴπερ ἐκσώσει γέ σε ('The deed's the better choice if it will save you'). [The text is doubted since ὁμοῦ γενήσεται could mean 'will come together' and require a plural subject. Diggle and Parker obelize ἕν τι...γενήσεται, and there are many conjectures (cf. Stockert 2000). Most involve altering ἕν τι τοῦθ', but that is idiomatic (see above) and unlikely to be corrupt.]

1000. and you can carry off the image: for the sense of οἴσεις see LSJ 'φέρω' VI.3. **on board your stout-sterned ship (ἐπ' εὐπρύμνου νεώς):** Homeric phrasing, also at 1357; cf. *Iliad* 4.247f. νῆες εὔπρυμνοι, E. *IA* 723, Bacchyl. 13.150.

1005–06. The truth is: οὐ γὰρ ἀλλ(ά) is roughly 'For (it is) not (otherwise) but', apparently colloquial (Denniston 31; Collard 2018, 106f.). **a man...is sorely missed:** male heirs provide protection and continuity for the family (*oikos*), cf. 57 n. **a woman is a feeble resource:** 'a woman's (attributes) are weak' (605– 7 n.), a conventional view (»» Dover 1974, 95–102); yet Orestes will insist that his sister should survive and she will take the lead in planning and executing their escape.

1007–08. I will not become your killer etc.: Euripides almost parodies this in *Or.* 1037–40 when Electra asks Orestes to kill her so as to save her from a public execution and he replies: 'My mother's blood is enough, I will not kill you – but you may die by your own hand however you wish.'

1008–09. I want to be your partner etc.: 'I would wish, like-minded with you, to get the same as you both while living and in dying.'

1013. that Loxias instructed me: see 942–44 n.

1014–15. Most recent editors have supposed with Köchly that one or more lines are missing between 1014 and 1015 since Apollo did not instruct Orestes to meet Iphigenia and **all this** seems to presuppose a fuller preceding argument. But Orestes might reasonably assume that Apollo expected him to find his sister, and **all this** might refer to his mission as a whole including their reunion. Athena herself says it was destined that Orestes should be sent by Apollo to retrieve his sister and bring the image of Artemis to Athens (1438–41).

1018. our return home is ailing (νοσεῖ): for the metaphor see 531–36 n.

1019. this is what we must plan for: 'this (is) the deliberation before (us)'. [Markland's ἥδε βούλευσις improves on L's ἡ δὲ βούλησις, 'but the wish (is) present'.]

1020–27. Orestes' proposals are rather absurd (killing Thoas will not do them much good and the temple is full of Taurians waiting to sacrifice him and Pylades), but they prepare the way for Iphigenia's revelation of her ingenious plan. Similarly *Ion* 971–77 (Creusa will not burn Apollo's temple or murder Xuthus), *Hel.* 1039–46 (fleeing on a chariot and murdering Theoclymenus are impractical, cf. *Hel.* 809–13).

234   COMMENTARY

1021. A dreadful suggestion: in Greek morality the host-guest relationship was highly valued (cf. 947–48 n.) and thought to be protected by Zeus Xenios. Violations could be considered 'barbarian' (e.g. *Hec.* 1247f.). Orestes' attitude here is perhaps another instance of the play's commenting ironically on Greek–barbarian stereotypes,. We might reflect that Thoas was about to have Orestes killed, but Orestes seems to have accepted that as due to the goddess (490f., 617–26, 644–46, 704f.; cf. 585–87 n.). At any rate, Iphigenia's sense of her own obligation to Thoas prevails.

1023. I commend your resolve: she briefly approves Orestes' boldness while rejecting his suggestion. For this use of the aorist ᾔνεσα see Lloyd 1999, 39; Rijksbaron 29f. Further discussion of the 'tragic aorist' in Bary 2012; Nijk 2021, 531–36.

1024. suppose you hid me: developing Pylades' suggestion in the prologue (110–12). τί δ᾿ εἰ... is colloquial (Collard 2018, 74).

[1025–26]. Most editors accept Markland's deletion of these lines. 1027 looks like a direct rebuttal of 1024, with οὐ λήσομεν, **we could not evade** responding to λάθρᾳ, **secretly**. Probably line 1025 was added to recall Pylades' suggestion in the prologue with 1026 as a filler to maintain the stichomythia. For defences of the lines see Schwinge 1968, 119f. with n. 14; Cropp 1997, 37f., and for counterarguments Kyriakou and Parker. Martin 2020, 198 suggests that the whole idea of their hiding in the temple is by now irrelevant and that all of 1024–27 should be deleted, but something is needed to prompt Orestes' despair in 1028 and Iphigenia's alternative scheme. **night belongs to thieves** has a proverbial ring, cf. *Iliad* 3.11 a mist 'better for a thief than night', I *Ep.Thess.* 5.2 'the day of the Lord comes like a thief in the night'.

1029. an ingenious new contrivance: see 42–43 n. on καινόν, here perhaps with a metadramatic hint at Euripides' own ingenuity.

1030. What sort etc.: the same kind of stichomythic prompt as 673, 734. ποῖόν τι; is colloquial (Collard 2018, 88), here suggesting surprise and curiosity as e.g. *Ion* 1418, Ar. *Frogs* 289. δόξης, **your thought** responds to Iphigenia's δοκῶ, **I think** (cf. *HF* 713f.).

1031. as a clever device: σοφίσματι is West's correction of L's σοφίσμασιν, 'devices', which was probably influenced by the following plural ἀνίαις, **torments**.

[1032–33]. The lines are probably an interpolation like 1025f. Line 1034 (**Make use of my troubles**) should respond directly to 1031 (**I'll use your torments**), like Menelaus responding to Helen's clever idea in *Hel.* 1049–52. Orestes can hardly ask what reason she will give (1036) if she has already described it in 1033. Line 1032, like 1026, uses a cliché to maintain the stichomythia. [The case for deletion is well made by Parker, preferring this to Czwalina's deletion of 1033f. for which West argued (1981, 63). *Hel.* 1049–52

COMMENTARY 235

makes it very likely that line 1034 is genuine. For defences of 1030–34 as a whole see Schwinge 1968, 122, Cropp 2000, Kyriakou.]

1034. Make use of my troubles if you'll profit by it (κερδανεῖς): Menelaus and Orestes allow false but ill-omened announcements of their own deaths in *Hel.* 1051f. ('speak, if I'll profit by it, εἰ κερδανῶ)', S. *El.* 59–61 ('No statement brings harm if it comes with profit, σὺν κέρδει)'.

1035. I'll say it's not lawful etc.: in simple order, λέξομεν ὡς (= ὅτι) οὐ θέμις (ἐστὶ) θύειν σε θεᾷ.

1036. What reason will you give: 'having (i.e. saying that you have) what reason', cf. 1037 n., 1039 (»» Diggle 1981, 88). **I think I can guess: ὑποπτεύω τι,** 'I have a suspicion' (τι internal accusative).

1037. I'll be making the sacrifice holy: 'I'll be giving (i.e. say that I'll be giving) that which is holy for sacrifice' (cf. 1194); or perhaps 'I'll be giving holiness to the sacrifice' (ὅσιον, 130–32 n.).

1038. So how does this help etc.: 'In what respect, then, is the goddess's image more captured?'

1039. to purify you with sea-water: sea-water with its saline content was valued for ritual cleansing and as a depository for pollution (cf. 1193, *Iliad* 1.313f.: »» R. Parker 1983, 226f., *ThesCRA* II.19f.).

1041. I'll say I'm going to wash it etc.: Iphigenia's plan would remind Euripides' audience of the practice of bathing a goddess's image annually at seashore or riverside, e.g. Hera at Samos, Artemis at Ephesus (probably) and at Athens Aphrodite Pandemos and (probably) Athena Polias in connection with her clothes-washing festival the Plynteria (»» R. Parker 1983, 26–28 and 1996, 307f.; Simon 1983, 46–51; Romano 1988, 129–31).[24] At Samos this was said to have begun when pirates stole the image of Hera from her temple but were foiled as a divine force prevented them from rowing their ship away (Menodotus *FGrH* 541 F 1 in Athenaeus 15.672), the inverse of Euripides' story in which the wind preventing the departure of Orestes' ship is calmed by Poseidon at Athena's request. **σοῦ θιγόντος ὥς,** 'as with you having touched it'. [L's aorist infinitive νίψαι would make this line a continuation from 1039 ('I'll say I want to purify you... and to wash the image since you've touched it as I shall say'), but 1041 must be a response to Orestes' question about the image in 1040.]

1042. along the sea's damp shore: πόντου νοτερὸν...παρ' ἔκβολον is an epic-style phrase like Homeric παρὰ θῖν' ἁλός 'along/beside the sea-shore', ἐπὶ ῥηγμῖνι θαλάσσης (253 n.). ἔκβολον has generally been misunderstood as 'inlet' or 'promontory', but the word, lit. 'offthrow', suggests surf and perhaps

---

[24] A similar ritual for the washing of the Athenian Palladion, an image sited in the Palladion court where killings of non-citizens were tried, might be relevant (see e.g. Ketterer 2013, 230f.), but Burkert's identification of such a ritual is unproven (»» R. Parker 1996, 307 n. 63; the only possible references to it are in *IG* II² 1006 (11f., 75f.), 1008 and 1011, all from 122–116 BC).

236   COMMENTARY

débris left by breakers on the shore. Euripides uses it of ship's wreckage (*Hel.* 422, 1214; *I.T.* 1424 ἐκβολάς) as well as babies abandoned (*Ion* 555) or 'cast' from a mother's womb (*Ba.* 91). In 1196 the sea 'falls out' (ἐκπίπτει) close to the temple, and in 107 it washes the nearby caves with its surf (νοτίδι). Lloyd 2002, 152 notes Aristot. *Meteor.* 367b13 ὅταν...κυμαίνουσα ἐκβάλλῃ 'when it (the sea) swells and breaks').

1043. with flax-woven cables: λινοδέτοις is 'flax-bound', i.e. 'made through the binding of flax';»» Diggle 1994, 343 on senses of -δετος (< δέω) compounds.

1045. It's untouchable for all but me: 'touching (it) is holy (ὅσιον, 130–32 n.) for me alone'.

1046. what role will he have: ποῦ τετάξεται, 'where will he be positioned', a military metaphor.

1047. I'll say he has etc.: 'he'll be said having' (»» LSJ 'λέγω' III.2 at end, Goodwin §910, Barrett on *Hipp.* 121f.).

1051, 1050. This order is needed since 1050 responds to 1051: 'Then the rest is up to you' – 'Yes, and our ship is all set to leave'.[25] **our fine-oared ship:** νεώς...πίτυλος εὐήρης, 'our ship's well-fitted oarbeat' (cf. 307 n., 1346 n., 1471–72 n.), suggesting readiness for a rapid departure. [δή in 1051 'marks the progression from one idea to a second of which the consideration naturally follows' (Denniston 239); cf. *Hel.* 1032–34. For καὶ μὴν, **And indeed** see Denniston 353f., *CGCG* 59.71.]

1056–88. The scene closes with appeals from Iphigenia to the Chorus and to Artemis which emphasize the moment of crisis (cf. *El.* 671–84, *Hel.* 1093–1107, *Or.* 1231–39). Appeals for a chorus's silence were a well-established ploy in tragedy, making their silence plausible but also useful for dramatic purposes. A chorus's complicity could be requested (*Med.* 259–66, *Hipp.* 710–12, *Hel.* 1385–89, S. *El.* 468–71), commanded (A. *Cho.* 581–84, E. *Ion* 666f., *IA* 542) or taken for granted (*El.* 272f., *Or.* 1103f.). A chorus could contribute actively to a conspiracy (persuading the Nurse to lure Aegisthus, A. *Cho.* 766–82), find itself concealing unforeseen crimes (*Med.*, *Hipp.*) or defy a command for silence as in *Ion* (»» Barrett on *Hipp.* 710–12, Lee on *Ion* 666f., Hose 1990, 299–307). Iphigenia's elaborate request both gives weight to the crisis and prepares for Thoas's threat to punish the Chorus which Athena must countermand (1431–34, 1467–69, 1482f.). In *Helen* 894–996 Helen and Menelaus persuade Theonoe with two elaborate speeches. Iphigenia rests her appeal on two arguments, loyalty amongst women and a promise that she will reward their help by rescuing them, and reinforces it with a formal supplication.

---

[25] Thus MacDonald 1963. Köchly had placed 1051 before 1050, assuming a line of Orestes lost before 1051 and assigning 1052 to Iphigenia. L's order is preferred by Platnauer, Schwinge (1968, 124 n. 27), Kyriakou and others.

COMMENTARY   237

1061–62. We are all women etc.: cf. *Med.* 822f., *Hel.* 329, 830, *Alope* F 108. Medea gains the Chorus's complicity with a more elaborate (and more sinister) appeal to women's solidarity, *Med.* 214–66.

1064. A loyal tongue is a credit to its possessor: 'It's a fine thing, in whom a loyal tongue is present', an interesting way of asking the women to lie to Thoas. For the subjunctive παρῇ see 670–71 n.

1068–[71]. by your right hand etc.: Iphigenia approaches the women in turn with standard gestures of supplication, grasping right hands (cf. 701 n.), cheeks and knees: »» Gould 1973, *ThesCRA* III.6.d, esp. pp. 193–98 (this scene not included in the literary catalogue). Physical contact was an essential element in such supplications. [Line 1071 must be inauthentic since the Chorus are unmarried women like Iphigenia (130; Introduction, p. 38). Line 1070 might perhaps be part of the interpolation (Cropp 1997, 39), but Kyriakou and Parker give reasons for retaining it.]

1072–73. Which of you will agree to this etc.: 'Which of you affirms (φησί) or which denies (οὔ φησι) that she wants these things?'

1077. may great Zeus witness ('know') **this:** i.e. be aware of my oath and ready to punish me if I break it (747–49 n.). The women swear by Zeus as Pylades did.

1079–81. It's up to you now etc.: σὸν ἔργον, '(It's) your task', is colloquial (Collard 2018, 91f.). Opinions differ on whether Orestes and Pylades should exit now or remain during Iphigenia's prayer. The prayer is more impressive if she is left alone to address the goddess.

1082–88. O mistress etc.: Iphigenia raises her arms to the sky and prays to Artemis in formal terms, appealing to the precedent of her previous help at Aulis, introducing her new appeal with **now too**, and explaining that it is in the goddess's interest to help her now so as to vindicate Apollo's truth and obtain a new and better home for herself. On this prayer form see Burkert 1985, 74f., Pulleyn 1997, 33–36, 65f.

1083. from a terrible child-killing hand: τεκνοκτόνου (Herwerden's conjecture, cf. *HF* 1155) is printed by England and Parker and has more impact than L's πατροκτόνου ('a father's killing hand'). [Most editors retain πατροκτόνου more or less doubtfully, but the word normally means 'father-killing' like other such compounds (cf. 53, 384, 389, 1113, 1200). Only *Med.* 1254 χέρ' αὐτοκτόνον (Medea's own hand killing her children) and [A.] *PV* 860f. θηλυκτόνῳ Ἄρει (a war of murdering females) are at all comparable.]

1084–85. the word of Loxias will no longer be true: resuming the question of Apollo's reliability raised earlier by Orestes and Pylades (105, 120f., 570f., 719–23). For the name see 942–44 n. The Third Stasimon will bring reassurance by telling how Apollo ('Loxias', 1280) took possession of Delphi with Zeus's support. Without reliable divine guidance and enforcement of rules mortals would

238   COMMENTARY

be helpless against evil and the gods not only shamed but deprived of the honours
brought by human worship. Cf. esp. S. *OT* 883–910.

1086–88. Be kind etc.: Iphigenia's appeal perhaps recalls Athena persuading
the Erinyes to adopt Athens as their new home at the end of Aeschylus's
Eumenides; Artemis should become εὐμενής, kind like the Eumenides (Kindly
Ones), distancing herself from her primitive nature to participate in the
blessedness of Athens.[26]

1089–1152. Second Stasimon: nostalgia and escape

Strophe 1: Like the halcyon lamenting her lost husband, the captive women sing
of their separation from Hellas and above all from the choral worship of Artemis
on the island of Delos. *Antistrophe 1:* Their mood shifts from nostalgia to pain as
they recall the fall of their own city, their capture and transportation into
servitude. *Strophe 2:* Now Iphigenia will sail happily back to Hellas, assisted by
Pan and Apollo but leaving her servants abandoned amongst the Taurians.
Antistrophe 2: Nostalgia and longing for escape converge: if only the women
could fly home like birds and rejoin their maiden dances.

This beautifully designed song returns to the play's nostalgic themes,
contrasting the happiness of Hellas and the Hellenic worship of Artemis with the
bleakness of the Taurian land and her worship there. The First Stasimon's
statement of these themes is repeated so that the two songs together frame the
recognition and planning scenes. The problem of the Chorus's own future once
Iphigenia has escaped is introduced. Each of the four self-contained strophes has a
clear and quite closely matched triadic structure (1089–93/1094–97/1098–1105 ~
1106–10/1111–16/1117–22;   1123–24/1125–31/1132–37   ~   1138–39/1140–
42/1143–52). Contrasts in imagery give striking effects and shifts of tone, colour
and movement. The halcyon's and the women's pining laments are contrasted
with the divine music of the Delian swans, Pan's pipe and Apollo's lyre; Delos
and its joys with the Taurian land and its sacrifices; the women's voyage into
slavery with Iphigenia's voyage to freedom; the returning ship's musical progress
with the festal dancing which the women cannot join. A profusion of decorated
word-pictures reflects the 'dithyrambic' mode of the late fifth century which is
found often in Euripides' later plays (cf. 1234–83 n. on the so-called 'dithyrambic
stasima') and is parodied in Aristophanes, *Frogs* 1309–21. In function and motifs
the song has many resemblances with the Third Stasimon of *Helen* (*Hel.* 1451–

---

[26] Parker denies the similarity, assuming with Brown 1984 that the identification
of Erinyes as Eumenides was invented shortly before 408 BC, when it is first
attested in Euripides' *Orestes*, and after the production of *Iphigenia* a few years
earlier. That assumption is far from certain (»» Lloyd-Jones 1990; Henrichs 1991,
167–79 and 1994, 46–54; Johnston 1999, 221–25). It is not surprising if in this
play Orestes' persecutors are never referred to as Kindly Ones. That the play-title
Eumenides was not yet in use is also uncertain, but that is beside the point here.

COMMENTARY   239

1511) where a chorus of captive Greek women again anticipate the heroine's voyage back to Greece. Choral music and dance are continually evoked in the dramatic chorus's language and movements: at Delos (1103–5 n.), in the divinely led procession across the sea (1125–30), and in the women's recollection of their girlhood dancing (also a symbol of Electra's deprivation in *Electra* 175ff.; on these emotive 'choral projections' see 427–29 n.). The song with its portrayal of the gracious Delian Artemis (rather than the bloodthirsty Artemis of Taurian cult) reinforces Iphigenia's prayer to the goddess (1082–88), balancing nostalgic pain with a tentative suggestion that their lost joys may after all be recovered. The suggestion will become stronger with the women's affirmation of Apollo's power to assist his worshippers in the Third Stasimon. For further analysis of the ode's design and significance see Kyriakou 349–52 with related commentary, Swift 2010, 207–13; Kowalzig 2013, 202–5; Taddei 2015, 159–62; Amiech 230–41.

The ode consists mainly of aeolo-choriambic cola (392–455 n.). The second pair ends with a dactylic coda (1134f. ~ 1150f.) and ithyphallic clausula (1136 ~ 1152, ≈ ◡ – ◡ – –): »» Parker 280–82.

1089–1105. A single sentence formally addressed to the halcyon shifts from the image of the mourning bird through the Chorus's yearning for their homeland to the image of the Delian sanctuary. *Helen* 1107–21 develops similarly, addressing the mourning nightingale. Aristophanes' parody of Euripides' choral lyric style in *Frogs* 1309–22 begins with 'Halcyons, who by the sea's ever-flowing waves...'.[27] Birds often image mourning in poetry, especially the swan (e.g. *El.* 151–55, *HF* 110f.) and the nightingale (»» Kannicht on *Hel.* 1107–12; Mastronarde on *Pho.* 1514–18), but sometimes more generally (e.g. *HF* 1039–40, *Tro.* 146–48, 829f.). The halcyon is a species of kingfisher (*Alceo atthis*), subject of much mythical and pseudo-scientific lore in ancient Greek writers (»» Amott 2007, 12f. 'Alkyôn', 93f. 'Kêrylos') and a proverbial symbol of lamentation, e.g. *Iliad* 9.563. In myth the uxorious human couple Ceyx and Alcyone were changed into a tern and a halcyon because they addressed each other as Zeus and Hera (Hesiod fr. 10(d) Merkelbach–West, Apollodorus 1.7.3f. etc.; Gantz 168), or both were changed into halcyons as she mourned over his death at sea (Ovid, *Met.* 11.410–748). For halcyon imagery in early Greek poetry (especially girls' songs) see now Steiner 2021, 119–41 (halcyons and mourning, pp. 121–28).

1091. sadly sing your fate: a Homeric reminiscence, cf. *Iliad* 9.563 ἀλκύονος...οἶτον 'the halcyon's fate', *Odyssey* 1.350 Δαναῶν κακὸν οἶτον ἀείδειν 'to sing the Danaans' ill fate', 8.489 Ἀχαιῶν οἶτον ἀείδεις 'you sing the Achaeans' fate' (Renehan 1976, 36). οἶτον is object of the phrase ἔλεγον ἀείδεις ('sing a lament (for) your fate'), cf. *Tro.* 335–37, A. *Ag.* 1191f., S. *Trach.* 49–51 (KG 1.

---

[27] *Frogs* 1309–12. The verses are attributed implausibly to *Iphigenia at Aulis* and have been assigned to Euripides as F 856 but are probably no more than a comic pastiche.

240 COMMENTARY

321, Diggle 1981, 58). [Parker prefers Barnes' conjecture οἰκτρόν, simplifying the syntax ('who sing a piteous lament').]

1092. well understood for those with understanding: compound and simple adjectives (**εὐξύνετον ξυνετοῖς**) are artfully linked, cf. 144–47 n., 218, *Pho.* 1506 δυσξύνετον ξυνετὸς μέλος ἔγνω (Oedipus 'with understanding recognized the hard-to-understand song' of the Sphinx): »» Breitenbach 228.

1095. an unwinged bird: an oxymoron like Aesch. F 312.4 'unwinged doves' (the Pleiades), *Ag.* 1257 'two-footed lioness' (Clytemnestra), E. *Or.* 621 'flameless fire' (emotional pain).

1097–99. pining for Artemis: i.e. for the worship of Artemis in the sanctuary on Delos, and especially the paeans performed by choruses of young men and women celebrating the births of Apollo and Artemis (*Hom.Hymn.* 3.146–64, E. *Hec.* 463–65, *HF* 687–90, Callim. *Hymn.* 4.279–82, 300–15). Joining one of these choruses would have been a high point in the lives of well-born girls from the many Greek communities which sent delegations (*theoriai*) to Delos: »» Kowalzig 2007, 56–128; Calame 2019, 174–90; Durvye 2021 (literary sources for the Delian Artemis). **bringer of births:** childbirth and nurture of the young were an important function of Artemis (Introduction, p. 28), who was worshipped as Loch(e)ia 'birth-bringer' and with other titles such as Eileithuia (originally an independent birth goddess), cf. *Supp.* 958 (»» Calame 291–94; Durvye 41–44). **who dwells by the Cynthian hill:** i.e. on Delos with Mount Kynthos at its centre. In *Homeric Hymn* 3.17f. Artemis is said to have given birth to Apollo 'leaning against the great mass of the Cynthian hill, close to the palm-tree beneath the streams of Inopus'. Identification of a small sanctuary on the eastern slope of Mount Kynthos with Artemis Lochia is uncertain (»» Moretti 2021; 78–81, Hermary 2021, 156–59).

1099–1102. the fine-haired palm: the sacred palm with its crest of foliage was a feature of the sanctuary at Delos and its iconography. Leto was supposed to have clung to or leaned against it as she gave birth to Apollo (cf. 1235 n., *Hom.Hymn.* 3.17f., 117f., Theognis 5f., E. *Hec.* 458–61, *Ion* 920–22, Callim. *Hymn.* 4.209–11; *LIMC* VI, 'Leto' no. 6, an early 4th C vase). **the burgeoning bay:** Apollo's sacred tree, also a feature of the Delian sanctuary (*Hec.* 459, *Ion* 919f.). According to *Hec.* 458–61 the palm and the bay tree first appeared on Delos to assist Leto in giving birth to Apollo. **the grey olive's sacred branch** is the earliest mention of the olive tree in connection with Leto's labour. In the second Delphic Paean (by the Athenian Limenios, 128 BC: *Coll.Alex.* 149–59) she clings to an olive branch, and in other sources either clings to the tree (e.g. Hyginus, *Fab.* 53, 140) or lies beside it (e.g. Catullus 34.7f., Ovid, *Met.* 6.335f.). The presence of the olive, symbol of Athena and Athens, in Delos helped to validate Athenian influence over the island and the Ionian states. It is seen in the iconography of Delos as early as the 430s, when Delos had for forty years been the official centre of the Athenian-dominated Delian League (cf. *LIMC* III, 'Delos

COMMENTARY 241

I' no. 1, the only certain depiction of the island's persona). Herodotus 4.34 mentions an olive tree growing on the tomb of the Hyperborean Maidens in the Delian Artemision, on which local young men and women offered their shorn hair before marriage. Ephesus later claimed to be Apollo's birthplace and exhibited an olive tree (Tacitus, *Annals* 3.61); likewise Tegyrae in Boeotia, which had two streams called Phoinix and Elaia ('Palm' and 'Olive': Plut. *Mor.* 412b). **dear to Leto's offspring: ὠδῖνι, offspring** rather than 'labour', though obviously there is an allusion to Leto's labour; cf. LSJ ὠδίς I.2, E. *Hec.* 460f. ὠδῖνος Δίας, 'offspring sired by Zeus'. [L's ὠδῖνα φίλαν would mean 'Leto's dear offspring' (in apposition to Ἄρτεμιν, 1097), but the syntax is tenuous and the reference out of place in this detailed pictorial description.]

1103–5. and the lake that whirls around etc.: i.e. the roughly circular Sacred Lake a little to the north of the sanctuary of Apollo, fed by the overflow from the river Inopos and now drained. The water's 'whirling' evokes choral dancing (cf. 1145 n.), the water dancing while the sacred swans sing (for their singing cf. *Ion* 164–69, Callim. *Hymn.* 2.5, 4.249–57). Swans are connected with Apollo and song in various ways: »» Allen–Halliday on *Hom.Hymn.* 21.1, Wilamowitz on *HF* 110, Diggle on *Pha.* 78.

1110. by enemies' oars and spears: hendiadys: the ships were manned by spear-bearing warriors who had seized them when their city was captured.

1111–12. Through gold-rich barter: i.e. the slave trade. **I reached this barbarous home: νόστον βάρβαρον ἦλθον,** 'I came a barbarous return', a bitter oxymoron; a νόστος is usually a return home.

1113–16. I attend the deer-slaying goddess's virgin servant etc.: ἐλαφοκτόνος, **deer-slaying** is a unique variant on Artemis's epithet ἐλαφηβόλος, 'deer-shooting' (Hes. F 23a.21, *Hom.Hymn.* 27.2, *Carm.Conv.* 886.3 *PMG* etc.; iconography, *LIMC* II 'Artemis', 635f. with nos 396–403a). For the adjective Ἀγαμεμνόνιον see 1 n. **altars where sheep are not slain:** 'non-sheep-sacrificing altars', an oxymoron (cf. 212); adjectives such as μηλοθύτης (*Alc.* 120, Bacchyl. 8.17), μηλοδόκος 'sheep-receiving' (Pind. *Pyth.* 3.27), βουθύτος 'ox-sacrificing' normally stress the sanctity of a sacred place or ritual.

1117–22. I envy one who is constantly ill-starred etc.: constant ill-fortune is less painful than good fortune lost: cf. *Hec.* 375f., *HF* 1291–93, *Tro.* 639f., *Hel.* 417–19, *Bellerophon* F 285.15–18, Thuc. 2.43.5. That constant good fortune is impossible for mortals is a conventional thought, memorably expressed in Achilles' consolation to Priam (*Iliad* 24.527–32: Zeus gives mortals either all bad luck or a mixture of good and bad, never all good). **σύντροφος ὤν, being raised with them:** i.e. afflicted by hardships since birth; cf. *HF* 1292 συγγενῶς δύστηνος ὤν, 'being congenitally wretched'. **[μεταβάλλει δ' εὐδαιμονία** is the simplest correction of L's μεταβάλλει δυσδαιμονία, 'ill fortune changes' (cf. Cropp 1997,

242 COMMENTARY

39f.).[28] It is however uncertain and there are some thirty conjectures. The best alternative is to read Bothe's σύντροφος ὤν...δυσδαιμονίᾳ, 'being raised... together with ill fortune' and suppose that μεταβάλλει has replaced a different word or phrase (Parker mentions Wecklein's ἐξ ἀρχᾶς, '(raised) from the beginning').[29]

1123–24. an Argive penteconter: the fifty-oared ship was the standard naval vessel of the Archaic period until superseded by the trireme during the sixth century, and of heroic poetry (cf. 1347 n.): »» Morrison–Williams 1968, 47, 67f., 128–31, 194, 246; Casson 1971, 60–63 with illustrations.

1125–27. With its shrill voice etc.: 'shrilling, the wax-bound reed...will cry to the oars'. Rowers took their rhythm from a *keleustês* (boatswain) and an aulete, responding with rhythmic song (»» Kannicht on *Hel.* 1575f.; Casson 1971, 302). Here Pan with his syrinx and Apollo with lyre and song will make the voyage a musical, dancing procession. The First Stasimon of *Electra* begins with a picture of the Achaean fleet setting out for Troy with Nereids and dolphins joining in as the ships dance with their oars to the rhythm of auloi (»» Cropp on *El.* 432–41).

1128. Phoebus the seer: see 570–71 n. Navigation was an aspect of seercraft, e.g. *Iliad* 1.68–72 (Calchas).

1131. safely to the Athenians' bright land: εὖ ('well', 'successfully') suggests untroubled passage as e.g. *Hec.* 1291, [E.] *Rhes.* 216. λιπαράν suggests lush prosperity as well as brilliancy, often referring to Attica (LSJ 'λιπαρός' V).

1134–35. †and with air etc.: L's text is incoherent in both sense and metre, probably because one or more copyists did not understand the nautical language. Comparison with the antistrophe (1150f.) suggests that the metre is dactylic, and this is clearly a conventional description of the ship's sail (ἱστία) billowing out against the mast's forestays (πρότονοι) as the breeze fills it and sail-power takes over from oar-power; cf. *Iliad* 1.479–81, *Odyssey* 2.424–27, E. *Hel.* 1612, *Phaethon* 79–86 (»» Diggle on *Pha.* 86; Morrison–Williams 1968, 55, 62, 200–204).

[For the metre, a run of dactyls with catalectic ending and following ithyphallic (1136, 1152), cf. *Hel.* 383–85, *Pho.* 830–33 (paroemiac clausula). As for the sense, the sail should billow *against* the forestays, 'with air' (ἀέρι) seems inappropriate, and πόδα has no construction. Parker prints a suggestion of Platnauer, ἱστία δ' ἐς προτόνους κατὰ πρῷραν ὑπὲρ στόλον ἐκπετάσουσι πόδες, 'and the sheets will spread out the sail against the forestays along the prow etc.');

---

[28] Parker objects, 'It has not been asserted that bad fortune does not ever change, nor can it be asserted that good fortune is generally more liable to change than bad'. But the first point is irrelevant and the second is what Achilles does assert in *Iliad* 24.527ff.

[29] Other current suggestions: μεταβάλλειν δυσδαιμονία, 'Changing (from good fortune to bad) is ill fortune' (Bergk; recently Diggle, Kyriakou); σύντροφος ᾧ μεταβάλῃ δυσδαιμονία, 'for whom familiar ill fortune changes' i.e. from one misfortune to another (Willink unpublished, Kovacs; μεταβάλλει Madvig).

COMMENTARY 243

but could the πόδες/sheets, i.e. the ropes attached to the lower corners of the sail to control it, be said to 'spread it out'?]

1136. of the fast-conveying ship (ναὸς ὠκυπόμπου): epic phrasing like e.g. νηῶν ὠκυπόρων 'fast-voyaging ships', *Iliad* 10.308.

1137–42. O that I might travel etc.: two poetic motifs are combined: the traveller's or exile's daydream of home (e.g. *Iliad* 15.80–82, »» Bannert 1998) and bird-flight imaging escape, especially over the sea (e.g. *Hipp.* 732–51, *Andr.* 861–5, *Hel.* 1478–94, cf. Barrett on *Hipp.* 732–34, 1290–93 for related types; *Odyssey* 20.61–65 is an antecedent). **the radiant chariot-road:** Helios drives his Sun-chariot daily through the sky, preceded by Dawn's and followed by Evening's. **the Sun's fine fire: εὐάλιον...πῦρ,** 'the fine-Sun fire' (»» Breitenbach 206). **the chambers of my home:** i.e. the women's rooms (LSJ 'θάλαμος' I.1), recalled by Iphigenia in her dream (45f.) and in reference to her birth (209).

1143–46. and might take my place etc.: the dream of home continues as the women imagine once again joining in choral dances with their age-mates as they did before their enslavement. **[δ' ἐνσταίην** is a likely adjustment of L's δὲ σταίην. In 1144 **δόμων, family** replaces L's γάμων 'marriage' which gives difficult syntax and limits the occasion for the dancing improbably. In 1145f. syntax and sense are both unclear. **παρά** is probably a prefix to **εἱλίσσουσα** (*tmêsis*, cf. 832–33 n.; ἑ(ι)λίσσειν 'whirl' often appears in descriptions of circular dancing, e.g. *El.* 180, *HF* 690, *IA* 1055), but that almost requires dative θιάσοις and the maidens should not be dancing with their mothers' age-mates. Parker obelizes all of 1145–51, Diggle all of 1144–52.]

1147–52. in rivalry of graces etc. the dance is a competitive display of the girls' beauty and adornments, as most famously in Alcman's Partheneion (fr. 1 *PMGF*). For the emphasis on their **finery (χλιδᾶς)** and **richly worked robes (πολυποίκιλα φάρεα)** cf. Alcman 64–70, E. *El.* 175–77, 190–92 and on their **tresses (πλοκάμους)** Alcman 51–54. **darkening my cheeks:** the flying robes and hair cast fleeting shadows over their faces; cf. Anacreon 347.1f. *PMG* καὶ κόμης ἥ τοι κατ' ἁβρὸν ἐσκίαζεν αὐχένα, 'and her hair which darkened her delicate neck'. [L's ἁβροπλούτοιο χαίτας is unmetrical and gives unlikely sense, 'contests of graces of luxurious hair'.]

1153–1233. Iphigenia deceives Thoas

Thoas arrives to see if the sacrifice has been completed. As he approaches the entrance of the temple, the doors open and he meets Iphigenia who is carrying out the image of Artemis into the open air. The action gathers pace as she fulfils the plan formulated in the previous scene. Stichomythic form adds urgency and allows humour and irony in the confrontation between the crafty Greek princess and the trusting barbarian ruler (on Thoas's character see Introduction, pp. 23, 26). A change of metre from iambic trimeters to trochaic tetrameters (1203–33 n.) marks Iphigenia's instructions to Thoas, with each tetrameter divided between her

244 COMMENTARY

instruction and his reply so that he seems entirely manipulated by her. The scene reaches its climax in her proclamation and ambiguous prayer as she leads off the procession towards the shore, carrying the image and followed by Orestes and Pylades (veiled and bound), some temple-servants carrying an array of ritual equipment (1222–25 n.) and an escort of Thoas's men. Thoas himself stands veiled against the pollution as they go, nicely signifying his unawareness. For artworks recalling this scene more or less loosely see *LIMC* V, 'Iphigeneia' nos 58–67, 77, 83–85.

1153. Where is the Hellene woman etc.: Thoas's question is brusque, but calling Iphigenia πυλωρός ('doorkeeper', cf. 1227) is not disrespectful. In fact he defers to her as priestess and guardian of the temple throughout this scene.

1154. Has she...consecrated the strangers: for the process see 54 n., 244–45 n.

[1155]. Are their bodies glowing ('are they body-glowing') **etc.**: an awkwardly phrased interpolation highlighting Thoas's bloodthirstiness and making him anticipate the last stage of the sacrifice, the burning of the victims' bodies on the altar (626 n.). For the phrasing cf. *Iliad* 15.623 'But he, glowing with/like fire (λαμπόμενος πυρί)', Ar. *Frogs* 293f. 'Her whole face glows with fire (πυρὶ... λάμπεται)'.

1159. hold still...in the doorway (ἐν παραστάσιν): Iphigenia bars Thoas's way into the temple as she comes out carrying the image. The παραστάδες are the projecting ends of the side-walls enclosing the porch at the front of the temple (LSJ 'παράστας' 2, »» Stieber 2011, 61–63); cf. ἐν πύλαις 'at the door', 1305.

1160. What's happened: 'What is there new' (καινόν, 42–43 n.).

1161. I spit it away (ἀπέπτυσα): the word substituted for actual spitting will repel the pollution which she wants Thoas to think is threatening them (also used in non-ritual contexts, e.g. *Hipp.* 614, *Hec.* 1276, *Telephus* F 727: »» R. Parker 1983, 219). For the aorist tense in such 'performative' expressions see Lloyd 1999, 26–33; Bary 2012, 43–51. **I say that for Holiness's sake**: 'I offer this saying to Holiness', i.e. to avoid offence or damage to the gods: cf. 130–32 n., 1037 n. and for the abstract Ὁσίᾳ, 1461. The power is virtually deified as in *Ba.* 370f., *TrGF* adesp. F 501. Such deifications are normal in Greek poetry and religion from Homer and Hesiod onwards (for tragedy see Mikalson 1991, 277 n. 7).

1163. The victims you caught: ἠγρεύσασθ(ε) denotes the catching of animal prey, continuing the imaging of Orestes as a hunted beast (77 n., 280) and stressing the treatment of humans as animals in the Taurian rites.

1165–67. The goddess's image turned away: the turning of statues is reported as a portent in historical as well as fictional contexts, e.g. Caesar, *Civil War* 3.105, Tacitus, *Hist.* 1.86, Cassius Dio 46.33 (»» Pritchett 1998, 317–23). **it closed its eyes**: 'it joined together the vision of its eyes' (LSJ 'ὄψις' II.1.a).

COMMENTARY 245

1170. some barbarian: here and at 1422 Thoas calls the Taurians 'barbarian' without implying 'alien and primitive' as the Greek characters do. The neutral sense is often used by non-Greek characters in Euripides' plays (e.g. *Tro.* 477, 771, 1277; also in Aeschylus's *Persians*) but can be exploited subversively (1174 n.).

1172. I feel a strong a desire to learn this: 'we have fallen into an *eros* for learning this'; the phrasing makes Thoas sound somewhat pompous. ἔρως (or poetic ἔρος) usually denotes a powerful desire, except in epic where it can refer to simple bodily appetites etc. This is generally true of tragedy, but in E. *El.* 297 the chorus-women feel an *eros* for learning about Electra's sufferings.

1173. sharing the sword: κοινωνῷ ξίφει is lit. 'with shared sword', as if Orestes and Pylades both held the sword that killed Clytemnestra. This of course does not have to be true and is merely an exaggeration designed to impress Thoas (likewise Clytemnestra was not really Pylades' mother). In *Orestes* Pylades says only that he 'shared in the killing' (*Or.* 406, 1073f., 1089f.). In both *Electra* and *Orestes* Electra says that she 'grasped the sword' along with Orestes (*El.* 1225, *Or.* 1235), but that too can be seen as an emotional exaggeration (cf. Willink on *Or.* 1235f.). There was no such tradition in either case. [If L's text is correct, the noun κοινωνός 'partner' is used uniquely as an adjective. Jackson 1955, 187 suggested κοινωνώ (dual) ξίφους, '(as) sharers of the sword'.]

1174. Apollo! Not even a barbarian etc.: Euripides' humour cuts several ways. Thoas calls on Apollo, god of purity, to witness his surprise, unaware that this is the god who ordered Orestes' crime. Greek ideas of Greek moral and intellectual superiority over barbarians are inverted (contrast, e.g., Jason's description of Medea's crime as impossible for any Greek woman, *Med.* 1339–40). The crudity of Orestes' crime and Apollo's role in ordering it are advertised and the credibility of the myth called into question (380–91 n.).

1177. to distance it from the blood: i.e. from Orestes' and Pylades' blood-pollution, but slyly hinting at her saving them from being sacrificed.

1180. Hellas raised you wise (σοφήν): Thoas naively admires Greek *sophia* (wisdom, cleverness) even as he is being fooled by it.

1181–82. they dropped a tempting bait: i.e. something that would lure her into sparing them. Thoas guesses what this might have been, and she assures him that of course she was not hooked. **By charming you with some news etc.**: 'Reporting to you something of the things from Argos as a charm'.

1185. And that my father lives: Iphigenia knows that her father is dead (543–48), but the lie adds weight to her deception. She invites Thoas to think that this news would further tempt her to spare the captives but that he knows better, as she confirms (again falsely) in her next answer.

1186–87. But you took the side of the goddess: 'But you leaned away (ἐξ-ένευσας < ἐκνεύω) towards the goddess's side', i.e. Artemis's demand for Greek victims. **Yes, for I hate all Hellas**: Iphigenia exploits the Taurians' belief that

246 COMMENTARY

she must hate all Greeks (336–39 n.). There is no reason to think that she really does so.

1189. We are obliged to respect the established law: i.e. to proceed with the sacrifices that the Taurians' *nomos* requires (585–87 n.).

1190. your lustrations and sword: for use in the sacrifice (54 n., 244–45 n.).

1192–94. with stream water etc.: water for ritual purifications had to be pure from a flowing source (e.g. *El.* 793f., *Hyps.* F 752h.29–32) or best, as Iphigenia's reply indicates, **from the sea** (1039 n.). For δρόσῳ denoting pure water see 255 n. **they'd be more acceptable:** 'they would fall more *hosioi*' (130–32 n., 1037 n.).

1195. And things would be better for me: i.e. she will be doing her duty as priestess, but with a sly allusion to the planned escape.

1197. a deserted place: i.e. where Orestes' ship is hidden. **We have other things to do:** a euphemism for secret rituals as Thoas understands it, but again slyly ambiguous. The demand for privacy would seem natural in a ritual exposing pollution and disrobing the goddess. In the Athenian Plynteria (cf. 1041 n.) two noble girls were permitted to wash Athena's image and its clothes.

1198. secret rites: τὰ ἄρρητα, 'the things unspoken of', i.e. not to be seen or spoken of profanely (cf. [41]).

1201–02. If not, I'd never have lifted it: Iphigenia finally answers Thoas's opening question (1157) to his satisfaction, and the iambic dialogue gives way to trochaics as the escape action begins.

1203–33. Trochaic tetrameters enliven the scene as it approaches its climax. These are said to have been the original, more lively, dialogue metre of tragedy (Aristot. *Poet.* 1449a21–23). They appear extensively in Aeschylus's earliest extant play, *Persians* (155–75 etc.), sparingly in *Agamemnon* (1344, 1346f., 1649–73), and are then unknown until the later plays of Sophocles (*Phil.* 1402–8, *OC* 887–90)[30] and of Euripides. Euripides' earliest uses bring a scene to a climax in a speech (*Tro.* 444–61) or in dialogue wholly or partly stichomythic as here (*HF* 855–73, *Hel.* 1621–41, cf. *Pho.* 588–637). In *Ion, Phoenician Women, Orestes, Bacchae* and *Iphigenia at Aulis* he uses them in more varied and elaborate ways. »» Krieg 1936; Imhof 1965; Drew-Bear 1968; West 1982, 78, 91f.; Parker lxxxv–lxxxvi.

1203. You know what I'd like done: 'Do you know what things are to come about for me'. The phrasing (οἶσθα with relative clause and imperative γενέσθω) is peculiar to drama and perhaps colloquial, though this has been questioned (»» Collard 2018, 84).

1204. Bind the strangers' hands: 'Attach bonds to the strangers'. They will be harnessed with their hands tied behind their backs and linked to a rope held by

---

[30] Soph. *OT* 1513–23 may be inauthentic, and 1524–30 almost certainly are. See Finglass's commentary.

COMMENTARY   247

Thoas's servants and later by Iphigenia (1329–34). They arrived similarly before being released by her (469f.).

1205. Hellas never can be trusted ('knows nothing trustworthy'): a double bluff, again inverting a Greek prejudice against barbarians, e.g. Hdt. 8.142.5 'There is nothing trustworthy (πιστόν) nor undeceiving (ἀληθές) in barbarians'.

1207. Covering their heads: otherwise their pollution will threaten the purity of natural elements (sky, sun etc.), as Thoas's comment indicates; cf. e.g. *HF* 1159–62, 1203f., S. *OT* 1424–28: »» R. Parker 1983, 293, 309–17.

1208. send some of your attendants with me: a surprising request given that Iphigenia's plan depends on eluding the Taurians. Kyriakou (p. 383) notes that the escorts are dramatically expedient since one of them must return to report the events at the shore. Just as importantly, without these escorts there would be no conflict at the shore providing the material for a spectacular report speech. Amiech 260 suggests that Iphigenia cunningly anticipates what Thoas would have ordered anyway, thus increasing his confidence in her.

1209. to our community (πόλει): see 38 n.; also in 1212, 1214.

1210. That all must stay inside their homes: again a feature of real rituals exposing pollution. The day of the Athenian Plynteria (1041 n.), in which the statue of Athena herself was undressed and veiled, was regarded as inauspicious for any public activity.

1213. the friends I most should care for: i.e. Orestes and Pylades. Thoas of course misunderstands.

1214. No wonder…: (ἴσθι) ὡς εἰκότως, '(Know) that understandably…'. This use of ὡς is colloquial (Collard 2018, 77). [Suggestions for Iphigenia's missing words include εὖ λέγεις 'You speak well' (Herwerden), εἰς φίλους 'To friends' (Geist).]

1216. cleanse the goddess's chamber with torch-fire: a process familiar from e.g. *Odyssey* 22.480–94. (Odysseus cleanses his hall with fire and sulphur after killing the suitors), E. *Hel.* 865–72 (Theonoe purifies air and ground similarly). R. Parker 1983, 57f., 227f. discusses the part-practical, part-symbolic function of such cleansing. There is some documentary evidence for shrines being ritually cleansed at the same time as cult images (R. Parker 27). »» *ThesCRA* II.21f.

1218. †get a guilty one (παλαμναῖον λάβω)†: παλαμναῖος means 'with a violent hand (παλάμη)', i.e. bearing the guilt of a violent deed; so 'receive some blood-guilt' is not a possible translation. [Weil's (ἐ)ς παλαμναῖον βάλω gives 'cast (my eyes) upon a guilty man, Bauer's παλαμναίους βλέπω 'look on guilty men' (Parker prints this). »» Diggle 1981, 88.]

1220. Take your time etc.: 'do the goddess's business well at leisure'.

1222–25. Now I see etc.: the procession that now emerges from the temple proves to be more elaborate (and must gave been more impressively staged) than we might have expected when Iphigenia spoke of cleansing with sea-water and performing 'other rites' (1191–99). **the goddess's adornments:** statues of Greek

248   COMMENTARY

goddesses were often clothed and adorned with offerings from worshippers
(»» Rouse 1902, 274–77; *ThesCRA* I.296f.); these would need to be washed along
with the image itself. **so I can wash off tainted blood with blood:** blood from
the lambs will 'wash' the matricidal blood-pollution from Orestes and Pylades,
just as Orestes was supposed to have been purified at Delphi with the blood of a
suckling pig (A. *Eum.* 282f., 449–52). »» Burkert 1985, 80–82; R. Parker 1983,
370–74; *ThesCRA* II.20f.; Georgoudi 2017, 120f., 125–32 (suggesting that the
blood of very young animals, such as **newborn lambs**, was used because it was
reliably pure). **flaring torches** ('flare of torches'): to be used for purifying the
surroundings (1216 n.) and especially the lustral water (*HF* 928f., Ar. *Peace* 959).

   1226–29. I call upon the citizens etc.: all must keep clear of the procession
so as to avoid the risk of pollution from the prisoners. Especially at risk are those
preparing for an initiation or fulfilling a vow of purity (**keeping clean hands for
the gods**), those **about to tie the marriage-knot** (another vulnerable transitional
process), and pregnant women (**childbearing** was considered both polluting and
open to pollution). »» R. Parker 1983, 345 (marriage), 48–52 (childbearing).

   1230–33. O maiden mistress etc.: Iphigenia prays publicly for the success of
the purification but includes cryptic appeals for the return to Greece (**sacrifice
where we should...enjoy good fortune...I do not say it**), exploiting the typical
vagueness of Greek prayers which encouraged the deity to give them the most
favourable interpretation. In *El.* 808f. Orestes prays for the opposite of what
Aegisthus has prayed for, 'not voicing the words'.

1234–83. Third Stasimon: Apollo's possession of Delphi

The Chorus sings a hymn of praise to Apollo, telling of his birth on Delos (1234–
36), his beauty and skills (1236–39), his arrival at Delphi (1239–44), and two
legendary events which confirmed his supremacy in the realm of prophecy: he
killed the earth-dragon to take possession of Delphi (1245–58), and when
Gaia/Earth (mother of the displaced goddess Themis/Right) retaliated by
producing dreams to compete with his prophecies, he persuaded Zeus to suppress
them (1259–82).

   This is one of Euripides' so-called 'dithyrambic stasima', a highly decorated
mythical narrative like the extant dithyrambs of Bacchylides.[31] The narratives in
these odes are set at some remove from the play's action but are thematically or
mythically relevant to it. Here the song resembles a hymn, seconding Iphigenia's
prayer to Artemis (1230–33) and aptly sung as the procession departs. The
beginning is virtually an invocation (1234–38 n.), and Apollo is directly addressed

---

[31] 'Dithyrambic stasimon' is a modern term characterizing the narrative style of
these odes. Furley and Bremer (2001, I.332–36) argue that this ode is less like a
real dithyramb (i.e. belonging to a Dionysiac context) than a kitharodic nome,
a hymn sung in praise of Apollo, his history and his powers, a form we know only
indirectly from ancient descriptions.

COMMENTARY   249

in 1252. The Chorus praises him and celebrates his birth, attributes, cult-places, achievements and powers so as to invite his favour and assistance in the present situation. Their hymn implies confidence in the god's power to help his worshippers in their escape and encourages him to use this power in their favour.[32]

The story in the *strophe* is broadly familiar from earlier (and later) accounts of Apollo's early life. The third *Homeric Hymn* tells in monumental style of his birth on Delos (14–18, 25–126), his claiming of lyre, bow and island (127–39), his complicated journey from Olympus to Delphi and founding of the sanctuary there (214–99), and his combat with the Python-dragon (300–4, 356–70). Alcaeus's *Hymn to Apollo* (fr. 307 Lobel–Page) also made him the first prophetic god at Delphi, arriving in a joyous procession from the land of the Hyperboreans. In the fifth century, by contrast, Pindar told of his taking Delphi by force against Gaia's opposition (fr. 55 Snell–Maehler in Schol. Aesch. *Eum.* 5b Smith), while Aeschylus, *Eumenides* 1–19 describes a peaceful transfer from Gaia to her daughter the Titaness Themis, then to Themis's sister Phoebe (Leto's mother) and so to Leto's son Apollo who arrived in a joyous procession from Delos through Attica. In Aristonous's *Paean* (4th C: *Coll.Alex.* 162–65) Apollo obtains Delphi from Gaia and Themis through persuasion and with Athena's supervision. Euripides' narrative pointedly differs from these as Gaia attempts to subvert the oracular power which Apollo has stolen from her daughter Themis (»» 1259–61 n.), only for Zeus to confirm his son's authority and control of divine truth. It is unlikely that any of the various myths of arrival and conquest reflect the actual development of the sanctuary at Delphi, although older scholarship generally assumed that they do. Rather, they are mythical constructs, all equally appropriate or 'true' in confirming Apollo's destiny as the oracular god (cf. Sourvinou-Inwood 1987, 234). That he kills the dragon as a babe in arms adds charm and humour to the story (cf. 1250–52 n.), but it also affirms the superhuman power of the Olympian god.

The story of Apollo's conflict with Gaia's dreams in the *antistrophe* is probably Euripides' own invention, although it too used to be taken as evidence that Delphi once possessed a dream-oracle. This episode is an elaboration of the myth's central idea, continuing the conceit of the young and vulnerable god (1270–72 n.) but reconfirming Zeus's endorsement of Apollo's rights and showing the 'new-order' father and son (Zeus and Apollo) asserting superiority over the 'old-order' mother and daughter (Gaia and Themis). The triumph of Olympian Apollo over Earth and her offspring (dragon, dreams) implies Orestes' ultimate escape from the Erinyes and his success in bringing Artemis and Iphigenia from the barbarian to the Hellenic realm.

The ode's myth affirms the play's myth in other ways too. The assertion of Apollo's authority in speaking from his **undeceiving throne** (1254, cf. 1281–83) suggests that Orestes has been rightly guided by the god. Dreams by contrast have

---

[32] Their confidence will promptly be challenged by the arrival of the Messenger with news that the escapers are in trouble, as Mastronarde (2010, 142) notes.

250 COMMENTARY

been prevented by Zeus from communicating their truths directly (1278–79 n.) and so are open to the kind of misinterpretation that led Iphigenia towards killing her brother. The god's journey to Delphi, combat with the dragon, and appropriation of the sanctuary from its primeval owners prefigure the quest of Orestes, who will appropriate Artemis from the Taurians and establish a sanctuary and rituals for the god's sister as Apollo did for himself. At the same time Orestes' subjection to trials and the threat of failure is prefigured in the resistance which impeded Apollo. He may still face some final difficulty (the adverse wind and wave, as it turns out) needing the superior power of Zeus, with Athena enforcing 'what must be' (1486), for its resolution. The humour and playfulness of the ode's narrative hint at a divinely sponsored fortune which is unpredictable yet possibly beneficent, and more burdensome to weak humans than to carefree gods. While the Chorus voices confidence in Apollo in order to assure his help, their story points a little uncomfortably to the god's ruthlessness in securing his **honours** or privileges (τιμάς, 1280) and to the arbitrariness of his favours (cf. Introduction, pp. 10f.).

»» *Myth:* Fontenrose 1959, esp. 1–22; Panagl 1969; Sourvinou-Inwood 1987; Gantz 88; Chappell 2006, 339–42. *Ode:* Burnett 1971, 69–71; Panagl 1971, 119–39; Sourvinou-Inwood 1987, 228–30 and 2003, 305; Furley–Bremer 2001, I.329–36, II.322–29; Kyriakou 391–94; Trieschnigg 2008, 472–75; Mastronarde 2010, 142f.; Parker 304–306; Amiech 270–82.

Strophe and antistrophe each have five parts which frame the narrative in epic style (matching its epic language, allusive and rich in noun-epithet phrases). Parallelism reinforces the demonstration of Apollo's supremacy: *Strophe* 1234–39 Apollo's birth and attributes, 1239–44 his journey to Delphi, 1245–49 he confronts the dragon, 1250–52 he prevails, 1253–58 he exercises prophetic power; *Antistrophe* 1259–62 Earth produces dreams, 1264–69 dreams reveal truths to humans, 1270–72 Apollo appeals to Zeus, 1274–80 he prevails (Zeus neutralizes dreams), 1281–83 he continues to exercise prophetic power.

The ode consists mainly of dactylic or dactylic-trochaic ('dactylo-epitrite') cola as often for lyric narrative, with iambics at beginning and end (1234~1259, 1257~1282) and marking the moments of divine intervention (1250 **An infant still...**, 1274 **Zeus laughed...**). Parker's colometry (adopted here) identifies some aeolo-choriambic cola (1236~1261, 1241–47~1266–71, 1251~1275). »» Parker lxxxix–xc, 306–9.

1234–38. A noble son is Leto's child etc.: a declaration of the god's virtue and parentage is followed by relative clauses mentioning his birth, cult-centre and chief attributes (golden hair, lyre, bow). These elements are characteristic of the invocations which typically introduce Greek hymns (Furley–Bremer 2001, I.52–56) but here lead directly into the narrative. εὔπαις, 'a fine-child one' (poetic pleonasm, cf. 436–37 n.), though εὔπαις normally means 'having good children'. For similar phrases see *HF* 689 τὸν Λατοῦς εὔπαιδα γόνον with Bond's note.

COMMENTARY   251

1235. whom once in Delos's fertile dell: cf. 1098–1102. The main accounts of Apollo's birth on Delos are in *Homeric Hymn* 3 and Callimachus, *Hymn* 4; »» Gantz 37f. The **fertile dell** is the sanctuary with its sacred trees ('Zeus's garden', *Ion* 922). Delos as a whole is far from fertile. Poetic γύαλα ('hollows') occurs often in topographical references, especially to Delphi, e.g. Pind. *Pyth.* 8.63, Soph. F 460, E. *Andr.* 1093, *Ion* 76 etc., *Pho.* 237. **[Δηλιάσιν γυάλοις:** feminine adjective with neuter noun as in *Hel.* 1301, *Pho.* 1024, *Or.* 270, 837. L's δηλιὰς ἐν gives 'whom once the Delian one (Leto) brought to birth in a fertile dell', but Leto has just been named and is not strictly Delian, and the place needs a geographic marker.]

1236. she brought to birth: ἔτικτε or something very like it is needed for metre and sense. L's text is slightly defective at 24-line intervals in 1236/1260, 1239/1263, 1380/1404, presumably through damage to its archetype.

1236–38. the gold-haired god etc.: Apollo's three most prominent attributes are mentioned in an ascending tricolon. The epithet **gold-haired** (χρυσοκόμης) belongs typically though not exclusively to Apollo, e.g. Pind. *Ol.* 6.41, 7.32, *Paean* 5.41, Bacchyl. 4.2, *Carm.Conv.* 886.2 *PMG*, E. *Supp.* 975. He claimed the **lyre** and **bow** at birth according to *Hom.Hymn.* 3.131. **[ὅστε, who:** the epic relative is used occasionally in later poetry (Diggle 1994, 172). L's ἅ τ', 'and her who…', would refer to Apollo's twin Artemis and her hunting-bow, but she is not relevant here.]

1240. the sea-bound crag: the rocky island of Delos with Mt. Kynthos at its centre.

1241–44. that mother of pouring waters: Euripides often personifies natural features as parents or nurses, e.g. *Hec.* 451f. τὸν καλλίστων ὑδάτων πατέρα, 'that father of most beautiful waters' (the river Apidanos): »» Breitenbach 166f. ἀστάκτων is lit. 'undripping' (*litotês*/understatement), an adjective seen only here and in lexical references; the adverb ἀστακτί refers to copious weeping, S. *OC* 1251, 1646, Pl. *Phd.* 117c7 and later. **who dances with Dionysus:** Parnassus was often the site of Bacchic revels celebrating Dionysus, who shared possession of Delphi with Apollo and could be imagined dancing with the revellers (e.g. *Ion* 714–17, *Ba.* 306–8, *Hyps.* F 752, cf. A. *Eum.* 22–24). Nature is often poetically identified with human celebrations, e.g. *Ba.* 114 (the whole earth will dance for Dionysus), *HF* 781–93 (the rivers of Thebes dancing and Parnassus singing for Heracles' victory): »» Breitenbach 168.

[L's text (see app. crit.) is confused: 'the mother of pouring waters brought her offspring…to Parnassus's crowning height which dances for Dionysus'. Diggle's μά|τηρ τὰν ἀστάκτων ὑδάτων | ⟨συμ⟩βακχεύουσαν Διονύ|σῳ etc. gives 'the mother brought her offspring…to the Parnassian peak of (i.e. endowed with) pouring waters which dances with Dionysus'. Sansone's **τὰν | ματέρ' ἀστάκτων ὑδάτων, that mother of pouring waters** gives better phrasing and sense. For ⟨συμ⟩βακχεύουσαν cf. *Ba.* 726, Pl. *Phaedr.* 234d6. Lines 1242–44 are three so-called

252   COMMENTARY

'choriambic dimeters', i.e. aeolic cola with choriambic ending (Parker's 'polyschematists', p. xciii).]

1245–49. where a mottle-backed dark-eyed serpent etc.: cf. the 'grey-eyed mottle-backed snake' (γλαυκῶπα...ποικιλόνωτον ὄφιν) of Pind. *Pyth.* 4.249. **οἰνωπός** (Homeric οἶνοψ) means 'dark and gleaming' as in Homer's 'wine-dark sea' etc. (Irwin 1974, 28, 202). **[possessed the grove etc.:** see app. crit. L's text would mean 'bronzed (i.e. with bronze-like scales) in shady verdant laurel', but that reads a lot into κατάχαλκος and the serpent is more likely on the ground. Burges (1807, 131) supplied the essential correction **κάτεχ' ἄλσος**. Most recent editors print this with L's σκιερᾷ...εὔφυλλον ('verdant with shady laurel'), but that seems less likely than **σκιερὸν...εὐφύλλῳ, shady with verdant laurel**; cf. *Odyssey* 20.278 ἄλσος ὕπο σκιερὸν ἑκατηβόλου Ἀπόλλωνος ('in far-shooting Apollo's shady grove'), *Iliad* 11.480 ἐν νέμεϊ σκιερῷ ('in a shady glade'), Theognis 1252 ἄλσεα...σκιερά ('shady groves'). **†*haunts the chthonic oracle†***: L's unmetrical **ἄμφεπει μαντεῖον χθόνιον** remains difficult to explain or emend.]

1250–52. An infant still etc.: the scene of Leto confronted by the Python while carrying her infant twins (sometimes with Apollo brandishing his bow) is represented in the art of the fifth century and later (*LIMC* II, 'Apollon' nos 988–997, especially the Attic vases nos 988, 993, 994). In *Hom.Hymn.* 3 Apollo breaks out of his swaddling bands to proclaim himself. In *Hom.Hymn.* 4 the child Hermes outwits Apollo in acquiring a divine role for himself.

1254–58. on the golden tripod you sit: in the prophetic ritual at Delphi Apollo's priestess sat in the bowl of the sacred tripod to deliver his words. The tripod-bowl is a 'throne' in A. *Eum.* 18, 29; Apollo sits on it, E. *Or.* 164, 329, 956, cf. Aristonous, *Paean* 9–16. It is 'Themis's tripod' at *Or.* 164, and it is she who sits in it in a vase-painting from the 430s (Berlin 2638 = *LIMC* VIII, 'Themis' no. 10). It carries Apollo across the sea (as Apollo Delphinios) in two vase-paintings of the late sixth and early fifth centuries (*LIMC* II, 'Apollon' nos 381, 382). **earth's midmost mansion:** the sacred Omphalos or 'navel'-stone in Apollo's temple at Delphi was supposed to be the Earth's centre, e.g. *Med.* 668, *Ion* 5f. etc., A. *Cho.* 1036, Pind. *Pyth.* 4.74, Pausanias 10.16.3. **Castalia's streams:** water from the Castalian spring, at the foot of the Phaedriades cliffs at the eastern end of the Delphic sanctuary, was used for purifications (e.g. *Ion* 95–97, 146–49).

1259–61. when he had displaced the Earth-child Themis etc.: Themis is the divine power motivating all that is right and lawful in the world (»» Rudhardt 1999, 43–57, *LIMC* VIII.1.1199–1205). According to Hesiod's *Theogony* (135) she was a Titaness, daughter of Gaia/Earth and Ouranos/Sky, and thus a fundamental element in the cosmos and possessed of Gaia's knowledge. She was coopted as a wife by Zeus when he overthrew the Titans, and bore him daughters Order, Justice, Peace and the Moirai (Hes. *Theog.* 901–6; for the Moirai see 207 n.); these now embody the beneficial order of the world under Zeus's control. Themis was usually seen as a guarantor of lawfulness in social and religious

COMMENTARY 253

contexts and associated with cults accordingly, including cults of Apollo and the Delphic oracle itself (»» Rudhardt 43, 47, 52–55). She assisted at Apollo's birth in the *Homeric Hymn* (94, 124f.). Euripides' story does not imply a conflict between Apollo and Themis; he simply supersedes her and now wields her authority, just as her daughters by Zeus now exercise the powers which stem from her. It is Gaia, mother of Themis (and of the slain Python), who resents this usurpation of the 'old order' and tries to subvert it, only to be outwitted (inevitably) by Zeus.

[For the form Γαῖαν ('Gaian') see 1 n.; L's ἐπὶ γᾶς ἰὼν 'going (masc.) upon earth' is obviously wrong. Some editors prefer Kviçala's Γαίων ('When he had removed her daughter Themis from the holy Earth-oracle'). For the missing word in 1260 Hermann guessed Πυθῶνος ('from Pytho's holy sanctuary'), Nauck ὁ Λατῷος ('when the Letoan, i.e. Apollo, had removed…'. **ἀπενάσσατο, displaced** ('made to dwell away from'): for the verb ἀποναίω see 175 n., and for the aorist middle used transitively A. *Eum.* 928f. (μεγάλας καὶ δυσαρέστους | δαίμονας αὐτοῦ κατανασσαμένη, 'causing great and hard-to-please spirits to dwell here'), Ap. Rhod. 1.1356, 4.567 (both νάσσατο, 'caused to dwell').]

1261–63. Earth spawned nocturnal dream-apparitions: i.e. dream-figures (ὄνειροι) who communicate with the dreamer as in e.g. *Iliad* 2.5–22 (Zeus sends an ὄνειρος to deceive Agamemnon), A. *Ag.* 274 (the Chorus asks Clytemnestra if her news from Troy was brought by dream-figures, ὀνείρων φάσματα). An ὄνειρος could also be more generally the content or experience of a dream, like Iphigenia's dream (55, 348, 569). Dreams were naturally associated with night and darkness and thought to come from the earth. In *Odyssey* 24.12 the underworld includes the neighbourhood of dreams (δῆμον ὀνείρων). In Hesiod's *Theogony* they are children of Earth's daughter Night (*Theog.* 212), and in Ar. *Frogs* 1331–35 (parodying Euripides) a dream is 'child of dark night, coming forth from unseen Hades' (ἀφανοῦς Ἀίδα πρόμολον…Νυκτὸς παῖδα μελαίνας). Earth herself is 'mother of black-winged dreams' in E. *Hec.* 71. »» Dodds 1951, Hanson 1980 on dreams in Greek culture. [Triclinius restored ὀ⟨νείρων⟩ in L (cf. 1236 n.) recalling similar phrases in A. *Ag.* 274 (above), S. *El.* 644f.]

1264. to communities of mortals: πόλεσιν μερόπων echoes the epic πόλεις μερόπων ἀνθρώπων (*Iliad* 18.342, 490, 20.217, *Hom.Hymn.* 3.42), using **μερόπων** substantively as in A. *Cho.* 1018 etc. The etymology of the word μέροψ is unknown (Beekes 'μέροψ', Silk 1983, 325). The phrase here presumably means 'mortals living in communities', including individuals in their own communities and not just 'envoys coming [to Delphi] from the cities of Greece' as Parker suggests. [The reading πόλεσιν **(to communities)** is strongly supported by the epic parallels noted above. Most editors have read πολέσιν (epic dative plural of πολύς: 'to many of mortals'), assuming that L's original reading was πολέσι (see also Kannicht on *Hel.* 1330–32). What L now has is πόλέσιᵛ, while P plainly has πόλεσι, which suggests that πόλεσι was the original reading of L and was altered by Triclinius to πολέσιν (Sansone ed. and 2008, 387).]

254 COMMENTARY

1264–65. the first things and things that followed etc.: a threefold time-division like *Iliad* 1.70 (Calchas knew 'things that were and would be and were before'), S. *Ant.* 611f. (the law of *âtê* holds 'for the next (τὸ ἔπειτα, i.e. events now unfolding), the future (τὸ μέλλον) and the before (τὸ πρίν)'). A simpler twofold distinction (τά τ' ὄντα καὶ μέλλοντα, 'things that are and are to come') is made at *Ion* 7, *Hel.* 14, 923, S. *El.* 1498. The past beyond human memory is, like the future, the preserve of divine knowledge, e.g. Hes. *Theog.* 104–15.

1266. as they slept in darkness on the ground: 'in sleep by darkened ground-beds'. The dream-figure stands over or beside the dreamer (e.g. *Iliad* 2.20). Sleeping on the ground enabled divinely inspired dreams in healing sanctuaries such as those at Epidauros and Oropos. The poetic adjective δνοφερός often refers to night or the darkness of the underworld, from which the dream-figures were supposed to come. [L's ὕπνου κατὰ δνοφερᾶς γᾶς εὐνάς makes difficult sense ('at their sleep-lyings on the dark earth'?), and γᾶς εὐνάς is unmetrical.]

1270–72. Then lord Apollo sped etc.: Apollo flying to Olympus to supplicate Zeus resembles Thetis doing so on her son Achilles' behalf in *Iliad* 1.496f. As a child-god appealing to an indulgent father he resembles Hermes in *Hom.Hymn.* 4.366–90 (1250–52 n.). **and coiled his youngster's arm etc.**: Apollo grasps the throne in supplication, as if to establish a bond with Zeus and enforce his claim for action. Greek suppliants would grasp the person supplicated or a god's altar, image etc. in this way (1068–[71] n.). **begging him to remove:** ἀφελεῖν is simply 'to remove', with 'begging' implied by the previous phrase. **the earth-goddess's wrath:** χθονίαν μῆνιν θεᾶς, 'the goddess's earth-wrath', with transferred epithet (*enallagê*, »» Breitenbach 182–86). [Nauck's χθονίας makes a more banal phrase but could be right, cf. Pind. *Pyth.* 4.159 ἀφελεῖν μᾶνιν χθονίων (Sansone 2008, 387).]

1274. Zeus laughed: as he laughed at the one-day-old Hermes' effrontery in claiming that he did not steal Apollo's cattle (*Hom.Hymn.* 4.389f.)

1276–77. He shook his hair etc.: a gesture of decision and authority. In *Iliad* 1.524–30 Zeus nods in assent to Thetis's request, shaking his hair over his brow ('for whatever I nod with my head is neither revocable nor deceptive nor unfulfilled'), and great Olympus trembles. ἐπὶ δ' ἔσεισεν...παῦσαι makes an indirect command as in 1272 ἀφελεῖν and 1330 ἐξένευσ' ἀποστῆναι. ἐπὶ belongs with ἔσεισεν (*tmêsis*, 832–33 n.) and suggests that Zeus shook his hair forward (ἐπ' ὄφρυσι νεῦσε, 'nodded forward with his brow', *Iliad* 1.528). [L's ἐπεὶ... παῦσε ('when he had shaken...he ended') is unmetrical. Musgrave suggested ἐπὶ δὲ σείσας...παῦσεν, 'shaking...he ended'.]

1278–79. and stole away...the night-figures' candour: Zeus has not abolished dreams but has cunningly stopped them from speaking plainly to humans (1264–67) and so from competing with Apollo's oracular utterances (which themselves were ἐνοπάς, **declarations**, cf. *El.* 1302). By depriving the dreams of their **candour** (ἀλαθοσύναν, 'unelusiveness') Zeus has left humans vulnerable to their

COMMENTARY   255

own misunderstandings of the dreams, like Iphigenia at the beginning of the play. ὑπό belongs with ἐξεῖλεν (*tmêsis* again). νυκτωπόν is 'night-faced', referring to the (speaking) faces of the dream-figures, cf. *HF* 112f. δόκημα νυκτερωπὸν ἐννύ-χων ὀνείρων, 'a night-faced fancy (consisting) of nocturnal dreams'. νυκτ(ερ)ωπ-ός is found nowhere else except in Plutarch's parody, δόκημα νυκτερωπὸν ἐννύχ-ων σοφιστῶν 'a night-faced fancy of nocturnal sophists', *Mor.* 1066c7.

1282–83. confidence for mortals: Zeus's decision caused mortals to trust Apollo's oracles instead of the revelations of the Earth-sent dreams. **the chantings of his decrees:** i.e. the chanted verses (dactylic hexameters) in which the Pythia's prophecies were conventionally supposed to have been given (simple spoken responses were in fact the norm for most of the historical period: »» Fontenrose 1978, 193–95, 233–36). [**πολυάνορι, crowded:** πολυάνωρ, 'with many men', is a poetic alternative for πολύανδρος, only here and Lyr. adesp. 19.13 *PMG* (the much-visited temple of Asclepius at Epidaurus), A. *Ag.* 62 (the promiscuous Helen), Ar. *Birds* 1313 (a populous city). **ξενόεντι, guest-frequented** is the only known instance of the adjective ξενόεις.[33] **θάρση** is the earliest instance of a plural form of the word θάρσος (Attic θάρρος), meaning 'feelings of confidence'. Later instances are nearly all philosophical and often in contrast with φόβοι, 'fears'.]

1284–1496. Final scenes

After the elaborate sequences of recognition and intrigue the action closes rapidly in scenes which highlight the narration of the escape and Athena's instructions for the foundation of sanctuaries and rituals for Artemis in Attica. 1284–1326 Mess-enger's arrival and dialogues with Chorus and Thoas – 1327–1421 Messenger's speech and Chorus's response – 1422–34 Thoas prepares to pursue the fugitives – 1435–74 intervention and speech of Athena – 1475–96 Athena's settlement accepted by Thoas and the Chorus.

1284–1434. The Messenger is one of the servants who escorted the 'purification' party to the shore. He arrives to report the offstage action according to a convent-ional tragic pattern, but the manner of his arrival is novel and includes humorous and parodic features. Messengers usually report to a receptive chorus, or to an individual who is present when they arrive or is summoned from inside. This Messenger's portentous call for Thoas ('Throw open these finely riveted doors…', 1286) is unsuccessful, and the Chorus intervenes only to reject the news ('That's an incredible story!'), hiding the fact that, unusually for a chorus, they know what to expect. Their attempt to send him off on a wild goose chase threatens to eliminate the Messenger speech, but the attempt fails as he sees

---

[33] Literally 'guested', like πτερόεις 'winged', νιφόεις 'snow-clad', ἰχθυόεις 'fish-inhabited', τεκνοῦς (< -όεις) 'having children' and many similar poetic adjectives (»» Buck–Petersen 1949, 460–63).

256 COMMENTARY

straight through it. In the ensuing quarrel he is reduced to hammering on the door, insisting on the importance of his news ('a load of new troubles', 1306), and then finds himself facing a distinctly irritated Thoas who is with difficulty persuaded to listen to the report (1311f., 1322). In the end the Messenger is allowed to deliver a long narrative speech despite his insistence that the fugitives must be pursued immediately.

Urgent approaches to a closed door (one of several ways in which the *skênê* door was dramatically exploited) may have been invented in A. *Cho.* 653–67 where Orestes reports his own death. In Euripides see e.g. *Pho.* 1067–71 (also a Messenger), *Med.* 1312–15, *Hipp.* 808–10, *Or.* 1561ff.»» Taplin 1977, 340f. and 1978, 33–35 (Aeschylus); Hourmouziades 1965, 14–25 (Euripides); Brown 2000 (tragedy) and 2008 (comedy).

1284. You temple-minders etc.: the Messenger at first ignores the Chorus and shouts through the closed door to the servants inside the temple.

1285. where is Thoas...to be found: ποῦ κυρεῖ βεβώς, 'where does he happen to have set himself'. For βεβώς see LSJ βαίνω A.I.2.

1289–90. that pair of young fellows (δίπτυχοι νεανίαι): for the phrasing see 124–25 n., and for Ἀγαμεμνονείας see 1 n.

1294. the one you want to see etc.: 'what lord you want to see'. ἄνακτα is incorporated in the relative clause and attracted into the case of the pronoun ὃν ('inverse attraction', *CGCG* §50.14–15).

1298. See how treacherous is womankind: ὁρᾶτε calls witness to evidence of a general truth as e.g. *HF* 508, *Ion* 1090. This one is proverbial, e.g. *Odyssey* 11.427–34, 456, Hes. *Works* 77–79, 375, E. *Med.* 421f.

1302. Not before I hear it stated plainly: 'Not before an interpreter makes this statement', i.e. reveals the true answer to his question (LSJ 'ἑρμηνεύς' II.1).

1306. reporting a load of new (καινῶν) troubles: like the Herdsman's 'strange new report' (239 n.). This confirms, if it wasn't already obvious, that the actor will deliver a messenger-speech.

1309. †*These women were saying falsely and...*†: the general sense is clear, but ψευδῶς ἔλεγον is unmetrical and καί only make sense if καί μ' ἀπήλαυνον δόμων is parenthetic. [Amongst many conjectures Pierson's ψευδῶς λέγουσαί μ' αἰδ' ('These women were driving me away from the temple saying falsely...') is printed for convenience by Kovacs and Parker.]

1312. what matters right now: τὰ ἐν ποσίν, 'the things at your feet' (LSJ 'πούς' I.4.c).

1316. The purification was a trick: the Taurian here and at 1336–38 suspects that there was no purification, but Iphigenia's dream suggested she would perform a lustration of Orestes, albeit for a purpose that she misunderstood (53–58), and the ritual paraphernalia which she has taken to the seashore included lambs whose blood would be used in cleansing the captives' bloodguilt. We may reasonably infer that she has purified them and the image of the goddess which their pollution

COMMENTARY   257

threatened, and that this implies a final cleansing of Orestes from his bloodguilt and of Artemis from her connection with human sacrifices (Latifses 2019).

1317. What breeze of fortune did she catch: wind is often an image for fortune: cf. Bond on *HF* 216. συμφορᾶς: see 618 n. κεκτημένη: κτάομαι 'take possession of' is often used for becoming subject to circumstances or divine influences, or bringing them upon oneself, e.g. *Med.* 1047, *Or.* 267, 543 etc.

1319. What Orestes: τὸν ποῖον, 'the one of what kind'. For ποῖον see 495 n., and for the added τόν e.g. *Pho.* 707, *IA* 517 (»» Collard 2018, 83).

1320. The man she dedicated to the goddess: καθωσιώσατο, 'made *hosios*' (130–32 n.), i.e. claimed as a victim. θεᾷ is the Aldine editor's correction of L's θεά, which makes Artemis the subject ('the man whom the goddess (had) made *hosios* for herself'). [θεά has been preferred by nearly all editors since Markland noticed L's reading in 1771, but the idea of a deity making a victim (or having a victim made) *hosios* is unparalleled so far as I know, and while the Taurian thinks Iphigenia has not really consecrated the victims, she has at least designated them for sacrifice (cf. Peels 2015, 239f.). Her ritual was supposed to make them 'more *hosioi* for the goddess' (ὁσιώτεροι τῇ θεῷ, 1194).]

1321. how can I find you a greater name: 'how can I hit the mark/succeed in naming you something greater?' 'Marvel' is the strongest term available, yet insufficient; cf. 839f., *Hec.* 714, *Hel.* 601 etc. For τύχω (or τύχοιμ' ἄν) in questions searching for a correct name see Barrett on *Hipp.* 826f. For questions or exclamations justifying a choice of terms cf. *Med.* 465f., *Sthen.* F 666 etc. »» Diggle 1981, 89f., Cropp 1997, 40f.

1325–26. The route they're fleeing on etc.: 'They are not fleeing a near-voyage route (pleonasm, 436–37 n.) so as to escape…'. The comment both emphasizes the continuing danger to the fugitives and serves to justify the length and detail of the report speech. **my armed pursuit:** δόρυ is a wooden shaft or stem, hence 'ship's plank', 'spear' etc., then by synecdoche 'ship' or 'army' or 'military power' (e.g. *Hipp.* 975). Euripides could use it for both 'army' and 'ship' in a single sentence (*Andr.* 789ff.), and he could have intended the sense 'ship' or 'fleet' here as some commentators think. But Thoas later envisages pursuit by both land and sea (1422–30), and in the end he will 'still the spear which I'm raising against the strangers, and my ships' oars' (1484f.).

1327–1419. The play's second report speech shares the standard features of its kind with the first which the Herdsman delivered (260–339 n. with 301–35 n. on mock-epic features of the battle). The narrative is carefully set out scene by scene as in epic: 1327–38 the mock ritual; 1339–53 discovery and description of the ship preparing to depart; 1355–78 confrontation and battle of Taurians and Greeks; 1379–1410 the ship departing and driven back to shore by wind and wave (see 1391–95 n.). The events are similar in pattern to those narrated by the Herdsman (the Taurians experience puzzling phenomena, decide to investigate, witness a remarkable scene, and join in an unequal battle with the heroic

258   COMMENTARY

Hellenes), but unlike the Herdsman Thoas's servant must excuse himself and his comrades from possible charges of negligence (1334f., 1342–44.) The first confrontation ended with the capture of Orestes and Pylades, and the second is about to do so as this report ends, but the divine protection which kept them unharmed during their capture will be reasserted in Athena's intervention. The escape report of *Helen* (1526–1618) is similarly designed. Several other plays feature speeches reporting the fulfilment of an intrigue (*mêchanêma*: *Med.*, *Andr.*, *El.*, *HF*, *Ion*, *Or.*, *Ba.*). »» de Jong 1991, 54–56, 104, 180f.

1331–32. hinting that the fire etc.: 'as burning an unmentionable (1198 n.) flame and the purification she was pursuing (being unmentionable)'. φλόγα is an internal object of θύουσα as in *HF* 936f., τί θύω…καθάρσιον πῦρ, 'why do I burn the purifying fire'. For this basic sense of θύειν see Casabona 1966, 73–75, Beekes 'θύω 2', Georgoudi 2017, 122–24.

1334–35. This was of course suspicious etc.: the king's gullibility in letting Iphigenia do as she pleased is neatly recalled. The Messenger in *Helen* (1549–53) likewise reminds Theoclymenus that he was the one who authorized Menelaus's command of the ship on which Menelaus and Helen are now escaping. The Taurian makes more of this in 1338–44.

1336. to give an impression, of course: here and in 1338 δή marks the Messenger's suggestion that this was all a pretence (»» Denniston 232, *CGCG* §59.44), although he has misunderstood what Iphigenia was actually doing (1316 n.).

1337–38. she raised an ululation etc.: aorist ἀνωλόλυξε (she ululated once) followed by 'immediative' imperfect κατῆδε (< κατ-αείδω), for which see 295–96 n. Women ululated in various contexts, especially ritual ones such as sacrifice, prayer and thanksgiving (»» Ziehen 1902, 393f.; Deubner 1941; Rudhardt 1958, 178–81). Iphigenia's ululation presumably followed the killing of the lambs whose blood would be used for the purification (Bremmer 2013, 96). **barbarian chants:** cf. the Chorus's 'barbarian clamour of Asian refrains' (178–81 n.). **playing the magus:** *magoi* were properly a Persian priestly caste, but the term came to be used for any 'oriental' priest or wizard. Foreign-sounding names and terms were often used in Greek magical incantations to give an impression of special knowledge and power (»» Graf 1997, 218–22).

1341–52, 1367–78. P. Oxy. 67.4565 (2nd C AD) has the first few letters of each of these lines (including 1346), with no new readings.

1339–43. it came to us that the foreigners…might kill her etc.: the messenger in *Helen* similarly reports that he and the Egyptian crew were suspicious when Menelaus allowed the disguised Greeks to come aboard their ship but did not object because their ruler (Theoclymenus) had foolishly put Menelaus in command (*Hel.* 1549–53).

1342. we sat on in silence: καθήμεθα imperfect (295–96 n.).

1345. vessel: νεὼς σκάφος, 'ship-hull' (pleonasm, cf. 370 n., 742).

COMMENTARY   259

1346. with oars spread out like wings in trim array: ταρσῷ κατήρει πίτυλον ἐπτερωμένον, 'oarbeat-winged with well-fitted array'. The phrasing is plausibly explained in Wecklein's commentary. πίτυλον 'oarbeat' stands for the **oars** themselves as in 1050 (νεώς...πίτυλος εὐήρης) and here is a 'retained accusative', equivalent to the object of an active verb ('I attach oars as wings to a ship'). ταρσός originally denoted wickerwork but was applied to other transverse arrays such as birds' wing-feathers, ships' oar-systems, Pan-pipes, eyelashes, the bones of hands or feet. Euripides elsewhere uses the rare adjective κατήρης with dative for 'equipped (with)' (*Supp.* 110, *El.* 498), but here it is simply 'fitted up', 'at the ready' like εὐήρης in 1050 (cf. Hdt. 8.21.1 πλοῖον κατῆρες, 'a fitted-up ship'). For ships 'winged' with oars cf. *Odyssey* 11.125 = 23.272, 'well-fitted (εὐήρεα) oars which are the wings of a ship' (and for great birds' wings as oars, A. *Ag.* 52, Ap.Rhod. 2.1255). Sails can also be a ship's wings (»» West on Hes. *Works* 628). [The verse is variously emended or obelized (Diggle, suggesting deletion) or transposed to follow 1394 (Hermann, Parker: see 1394–95 n.). I think it belongs in this vivid picture of the ship preparing to depart. Its first three letters are visible after line 1345 in P. Oxy. 4565.]

1347. fifty sailors: fifty is the number of a penteconter's oarsmen (1123–24 n.), commonly mentioned in Greek epic, e.g. *Iliad* 16.169f., 'in each [of Achilles' ships] there were fifty comrades at the tholepins'. The **thole-pins** are vertical pins giving leverage for the oar which was attached to the pin by a leather loop or passed between two of them. »» Morrison–Williams 1968, 52 and Index 'tholepins', Casson 1971, 46, 55, both with illustrations.

1348–53. This description with others such as *Helen* 1530–36 illustrates the handling and equipment of ships in this period. L's text is however confused, partly because the technical language was not well understood by copyists. The text printed here is as proposed by Köchly[34] and printed by Parker but with an additional loss marked after 1352. The Taurians see Orestes and Pylades waiting on the shore with Iphigenia and the image (1348f., end of description lost), some sailors on the afterdeck hauling in the stern-cables which moored the ship to rocks or trees on the shore (1349, 1352, beginning of description lost), some holding the prow steady with poles to stop it drifting now that the anchor has been raised (1350a: see below), some hanging the raised anchor from the catheads (1350b–1351a), and some lowering a ladder for Orestes and Pylades (1351b, 1353 n.). This is consistent with the following narrative in which the Taurians try to seize Iphigenia from Orestes and Pylades and hold the ship back by grabbing the stern-cables and steering-oars.

[L's text with a few incidental adjustments gives: 'and (we saw) the young men, free from their bonds, standing on the ship's afterdeck (or 'astern of the

---

[34] Köchly 1860, 10–13 and in his editions of the play (Schöne–Köchly 1863, 1872). The passage is treated differently in Bruhn's revision (Schöne–Köchly–Bruhn 1894).

260 COMMENTARY

ship') (1348f.); and they were holding the prow steady with poles while others were lashing the anchor to the cat-heads (1350–51a), and others hurrying ladders were drawing the stern-cables through their hands, were lowering them into the sea etc. (1351b–53). But (1) Orestes and Pylades must still be on the shore and hardly just 'standing', while Iphigenia and the image are not mentioned at all, (2) 'they' in 1350 are unidentified, and (3) the syntax of 1351b–53 is confused. Changing **πρυμνήσια** to πρύμνης δ' ἀπό in 1352 with L's line-order unchanged gives 'and others were hurriedly passing ladders through their hands and lowering them from the afterdeck into the sea' (Musgrave, Diggle), but this only addresses the third point. Köchly's transpositions resolve the first and third, but I think the second can only be resolved by supposing that **and were holding the prow steady with poles** is the end of a sentence which began by identifying sailors active on the foredeck.]

1350–51. lashing the anchor to the catheads: ships usually had two anchors (a single one could symbolize insufficient support: »» Diggle on *Pha.* 124–26). The Argo has one at Pind. *Pyth.* 4.24, and two at 4.192. **catheads** (ἐπωτίδες, 'earpieces') were the projecting ends of a transverse beam set into a ship's prow, from which the anchor was suspended when not in use (»» Morrison–Williams 1968, 198, Casson 1971, 85f.).

1351, 1353. others were lowering a ladder: plural κλίμακας probably means a single ladder with multiple steps as in *Supp.* 497, 729, *Pho.* 104, 1182 (see also 97–98 n.). **for the two strangers (τοῖν ξένοιν):** i.e. for Orestes and Pylades. Seidler's conjecture seems more likely than Musgrave's τῇ ξένῃ, as Parker notes.[35] At this point the Taurians think the two strangers are kidnapping Iphigenia and the image (1358f.), not that she is about to go aboard voluntarily.

1356–57. pulling out...the steering-oars: ships normally had two steering-oars projecting from either side of the stern and handled by a single helmsman by means of a tiller (»» Casson 1971, 224–28 with illustrations). **through their sockets (εὐθυντηρίας):** the word εὐθυντηρία (< εὐθύνειν 'keep straight, direct') is found only here and presumably means the opening through which the steering-oar projected. Elsewhere the oars themselves are εὐθυντῆρες ('steerers', Hesychius π 4207), cf. A. *Supp.* 717 'the guiding oar (οἴακος εὐθυντῆρος) at the ship's stern'. **of the stout-sterned ship:** εὐπρύμνου νεώς, cf. 1000 n.

1359. carved images and priestesses: plurals implying indignation at such behaviour. The word ξόανον, 'carving' (< ξέω), is used only here in this play (87–88 n.).

1360. Who are you...to be trafficking: 'Being who (son) of whom are you trafficking', i.e. kidnapping for sale into slavery (LSJ 'ἀπεμπολάω'; Parker).

---

[35] Seidler however was reading 1352 before 1353 and thought the sailors were lowering the stern-cables (πρυμνήσια...καθίεσαν) so that Orestes and Pylades could pull the ship closer to the shore.

COMMENTARY   261

1368–70. fists were being thumped and legs launched etc.: the barbarians
are easy meat for the Hellenic youths trained in athletics and combat. Athletic
games included boxing and the pankration (ancient mixed martial arts). Combat
training seems to have been reflected in the rituals for Artemis in the sanctuary at
Halai supposedly founded by Orestes (Graf 1985, 414f.). ἦσαν ἐγκροτούμεναι is
a periphrastic imperfect tense adding vividness (cf. 721–22 n.). ἠκοντίζετο is a
metaphor from javelin-throwing (362 n.).

1371. ached and seized up altogether: ξυναλγεῖν is a present infinitive with
imperfect force ('were aching'), ξυναποκαμεῖν aorist ('reached exhaustion'). This
combination and the repeated ξυν- (**together**) show the Taurians' strength failing
rapidly and completely.

1377. archers: ancient warships normally carried a few archers and a number
of marines (*epibatai*: »» Morrison–Williams 1968, 254–56, 263–66, 276f.; Casson
1971, 304).

1379–80. a terrible wave etc.: the wave drives the ship aground stern-first.
The oarsmen row vigorously to release it and the ship makes headway until it is
checked at the harbour mouth by 'a violent wave' and 'a terrible wind' which
again drive it back towards the shore (1390–97; see 1391–95 n. on the cause of
this resistance). **the maiden was afraid:** φόβος...ἦν παρθένῳ, 'there was fear in
the maiden'. [Badham's παρθένῳ fills the gap in L's text suitably (cf. 1236 n.).]

1383. the fine-decked ship (εὐσέλμου νεώς): an epic phrase (»» LSJ
'εὔσελμος') referring to a ship's decking (*selma, selmata*, »» Casson 1971, 220).
Orestes presumably placed Iphigenia on the afterdeck from which the ladder was
lowered (1352).

1384–85. that bolt from the sky: cf. 87–88 n. πέσημα, 'a thing fallen'.

1385–86. from mid-ship a voice cried out: we have to intuit the identity of
this voice. Earlier commentators took it to be a divine voice, comparing Apollo
encouraging Neoptolemus's killers at Delphi (*Andr.* 1147–49), Dionysus urging
his maenads to attack Pentheus (*Ba.* 1078–81) and the deity summoning Oedipus
to his death (S. *OC* 1623–28); similarly Cropp 2000; Sansone 2000, 170;
Mastronarde 2010, 196f. The voice might then be Apollo's, which Orestes heard
at Delphi (976–78) and which the Chorus imagines singing while conducting the
ship safely back to Athens (1128–31). There is however no clear indication that
this was a divine voice, and a stirring cry from the ship is more like those heard
from the Greek ships at Salamis (A. *Pers.* 401–5) or Menelaus and Helen
encouraging their fellow Greeks to attack the Egyptian crew as they escape from
Egypt (*Hel.* 1592–95, 1603f.). Here it presumably comes from the ship's captain
or boatswain (1125–27 n.): »» Kyriakou, Parker. **O you...from Hellas land:**
similar phrasing in A. *Pers.* 402, *Hel.* 1593, *Pho.* 1225. **sailor folk:** like *IA* 294f.
ναυβάταν λεών 'ship-board folk, *Hec.* 921 ναύταν ὅμιλον 'sailor company',
A. *Pers.* 383 ναυτικὸν λεών 'nautical folk' etc. [L's ναῦται νεώς 'ship's sailors'
is unlikely: »» Diggle 1994, 219 on *Supp.* 509.]

262   COMMENTARY

1387. stir up a whitening surf: ῥόθια…ἐκλευκαίνετε, 'whiten up surges', cf. 407 n., *Odyssey* 12.172 'they whitened the water with smooth oars', E. *Cyc.* 16f. 'whitening the gray brine with surging strokes (ῥοθίοισι)', A. *Pers.* 396f. 'they struck the deep brine (ἔπαισαν ἅλμην βρύχιον) with onset of surging oar (κώπης ῥοθιάδος)'.

1390–91. they bellowed out a cheerful roar (στεναγμὸν ἡδύν): an oxymoron; στεναγμός is normally 'groaning' but here the sound of fifty men exerting themselves as they strike out for home. **and struck the brine (ἔπαισαν ἅλμην):** cf. A. *Pers.* 397 cited above. The epic formula is πολίην ἅλα τύπτον ἐρετμοῖς 'they struck the brine with their oars' (*Odyssey* 4.580, 9.104 etc.).

1391–95. The ship…made way etc.: the ship again meets powerful resistance (cf. 1379f.) as wind and wave drive it back from the harbour entrance. The reason for this resistance is not stated. The Messenger guesses that Poseidon is angry at Agamemnon's family because of the sack of Troy (1414–19 n.), and there are suggestions that Artemis may be angry with Iphigenia for stealing her image and abandoning her Taurian cult (Iphigenia prays for her forgiveness, 1398–1402; the Messenger talks of her 'betraying the goddess', 1418f.; Thoas assumes that Artemis wants the 'impious' fugitives hunted down, 1425f.). These guesses are not verified by Athena, who says simply that Orestes' mission was required by destiny and that Poseidon has put an end to the resistance as a favour to her (1438–45). Kyriakou (pp. 16f., 438f.) argues that the resistance should be understood as due either to chance (*tuchê*) or to an intervention by an unidentified god (which from the human point of view is almost the same thing), but Duranti notes that it fits a pattern in which a sacrilegious theft provokes a natural reaction, most notably in the stories of the abortive theft of Hera's image from her temple on Samos (see 1041 n.) and Pyrrhus's theft of treasures from Persephone's temple at Locri which led to the wreck of his fleet (Diodorus 27.4.3, cf. Livy 29.18).[36] Duranti infers that the resistance is provoked by Artemis and enforced by Poseidon, just as in the prologue of *Trojan Women* Poseidon agrees to wreck the Greek fleet at Athena's request in response to the Lesser Ajax's sacrilege. Athena however says nothing about alleviating the two gods' resentments, as one would expect if these were important factors (cf. 1444–45 n.). In this and similar cases the disturbances are better seen, I think, as reactions of the elements themselves to the sacred items' presence on the ships.

1392. [but as it crossed the mouth: L's punctuation gives 'it made way towards the mouth, but as it crossed it'. For the postponed δέ see Denniston 187f.]

1394–95. and pushed the ship's †stern-cables back†: ὠθεῖ replaces L's imperfect ὤθει, the historic present marking this crucial point in the narrative (cf. 16 n.). νεὼς…πρυμνήσι(α) recalls the epic formula πρυμνήσια νηός, but winds do not push back stern-cables. [Hermann's παλιμπρυμνηδόν ('pushed the

---

[36] Duranti 2022, 183–86 citing Wolff 1992, 314 with note 14.

COMMENTARY   263

ship back stern-first' is known only from Hesychius π 187 and leaves ὠθεῖ without an object. Hermann supplied one by inserting line 1346 before 1395, but the transposition is unlikely (see 1346 n.). Paley instead suggested replacing νεώς with σκάφος ('pushed back the bark stern-first'), while Bruhn printed a lacuna between 1394 and 1395. More recent editors have printed Mekler's παλίμπρυμν' ἱστί(α), 'pushed the sail sternwards', but 'No one in his senses would have hoisted sail under these conditions' (Morrison) and there are no grounds for taking 'sail' as a synecdoche for 'ship'.][37]

1396. and kicked against the wave: not an athlete's kick but the proverbial 'kick against the goad' symbolizing painful struggle against a superior force. The proverb is found in earlier Greek poetry: Pind. *Pyth.* 2.94 (where the scholia explain it), A. *Ag.* 1624, [A.] *PV* 323, E. *Ba.* 795, F 604.

1397–1402. Agamemnon's daughter stood and prayed: the ship is now close enough to the shore for the Taurian to hear Iphigenia's prayer, as he heard the earlier cry from the ship. **O daughter of Leto, etc.:** again Iphigenia uses formal prayer-terms (1082–88 n.) including invocation, request, indication of her claim on Artemis (**your priestess**), an apology for possible offence (cf. Pulleyn 1997, 66–68) and a precedent reinforcing her demand for understanding and support from the goddess.

1403–4. The sailors followed…with an auspicious paean: 'properly-uttered a paean upon the maiden's prayers'. The paean (182–85 n.) was often used in moments of danger or impending struggle. The simple cry 'Hié Paian' could follow prayers as a refrain, calling for the deity's favour and protection. Cf. *IA* 1467–69, A. *Pers.* 392f., *Sept.* 635, Ar. *Wasps* 874, Xen. *Anab.* 3.2.9. »» Käppel 1992, 45–49, 300–3, 310, Ford 2006, 286–89.

1404–5. at the command: from the *keleustês* or boatswain (1390 n.). [ἐκ ⟨πέπλων⟩: the gap in the Greek text (1236 n.) is filled by reference to *Ion* 1208 γυμνὰ δ' ἐκ πέπλων μέλη, 'limbs stripped of clothing'.]

1407–8. one of us ran forward: the Taurians use their wreckers' skills to snare the ship as it drifts onto the rocks. ὁ μέν τις: definite and indefinite articles together denote a specific but unidentified individual as e.g. *Med.* 1141, *Hel.* 1597 (»» Kannicht on *Hel.* 98).

1414–19. The ocean's ruler was watching over Troy etc.: the Taurian assumes that Poseidon, already angry at the destruction of his city, now (καὶ νῦν) wishes to punish its destroyer's children; Thoas, then, can help to avenge the sack of Troy and punish Iphigenia's disloyalty to Artemis. He misconceives the direction of events and the divine intent which Athena will explain, like the Herdsman

---

[37] Unger's πρῳρήσι(α) (Marshall 2007) is a very rare word and gives unlikely sense. In Schol. Lycophron 295 (ed. Leone, 2002) it refers to some part(s) of the prow, a comment recycled more or less accurately in lexica (incompletely in Etym. Magn. 177.47 which Marshall cites). Gennadius Scholarius (15th C) identified a πρῳρήσιον as a cable (*TLG*).

264   COMMENTARY

who finished his report by inviting Iphigenia to treat the killing of Orestes and
Pylades as a heaven-sent revenge for her own suffering. Poseidon was a co-
founder and protector of Troy with Apollo (*Iliad* 7.451–53, E. *Tro.* 4–8). The verb
ἐπισκοπεῖν denotes protection by tutelary gods (e.g. S. *Ant.* 1136, cf. ἐποπτεύειν
A. *Cho.* 1, 1063) or their supervision of events (notably *Hec.* 491) or observance
of human behaviour with a view to reward and punishment (A. *Supp.* 402, *Cho.*
61, 985, E. *Hcld.* 869, ἐποπτεύειν A. *Ag.* 1579). **Pelops' descendants:** i.e. his
grandsons Agamemnon and Menelaus who attacked and destroyed Troy.[38]

   1418–19. forgetting the sacrifice at Aulis: i.e., that Artemis rescued her from
the sacrifice.

   1423. Come on now: εἷα is probably colloquial and appears in a few fixed
expressions in the dramatists and Plato (»» Collard 2018, 79; Diggle on *Phaethon*
221). Aspirated εἷα seems to be correct (»» Radt on Aesch. F 78a.18; Mastronarde
on *Pho.* 970).

   1424. the wreckage (ἐκβολάς): see 1042 n.

   1425–26. then with the goddess's help etc.: Thoas shares the Messenger's
misconceptions (1414–19 n.).

   1427. and others drag swift vessels: ὠκυπόμπους...πλάτας 'swift-
conveying oarblades' (116–17 n.). Herodotus 4.103.1 mentions that the Taurians
used boats to plunder passing ships as well as seizing shipwrecked mariners.

   1429–30. hurl them down...skewer their bodies: this reflects Herodotus's
account of the Taurians' treatment of their captives (4.103 cited above, pp. 19f.).
Such extreme measures are associated with 'barbarians' in Greek historical and
poetic texts (»» Hall 1989b, 111f., 158f.).

   1431–33. As for you...you women: threatening the Chorus is often the mark
of hybristic and ill-fated tragic tyrants such as Aegisthus (A. *Ag.* 1617–71), Lycus
(E. *HF* 247–51) and Pentheus (*Ba.* 511–14), but Thoas will be saved by Athena's
good will and his deference to her authority.

1435–89. The goddess Athena appears abruptly to guide the events of the drama
to a close and give instructions about their proper outcomes. Orestes must take the
image to Halai in Attica and establish the cult of Artemis Tauropolos with its
annual festival, the Tauropolia. Iphigenia will continue as priestess of Artemis at
Brauron and receive her own cult there after her death. Thoas must allow the
women of the Chorus to return, presumably to their home city (1467–71 n.), and
at Athens the principle that equal votes mean acquittal must be established (1471–
72 n.). Thoas readily accepts the goddess's instructions, Athena flies off to escort

---

[38] '[I]n all genres throughout the classical period the term [Pelopidai] refers
exclusively to the sons of Atreus and Thyestes, principally of the former. It is thus
shorthand for the leaders of the Greeks against Troy/the Trojan War period of
Greek history'' (Fowler 2013, 428).

COMMENTARY   265

the fugitives safely on their voyage, and the Chorus welcomes these outcomes. On the cult details and aetiologies see notes below with Introduction, pp. 27–34.

Euripides used divine appearances in the closing scenes of many other extant plays (*Hippolytus, Andromache, Suppliant Women, Electra, Ion, Helen, Orestes, Bacchae*; also in the lost ending of *Iphigenia at Aulis*). There are others in the fragments of *Antiope, Erechtheus* and *Hypsipyle*, as well as in *Rhesus* and Sophocles' *Philoctetes*. With some significant exceptions (*Hippolytus, Electra, Bacchae*) they are stylized and simple in structure: the god's speech, brief human response(s) and the Chorus's play-closing lines. The god's speech may forbid the continuation of violence (such as the murders of Theonoe by her brother in *Helen*, Hermione by Orestes in *Orestes*, Lykos by the twins in *Antiope*: the motif goes back to the ending of the *Odyssey*), or avert divine affliction (Poseidon's attempt to destroy Athens with an earthquake in *Erechtheus*), or redirect an ill-judged human decision (Ion's determination to confront Apollo, Philoctetes' refusal to go to Troy: cf. Zeus's correction of Achilles at the end of the *Iliad*). In other cases the god may only try to explain or console (e.g. Artemis on Hippolytus' death, Thetis on Neoptolemus' death in *Andromache*, Castor in *Electra* on the matricide which he and his brother have failed to avert). The god reveals divine or universal influences on the tragic events and future outcomes which may suggest a kind of meaning or purpose in them. All of these factors are at work in Athena's appearance. She has already arranged the quelling of the storm but must also prevent Thoas from pursuing the fugitives and punishing the Chorus, thus ensuring the rescue of all the Hellenes from the barbarians. She provides final confirmation of the rightness of Apollo's plan for Orestes and reveals its outcomes in the Hellenization of Artemis, the founding of the cults at Halai and Brauron, the destiny of Iphigenia (and probably the Chorus, 1467–71 n.) and the settlement of Orestes' trial with its implications for the Athenian legal system. Her status gives her authority in all of this, both as mistress of Attica and as Zeus's special daughter who can operate on at least equal terms with Poseidon and Apollo. It is likewise Athena who announces settlements in other tragedies of Euripides based in Athenian myth and ideology (*Suppliant Women, Ion, Erechtheus*) and of course in Aeschylus's *Eumenides*, whose linking of the Orestes story with the development of Athenian culture Euripides is here reformulating (Introduction, pp. 7, 12f.).

Scenes of this kind are usually called *deus ex machina* ('god from the machine') scenes, though the 'machine' (*mēchanē*) or crane may not always have been used for divine appearances in late fifth century productions. It is explicitly mentioned in several comic texts dating from 425 onwards. In tragedy its use is sometimes evident from references to flying (e.g. *El.* 1233–36). In *Iphigenia* the only textual indication that Athena may be airborne is in her exit lines (1488 n.), but even without this the use of the crane seems natural and expected as she arrives to exercise her heavenly power. She may have remained suspended throughout the scene or landed on the roof of the stage-building (or the

266   COMMENTARY

theologeion, a special platform for gods, if that existed at the time). Suspension
might make her addresses to the distant Orestes and Iphigenia seem more natural
(cf. 1447; in *Erech*. F 370.45ff. she probably stayed suspended since the palace/
stage-building is supposedly collapsing just as she arrives.) »» Mastronarde 1990
(detailed study with cogent argument for use of the crane in some cases where
others have doubted it: see pp. 280, 283 on *Iphigenia*); Newiger 1990; Csapo–
Slater 1994, 268–70 (ancient refs.).

   1435. Where, where etc.: Athena's tone is urgent and commanding but also
respectful **(lord Thoas)**. **are you carrying (πορθμεύεις) this pursuit**: cf. 266 n.

   1436. I, Athena: arriving gods normally identify themselves in tragedy even
if they are easily recognizable to the audience, as Athena presumably was with her
helmet and aegis. Gods were supposed to be overawing and hard to recognize.

   1437. launching the flood of your forces: Athena's language seems
ironically exaggerated (similar language describes Xerxes' forces in A. *Pers*. 88,
412 and the Seven against Thebes in S. *Ant*. 129), and might hint at a comparison
with Menelaus whose pursuit of the abducted Helen led to the Trojan War.

   1438–39. It was destined etc.: '(As something) destined…did Orestes come
etc.' (πεπρωμένον in apposition to the sentence, 452–55 n.). τὸ πεπρωμένον 'the
given (by destiny)' and τὸ χρή/χρεών 'the necessary' (cf. 1486) represent a
vaguely defined natural order of things which even the gods must observe and
which the most authoritative gods (Zeus, Athena, Apollo) best understand. It is
often invoked by Euripides' play-closing gods (*Andr*. 1268, *El*. 1290, *Ion* 1582
(cf. 1388), *Hel*. 1646, 1660, *Or*. 1654). **Loxias's oracles**: see 942–44 n. [πεπρω-
μένον is Monk's correction of L's πεπρωμένοις ('through Apollo's destined
instructions'). Parker argues for Hermann's πεπρωμένος ('destined by Apollo's
instructions'), but the word rarely refers to people rather than events (once in
tragedy, *Tro*. 340) and (as Monk noted) Apollo can proclaim what is destined but
cannot dictate it. Etymology and meaning: LSJ '*πόρω' II.2, Beekes 'πορέω').]

   1440. to convey his sister's person back to Argos: Euripides' adaptation of
the myth seems slightly indecisive as Athena is about to announce that Iphigenia
will reside at Brauron in Attica (1462–67). There was always room for competing
traditions, e.g. Pausanias 1.33.1 (return to Argos *via* Athens after depositing the
image at Brauron), 1.43.1 (death at Megara, or in Arcadia), not to mention the
vastly elaborated accounts of the wanderings of Orestes and Iphigenia which later
connected them with cult sites in Asia (Introduction, p. 43).

   1441b. achieving respite: ἀναψυχάς is in apposition to the sentence (452–
55 n.). [The line was accidentally omitted in ms. P and in the early printed
editions which depended on it, hence the need for the number 1441b. Some 18th
and 19th C editors thought it was an interpolation based on *Hipp*. 600, but it is
entirely appropriate here (cf. 92).]

   1444–45. already Poseidon at my request ('as a *charis*/favour to me'):
Athena, it seems, has politely asked for Poseidon's help as she does for a different

COMMENTARY 267

purpose in the prologue of *Trojan Women*. In other contexts she foils his attacks on Odysseus (e.g. *Odyssey* 5.382–87) or orders him to end his earthquake afflicting Athens (E. *Erech.* F 370.55–62), but there is no suggestion here of conflict between them. **is making the ocean's surface calm for his voyage:** for the sense of **τίθησι** see LSJ 'τίθημι' B.I. **πορθμεύειν πλάτῃ** is lit. 'for travelling over (or 'for him to travel over') by ship'; cf. 266 n. with LSJ 'πορθμεύω' II, and 116–17 n. for πλάτη 'oar-blade' = 'ship'. [L's πορθμεύων πλάτη has Poseidon 'conveying him by ship', but the god is not actually doing this and the calming should precede the voyaging. Most modern editors accept Tyrwhitt's **πορθμεύειν πλάτῃ**, but Diggle's πορθμεύειν πλάτην ('for him to conduct his ship') is also possible. The phrasing makes it unlikely that the object of **τίθησι** is either Orestes ('is making him travel', Köchly) or the ship ('makes his ship carry him over a waveless surface of the sea', Parker reading πορθμεύειν πλάτην).]

1446–47. And you, Orestes: Athena addresses the rest of her speech to Orestes and Iphigenia as they sail away, like Castor instructing Helen in *Hel.* 166–79. In *Erech.* F 370.55–62 Poseidon is not present to hear Athena's instructions. In *Eum.* 297 Orestes declares that the absent Athena will hear him wherever she is.

1449. And when you reach god-built (θεοδμήτους) Athens: θεόδμητος is a poetic epithet showing Athens' special status as at *Hipp.* 974, S. *El.* 707; also for Delphi (*Andr.* 1263) as for Troy (*Iliad* 8.519), Delos (Pind. *Ol.* 6.59), Tiryns (Bacchyl. 11.58), Aegina (Bacchyl. 12.7). Gods are not in fact linked specifically with the building of Athens in Athenian myths.

1450–57. Athena ordains the founding of a sanctuary and rituals of Artemis at Halai where she will have the title Tauropolos. On the cult legend (invented or developed by Euripides) and the worship of Artemis Tauropolos there and elsewhere, see Introduction, pp. 31–33.

1450–52. a place near the furthest borders of Attica: Halai Araphenides (modern Loutsa) is on the east coast of Attica, 25 km from Athens and about half-way between Araphen (Rafina) and Brauron (Vravrona). The name **Halai** refers to the salt-water lagoon (now dry) adjoining the sanctuary. This association with the remote and wild margins between land and sea is typical for Artemis (»» Barrett on *Hipp.* 148–50). **the crags of Carystos:** the mountainous coastal promontory of Euboea (called Mt. Okhé by Strabo 9.1.6), about 30 km across the water from Halai. Carystos (Karistos), Euboea's southernmost port, is in the bay beyond the promontory.

1453–57. There build a temple: a temple about 19 m by 12 m with peristyle and bipartite cella was discovered by N. Kyparissis in 1930 or 1931, re-excavated by J. Papadimitriou in 1956–57 and re-examined by Hollinshead and Travlos. Travlos dated it to the sixth century; Hollinshead offers a range from the late sixth through the fourth. No sixth-century material seems to be known (R. Parker 1996, 74 n. 29). »» Travlos 1988, 211–15 (illustrated); Hollinshead 1985, 435–39; Kalogeropoulos 2010, 2013; Bathrellou 2012, 156–60. **named for the Tauric**

268   COMMENTARY

land etc.: Artemis's title Tauropolos is linked with Orestes' story by this artificial etymology deriving 'Tauro-' from the Taurians and '-polos' from πολέω 'roam' (περιπολῶν, 1455). In fact ταυροπόλος means 'bull-herd', like αἰπόλος 'goatherd, βουκόλος 'oxherd', οἰοπόλος 'shepherd' (also a title of Artemis and other gods), ἱπποπόλος 'horse-herding', and may include her role in the social and sexual development of young men ('bulls': »» Graf 1979, 41; Lloyd-Jones 1983, 97, Lo Monaco 2018, 532–37). Phanodemus *FGrH* 325 F 14 gives other false etymologies. **in Fury-goaded frenzy**: the phrase evokes the persecution of Io by Hera's gadfly. Like Io, Orestes is achieving a final respite and a divinely ordained role in 'history'. [Line 1455 is the basis for the interpolated line 84: see note there.]

    1458–61. when the people keep her festival: i.e. at the Tauropolia, the Athenian festival (ἑορτή) which will recall the Taurian one without the reality of human sacrifice (35–37 n.; Introduction, pp. 13, 33). **as recompense for your slaughter**: i.e. the unfulfilled sacrifice of Orestes (cf. 994 σφαγῆς...σῆς). Wolff suggested that a reference to Orestes' killing of Clytemnestra 'is not entirely erased' (1992, 314, cf. Henrichs 2013, 134), but that is remote at best; an atonement for the matricide is not Artemis's concern. **let a sword be held etc.**: 'let him hold a sword...and draw blood'; the officiant is unspecified as often in ritual regulations. A sword is used as in human sacrifices (26–27 n.). **for the sake of holiness (ὁσίας) etc.**: cf. 130–32 n., 1037 n., 1161 (similar abstraction), 1194.

    The goddess will still be honoured with an offering of human blood, but in a form which is permitted (*hosios*) according to the Greek *nomos* (1458) rather than the Taurian one (463–66 n.). This is the only evidence for such a practice, and opinions are divided between those who see it as an invented *aition* for a rite actually performed at the Tauropolia and those who think that the rite too is a poetic invention designed either to reinforce the play's themes or to advertise its own fictitiousness and thus subvert the expectation of a stable conclusion to the play.[39] The same question arises regarding the tomb of Iphigenia and dedications to her at Brauron (1464–67 n.). The case for invention of the rite at Halai depends essentially on the absence of other evidence for it and the difference between the grimness of this rite and the other known features of the Tauropolia (see Introduction, pp. 32f.). These points are not conclusive, and it seems unlikely that Euripides would have capped a plot devoted to the bringing of Artemis and her cult to Halai with a feature of the cult that was obviously fictitious. The issue is

---

[39] For these interpretations see respectively Scullion 1999–2000, 227f. (the ritual bloodletting a continuing reminder of the dark side of Artemis's character) and Dunn 1996, 62f. with 2000, 18–21. Both argue that Euripides invented other such rites. For positions similar to Scullion's see Kyriakou 23–30, 457; Torrance 2019, 85–90. For the reality of these practices see Bonnechere 1994, 48f.; Sourvinou-Inwood 2003, 414–22 (responding to Dunn in particular); R. Parker 2005, 140–43, 374–83; Wright 2005, 357–62; Seaford 2009; Parker 346f.; Henrichs 2013, 134 (the Halai rite).

COMMENTARY 269

important for our assessment of the play's apparently happy ending (see further the Introduction, pp. 13–15).

1462–63. You, Iphigenia etc.: Athena turns to Iphigenia's new role as priestess (**key-keeper**, 130–32 n.) of Artemis at Brauron, where she will herself receive cult after her death (»» Introduction, pp. 27–31). Her appointment is like Praxithea's as priestess of Athena Polias at the end of *Erechtheus* (F 370.95–97), where Athenas's words are vague but clearly imply that Praxithea will be the first priestess of that cult. The same is probably true of Iphigenia's appointment at Brauron, although this is denied by e.g. Wolff 1992, 319; Ekroth 2003, 96; Kyriakou 459. It suits Iphigenia's cult status as a mythical princess with a tomb in the sanctuary; cf. Sourvinou-Inwood 1997, 174f. (~ 2003, 36). **the holy meadows of Brauron:** see Introduction, p. 27.

1464–67. There you will also lie buried etc.: these lines are our only explicit evidence for a tomb and cult of Iphigenia at Brauron and for dedications to her of the clothing of women who had died in childbirth. Their reality is disputed as for the rite at Halai (»» 1458–61 n.). It has been argued either that the dedications are Euripides' invention based on dedications to Artemis in thanks for successful childbirths, or that tomb, cult and dedications are all his invention.[40] A possible site for the tomb and shrine was identified by the excavator of Brauron (J. Papadimitriou) but remains unproven and disputed (»» Ekroth 2003, 74–79).[41] The dedications are not otherwise documented, and dedications of this kind are unparalleled, but records inscribed in the 340s and 330s for the Brauronion in Athens (*IG* II² 1514–1530) show abundantly that living women dedicated their and their children's clothes and accessories as thank-offerings to Artemis at Brauron as to Artemis or similar deities elsewhere.[42] Similar dedications in thanks for safe childbirths are also known from epigrams (*Anth.Pal.* 6.59, 200–2, 270–74). If the tomb and cult existed, Iphigenia might have been a recipient of clothes which would have been dedicated to Artemis if their owners had lived. Nothing in

---

[40] For the first option see Scullion 1999–2000, 228f.; Romano 2012, 139; for the second e.g. Dunn 2000, 21f.; Ekroth 2003, 70–72, 96f., 98f.; Kyriakou 459f.; Zeitlin 2011, 462; Torrance 2019, 88–90. Against these interpretations see Sourvinou-Inwood 2003, 420f. with n. 540; Seaford 2009, 232f.; Parker 346f. R. Parker (2005, 232 n. 61) finds the dedications 'not necessarily inauthentic'.

[41] The Hellenistic poet Euphorion apparently referred to Brauron as 'Iphigenia's cenotaph' (ἀγχίαλον Βραυρῶνα, κενήριον Ἰφιγενείης: fr. 91 Powell, 85 Lightfoot in Schol. Ar. *Lys.* 645). This probably implies that there was a so-called 'tomb' of Iphigenia at Brauron in which (according to Euphorion) she was not really buried. Ekroth argues that this may merely reflect Euripides and is not necessarily evidence for an actual tomb (Ekroth 2003, 62, 95, 113), but that seems unlikely. Euphorion came from Chalcis in Euboea, just 90 km from Brauron, and will have known the site.

[42] For the Brauron records see Linders 1972, Cleland 2005, Lo Monaco 2018, 501–5. For Brauron and elsewhere, Brøns 2015.

270   COMMENTARY

the text suggests that these were clothes worn during or polluted by the women's
fatal childbirths or that they were the unfinished weavings sometimes mentioned
in the inventories (Johnston 1999, 238–41 disputed by Ekroth 2003, 70–72).

1467–71. And I give instruction etc.: Athena now turns to the fate of the
Chorus. The text does not say who she is addressing,[43] but **these Hellene women**
suggests it is a Taurian, and it is Thoas who threatened the women with punishment (1431–33) and must now be told to release them **because of their righteous
judgment** (i.e. in assisting Iphigenia's scheme). Thoas responds to the instruction
almost word for word in lines 1282f. ἐκπέμπειν has its usual meaning **send out**.
Kovacs translates 'to escort them from the country', so that Athena tells Orestes to
take the women away on board his ship (cf. Kovacs 2000; Catrambone 2013), but
the ship has already left (and Athena will leave to join it, 1487–89), while the
women are still with Thoas in front of the temple. How they will get back to
Greece and what they will do there may have been left unexplained (as Kyriakou
and Parker assume), but something could have been said about their future in the
text now lost (see below). Their promise to obey Athena's instructions (1494)
suggests that something was said since it does not respond to anything in the
extant text of her speech.[44]

Most editors assume that some text has been lost either after the end of 1468
or after the first three words of 1469 (as printed here: Diggle and Parker print a
continuous text, the latter noting that 'something may well have gone missing').
A continuous text only makes sense if the reading ἐξέσωσα δὲ καὶ πρίν σ(ε) ('and
I rescued you also before') is adopted from the scholia on Aristophanes' *Frogs*,
but it is unlikely that this would have been replaced by ἐκσώσασά σε καὶ πρίν
γ(ε) (**having rescued you...**) in the direct manuscript tradition (cf. Kovacs 2000,
22), and even if it did the transition from the topic of the Chorus's fate to that of
the Areopagus's vote is improbably abrupt. If the loss began after line 1468,
γνώμης δικαίας οὕνεκ(α) would presumably be addressed to Orestes and refer to
his righteous judgment in obeying Apollo and killing his mother, but that point is
only remotely relevant here. For the reference to the Chorus cf. *Erech.* F 370.68f.,
'And bury these sisters of hers in the same earth-tomb, because of their nobility
(γενναιότητος οὕνεκα)', also in a play-ending aetiological speech of Athena and
with some added explanation. The missing text could have said more about the
Chorus's righteousness and/or their future, or about Orestes' final release from his

---

[43] The only other instance of the compound ἐξεφίεμαι also has no object: S. *Ajax*
795, 'Teucer has given instruction (ἐξεφίεται) to confine him within his tent'.

[44] Wolff 1992, 322 suggested that they could be imagined as rejoining the cycle of
girls' lives in their home city, like Athenian girls returning from their temporary
captivity as 'bears' at Brauron (cf. Swift 2010, 213). The past capture of their city
should probably be overlooked. Lines 1108f. do not imply that it has been totally
destroyed. Kyriakou notes that they can still imagine returning to it (452–55,
1138–52).

COMMENTARY 271

bloodguilt and the Erinyes' pursuit, thus leading into the topic of his previous
rescue and the outcome of the Areopagus trial.

1471–72. And this too will be a rule: Euripides completes the mythical
innovation which began with the dissenting Erinyes' rejection of Orestes'
acquittal on a tied vote at his Areopagus trial (965–71 nn.). The precedent of the
Vote of Athena is confirmed as their pursuit is finally ended. [**equally balanced**:
the word ἰσήρης was perhaps invented by Euripides here (otherwise only in
Nicander, *Ther.* 643, 788). The suffix -ηρης from stem ἀρ- 'fit' (εὐήρης 1050,
κατήρει 1346) is often used loosely.]

1475–85. Queen Athena etc.: Thoas responds in the same accepting spirit
and almost formulaic manner as most subjects of divine conflict resolution in
tragedy, especially Theoclymenus (*Hel.* 1680–87), Orestes and Menelaus (*Or.*
1666–81), Lykos (*Antiope* F 223.104–16); cf. Theseus (*Supp.* 1227–31), Peleus
(*Andr.* 1273–83), Ion and Creusa (*Ion* 1606–18), Philoctetes and Neoptolemus
(S. *Phil.* 1445–48). He responds precisely to each of Athena's instructions that
concerned him: he will obey her commands, allow Orestes and Iphigenia to depart
with the image, release the women of the Chorus and call off the pursuit. The last
point matches Athena's opening instruction in ring-composition.

1478–79. Where is the credit in struggling etc.: 'In what respect is it fine to
struggle'. [This is probably a single sentence. Reiske took τί γάρ as 'of course
not' (»» Denniston 85f.) and 1479 as a separate question. Diggle and Parker
punctuate accordingly, and Diggle then deletes 1479 as an unneeded explanation
while Parker retains it since in her view Thoas must explain why he is no longer
angry ('there is no 'of course' about it'). Either choice would be possible if τί γάρ
had the nuance 'What else can I do?' (»» Collard 2018, 124), but a bare τί γάρ; at
line-end is unparalleled in Euripides (in tragedy only A. *Ag.* 1139, 1239, *Cho.*
880, F 94, Soph. F 93) and a separate question ('Is it a fine thing to struggle...?'
seems rather lame.]

1486. What must be controls you and the gods: see 1438–39 n. on this idea.
τὸ χρεών = τὸ χρὴ ὄν, 'that which is necessary', χρή being originally a noun.

1487–89. Go, winds etc.: Athena has persuaded Poseidon to calm the sea
(1444f.). Now she takes command of the formerly unruly winds. **ναυσθλοῦτε**,
'cause to be shipped'. [The verb ναυσθλόω, properly 'hire a ship' according to
ancient lexicographers, is found five times in Euripides, in Ar. *Peace* 126 and
three times in Lycophron's *Alexandra*. These lines are carelessly assigned to
Apollo in L despite the feminine σῴζουσ(α) in 1489, presumably because of the
reference there to **my sister** (Artemis being Athena's half-sister).]

1488. I will go with them: Athena probably flies away on the crane and
disappears behind the stage-building. The mood of safe homeward passage
anticipated by the Chorus before the crisis (1123–31) now prevails. Departing
gods mention their flight paths in other plays of Euripides (*El.* 1347–49, *Ion* 1616,
Hel. 1664f., *Or.* 1683–85; cf. *HF* 872, *Tro.* 92), and sometimes promise to escort

272   COMMENTARY

their human protégés safely home (*Ion*, *Helen*) or to heaven (*Orestes*). Such announcements seem to confirm that the crane was used (Mastronarde 1990, 280).

1490–99. The metre shifts to 'marching' anapaests, tragedy's commonest metre for final closure and departure. The accumulation of closing motifs and some awkward language have raised doubts about the authenticity of some or all of these lines. The formulaic prayer to Victory (1497–99) is in any case not part of the drama. Barrett (on *Hipp*. 1462–66) noted that 1490f. and 1492–96 'seem to be two other alternative anapaestic tail-pieces, neither of them laudable and the first barely intelligible'. The case against them is not conclusive: see notes below.

1490–91. Go on your way in good fortune: ἐπί here is 'on the basis of, in a state of' as e.g. *Ba*. 1369, *El.* 133. **happy in attaining your salvation:** τῆς σῳζομένης μοίρας εὐδαίμονες ὄντες, 'fortunate (in) being of the portion being preserved', as opposed to those continuing in misfortune. The wording perhaps reflects the language of the mysteries in which initiation led to increased happiness before and after death. It is repeated in Aristides, *Or.* 33.31 Keil (II.582 Dindorf), εἰ μὲν τῆς σῳζομένης μοίρας εἴημεν 'if we were of the portion being preserved (i.e. amongst those living on after death)'. Editors also compare Pindar, *Pyth*. 3.60 γνόντα...οἵας εἰμὲν αἴσας 'recognizing what dispensation we belong to (i.e. the human one)', Plut. *Numa* 2.3 (Romulus κρείττονος ὄντα μοίρας, 'being of a superior (i.e. non-mortal) portion'), and for μοῖρα denoting a group or sub-group E. *Supp*. 244, Hdt. 1.146.1.

[These lines are mistakenly assigned to Athena in L, probably after lines 1487–89 were mistakenly assigned to Apollo so that Athena had to be given something for the Chorus to respond to in 1492–96. Kovacs gives them to Athena, assuming that the Chorus will leave with Orestes and company, but see 1467–71 n. Catrambone 2013 argues for Thoas as speaker).]

1492–96. O Lady revered etc.: the women give their own response to the divine settlement (ἀλλ(ά) marks their turning from addressing Orestes and company to addressing her). They are interested parties, like the Argive mothers pressing their king to swear alliance with Athens (*Supp*. 1232–34) or the Athenian women welcoming their royal family's restoration (*Ion* 1619–22).

[1497–99]. Venerable Victory etc.: the same lines appear at the end of *Phoenician Women* and *Orestes*, and incidentally in two manuscripts of *Hippolytus*. Many see them and the sententious 'tags' which end most of Euripides' other plays as insertions by later actors or editors (cf. Barrett on *Hipp*. 1462–66), although it has been argued that they served to mark closure (or sometimes its incompleteness) and that some at least may be authentic (»» Willink on *Or.* 1691–93; Roberts 1987; Dunn 1996, 14–25). The prayer to Victory is the least dramatically significant. Parker notes that it might nevertheless have been meant for delivery by the play's Chorus, and Sourvinou-Inwood 2003, 417 argues that here and in *Orestes* it emphasized the religious nature of their performance.

ABBREVIATIONS AND REFERENCES

1. ABBREVIATIONS

For standard abbreviations of classical authors and works, inscriptions and papyri see LSJ xvi–xlii with LSJ Supp. x–xxvii.

Beekes   R. Beekes, *Etymological Dictionary of Greek*. Two volumes. Leiden, 2010.

BNP   *Brill's New Pauly. Encyclopaedia of the Ancient World*. Many volumes. Leiden, 2002 etc. and online. Orig. German, *Der Neue Pauly*, Stuttgart, 1996 etc.

Breitenbach   W. Breitenbach, *Untersuchungen zur Sprache der euripideischen Lyrik*. Stuttgart, 1934.

CGCG   *The Cambridge Grammar of Classical Greek*, ed. E. van Emde Boas, A. Rijksbaron, L. Huitink, M. de Bakker. Cambridge, 2019.

Coll.Alex.   J. U. Powell, *Collectanea Alexandrina*. Oxford, 1925.

CQ   *Classical Quarterly*

Denniston   J. D. Denniston, *The Greek Particles*. Second edition. Oxford, 1954.

DK   Diels, H., W. Kranz, *Die Fragmente der Vorsokratiker*. Two volumes. Sixth edition. Berlin, 1951–52.

FGrH   F. Jacoby et al., *Die Fragmente der griechischen Historiker*. Many volumes. Berlin, 1923–99. Also BrillOnline.

Gantz   T. Gantz, *Early Greek Myth*. Baltimore, 1993.

GEF   M. L. West, *Greek Epic Fragments from the Seventh to the Fifth Centuries BC*. Cambridge MA and London, 2003.

Gildersleeve   B. Gildersleeve, *Syntax of Classical Greek from Homer to Demosthenes*. New York, 1900, 1911. Reprinted with index of passages cited, Groningen, 1980.

Goodwin   W. W. Goodwin, *Syntax of the Moods and Tenses of the Greek Verb*. London, New York, 1889.

IEG   M. L. West, *Iambi et Elegi Graeci ante Alexandrum Cantati*. Second edition. Oxford, 1989.

KG   R. Kühner, B. Gerth, *Ausführliche Grammatik der griechischen Sprache*. Teil II. Two volumes. Third edition. Hannover, 1898.

LIMC   *Lexicon Iconographicum Mythologiae Classicae*. Nine volumes, each in two parts. Zurich. 1981–98.

LIMC Supp.   *Lexicon Iconographicum Mythologiae Classicae. Supplementum*. Düsseldorf. 2009.

274 ABBREVIATIONS & REFERENCES

LSJ	H. G. Liddell, R. Scott, *A Greek–English Lexicon*. Ninth edition, revised by H. Stuart Jones and R. McKenzie. Oxford, 1940.
LSJ Supp.	P. G. W. Glare, A. Thompson (eds), *Greek-English Lexicon, Revised Supplement*. Oxford, 1996.
PCG	R. Kassel, C. Austin, *Poetae Comici Graeci*. Eight volumes. Berlin, 1983–2023
PMG	D. L. Page, *Poetae Melici Graeci*. Oxford, 1962.
PMGF	M. Davies, *Poetarum Melicorum Graecorum Fragmenta*. Oxford, 1991.
Rijksbaron	A. Rijksbaron, *The Syntax and Semantics of the Verb in Classical Greek*. Third edition. Chicago, 2006.
SEG	*Supplementum Epigraphicum Graecum*. Many volumes. Amsterdam, Leiden, 1923– .
Smyth	H. W. Smyth, *Greek Grammar*. Cambridge MA, 1956.
ThesCRA	*Thesaurus Cultus et Rituum Antiquorum*. Eight volumes. Malibu, 2004–12.
TLG	*Thesaurus Linguae Graecae*. University of California, online.
TrGF	B. Snell, R. Kannicht, S. Radt, *Tragicorum Graecorum Fragmenta*. Five volumes in six. Göttingen, 1971–2004.
van Straten	F. van Straten, *HIERA KALA. Images of animal sacrifice in archaic and classical Greece*. Leiden, 1995.

2. RECENT EDITIONS AND COMMENTARIES

Usually cited by editor's/commentator's name only (e.g. 'Fraenkel on A. *Ag.* 218'). For other editions see Sansone IX, Parker 359; for textual studies, Sansone IX-XIII.

Grégoire, H. 1925. In *Euripide*, IV (Collection Budé). Paris.

Platnauer, M. 1938. *Euripides: Iphigenia in Tauris*. Oxford.

Strohm, H. 1949. *Euripides: Iphigenie im Taurerlande*. Munich.

Sansone, D. 1981. *Euripides: Iphigenia in Tauris*. Leipzig.

Diggle. 1981. In *Euripidis Fabulae*, II (Oxford Classical Texts). Oxford.

Kovacs, D. 1999. In *Euripides*, IV (Loeb Classical Library). Cambridge MA and London.

Cropp, M. J. 2000. *Euripides: Iphigenia in Tauris*. First edition. Warminster.

Kyriakou, P. 2006. *A Commentary on Euripides' Iphigenia in Tauris*. Berlin.

Parker, L. P. E. 2016. *Euripides: Iphigenia in Tauris*. Oxford.

Amiech, C. and L. 2017. *Euripide: Iphigénie en Tauride*. Paris.

ABBREVIATIONS & REFERENCES 275

3. OTHER REFERENCES

* Denotes items which discuss the play extensively.

Allan, A. and J. Potter. 2014. Loxias and Phoebus in tragedy: Convention and violation. *American Journal of Philology* 135: 1–27.

Allen, W. S. 1947. The name of the Black Sea in Greek. *CQ* 41: 86–88.

Allen, W. S. 1948. Supplementary note on the name of the Black Sea. *CQ* 42: 60.

Aloni, A. 2009. Elegy. In F. Budelmann (ed.), *The Cambridge Companion to Greek Lyric* (Cambridge): 168–88.

Andronikos, M. 1968. *Totenkult. Archeologia Homerica* W. Göttingen.

Aretz, S. 1999. *Die Opferung der Iphigeneia in Aulis. Die Rezeption des Mythos in antiken und modernen Dramen.* Stuttgart, Leipzig.

Armstrong, D., E. Ratchford. 1985. Iphigenia's veil. Aeschylus, *Agamemnon* 228–248. *Bulletin of the Institute of Classical Studies* 32: 1–12.

Arnott, W. G. 2007. *Birds in the Ancient World from A to Z.* London.

Aurigny, H., C. Durvye. 2021. *Artémis près d'Apollon. Culte et représentation d'Artémis à Délos, Delphes, Claros et Didymes.* Liège.

Austin, C. 1987. Textual problems in Ar. *Thesm. Dodoni* 16: 61–92.

Bacon, H. 1961. *Barbarians in Greek Tragedy.* New Haven.

Bain, D. 1977. *Actors and Audience: A study of asides and related conventions in Greek drama.* Oxford.

Bain, D. 1981. *Masters, Servants and Orders in Greek Tragedy.* Manchester.

Bannert, H. 1998. Der Tagtraum der griechischen Mädchen: *Iphigenie bei den Taurern*, 1089–1151. *Wiener Humanistische Blätter* 40: 5–14.

Barber, E. 1992. The Peplos of Athena. In J. Neils, *Goddess and Polis: The Panathenaic Festival in Ancient Athens* (Princeton): 103–17.

Barrenechea, F. 2012. At the feet of the gods: myth, tragedy, and redemption in Alfonso Reyes's *Ifigenia cruel. Romance Quarterly* 59: 6–18.

Barrett, W. S. 2007. *Greek Lyric, Tragedy, and Textual Criticism: Collected Papers.* Edited by M. L. West. Oxford.

Barringer, J. 1995. *Divine Escorts: Nereids in Archaic and Classical Greek Art.* Ann Arbor.

Bary, C. 2012. The Ancient Greek tragic aorist revisited. *Glotta* 88: 31–53.

Bathrellou, E. 2012. Menander's *Epitrepontes* and the festival of the Tauropolia. *Classical Antiquity* 31: 151–92.

Battezzato, L. 2000. Livineius' unpublished Euripidean *marginalia. Revue d'Histoire des Textes* 30: 323–48.

Battezzato, L. 2016. 'Shall I sing with the Delian maidens?': Trojan and Greek identities in the songs of Euripides' *Hecuba. Materiali e discussioni per l'analisi dei testi classici* 76: 139–55.

Bauer, W. 1872. *Zu Euripides' Iphigenie auf Taurien: Kritisches und Exegetisches.* Diss. Munich.

276 ABBREVIATIONS & REFERENCES

* Belfiore, E. 1992. Aristotle and Iphigeneia. In Rorty (ed.) 1992: 359–78.

* Belfiore, E. 2000. *Murder Among Friends: Violation of* Philia *in Greek Tragedy*. New York and Oxford.

Bentein, K. 2016. *Verbal Periphrasis in Ancient Greek. Have- and Be- constructions*. Oxford.

Bevan, E. 1987. The goddess Artemis, and the dedication of bears in sanctuaries. *Annual of the British School at Athens* 82: 17–21.

Bielfeldt, R. 2005. *Orestes auf Römischen Sarkophagen*. Berlin.

Bietolini, N. Avamposti del mito greco. La *Ifigenia cruel* del messicano Alfonso Reyes. In Secci (ed.) 2008: 189–208.

Boardman, J. 1999. *The Greeks Overseas*. Fourth edition. London.

Bobrick, E. 1991. Iphigeneia revisited: *Thesmophoriazusae* 1160–1225. *Arethusa* 24: 67–76.

Bonanno Aravantinos, M. 2008. Ifigenia nell'arte greca e romana. In Secci (ed.) 2008: 75–109.

Bonnechere, P. 1994. *Le sacrifice humain en Grèce ancienne*. Liège.

Bonnechere, P. 2013. Victime humaine et absolue perfection dans la mentalité grecque. In Bonnechere–Gagné 2013, 21–60.

Bonnechere, P., R Gagné (eds). 2013. *Sacrifices humains. Perspectives croisées et représentations*. Liège.

Borthwick, E. 1976. The 'flower of the Argives' and a neglected meaning of ἄνθος. *Journal of Hellenic Studies* 96: 1–7.

Bowersock, G., C. P. Jones. 2006. A New Inscription from Panticapaeum. *Zeitschrift für Papyrologie und Epigraphik* 156: 117–28.

Bowie, E. 1986. Early Greek elegy, symposium, and public festival. *Journal of Hellenic Studies* 106: 13–35.

Braund, D. 2018. *Greek Religion and Cults in the Black Sea Region*. Cambridge.

Braund, D., E. Hall, R. Wyles (eds). 2019. *Ancient Theatre and Performance Culture around the Black Sea*. Oxford.

Brelich, A. 1969. *Paides e Parthenoi*. Rome. (Revised edition, Rome, 2013.)

Bremmer, J. N. 2002. Sacrificing a child in Ancient Greece: the case of Iphigeneia. In E. Noort, E. Tigchelaar (eds), *The Sacrifice of Isaac: the Aqedah (Genesis 22) and its interpretations* (Leiden): 21–43. Reprinted with revisions in Bremmer 2019a: 373–90.

* Bremmer, J. N. 2013. Human Sacrifice in Euripides' *Iphigeneia in Tauris*: Greek and Barbarian. In Bonnechere–Gagné 2013, 87–100. Reprinted with revised notes in Bremmer 2019a: 403–18.

Bremmer, J. N. 2019a. *The World of Greek Religion and Mythology. Collected Essays II*. Tübingen.

Bremmer, J. N. 2019b. Imagining human sacrifice in Euripides' *Iphigenia in Aulis*. In Bremmer 2019a: 391–402.

Bremmer, J. N. 2019c. Myth and ritual in Greek human sacrifice: Lykaon, Polyxena and the case of the Rhodian criminal. In Bremmer 2019a, 349–71.

ABBREVIATIONS & REFERENCES 277

Brendel, O. J. 1950. Iphigenie auf Tauris. In H. Meesen (ed.), Goethe Bicentennial Studies by Members of the Faculty of Indiana University (Bloomington): 1–47. German translation in *Antike und Abendland* 27: 52–97.

Brøns. C. 2015. Textiles and temple inventories. Detecting an invisible votive tradition in Greek sanctuaries in the second half of the first millennium BC. *Acta Hyperborea* 14: 43–83.

Brown, A. L. 1984. Eumenides in Greek Tragedy. *CQ* 34: 260–81.

Brown, P. G. McC. 2000. Knocking at the door in fifth-century Greek tragedy. In S. Gödde, T. Heinze (eds), *Skenika: Beiträge zum antiken Theater und seiner Rezeption* (Darmstadt): 1–16.

Brown, P. G. McC. 2008. Scenes at the door in Aristophanic comedy. In M. Revermann, P. Wilson (eds), *Performance, Iconography, Reception. Studies in Honour of Oliver Taplin* (Oxford): 349–73.

Brown, P., S. Ograjenšek (eds) 2010. *Ancient Drama in Music for the Modern Stage*. Oxford.

Brulé, P. 1987. *La Fille d'Athènes*. Paris.

Buck, C. D., W. Petersen. 1949. *A Reverse Index of Greek Nouns and Adjectives*. Chicago.

* Budelmann, F. 2019. Dare to believe: wonder, trust and the limitations of human cognition in Euripides' *Iphigenia in Tauris*. In Braund et al. (eds) 2019: 289–304.

Burges, G. 1817. *Euripidis Troades etc.* Cambridge.

Burgess, J. 2009. *The Death and Afterlife of Achilles*. Baltimore.

Burkert, W. 1983. *Homo Necans*, transl. P. Bing. Berkeley.

Burkert, W. 1985. *Greek Religion: Archaic and Classical*, trans. J. Raffan. Oxford.

* Burnett, A. P. 1971. *Catastrophe Survived: Euripides' plays of mixed reversal*. Oxford.

Burrell, B. 2005. Iphigeneia in Philadelphia. *Classical Antiquity* 24: 223–56.

Bury, R. 1941–5. On the Greek fleet at Aulis (Soph. *El.* 564; Eurip. *I.T.* 15). *Proceedings of the Cambridge Philological Society* 178: 4–6.

Buxton, R. 1992. Iphigénie au bord de la mer. *Pallas* 38: 9–15.

Cairns, D. 1993. *Aidos*. Oxford.

Cairns, D. 1996. Veiling, αἰδώς and a red-figure amphora by Phintias. *Journal of Hellenic Studies* 116: 152–58.

Calame, C. 2009. Iphigénie à Brauron: étiologie poétique et paysage artémisien. In L. Bodiou, V. Mehl (eds), *La religion des femmes en Grèce ancienne: mythes, cultes et société* (Rennes): 83–92.

Calame, C. 2017. *La tragédie chorale: poésie grecque et rituel musical*. Paris.

Calame, C. 2019. *Les choeurs de jeunes filles en Grèce ancienne*. Second French edition. Paris.

* Caldwell, R. 1974–75. Tragedy Romanticized: The *Iphigenia Taurica*. *Classical Journal* 70: 23–40.

278 ABBREVIATIONS & REFERENCES

Cambitoglou, A. 1975. Iphigeneia in Tauris. The question of the influence of the Euripidean play in the representations of the subject in Attic and Italiote vase-painting. *Antike Kunst* 18: 56–66.

Carrara, P. 2009. *Il testo di Euripide nell'antichità. Ricerche sulla tradizione testuale euripidea antica (sec. IV.a.C.–sec. VIII.d.C)*. Florence.

Carrara, P. 2020. Poliido di Selymbria: qualche precisazione sulla sua opera. *Prometheus* 46: 112–27.

Casabona, J. 1966. *Recherches sur le vocabulaire des sacrifices en grec*. Aix-en-Provence.

Casson, L. 1971. *Ships and Seamanship in the Ancient World*. Princeton.

Catrambone, M. 2013. Toante e il Coro: nota a Eur. *IT* 1490–1. *Philologus* 157: 16–34.

Ceccarelli, P. 2013. *Ancient Greek Letter Writing: A cultural history (600 BC–150 BC)*. Oxford.

Chadwick, J. 1996. *Lexicographica Graeca. Contributions to the lexicography of Ancient Greek*. Oxford.

Chappell, M. 2006. Delphi and the *Homeric Hymn to Apollo. CQ* 56: 331–48.

Chatzivasiliou, D. 2019. Retour sur l'*arkteia*: lieux de culte et pratiques rituelles en Attique. *Métis* 17: 203–22.

Chong-Gossard, J. 2006. Female song and female knowledge in the recognition duets of Euripides. In J. Davidson, F. Muecke, P. Wilson (eds), *Greek Drama III: Essays in honour of Kevin Lee* (London): 27–48.

Cleland, L. 2005. *The Brauron Clothing Catalogues. Text, analysis, glossary and translation*. Oxford.

Clement, P. 1934. New evidence for the origin of the Iphigeneia legend. *L'Antiquité Classique* 3: 393–409.

Collard, C. 1980. On stichomythia. *Liverpool Classical Monthly* 5: 77–85. Reprinted with addenda and recent bibliography in Collard, *Tragedy, Euripides and Euripideans: Selected Papers* (Bristol, 2007): 16–30.

Collard, C. 2018. *Colloquial Expressions in Greek Tragedy*. Revised and enlarged edition of P. T. Stevens's *Colloquial Expressions in Greek Tragedy*. Stuttgart.

Collard, C., M. Cropp, K. Lee. 1995. *Euripides. Selected Fragmentary Plays I.* Warminster. Reprinted with corrections and addenda, Oxford, 2009.

Collard, C., M. Cropp, J. Gibert. 2004. *Euripides. Selected Fragmentary Plays II.* Oxford.

Collard, C., J. Morwood. 2017. *Euripides:* Iphigenia at Aulis. Two volumes. Liverpool.

Colombati, C. 2008. Ifigenia tra mito e musica. In Secci (ed.) 2008: 111–27.

Colvin, S. 1999. *Dialect in Aristophanes and the Politics of Language in Ancient Greek Literature*. Oxford.

Connelly, J. B. 2007. *Portrait of a Priestess: Women and ritual in ancient Greece*. Princeton.

ABBREVIATIONS & REFERENCES 279

Corbett, P. E. 1970. Greek temples and Greek worshippers. The literary and archaeological evidence. *Bulletin of the Institute of Classical Studies* 17: 14–58.

Cousland, J. R. C., J. R. Hume (eds). 2009. *The Play of Texts and Fragments: Essays in honour of Martin Cropp*. Leiden.

Cropp, M. J. 1997. Notes on Euripides, *Iphigenia in Tauris*. *Illinois Classical Studies* 22: 25–41.

Cropp, M. J. 2013. *Euripides: Electra*. Second edition. Oxford.

Cropp, M. J. 2021. *Minor Greek Tragedians, Volume 2: Fourth-century and Hellenistic poets*. Liverpool.

Cropp, M. J., G. H. Fick. 1985. *Resolutions and Chronology in Euripides: The fragmentary tragedies*. London.

Csapo, E., W. J. Slater. 1994. *The Context of Ancient Drama*. Ann Arbor.

Cunningham, M. 1994. Thoughts on Aeschylus: the satyr play *Proteus* – the ending of the *Oresteia*. *Liverpool Classical Monthly* 19: 67–68.

Dale, A. M. 1967. *Euripides: Helen*. Oxford.

Dale, A. M. 1968. *The Lyric Metres of Greek Drama*. Second edition. Cambridge.

Dana, M. 2007. Cultes locaux et identité grecque dans les cités du Pont-Euxin. *Les Études Classiques* 75: 171–86.

Dangel, J. 2002. *Accius, Oeuvres. Fragments*. Second edition. Paris.

D'Anna, G. 1967. *M. Pacuvii Fragmenta*. Rome.

Davidson, J. 1997. *Courtesans and Fishcakes*. London.

Davies, M. 2010. 'Sins of the fathers': omitted sacrifices and offended deities in Greek literature and the folk-tale. *Eikasmos* 21: 331–55.

Davies, M. 2019. *The Cypria*. Cambridge MA.

Davies, M., P. Finglass. 2014. *Stesichorus: The Poems*. Cambridge.

de Jong, I. 1991. *Narrative in Drama: The art of the Euripidean messenger-speech*. Leiden.

De Poli, M. 2017. A Case of Aposiopesis. Note on Euripides, *Iphigenia among the Taurians* 827–836. In M. de Poli (ed.), *Euripides: Stories, texts and stage-craft* (Padova): 79–84.

Degiovanni, L. 2011. L'*Orestes* di Pacuvio. Alcune ipotesi di ricostruzione. *Rheinisches Museum* 154: 256–84.

Despinis, G. 2005. Iphigeneia und Orestes: Vorschläge zur Interpretation zweier Skulpturenfunde aus Brauron. *Mitteilungen des Deutschen Archäologischen Instituts, Athenische Abteilung* 120: 241–67 with illustrations.

Deubner, L. 1941. *Ololyge und Verwandtes*. Berlin.

Devereux, G. 1976. *Dreams in Greek Tragedy: An ethno-psycho-analytical study*. Oxford.

Dickey, E. 1996. *Greek Forms of Address: From Herodotus to Lucian*. Oxford.

Diggle, J. 1981. *Studies on the Text of Euripides*. Oxford.

Diggle, J. 1994. *Euripidea: Collected Essays*. Oxford.

280 ABBREVIATIONS & REFERENCES

Diggle, J. 2007. Housman's Greek. In P. J. Finglass et al. (eds), *Hesperos. Studies in Ancient Greek Poetry presented to M. L. West on his Seventieth Birthday* (Oxford): 145–69.

Dillon, M. 2008. 'Xenophon sacrificed on account of an expedition': divination and the *sphagia* before ancient Greek battles. In V. Mehl. P. Brulé, R. Parker (eds), *Le sacrifice antique: vestiges, procédures et stratégies* (Rennes): 235–51.

Dodds, E. R. 1951. Dream-pattern and culture-pattern. In Dodds, *The Greeks and the Irrational* (Berkeley): 102–34.

Donzelli, G. Basta. 1989. Euripide, *Elettra*. Dai codici alle prime edizioni a stampa. *Bollettino dei Classici* 10: 70–105.

Dover, K. J. 1974. *Greek Popular Morality in the Time of Plato and Aristotle.* Oxford.

Dowden, K. 1989. *Death and the Maiden. Girls' initiation rites in Greek mythology.* London.

Dowden, K. 1990. Myth: Brauron and beyond. *Dialogues d'Histoire Ancienne* 16: 29–43.

Dowden, K. 2011. Initiation: the key to myth? In Dowden–Livingstone 2011: 487–505.

Dowden, K., N. Livingstone (eds). 2011. *A Companion to Greek Mythology.* Malden MA and Oxford.

Drew-Bear, T. 1968. The trochaic tetrameter in Greek tragedy. *American Journal of Philology* 89: 385–405.

Dunn, F. 1996. *Tragedy's End: Closure and innovation in Euripidean drama.* New York.

Dunn, F. 2000. Euripidean aetiologies. *Classical Bulletin* 76: 3–28.

Duranti, M. 2022. The meaning of the wave in the final scene of Euripides' *Iphigenia Taurica. Greece & Rome* 69: 179–202.

Durvye, C. L'Artémis délienne dans la littérature antique. In Aurigny–Durvye 2021: 31–59.

Egli, F. 2003. *Euripides im Kontext zeitgenössischer intellektueller Strömungen.* Leipzig.

Ekroth, G. 2003. Inventing Iphigeneia? On Euripides and the cultic construction of Brauron. *Kernos* 16: 59–118.

Ekroth, G. 2005. Blood on the altars? On the treatment of blood at Greek sacrifices and the iconographical evidence. *Antike Kunst* 48: 9–29.

* Erbse, H. 1984. *Studien zum Prolog der euripideischen Tragödie.* Berlin.

Ewans, M. 2007. *Opera from the Greek. Studies in the poetics of appropriation.* Aldershot.

Fantham, E. 1992. Ovidius in Tauris: Ovid *Tr.* 4.4 and *Ex P.* 3.2. In R. McKay et al. (eds), *The Two worlds of the Poet. New perspectives on Vergil* (Detroit): 268–80.

ABBREVIATIONS & REFERENCES 281

Fantham, E. 2003. Pacuvius: melodrama, reversals and recognitions. In D. Braund, C. Gill (eds), *Myth, History and Culture in Republican Rome: Studies in honour of T. P. Wiseman* (Exeter): 98–118.

Faraone, C. 2003. Playing the bear and the fawn for Artemis: female initiation or substitute sacrifice? In D. Dodd, C. Faraone (eds), *Initiation in Ancient Greek Rituals and Narratives: New critical perspectives* (London): 43–68.

Fehling, D. 1968. Νυκτὸς παῖδες ἄπαιδες. A. Eum. 1034 und das sogenannte Oxymoron in der Tragödie. *Hermes* 96: 142–55.

Finglass, P. J. 2020. The textual tradition of Euripides' dramas. In A. Markantonatos (ed.), *Brill's Companion to Euripides* (Leiden, Boston): 29–48.

Fletcher, J. 2012. *Performing Oaths in Classical Greek Drama*. Cambridge.

Fontenrose, J. 1959. *The Delphic Oracle: its responses and operations*. Berkeley.

Fontenrose, J. 1978. *Python. A study of Delphic myth and its origins*. Berkeley.

Ford, A. 2006. The genre of genres: Paeans and *paian* in early Greek poetry. *Poetica* 38: 277–95.

Fowler, R. L. 1987. The rhetoric of desperation. *Harvard Studies in Classical Philology* 91: 6–38.

Fowler, R. L. 1995. Greek magic, Greek religion. *Illinois Classical Studies* 20: 1–22.

Fowler, R. L. 2013. *Early Greek Mythography, II: Commentary*. Oxford.

Furley, W. D. 2013. *Menander:* Epitrepontes. London.

Furley, W. D., J. M. Bremer. 2001. *Greek Hymns. Selected cult songs from the Archaic to the Hellenistic period*. Two volumes. Tübingen.

Gallo, L. 2020. La Crimea e la colonizzazione greca. In M. Bernardini et al. (eds), *La Crimea in una prospettiva storica* (Naples): 11–25.

Garland, R. 2001. *The Greek Way of Death*. Second edition. London.

Georgoudi, S. 2017. Reflections on sacrifice and purification in the Greek world. In S. Hitch, I. Rutherford (eds), *Animal Sacrifice in the Ancient Greek World* (Cambridge): 105–35.

Gerber, D. 1982. *Pindar's Olympian One*. Toronto.

Giannopoulou, V. 1999–2000. Divine agency and *Tyche* in Euripides' *Ion*: Ambiguity and shifting perspectives. *Illinois Classical Studies* 24–25: 257–72.

Gliksohn, J.-M. 1985. *Iphigénie de la Grèce antique a l'Europe des Lumières*. Paris.

Goette, H. R. 2005. Überlegungen zur Topothese von Gebäuden im antiken Brauron. *Archäologischer Anzeiger* 2005.1: 25–38.

* Goff, B. 1999. The violence of community: ritual in the *Iphigenia in Tauris*. *Bucknell Review* 43: 109–28.

Goldhill, S. 2010. Who killed Gluck? In Brown–Ograjenšek 2010: 210–39.

Gould, J. P. 1973. Hiketeia. *Journal of Hellenic Studies* 93: 74–103.

Graf, F. 1979. Das Götterbild aus Taurerland. *Die Antike Welt* 10: 33–41.

282 ABBREVIATIONS & REFERENCES

Graf, F. 1980. Milch, Honig und Wein. Zum Verständnis der Libation im griechischen Ritual. In *Perennitas: studi in onore di A. Brelich* (Rome): 209–21.

Graf, F. 1985. *Nordionische Kulte.* Rome.

Graf, F. 1997. *Magic in the Ancient World.* Cambridge MA.

Graninger, D. 2007. Studies in the Cult of Artemis Throsia. *Zeitschrift für Papyrologie und Epigraphik* 162: 151–64.

Guldager Bilde, P. 2003. Wandering images: from Taurian (and Chersonesean) Parthenos to (Artemis) Tauropolos and (Artemis) Persike. In P. Guldager Bilde et al. (eds), *The Cauldron of Ariantas: Studies presented to A. N. Ščeglov* (Aarhus): 165–83.

Guldager Bilde, P., S. Handberg, J. Hjarl Petersen. 2020. The Black Sea. In F. de Angelis (ed.), *A Companion to Greeks Across the Ancient World* (Hoboken NJ): 431–58.

Gutzwiller, K. 2004. Seeing thought: Timomachus' Medea and ecphrastic epigram. *American Journal of Philology* 125: 339–86.

Hadzisteliou Price, Th. 1978. *Kourotrophos.* Leiden.

Hall, E. 1987. The geography of Euripides' *Iphigeneia among the Taurians. American Journal of Philology* 107: 427–33.

Hall, E. 1989a. The archer scene in Aristophanes' *Thesmophoriazusae. Philologus* 133: 38–54.

Hall, E. 1989b. *Inventing the Barbarian. Greek self-definition through tragedy.* Oxford.

* Hall, E. 2013. *Adventures with Iphigenia in Tauris: a cultural history of Euripides' Black Sea tragedy.* Oxford.

Hall, E. 2019. Visualising Euripides' Tauric temple of the Maiden Goddess. In Braund–Wyles 2019: 305–27.

Hamilton, R. 1978. Prologue, prophecy and plot in four plays of Euripides. *American Journal of Philology* 99: 277–302.

Hamilton, R. 1989. Alkman and the Athenian Arkteia. *Hesperia* 58: 449–72.

Hamilton, R. 1992. *Choes and Anthesteria. Athenian iconography and ritual.* Ann Arbor.

Hanson, J. S. 1980. Dreams and visions in the Graeco-Roman world and early Christianity. *Aufstieg und Niedergang der römischen Welt* II.23.2: 1395–1427.

Harris, E. M. 2017. Aeschylus' *Eumenides*: the role of the Areopagus, the rule of law and political discourse in Attic tragedy. In A. Markantonatos, E. Volonaki (eds), *Poet and Orator: A symbiotic relationship in democratic Athens* (Berlin): 389–419.

Harris, E. M., D. Leão, P. J. Rhodes. 2010. *Law and Drama in Ancient Greece.* London.

Harris, W. V. 1989. *Ancient Literacy.* Cambridge MA.

Hartog, F. 1980. *Le Miroir d'Hérodote.* Paris. Transl. J. Lloyd, Berkeley, 1988.

Hedreen, G. 1991. The cult of Achilles in the Euxine. *Hesperia* 60: 313–30.

ABBREVIATIONS & REFERENCES   283

Heitner, R. 1964. The Iphigeneia in Tauris Theme in Drama of the Eighteenth century. *Comparative Literature* 76: 289–309.

Henrichs, A. 1983. The 'sobriety' of Oedipus. Sophocles *OC* 100 misunderstood. *Harvard Studies in Classical Philology* 87: 87–100.

Henrichs, A. 1991. Namenlosigkeit und Euphemismus: zur Ambivalenz der chthonischen Mächte im attischen Drama. In H. Hofmann (ed.), *Fragmenta dramatica: Beiträge zur Interpretation der griechischen Tragikerfragmente und ihrer Wirkungsgeschichte* (Göttingen): 161–202.

Henrichs, A. 1994. Anonymity and polarity: unknown gods and nameless altars at the Areopagus. *Illinois Classical Studies* 19: 27–58.

Henrichs, A. 1996. Dancing in Athens, dancing on Delos: some patterns of choral projection in Euripides. *Philologus* 140: 48–62.

Henrichs, A. 2000. Drama and *dromena*. bloodshed, violence and sacrificial metaphor in Euripides. *Harvard Studies in Classical Philology* 100: 173–88.

Henrichs, A. 2013. Répandre le sang sur l'autel: ritualisation de la violence dans le sacrifice grec. In Bonnechere–Gagné 2013: 119–44. (Orig. German, 2006).

Hermann, C. 2005. *Iphigenie: Metamorphosen eines Mythos im 20. Jahrhundert.* Munich.

Hermary, A. 2021. L'iconographie d'Artémis à Délos. In Aurigny–Durvye 2021: 137–64.

Hind, J. 1983–84. Greek and barbarian peoples on the shores of the Black Sea. *Archaeological Reports* 30: 71–97.

Hind, J. 1992–93. Archaeology of the Greeks and barbarian peoples around the Black Sea (1982–1992). *Archaeological Reports* 39: 82–112.

Hind, J. 1994. The Bosporan kingdom. In *The Cambridge Ancient History*, VI^2: 476–511.

Hollinshead, M. 1985. Against Iphigeneia's adyton in three mainland temples. *American Journal of Archaeology* 89: 419–40.

Hommel, H. 1980 *Der Gott Achilleus.* Heidelberg.

Hose, M. 1990, 1991. *Studien zum Chor bei Euripides.* Two volumes. Stuttgart.

Hose, M. 1995. *Drama und Gesellschaft.* Stuttgart.

Hourmouziades, N. 1965. *Production and Imagination in Euripides.* Athens.

Hubbard, T. 1987. The 'cooking' of Pelops. Pindar and the process of mythological revisionism. *Helios* 14: 3–21.

Hughes, D. 2007. *Culture and Sacrifice. Ritual death in literature and opera.* Cambridge.

Hurwit, J. 1999. *The Athenian Acropolis.* Cambridge.

Imhof, M. 1956. Tetrameterszenen in der Tragödie. *Museum Helveticum* 13: 125–43.

Ingleheart, J. 2010. 'I'm a celebrity, get me out of here': the reception of Euripides' *Iphigenia among the Taurians* in Ovid's exile poetry. In I. Gildenhard, M.Revermann (eds), *Beyond the Fifth Century: interactions with Greek tragedy from the fourth century BCE to the Middle Ages* (Berlin, New York): 219–46.

284 ABBREVIATIONS & REFERENCES

Irwin, E. 1974. *Colour Terms in Greek Poetry*. Toronto.

Itsumi, K. 1982. The choriambic dimeter of Euripides. *CQ* 32: 59–74.

Jackson, J. 1955. *Marginalia Scaenica*. Oxford.

Jameson, M. 1991. Sacrifice before battle. In V. Hanson (ed.), *Hoplites: the classical Greek battle experience* (London): 197–227.

Jameson, M., D. Jordan, R. Kotansky. 1993. *A Lex Sacra from Selinous*. Durham NC.

Jens, W. (ed.). 1971. *Die Bauformen der griechischen Tragödie*. Munich.

Jiménez Justicia, L. 2017. El primer discurso de mensajero de *Ifigenia entre los tauros*, una pequeña *Ilíada*. *Euphrosyne* 45: 231–40.

Johnston, S. I. 1999. *Restless Dead: encounters between the living and the dead in ancient Greece*. Berkeley.

Jucker, I. 1998. Euripides und der Mythos von Orest und Iphigenie in der bildenden Kunst. In B. Zimmermann (ed.), *Euripides, Iphigenie bei den Taurern, übersetzt.von Georg Finsler* (Stuttgart): 105–38 with illustrations.

Jurgensen, J.-D. 1977. L''Iphigénie en Tauride' de Racine. *Revue d'Histoire littéraire de la France* 77: 749–74.

Kahil, L. 1963. Quelques vases du sanctuaire d'Artémis à Brauron. *Antike Kunst*, Beiheft 1: 5–29.

Kahil, L. 1977. L'Artémis de Brauron: rites et mystère. *Antike Kunst* 20: 86–98.

Kahil, L. 1983. Mythological Repertoire of Brauron. In W. Moon (ed.), *Ancient Greek Art and Iconography* (Madison): 231–44.

Kahil, L. 1988. Le sanctuaire de Brauron et la religion grecque. *Comptes rendus de l'Académie des Inscriptions et Belles-lettres*, 1988: 799–813.

Kalogeropoulos, K. 2010. Die Entwicklung des attischen Artemis-Kultes anhand der Funde des Heiligtums der Artemis Tauropolos in Halai Araphenides (Loutsa). In H. Lohmann, T. Mattern (eds), *Attika: Archäologie einer 'zentralen' Kulturlandschaft* (Wiesbaden, 2010): 167–82.

Kalogeropoulos, K. 2013. Το ιερό της Αρτέμιδος Ταυροπόλου στις Αλές Αραφηνίδες (Λούτσα). Two volumes. Athens.

Kalogeropoulos, K. 2019. Reflections on pilgrimage at the Acropolis of Brauron during the Late Helladic period. In W. Friese et al. (eds), *Ascending and Descending the Acropolis. Movement in Athenian religion* (Aarhus): 221–52.

Kannicht, R. 1956. Das erste Stasimon der Iphigenie bei den Taurern. *Herrn. Prof. Dr. Otto Regenbogen zum 65. Geburtstage* (Heidelberg): 100–16.

Kannicht, R. 1969. *Euripides: Helena*. Heidelberg.

Käppel, L. 1992. *Paian: Studien zur Geschichte einer Gattung*. Berlin.

Kavoulaki, A. 2009. Coming from Delphi: Apolline action and tragic interaction. In L. Athanassaki, R. Martin, J. Miller (eds), *Apolline Politics and Poetics* (Athens): 229–48.

Kearns, E. 1989. *The Heroes of Attica*. London.

ABBREVIATIONS & REFERENCES 285

* Ketterer, R. 2013. Skēnē, altar and image in Euripides' *Iphigenia among the Taurians*. In G. Harrison, V. Liapis (eds), *Performance in Greek and Roman Theatre* (Leiden): 217–33.

* Knox, B. 1970. Euripidean Comedy. In A. Cheuse, R. Koffler (eds), *The Rarer Action* (New Brunswick): 68–96. Reprinted in Knox, *Word and Action* (Baltimore, 1979): 250–74.

Köchly, A. 1860. *Emendationum in Euripidis Iphigeniam Tauricam, pars 2*. Zurich.

Kondis, J. 1967. Artémis Brauronia. *Archaiologikon Deltion, ser. A.*, 22: 156–226.

Kovacs, D. 2000. One ship or two: the end of the *Iphigenia in Tauris*. Echos du Monde Classique: *Classical Views* 19: 19–23.

Kovacs, D. 2003. *Euripidea tertia*. Leiden.

Kowalzig, B. 2006. The aetiology of empire? Hero-cult and Athenian tragedy. In J. F. Davidson et al. (eds), *Greek Drama III. Essays in honour of Kevin Lee* (London): 79–98.

Kowalzig, B. 2007. *Singing for the Gods: Performances of myth and ritual in archaic and classical Greece*. Oxford.

* Kowalzig, B. 2013. Transcultural chorality: *Iphigenia in Tauris* and Athenian imperial economics in a polytheistic world. In R. Gagné, M. Govers Hopman (eds), *Choral Mediations in Greek Tragedy* (Cambridge): 178–210.

Krieg, W. 1936. Der trochäische Tetrameter bei Euripides. *Philologus* 91: 42–51.

Krummen, E. 1993. Athens and Attica: polis and countryside in Greek tragedy. In Sommerstein et al. 1993: 191–217.

Kurtz, D., J. Boardman. 1971. *Greek Burial Customs*. London.

Larson, J. 1995. *Greek Heroine Cults*. Madison.

Larson, J. 2017. Venison for Artemis? The problem of deer sacrifice. In S. Hitch, I. Rutherford (eds), *Animal Sacrifice in the Ancient Greek World* (Cambridge): 48–62.

* Latifses, A. 2019. Le sang et l'eau: du sacrifice à la purification dans *Iphigénie en Tauride* d'Euripide. *Métis* 16: 335–55.

Lattimore, R. 1962. *Themes in Greek and Latin Epitaphs*. Urbana.

Leão, D. 2010. The legal horizon of the *Oresteia*: the crime of homicide and the founding of the Areopagus. In Harris et al. 2010: 39–60.

Lee, K. H. 2003. Goethe's *Iphigenie* and Euripides' *Iphigenia in Tauris. AUMLA: Journal of the Australasian Universities Modern Language Association*, Special issue, Feb 2003: 64–74.

* Lefkowitz, M. 2016. *Euripides and the Gods*. New York.

Leskov, A. 1980. Die Taurer. *Die Antike Welt* 11: 39–53.

* Lesky, A. 1983. *Greek Tragic Poetry*, transl. M. Dillon. New Haven.

Linders, T. 1972. *Studies in the Treasure Records of Artemis Brauronia Found in Athens*. Stockholm.

Llewellyn-Jones, L. 2003. *Aphrodite's Tortoise: The veiled woman of ancient Greece*. Swansea.

286 ABBREVIATIONS & REFERENCES

Lloyd, M. 1999. The tragic aorist. *CQ* 49: 24–45.

Lloyd, M. 2002. Review of Cropp 2000. *CR* 52: 151–52.

Lloyd, M. 2013. The mutability of fortune in Euripides. In D. Cairns, W. Allan (eds), *Tragedy and Archaic Greek Thought* (Swansea): 205–26.

Lloyd-Jones, H. 1983. Artemis and Iphigeneia. *Journal of Hellenic Studies* 103: 87–102. Reprinted in Lloyd-Jones, *Greek Comedy, Hellenistic Literature, Greek Religion, and Miscellanea* (Oxford, 1990): 306–30.

Lloyd-Jones, H. 1990. Erinyes, Semnai Theai, Eumenides. In E. Craik (ed.), *Owls to Athens. Essays on classical subjects presented to Sir Kenneth Dover* (Oxford): 203–11. Reprinted in *The Further Academic Papers of Sir Hugh Lloyd-Jones* (Oxford, 2002): 91–99.

Lo Monaco, A. 2018. *L'Artemide venuta da lontano: Artemide Taurica, La Tauropolos e le altre*. Rome (*Atti della Accademia Nazionali dei Lincei* IX.38.3).

Lucas, D. W. 1968. *Aristotle*: Poetics. Oxford.

Ludwig, W. 1954. *Sapheneia. Ein Beitrag zur Formkunst im Spätwerk des Euripides*. Diss. Tübingen.

MacDonald, A. D. 1963. A Note on *Iphigenia in Tauris* 1050–52. *Transactions of the American Philological Association* 94: 154–56.

MacDowell, D. 1978. *The Law in Classical Athens*. London.

Maltby, R., N. Slater. 2022. *Fragmentary Republican Latin, VI: Livius Andronicus, Naevius, Caecilius*. Loeb Classical Library 314. Cambridge MA and London.

Manuwald, G. 2011. *Roman Republican Theatre: a history*. Cambridge.

Marinatos, N. 1998. Goddess and monster: an investigation of Artemis. In F. Graf (ed.), *Ansichten griechischer Ritualen* (Stuttgart, Leipzig): 114–25.

Marshall, C. W. 2007. Euripides, *Iphigenia in Tauris* 1391–7. *CQ* 57: 749–52.

Marshall, C. W. 2009. Sophocles' *Chryses* and the date of *Iphigenia in Tauris*. In Cousland and Hume 2009: 141–56.

Martin, G. 2020. Review of Parker. *Gnomon* 92: 196–201.

* Masaracchia, E. 1984. *Ifigenia Taurica*: un dramma a lieto fine? *Quaderni Urbinati di Cultura Classica* 18.3: 111–23.

Mastronarde, D. 1990. Actors on high: the skene roof, the crane, and the gods in Attic drama. *Classical Antiquity* 9: 247–94.

* Mastronarde, D. 2010. *The Art of Euripides. Dramatic technique and social context*. Cambridge, New York.

* Matthiessen, K. 1964. *Elektra, Taurische Iphigenie und Helena*. Göttingen.

Matthiessen, K. 2000. Die *Taurische Iphigenie* bei Euripides, bei Goethe und anderswo. In *Skenika: Beiträge zum antiken Theater und seiner Rezeption: Festschrift für H.-D. Blume* (Darmstadt): 363–80.

McClure, L. 2017. Priestess and polis in Euripides' *Iphigeneia in Tauris*. In M. Dillon, E. Eidinow, L. Maurizio (eds), *Women's Ritual Competence in the Greco-Roman Mediterranean* (London, New York): 115–30.

ABBREVIATIONS & REFERENCES 287

McInerney, J. 2014. 'There will be blood...': the cult of Artemis Tauropolos at Halai Araphenides. In K. Daly, L. E. Riccardi (eds), *Cities Called Athens: Studies honoring John McK. Camp II* (Lewisburg PA): 289–320.

Meiggs, R. 1972. *The Athenian Empire*. Oxford.

Mikalson, J. 1982. The *Heorte* of Heortology. *Greek, Roman and Byzantine Studies* 23: 213–21.

Mikalson, J. 1991. *Honor Thy Gods: Popular religion in Greek tragedy*. Chapel Hill.

Miller, T. 1929–32. *Daedalus and Thespis. The contributions of the ancient dramatic poets to our knowledge of the arts and crafts of Greece*. Three volumes. New York.

Millis, B., D. Olson. 2012. *Inscriptional records for the dramatic festivals in Athens: IG II² 2318–2325 and related texts*. Leiden.

Mills, S. 2015. Iphigenia in Tauris. In R. Lauriola, K. Demetriou (eds), *Brill's Companion to the Reception of Euripides* (Leiden): 259–91.

* Mirto, M. S. 1994. Salvare il γένος e riformare il culto: divinazione e razionalità nell'Ifigenia Taurica. *Materiali e discussioni per l'analisi dei testi classici* 32: 55–98.

Moorhouse. A. C. 1940. The name of the Euxine Pontus. *CQ* 34: 123–28.

Moorhouse. A. C. 1948. The name of the Euxine Pontus again. *CQ* 42: 59–60.

Moretti, J.-Ch. 2021. Les sanctuaires d'Artémis à Délos. In Aurigny–Durvye 2021: 61–86.

Morrison, J., R. T. Williams. 1968. *Greek Oared Ships, 900–322 B.C.* Cambridge.

Mossman, J. 1995. *Wild Justice: a study of Euripides' Hecuba*. Oxford.

Most, G. 2000. Two Notes on Euripides' *Iphigenia among the Taurians. Acta Antiqua Academiae Scientiarum Hungaricae* 40: 349–56.

Moutsopoulos, E. 1992. Musique tragique, mais laquelle? (Eurip., *Iph. Taur.* 179–184). *Pallas* 38: 109–15.

Mueller, M. 2016. *Objects as Actors: props and the poetics of performance in Greek tragedy*. Chicago.

Murnaghan, S. 1995. Sucking the juice without biting the rind: Aristotle and tragic mimesis. *New Literary History* 26: 755–73.

Mylonopoulos, I. 2013. Gory Details? The Iconography of Human Sacrifice in Greek Art. In Bonnechere–Gagné 2013: 61–86.

Nagy, G. 1990. *Pindar's Homer*. Baltimore.

Napolitano, M. 2010. Greek tragedy and opera: notes on a marriage manqué. In Brown–Ograjenšek 2010: 31–46.

Neumann, G. 1985. i-pe-me-de-ja, eine mykenische Göttin. *Münchener Studien zur Sprachwissenschaft* 46: 165–71.

Newby, Z. 2011. Myth and death: Roman mythological sarcophagi. In Dowden–Livingstone 2011: 301–18.

Newiger, H.-J. 1990. Ekkyklema und Mechané in der Inszenierung des griechischen Dramas. *Würzburger Jahrbücher für die Altertumswissenschaft* 16: 33–42.

288 ABBREVIATIONS & REFERENCES

Nielsen, I. 2009. The sanctuary of Artemis Brauronia: can architecture and iconography help to locate the settings of the rituals? In T. Fischer-Hansen, B. Poulsen (eds), *From Artemis to Diana: the goddess of man and beast* (Copenhagen): 83–116.

Nijk, C. 2021. The 'polite' aorist: tense or aspect? *CQ* 71: 520–37.

Nikolaenko, G. 2006. The *chora* of Tauric Chersonesos and the cadastre of the 4th–2nd century BC. In P. Guldager Bilde, V. F. Stolba (eds), *Surveying the Greek Chora: the Black Sea region in a comparative perspective* (Aarhus): 151–73.

Oakley, J., R. Sinos. 1993. *The Wedding in Ancient Athens*. Madison.

* O'Brien, M. J. 1988a. Pelopid History and the Plot of *Iphigenia in Tauris*. *CQ* 38: 98–115.

O'Brien, M. J. 1988b. Tantalus in Euripides' *Orestes*. *Rheinisches Museum* 131: 30–45.

Okhotnikov, S., A. Ostroverkhov. 2007. Achilles on the island of Leuke. In D. Grammenos, E. Petropoulos (eds), *Ancient Greek Colonies in the Black Sea 2* (Thessaloniki): I.537–62.

Osborne, R. 1985. *Demos. The discovery of classical Attika*. Cambridge.

Osborne, R. 1993. Women and sacrifice in classical Greece. *CQ* 43: 392–405.

Osborne, R. 2016. Sacrificial theologies. In E. Eidinow, J. Kindt (eds), *Theologies of Ancient Greek Religion* (Cambridge): 233–48.

Pache, C. 2004. *Baby and Child Heroes in Ancient Greece*. Urbana.

Page, D. L. 1934. *Actors' Interpolations in Greek Tragedy*. Oxford.

Palaiokrassa, L. 1991. *Τὸ Ἱερὸ τῆς Ἀρτέμιδος Μουνιχίας*. Athens.

Panagl, O. 1969. Stationen hellenischer Religiosität am Beispiel des delphischen Sukzessionsmythos. *Kairos* 11: 161–71.

Panagl, O. 1971. *Die 'dithyrambischen Stasima' des Euripides*. Vienna.

Papadimitriou, J. 1963. The sanctuary of Artemis at Brauron. *Scientific American* 208: 111–20.

Parker, R. 1983. *Miasma. Pollution and purification in early Greek religion*. Oxford.

Parker, R. 1996. *Athenian Religion: A history*. Oxford.

Parker, R. 1997. *Gods cruel and kind: tragic and civic theology*. In C. Pelling (ed.), *Greek Tragedy and the Historian* (Oxford): 143–60.

Parker, R. 2000. Sacrifice and battle. In H. van Wees (ed.), *War and Violence in Ancient Greece* (Swansea): 299–314.

Parker, R. 2005. *Polytheism and Society at Athens*. Oxford.

Parra, M. C. 1991–92. Artemide tra Locri Reggio e Siracusa: un contributo da Francavilla di Sicilia? *Klearchos* 34: 77–90.

Parra, M. C. 2005. I culti dello stretto: Reggio e il suo territorio. In F. Ghedini et al. (eds), *Lo Stretto di Messina nell'Antichità* (Rome): 423–41.

Peels, S. 2015. *Hosios. A semantic study of Greek piety*. Leiden.

ABBREVIATIONS & REFERENCES 289

* Perrotta, G. 1928. Studi Euripidei, I: L' *Elena* e l' *Ifigenia taurica* dell' Euripide. *Studi Italiani di Filologia Classica* 6: 5–53.

Philippart, H. 1925. Iconographie de l''Iphigénie en Tauride' d'Euripide. *Revue Belge de Philologie et d'Histoire* 4: 5–33.

Phillips, D. 2008. *Avengers of Blood: Homicide in Athenian law and custom from Draco to Demosthenes.* Stuttgart.

Phillips, D. 2013. *The Law of Ancient Athens.* Ann Arbor.

Pickard-Cambridge, A. W. 1988. *The Dramatic Festivals of Athens.* Second edition revised by J. Gould and D. M. Lewis (1968), with supplement and corrections. Oxford.

Poe, J. Park. 1989. The altar in the fifth-century theater. *Classical Antiquity* 8: 116–39.

Pöhlmann, E., M. L. West. 2012. The Oldest Greek papyrus and writing tablets: fifth-century documents from the 'Tomb of the Musician' in Attica. *ZPE* 180: 1–16.

Popp. H. 1971. Das Amoibaion. In Jens 1971: 221–75.

Porucznik, J. 2021. *Cultural Identity with the Northern Black Sea Region in Antiquity.* Leuven.

Pritchett, W. K. 1979, 1991. *The Greek State at War. Parts III, V.* Berkeley.

Pritchett, W. K. 1998, 1999. *Pausanias Periegetes, I, II.* Amsterdam.

Pulleyn, S. 1997. *Prayer in Greek Religion.* Oxford.

Reeder, E. (ed.). 1995. *Pandora. Women in Classical Greece.* Princeton.

Rehm, R. 1988. The staging of suppliant plays. *Greek, Roman and Byzantine Studies* 29: 263–308

Rehm, R. 1995. *Marriage to Death.* Princeton.

Reid, J. D. 1993. *The Oxford Guide to Classical Mythology in the Arts.* Two volumes. Oxford.

Renehan, R. 1976. *Studies in Greek Texts.* Göttingen.

Risch, E. 1992. À propos de la formation du vocabulaire poétique Grec entre le 12e et le 8e siècle. In F. Létoublon (ed.), *La langue et les textes en Grec ancien. Actes du Colloque P. Chantraine (Grenoble, 5–8 Sept. 1989)* (Amsterdam): 91.

Roberts, D. 1987. Parting words. Final lines in Sophocles and Euripides. *CQ* 37: 51–64.

Rocchi, M. 1996. Osservazioni a proposito di *I-pe-me-de-ja.* In E. De Miro et al., *Atti e memorie del secondo congresso internazionale di micenologia: Roma–Napoli, 14–20 ottobre 1991* (Rome): 861–67.

Romano, A. 2012. Euripidean explainers. In J. Marincola et al. (eds), *Greek Notions of the Past in the Archaic and Classical Eras* (Edinburgh): 127–43.

Romano, I. 1988. Early Greek Cult Images and Cult Practices. In R. Hägg (ed.), *Early Greek Cult Practice* (Stockholm): 127–33.

Rorty, A. O. (ed.). 1992. *Essays on Aristotle's Poetics.* Princeton.

290 ABBREVIATIONS & REFERENCES

Rossi, F. 2007. Dalla Grecia a San Pietroburgo: Ifigenia non si ferma in Tauride. In R. Tibaldi (ed.), *Baldassare Galuppi, il Buranello, aspetti e vicende della vita e dell'arte* (Venice): 13–32.

Rouse, W. H. D. 1902. *Greek Votive Offerings*. Cambridge.

Rudhardt, J. 1958. *Notions fondamentales de la pensée religieuse etc.* Geneva.

Rudhardt, J. 1999. *Thémis et les Hôrai. Recherche sur les divinités grecques de la justice et de la paix.* Geneva.

Rusten, J., I. Cunningham. 2002. *Theophrastus,* Characters; *Herodas, Mimes; Sophron and other mime fragments.* Loeb Classical Library 225. Cambridge MA and London.

Rusyaeva, A. 2003. The temple of Achilles on the island of Leuke in the Black Sea. *Ancient Civilizations from Scythia to the Black Sea* 9: 1–16.

Rutherford, I. 1995. Apollo in ivy: the tragic paean. *Arion* n.s. 3: 112–35.

Rutherford, R. 2012. *Greek Tragic Style. Form, language and interpretation.* Oxford.

Said, S. 1984. Grecs et Barbares dans les tragédies d'Euripide. La fin des différences? *Ktema* 9: 27–53.

Said, S. 1993. Tragic Argos. In Sommerstein et al. 1993: 167–190.

* Said, S. 2002. Exotic space in *Iphigeneia in Tauris. Dioniso* 1: 48–61.

Sale, W. 1975. The temple-legends of the Arkteia. *Rheinisches Museum* 118: 265–84.

* Sansone, D. 1975. The Sacrifice-Motif in Euripides' *Iphigenia in Tauris. Transactions of the American Philological Association* 105: 283–95.

Sansone, D. 1978. A Problem in Euripides' *Iphigenia in Tauris. Rheinisches Museum* 121: 35–47.

Sansone, D. 1979. Euripides, Friederich Bothe and Mr. Diggle. *Quaderni Urbinati di Cultura Classica* 1: 157–59.

Sansone, D. 1982. Review of Diggle 1981. *Göttingsche Gelehrte Anzeigen* 234: 31–41.

Sansone, D. 1988. The survival of the Bronze-Age demon. *Illinois Classical Studies* 13: 1–17.

Sansone, D. 2000. Iphigenia in Colchis. In M. A. Harder, R. Regtuit, G. Wakker (eds), *Apollonius Rhodius* (Leuven): 155–72.

Sansone, D. 2008. Review of Kyriakou. *Gnomon* 80: 385–87.

Schierl, P. 2006. *Die Tragödien des Pacuvius.* Berlin.

Schmidt, V. 1968. *Sprachliche Untersuchungen zu Herondas.* Berlin.

Schwinge, E.-R. 1968. *Die Verwendung der Stichomythie in den Dramen des Euripides.* Heidelberg.

Scullion, S. 1999–2000. Tradition and invention in Euripidean aitiology. *Illinois Classical Studies* 24–25: 217–34.

Seaford, R. 1987. The Tragic Wedding. *Journal of Hellenic Studies* 107: 106–30.

ABBREVIATIONS & REFERENCES 291

Seaford, R. 2009. Aitiologies of cult in Euripides: a response to Scott Scullion. In Cousland and Hume 2009: 221–34.

Secci, L. (ed.). 2008. *Il mito di Ifigenia da Euripide al novecento*. Rome.

Séchan, L. 1926. *Études sur la tragédie grecque dans ses rapports avec la céramique*. Paris.

Segal, E. 1995. 'The comic catastrophe': an essay on Euripidean comedy. In A. Griffiths (ed.), *Stage Directions: Essays in ancient drama in honour of E. W. Handley* (London): 46–55.

Seidensticker, B. 1971. Die Stichomythie. In Jens (ed.) 1971: 183–220.

Shear, J. 2021. *Serving Athena: the festival of the Panathenaia and the construction of Athenian identities*. Cambridge, New York.

Silk, M. 1983. LSJ and the problem of poetic archaism. From meaning to iconyms. *CQ* 33: 303–30.

Simon, E. 1983. *Festivals of Attica*. Madison.

Slater, W. J. 1989. Pelops at Olympia. *Greek, Roman and Byzantine Studies* 30: 485–501.

Sommerstein, A. H. 2010. Orestes' trial and Athenian homicide procedure. In Harris et al. 2010: 25–38.

Sommerstein, A. H. et al. (eds). 1993. *Tragedy, Comedy and the Polis*. Bari.

Sommerstein, A. H., I. C. Torrance. 2014. *Oaths and Swearing in Ancient Greece*. Berlin.

Sourvinou-Inwood, C. 1987. Myth as history: the previous owners of the Delphic Oracle. In J. Bremmer (ed.), *Interpretations of Greek Mythology* (London): 215–41. Reprinted in Sourvinou-Inwood, *'Reading' Greek culture: Texts and images, rituals and myths* (Oxford, 1991), 217–43.

Sourvinou-Inwood, C. 1988. *Studies in Girls' Transitions*. Athens.

Sourvinou-Inwood, C. 1990. Lire l'arkteia: lire les images, les textes, l'animalité. *Dialogues d'Histoire Ancienne* 16: 45–60.

* Sourvinou-Inwood, C. 1997. Tragedy and Religion: constructs and readings. In C. Pelling (ed.), *Greek Tragedy and the Historian* (Oxford): 161–86.

* Sourvinou-Inwood, C. 2003. *Tragedy and Athenian Religion*. Lanham MD.

Spranger, J. A. 1920. *Euripidis quae inveniuntur in codice Laurentiano, pl. XXXII 2*. Florence.

Spranger, J. A. 1939, 1946. *Euripidis quae in codicibus Palatino Graeco inter Vaticanos 287 et Laurentiano Conv. Soppr. 172...inveniuntur phototypice expressa etc*. Two volumes. Florence.

Steiner, D. 2021. *Choral constructions in Greek culture. The idea of the chorus in the poetry, art and social practices of the archaic and early classical period*. Cambridge.

* Stern-Gillet, S. 2001. Exile, displacement and barbarity in Euripides' *Iphigeneia amongst the Taurians*. *Scholia* 10: 4–21.

Stieber, M. 2011. *Euripides and the Language of Craft*. Leiden.

292 ABBREVIATIONS & REFERENCES

Stinton, T. C. W. 1976. 'Si credere dignum est'. Some expressions of disbelief in Euripides and others. *Proceedings of the Cambridge Philological Society* 22: 60–89. Reprinted in Stinton 1990: 236–64.

Stinton, T. C. W. 1977. *Notes on Greek Tragedy, II. Journal of Hellenic Studies* 97: 127–54. Reprinted in Stinton 1990: 271–309.

Stinton, T. C. W. 1990. *Collected Papers on Greek Tragedy.* Oxford.

Stockert, W. 1992. *Euripides: Iphigenie in Aulis.* Vienna.

Stockert, W. 2000. Zu einer Korruptel in der Taurischen Iphigenie (Vers 999). *Wiener Studien* 113: 71–74.

Suk Fong Jim, Th. 2022. *Saviour Gods and Soteria in Ancient Greece.* Oxford.

Sutton, D. F. 1972. Satyric qualities in Euripides' *Iphigeneia at Tauris* and *Helen. Rivista di Studi Classici* 20: 321–30.

Swift, L. A. 2010. *The Hidden Chorus. Echoes of genre in tragic lyric.* Oxford.

Taddei, A. 2015. Ifigenia e il Coro nella *Ifigenia tra i Tauri.* Destini rituali incrociati. *Lexis* 33: 150–67.

Taplin, O. 1977. *The Stagecraft of Aeschylus.* Oxford.

Taplin, O. 1978. *Greek Tragedy in Action.* London.

Taplin, O. 2007. *Pots & Plays. Interactions between tragedy and Greek vase-painting of the fourth century B.C.*

Tarán, S. 1979. *The Art of Variation in the Hellenistic Epigram.* Leiden.

Telò, M. 2003. Eur. I.T. 798–9: un'attribuzione problematica. *Rheinisches Museum* 146: 103–7.

Themelis, P. 1971. *Brauron. Guide to the Site and Museum.* Athens.

Themelis, P. 2002. Contribution to the study of the sanctuary at Brauron. In B. Gentili, F. Perusino (eds), *Le Orse di Brauron* (Pisa): 103–116, 223–232.

Thompson, W. D. 1947. *A Glossary of Greek Fishes.* Oxford.

Todd, S. C. 1993. *The Shape of Athenian Law.* Oxford.

Torrance, I. C. 2009. Euripides' *IT* 72–5 and a *skene* of slaughter. *Hermes* 137: 21–27.

* Torrance, I. C. 2019. *Euripides:* Iphigenia among the Taurians. London

Travlos, J. 1988. *Bildlexikon zur Topographie des antiken Attika.* Tübingen.

Trédé-Boulmer, M. 2015. *Kairos: l'àpropos et l'occasion.* Revised edition (orig. 1992). Paris.

Trejster, M., U. Vinogradov. 1993. Archaeology on the northern coast of the Black Sea. *American Journal of Archaeology* 97: 521–63.

Trendall, A. D., T. B. L. Webster. 1971. *Illustrations of Greek Drama.* London.

* Trieschnigg, C. 2008. Iphigenia's dream in Euripides' *Iphigenia Taurica. CQ* 58: 461–78

Tsetskhladze, G. 1994. Greek penetration of the Black Sea'. In G. Tsetskhladze, F. de Angelis (eds), *The Archaeology of Greek Colonisation* (Oxford): 111–35.

Tsetskhladze, G. (ed.). 1998. *The Greek Colonisation of the Black Sea Area.* Stuttgart.

ABBREVIATIONS & REFERENCES 293

Turyn, A. 1957. *The Byzantine Manuscript Tradition of the Tragedies of Euripides*. Urbana.

* Tzanetou, A. 1999–2000. Almost dying, dying twice: ritual and audience in Euripides' *Iphigenia in Tauris*. *Illinois Classical Studies* 24–25: 199–216.

Ventris, M., J. Chadwick. 1983. *Documents in Mycenean Greek*. Second edition. Cambridge.

Verdenius, W. J. 1975. Adversative καί again. *Mnemosyne* 28: 189–90.

Vikela, E. 2015. *Apollon, Artemis, Leto. Eine Untersuchung zur Typologie, Ikonographie und Hermeneutik der drei Gottheiten auf griechischen Weihreliefs*. Munich.

Warmington, E. H. 1936. *Remains of Old Latin, II*. Cambridge MA, London.

West, M. L. 1981. Tragica V. *Bulletin of the Institute of Classical Studies* 28: 61–78.

West, M. L. 1982. *Greek Metre*. Oxford.

West, M. L. 1992. *Ancient Greek Music*. Oxford.

West, M. L. 1997. *The East Face of Helicon. West Asiatic elements in Greek poetry and myth*. Oxford.

West, M. L. 2013. *The Epic Cycle: A commentary on the lost Troy epics*. Oxford.

West, S. 2003. The most marvellous of all seas: the Greek encounter with the Euxine. *Greece & Rome* 50: 151–167.

West, S. 2019. The northward advance of Greek horizons. In Braund et al. 2019: 26–41.

* White, S. 1992. Aristotle's favorite tragedies. In Rorty (ed.) 1992: 221–40.

Wilamowitz-Moellendorff, U. von. 1921 *Griechische Verskunst*. Berlin.

Wiles, D. 1997. *Tragedy in Athens. Performance space and theatrical meaning*. Cambridge.

Willink, C. 2009. Euripides, *Electra* 432–486 and *Iphigenia in Tauris* 827–899. In Cousland and Hume 2009: 205–17.

Wilson, J. R. 1971. Τόλμα and the meaning of τάλας. *AJP* 92: 292–300.

* Wolff, C. 1992. Euripides' *Iphigeneia among the Taurians*: aetiology, ritual, and myth. *Classical Antiquity* 11: 308–34.

* Wright, M. 2005. *Euripides' Escape-Tragedies. A study of* Helen, Andromeda *and* Iphigenia among the Taurians. Oxford.

Xian Ruobing. 2020. Scepter and Spear in Euripides' *Iphigenia in Tauris*. *Museum Helveticum* 77: 188–93.

* Zeitlin, F. 2005. Redeeming matricide? Euripides rereads the *Oresteia*. In V. Pedrick, S. Oberhelman (eds), *The Soul of Tragedy: Essays on Athenian drama* (Chicago): 199–225.

* Zeitlin, F. 2011. Sacrifices holy and unholy in Euripides' *Iphigenia in Tauris*. In F. Prescendi et al. (eds), *Dans le laboratoire de l'historien des religions: Mélanges offerts à Philippe Borgeaud* (Geneva): 449–66.

294   ABBREVIATIONS & REFERENCES

Zeitlin, F. 2019. Life trajectories: Iphigenia, Helen and Achilles on the Black Sea. In Braund et al. 2019: 453–69.

Zgoll, C. 2021. Göttergaben und Götterstürze. In G. Gabriel et al. (eds), *Was vom Himmel kommt. Stoffanalytische Zugänge zu antiken Mythen* (Berlin): 221–70.

Ziehen, L. 1902. ΟΥΛΟΧΥΤΑΙ. *Hermes* 37: 391–400.

Zielinski, Th. 1925. *Tragodoumenon Libri Tres.* Cracow.

Zolotarev, M. 2003. Chersonesus Tauricus. In D. Grammenos, E. Petropoulos (eds), *Ancient Greek Colonies in the Black Sea* (Thessaloniki): I.603–44.

Zuntz, G. 1965. *An Inquiry into the Transmission of the Plays of Euripides.* Cambridge.

INDEXES

Bold face indicates pages and footnotes on those pages in the Introduction. Other references are to the notes in the Commentary (* indicates two or more notes within the range cited).

1. Ancient authors and texts

Accius **43n.**

Aeschylus, *Oresteia* **6–8, 17, 20–22,** 157, 223; *Agamemnon* **7n, 20n,** 10–27*, 50–52, 199–201, 214–17, 300, 359–60, 442–45, 553, 620, 621, 866–72, 1261–62, 1431–33; *Choephori* 42–66, 50–52, 77, 105, 123–235, 133–36, 159–61, 172–74, 281–300, 288, 456–560, 570–71, 702–5, 811–26, 942–44 1056–88, 1083, 1284–1434; *Eumenides* **12, 20,** 35–37, 77, 85–92, 92, 120–21, 285–94*, 570–71, 942–44, 945–46, 962–71*, 1222–25, 1086–88, 1234–83, 1435–89, 1446–47; *Iphigenia* **20**; *Persians* 236–391, 1385–91*; *Seven against Thebes* 236–391

[Aeschylus], *Prometheus Bound* 236–391, 393–97

Aethiopis (epic) 435–36

Alcaeus 1234–83

Ammianus Marcellinus 75

Anthology, Greek **45n,** 695–98, 1464–67

Apollodorus, *Library* **21n,** 87–88, 626

Aristonous, *Paean* 1234–83

Aristophanes 482–83; *Acharnians* 947–60; *Clouds* 380–91; *Frogs* 1–5, 392, 450–51, 827–99, 1089–1152, 1089–1105, 1261–62; *Thesmophoriazusae* **41,** 701, 827–99; *Women of Lemnos* 32–33

Aristotle, *Nicomachean Ethics* 585–87, 687–88; *Poetics* **1n, 4n, 15, 16, 42,** 811–26; *Rhetoric* 500–1, 559, 727

[Aristotle], *Constitution of Athens* **29n,** 965–66

Artemidorus 47–49, 57

Callimachus, *Hymn to Apollo* 1103–5; *to Artemis* 127, 362, 1099–1105*; *to Delos* 1097–1105*, 1235

Charition-Mime **42f.**

Cypria (epic) **17–19,** 15, 24–25

Euphorion 1464–67 n.

Euripides, *Alexandros* 456–826; *Andromache* 42–43, 301–35, 385–86, 435–36, 1327–1419, 1385–86, 1435–89, 1475–85; *Antiope* 1435–89, 1475–85; *Bacchae* **16,** 123–36, 236–391, 260–339, 301–35, 385–91, 1241–44, 1327–1419, 1385–86, 1435–89; *Bellerophon* 380–91; *Cresphontes* **4n,** 456–826; *Cretans* 123–36; *Electra* **7, 10, 15n, 20, 22n, 41,** 42–66*, 77, 92, 120–21, 123–235, 139–42, 172–74, 191–94*, 208, 214–17, 221, 281–300, 456–826, 552–71*, 695–98, 702–5, 798–810, 827–99, 902–1088, 907–11*, 942–44, 964–71*, 1056–88, 1125–27, 1327–1419, 1435–89; *Erechtheus* **13,** 47–49, 1435–89, 1444–47*, 1462–63 *Hecuba* 222–24, 354–60*, 392, 500–1, 585–87, 1099–1102; *Helen* **7, 14n, 16, 40f.,** 29, 123–235, 301–35, 354–58, 456–826, 504, 543, 713, 798–802, 827–99, 902–1088, 1020–27, 1041–46, 1032–34*,

INDEXES

1056–88, 1089–1152, 1089–1105, 1327–1419, 1334–43*, 1348–53, 1385–86, 1435–89, 1446–7, 1475–85, 1488; *Heracles* **13n, 17**, 47–49, 281–300, 282–84, 296–98, 307–8*, 380–91, 486–89, 502, 965–66, 1241–44; *Heraclidae* 359–60; *Hippolytus* 380–91, 578–96, 1056–88, 1435–89; *Hypsipyle* 472–73, 827–99, 1435–89; *Ion* **4n, 11, 12, 16, 17**, 380–91, 456–826, 472–73, 713, 811–26, 827–99, 902–1088, 1020–27, 1056–88, 1327–1419, 1435–89, 1475–85, 1488; *Iphigenia at Aulis (IA)* **1n, 11n, 21, 42**, 8, 24–25, 214–17, 230–36, 359–60, 366–69*, 856–59, 1056–88, 1435–89; *Medea* 124–25, 1056–88, 1061–62, 1174, 1284–1434, 1327–1419; *Melanippe Captive* 301–39*; *Oenomaus* 75; *Orestes* **22n**, 191–94*, 193–94, 281–335*, 386–91, 552, 559, 570–71, 675, 695–98, 929, 942–44, 973–75, 1007–8, 1056–88, 1173, 1327–1419, 1435–89, 1475–85, 1488; *Palamedes* 578–96; *Phoenician Women* 26–27, 67–68, 123–36, 236–391, 827–99; *Suppliant Women* **12, 13n**, 1435–89, 1475–85; *Theseus* 578–96; *Trojan Women* 24–25, 380–91*, 1391–95, 1444–45

Hellanicus 695–98

Herodotus **17, 19–23, 25**, 75, 133–36, 208, 625–35, 1099–1102, 1205, 1427–30*

Hesiod, *Theogony* 385–91

[Hesiod], *Catalogue of Women* **17f.**

Homer **17**; *Iliad* **15, 17n**, 312, 691–92, 1271, 1276, 1395, 1435–89; *Odyssey* **4, 7n, 26n**, 270–71, 296–98, 386–8, 531–36, 798–810, 823–25, 1216, 1435–89, 1444–45

Homeric Hymn to Demeter 230–35; *to Apollo* 1097–1102*, 1234–83*; *to Hermes* 1250–52, 1270–74*

Hyginus, *Fabulae* **4n, 21n, 43**, 270–71, 386–91, 1099–1102

inscriptions **20n**, 28, **29n, 42n**, 87–88n, 934, 1041n

Limenios, *Paean* 1099–1102

Lucian, *Toxaris* **44, 45f., 47n**

Lycophron, *Alexandra* 435–36

Menander **32**, 482–83

Naevius **42**

Ovid **43**, 1089–1105*, 1099–1102

Pacuvius **42, 43n**

Pausanias, *Description of Greece* **18n, 28n, 30n, 33n**, 87–88n, 191–93, 435–36, 962–63, 1440

Pindar 438, 678; *Nemean 1* 435–37; *Nemean 4* 435–36; *Olympian 1* 1–5, 191–93, 386–91; *Pythian 11* **7n, 20**; fr. 55 1234–83

Plato 380–91

Ptolemy Chennos 354–58

Rhinthon **42f.**

Sack of Troy (epic) 24–25

Solon 380–91, 407–21, 475–78

Sophocles, *Ajax* 281–300, 296–98; *Antigone* 236–391, 260–339, 423–24, 548; *Chryses* **21n, 43n**; *Electra* **7n, 17n, 20**, 15, 42–66, 191–93, 456–826, 553, 702–5, 827–99, 1056–88; *Iphigenia* **20f.**, 24–25; *Oedipus at Colonus* **17**; *Oedipus Tyrannus* **4n, 16**, 456–826, 1084–85; *Oenomaus* 75; *Philoctetes* 1435–89, 1475–85; *Trachiniae* 92

Stesichorus, *Oresteia* **18f.**, 42–66

Strabo, *Geography* **20n, 32n**, 422–38, 436–37

Timesitheos (tragedian) **43n**

Timotheus (poet) **28n**

Xenophanes 380–91

Xenophon **25n**

INDEXES

2. Language, style, metre

αἰδώς see Index 4, 'aidôs'
αἱμακτός 645
ἀκοντίζω 362
ἀκροθίνια 75, 459–62
ἀμαθία: see Index 4, 'amathia'
ἀμφίβληστρα 96
ἄνθος 300
ἄξε(ι)νος 124–25, 218–19
ἄπλοια 15
γύναι 482–83
δή 320, 459–62, 682, 1051
δίκροτος 407
δόρυ
δρόσος 255
δυσ- 144–47
εἷα 1423
ἔκβολον 1042
ἐλαστρέω 934
ἑορτή 35–37, 1458–61
ἐπίκρανον 50–52
ἔρως 1172
εὐφημία 123, 458, 687–88
θρίγκοι, θριγκώματα 47–49, 73, 74
θύω, θῦμα 209–13, 1331–32
ἰσήρης 1471–72
καινός 42–43, 239, 1306
καιρός 420
καίτοι γε 720
κατάρχομαι 38–41
κατήρης 1346
κλίμακες 97–98, 1351
κληδοῦχος: see Index 4, 'key-keeper'
κυάνεος 6–7
λαμπρός 29
λουτρά: see Index 4, 'lustration'
λέγοιμ' ἄν 811, 939
μέλεος 645, 852–53

ναυσθλόω 1487–89
νεᾶνις 336–39
νυκτ(ερ)ωπός 1278–79
νοσέω 531–36, 1018
ξανθός 50–52
ξενία: see Index 4, 'hospitality'
ξίφος: see Index 4, 'sword'
ξόανον 87–88, 1359
ξουθός 165
ὅσιος 130–32, 342–43, 463–66, 1037,
    1045, 1161
παλαμναῖος 1218
παρθενών 45
πατροκτόνος 1083
πεπρωμένος 1438–39
πίτυλος 307, 1050, 1346
ποῖος 495, 1319
πόλις 38, 595, 876–80, 1209, 1264
πορθμεύω 266, 936, 1435, 1444–45
πρόσφαγμα 243, 458
ῥόθιον 407, 425–26, 1387
συμφορά 618, 1317
σφάζω, σφαγή etc. 8, 552, 1458–61
σῶμα 753–58, 765
τάλας 805, 866–72, 894
τάχ' οὖν 782
τηλύγετος 828–30
τί γάρ 1478–79
τύχη: see Index 4, 'fortune'
φιλία: see Index 4, 'friendship'
φῶς 20–21, 187–88
χάρις 14, 566, 630–31, 1444–45
χέρνιψ: see Index 4, 'lustration'
χρή, χρεών 1438–39, 1486
ψῆφος 945–46
ὠλένη 965–66

INDEXES

accusative, retained 442–45, 456–57, 1346

anacoluthon 675, 695–98, 947–48, 964–65

anadiplosis 138, 392

anaphora 827–99, 876–80

asyndeton 209–13, 220, 230–35

colloquialisms 244–45, 932, 1005–6, 1024, 1030, 1079–81, 1203, 1214, 1319, 1423

dithyrambic style 1089–1152, 1234–83

epic style 1, 133–36, 170–71, 235, 236–391, 253, 260–339, 260–64, 300, 301–35, 325–27, 344–50, 407, 409, 425–26, 430–32, 456–826, 655, 663, 700, 828–30, 1000, 1042, 1091, 1136, 1234–83, 1264, 1327–1419, 1383, 1390–91, 1394–95

etymological figure 201–2, 753–58, 765

etymology 32–33, 35–37, 84, 307, 393–97, 828–30, 942–44, 1264, 1438–39, 1453–57

euphemisms 124–25, 942–44, 1197

hendiadys 876–80, 1110

inverse attraction 1294

litotês 144–47, 1241–44

metre **40, 49**; aeolic 1089–1152*; aeolo-choriambic 392–455, 1089–1152, 1234–83; anapaestic 123–235*, 456–66, 1490–99; archilochean 392–455; 'choriambic dimeter' **40**, 1241–44; cretic 827–99; dactylic 827–99, 876–80, 1089–1152, 1134–35, 1234–83; dactylo-epitrite 1234–83; dochmiac 643–57*, 827–99, 852–53; iambic 209–13, 392–455, 827–99, 828–30, 861–72, 1234–83, (resolutions in trimeters) **40**; ithyphallic 1089–1152, 1134–35; pherecratean 392–455; trochaic **40**, 1153–1233, 1203–33

moods: imperative 1203; optative 325–27, 811, 695–98, 895–99; subjunctive 442–45, 637, 670–71, 912, 1064

oxymoron 144–47, 182–85, 201–2, 209–13, 218–19, 512, 566, 886–89, 897, 1095, 1111–16*, 1390–91

patronymics 1

pleonasm 124–25, 300, 370, 409–10, 436–37, 856–59, 1234–38, 1325–26, 1345

plural for singular 50–52, 97–98, 128–29, 187–88, 312, 370, 537–39, 856–59, 987–88, 1282–83, 1351, 1359

synecdoche 116–17, 124–25, 945–46, 1050, 1102, 1325–26, 1346, 1394–95, 1427, 1445

tenses: aorist 357, 1023, 1161; future 999; imperfect 26–27, 295–96, 324–35*, 1337–42*, 1368–71*; present 999, (historic) 2, 16, 42–66, 282–84, 330–35*, 1394–95, (registering) 22–23, 34, 207, 682, 926, 931

tmêsis 832–33, 876–80, 1143–46, 1276–79*

tricolon 1236–38

word-play 504, 512, 646, 765. See also 'etymological figure'.

INDEXES

3. Names and Places

Achilles 24–25, 32–33, 214–17, 273–74, 369, 435–37*, 537–39, 632–35, 663, 695–98, 856–59, 1117–22

Aegisthus **7n, 8n,** 924–27

Agamemnon **6, 8, 17–19, 30,** 3, 8, 20–21, 26–27, 42–66, 50–52, [59–60], 139–42, 170–74*, 214–17, 442–45, 521–22, 543, 552, 620, 992, 1414–19

Ajax 281–300, 296–98

Amphitrite 273–74, 425–26

Apollo **2, 5–6, 7, 9–12, 15, 17, 21, 34, 39, 48,** 67–122, 77–92*, 182–85, 570–75*, 711–23*, 942–44, 964–82*, 1014–15, 1082–88*, 1097–1105*, 1125–27, 1174, 1234–83*, 1385–86, 1435–89, 1438–39. See also 'Loxias', 'Phoebus'.

Areopagus **7, 21,** 945–46, 962–63, 968–71, 1467–72*

Argonauts **25,** 124–25, 423–24

Argos **13, 21, 22n, 49,** 42–66, 157–59, 221–24*, 235, 366–75*, 393–402*, 506–8, 567–68, 583, 590, 638, 700, 804, 818, 929, 942–44, 1440

arkteia (ritual) **27–31, 32n**

Artemis **5, 8, 11–14, 18f., 36,** 8, 20–41*, 87–88, 127–36*, 344–91, 359–60, 380–91*, 463–66, 531–36, 747–49, 989–1019, 1082–88*, 1089–1152, 1097–99, 1113–16, 1316, 1391–95, 1397–1402, 1425, 1435–89; cults in Attica **8, 11–14, 27–34,** 20–24, 26–27, 1368–70, 1440, 1450–67*; of Ephesus 1041; Taurian cult **12n, 23f., 25,** 26–27, 35–37, 72–75*, 243–45*, 280, 380–91, 463–66, 585–87, 625–35, 1163, 1189, 1458–61; Taurian image **21, 33, 35, 45, 48,** 87–88, 111, 876–80, 977–78, 989–1019, 1041, 1153–1233, 1165–67, 1222–25, 1348–53*,

1440; Taurian temple and altar **34f., 44,** 65–66, 72–75*, 96–100*, 113–14, 128–29, 403–6, 625–35*, 1159, 1284; Tauropolos **31–33,** 1453–61*

Asia(n) **32,** 178–81, 393–97, 1440

Athena **3, 10, 11, 12f., 15, 32, 34, 37, 38,** 91, 133–36, 222–24, 942–46*, 965–71*, 1014–15, 1041, 1086–88, 1197, 1210, 1391–95, 1431–33, 1435–89*

Athens **11–13, 21, 27–31, 38f.,** 222–24, 399–402, 902–1088, 942–71*, 1041, 1086–88, 1099–1102, 1440–52*

Atreus **7,** 192–8*, 811–26, 812, 987–8. See also 'Pelopids'.

Attica **3, 12f., 17,** 1131, 1450–52

Aulis **7, 11, 19–22, 30, 37,** 6–7, 24–25, 214–17, 336–39, 358, 818, 1082–88, 1418–19

Black Sea **24f., 37,** 124–25, 218–19, 392, 422–38, 435–36

Bosporus 124–25, 133–36, 260–4, 392–406, 392–406*, 422–38

Brauron, Brauronia **3, 12f., 21f., 27–34,** 20–21, 1440, 1450–52, 1462–67*

Calchas **11, 19f.,** 8, 20–23*, 531–36, 662, 1128, 1264–65

Castor **20,** 92, 208, 1435–89, 1446–47; and Pollux 268–74*

Chersonesos **20, 24**

Choes (ritual) **13, 34,** 947–60*

Clashing/Dark Rocks (*Symplêgades*) **25, 36, 37,** 124–25, 241–42, 393–97, 746

Clytemnestra **6, 7n, 8, 10,** 5, 42–66, 50–52, 203–17*, 289–90, 442–45, 521–22, 552–59*, 621, 924–27*, 1095, 1173, 1458–61

Colchis **25**

INDEXES

Delos **12n**, **39**, 1089–1152, 1097–1105*, 1234–83, 1235–40*, 1449

Delphi **11**, **13**, **39**, 87–88, 92, 128–29, 942–44, 972–76*, 1222–25, 1234–83*

Dictynna 127

Dionysus 947–60, 1241–44, 1385–86

Dioscuri: see 'Castor and Pollux'

Dirce 399–402

Electra **4n**, **7n**, 42–66, 123–235, 148–56, 172–74, 208, 230–35, 296–98, 308, 456–826, 562, 627–31*, 682, 695–98, 702–7*, 798–810, 811–26, 898, 902–1088, 920, 939, 984–85, 1007–8, 1173

Ephesus **45**, 1041, 1099–1102

Erinyes **1f.**, **3**, **6**, **8**, **12f.**, **21**, **34**, **37**, **39**, 77–83*, 199–201, 230–35, 260–339, 281–300*, 778, 932–44*, 962–72*, 1086–88, 1234–83, 1467–72*

Eumenides 968–71, 1086–88

Euripus 6–7

Europe 133–36, 393–97

Eurotas 133–36, 399–402

Fates (*Moirai*) 203–7*, 1259–61

Gaia (Earth) 1234–83, 1254–72*

Gluck, C. W. **47f.**

Goethe, J. W. **47**, **48f.**

Halai Araphenides **3**, **8**, **12**, **13**, **15**, **22**, **23**, **27**, **29n**, **31n**, 31–34, **37**, 26–27, 1368–70, 1450–61*

Hecate **18**, **25**, **31**, 20–21

Helen 2, **6**, **7f.**, **18**, **36**, **38**, **39**, 14, 29, 354–58*, 435–36, 439–55, 521–26*, 566, 902–1088, 1056–88. See also Index 1, 'Euripides, *Helen*'.

Hera **13**, 221, 393–97, 1041, 1453–57

Heracles **26**, 92, 114–15. See also Index 1, 'Euripides, *Heracles*'.

Heraea (festival) 221–24*

Hermes 29, 1250–52, 1270–74*

Hippodameia 1–5*, 811–26

Io 45, 130–36*, 393–97, 1453–57

Iphianassa **17n**

Iphigenia: and family/home **6**, **48**, 42–66*, 143–77*, 178–202, 229–35*, 378–79, 553, 565–68*, 590, 612–13, 778, 850, 865–67, 1005–6; as priestess **9n**, **21**, **27**, **31**, **35f.**, 35–41*, 65–66, 130–32, 467–69, 1462–63; ingenuity **9n**, 1005–6, 1029–49*, 1153–1221*, 1334–35; longs for Greece 175, 218–24*, 439–55, 553, 1186–87, 1230–33; marriage to Achilles 24–25, 214–17, 369–75*, 435–36, 537–39, 818–21, 856–59*; myth and cult **17–22**, **27–31**, 1462–67*; sacrifice of **6f.**, **10**, **11**, **14**, **17–21**, **29–31**, **49**, 6–30*, 207–17*, 336–39, 358–75*, 521–41*, 620, 920–27*, 1082–88, 1083, 1418–19; views on gods **9**, 344–91, 380–91*, 1418–19

Iphimede(ia) **18**

Lagrange-Chancel, F. J. **46n**

Leto 380–91*, 1099–1102, 1234–83, 1234–38*, 1250–52

Leucothea 270–1

Leukê: see 'White Island'

Loxias 105, 570–71, 942–44, 1084–85, 1438–39

Menelaus **10n**, 1–66, 14, 50–52, 352–58, 929, 1414–19, 1437, 1475–85. See also Index 1, 'Euripides, *Helen*'.

Moirai: see 'Fates'

Moon 110

Mounychia **29–31**, **37**, 20–21

Mycenae 510, 845

Nereids 273–74, 427–29, 632–35, 1125–27

Odysseus **11n**, **12n**, **26**, 1–66, 22–25*, 531–36. See also Index 1, 'Homer, *Odyssey*'.

Oenomaus 1–5, 75

INDEXES

Orestes: age 230–35; and Apollo **5f**,,
67–122, 77–92*, 120–21, 570–71,
[572–75], 711–23*, 942–44, 964–82*,
1013–15*, 1084–85, 1174, 1234–83,
1438–39; and Erinyes **6**, **21**, 77–83*,
230–35, 281–300*, 932–44*, 962–
72*, 1467–72*; and Halai **22**, **32f.**,
1450–61*; character **9f.**, **44**, 67–122,
456–826, 482–89*, 500–8*, 597–642,
605–10*, 658–724, 687–715*, 1021;
madness **34**, **45**, 81–83, 260–339,
281–300*, 307–8*, 932; matricide **6**,
7f., **10f.**, **14**, **48**, 924–46*, 957, 964–
65; trial at Athens **7**, 947–67*, 1471–
72

Palaemon 270–71

Panathenaea **29**, 222–24

Parthenos (goddess) **19f.**, **23**, **24**

Pelops, Pelopids **3**, **10**, **13**, 1–5*, 157–
59, 192–202*, 235, 386–91, 811–25*,
865–67, 984–85, 1414–19. See also
'Atreus', 'Thyestes'.

Phineus 423–24

Phoebus 711–15, 723, 942–44, 972,
1128

Plynteria (festival) 1041, 1197, 1210

Polyidus ('sophist') **42n**, **47n**

Pompeii **44f.**, 26–27, 456–66

Poseidon 1–5, 191–93, 328–29, 386–
91, 425–26, 531–36, 945–46, 1391–
95, 1414–19, 1444–47*

Pylades **2f.**, **5**, **9f.**, **13**, **34f.**, **36**, **43n**,
44f., **46n**, **48**, [59–60], 67–76*, 105–
122*, 248–51, 301–35*, 340–43*,
472–73, 498, 562, 570–71, 578–96,
609–10, 638, 643–797*, 902–1088,
915–20*

Racine, Jean **47n**

Reyes, Alfonso **49**

Scythians **19**, **24**, **26**, **41f.**, **44**, **46**

Strophius 498, 695–98, 917

Sun 110, 191–94*, 812, 1137–42

Tantalus, Tantalids **49**, 1, 199–201,
289–90, 386–91, 987–88

Taurians **1**, **12**, **13**, **15f.**, **19f.**, **22–27**,
32, **33**, **34f.**, **36f.**, **48f.**, 35–38*, 75,
124–25, 133–36, 244–45, 280, 336–
39, 380–91, 392–455, 399–402, 463–
66, 585–87, 625–35, 725–26, 1089–
1152, 1163, 1170, 1186–89*, 1327–
1419, 1407–8, 1427–30*

Tauropolia **27**, **32**, 35–37, 1458–61.
See also 'Artemis, Tauropolos'.

Themis 207, 1234–83, 1254–61*

Thetis 214–17, 273–74, 369, 427–29,
435–36, 537–39, 570–71, 632–35,
1270–77*

Thoas **3**, **14**, **15n**, **21n**, **22n**, **23**, **26**,
34f., **36**, **43n**, **46n**, **47f.**, 32–33, 336–
39, 638, 1020–27*, 1153–1233*,
1284–1434, 1325–26, 1391–95, 1414–
33*, 1435–89, 1467–85*

Thyestes 178–202*, 812. See also
'Pelopids'.

Timomachus (painter) **45**

Titans 222–24, 844–45, 1259–61.

Triclinius, Demetrius **46**, **50**, 423–24,
1261–63, 1264

Troy, Trojan War **1**, **2**, **6**, **8**, **17–19**, 10–
14*, 139–42, 354–58, 514, 543, 670–
71, 702–5, 1125–27, 1414–19, 1437

White Island 435–37*

Zeus **11**, 1, 193–94, 222–24, 235, 272,
393–97, 403–6, 747–49, 934, 945–46,
1021, 1077, 1117–22, 1234–83, 1259–
61, 1270–83*, 1438–39

INDEXES

4. Topics

actors **34, 38, 42**, 74, 342–43, 827–99, 1306, [1497–9]

aether 29

aetiologies **29f.**, **31, 34**, 902–88, 947–60, 1435–89, 1458–61

aidôs (shame) 372–75, 500–1, 713

altars **23, 29, 35, 44**, 16, 26–27, 72–74*, 243, 625–35*, 1270–72

amathia (ignorance) 385–86

amoibaion 123–235, 827–99

audience **4, 8n, 13n, 14, 15, 25, 37, 38**, 1–66, 42–66, 42–43, 50–52, 62, 74, 123–235, 621, 1041, 1436

barbarian(s) **22, 25, 26f., 40f.**, 49, 178–81, 1021, 1153–1233, 1170–74*, 1205, 1337–38, 1368–70, 1429–30

bears **29, 31**

childbirth **14, 27, 28**, 381–83, 1097–99, 1226–29, 1464–67

chorus **1–3, 5, 7, 10, 12, 14f., 20n, 26, 34, 36f., 37–39, 41f.**, 47, 65–66, 123–235, 123–38*, 178–202, 178–81, 236–37, 344–91, 427–29, 439–55, 456–66, 576–77, 643–57, 798–802, 900–1, 1056–88*, 1089–1152*, 1284–1434, 1431–33, 1435–89, 1467–71, 1490–99

comedy **15, 16, 32**, 827–99, 1284–1434, 1435–89

daimon **9**, 157–59, 178–81, 201–5*, 865–67, 987–88

dancing **14, 29, 32, 36, 38, 39**, 35–37, 273–74, 366–68, 427–29, 1089–1152, 1103–5, 1125–27, 1143–52*, 1241–44

date of *Iph. Taur.* **40–42**

deer **1, 18f., 21, 30, 31**, 28–30. 1113–16

destiny: see Index 1, 'χρή, χρεών', Index 3, 'Fates'

deus ex machina: see 'gods'

divination 16

dreams **1f., 2, 5f.**, 11, 15, 36, 37, 47, **48n**, 37, 42–66*, 73, 148–56, 452–55, 569, 622, 823–25, 1137–46, 1234–83, 1261–83*

elegos 144–47

entrances, dramatic **36**, 67–68, 123–36

epitaphs 128–29, 695–98, 702–5

fire 626, 1137–42, [1155], 1216, 1331–32

fortune (*tuchê*) **5, 9f., 14f.**, 352–53, 407–21, 477, 486–89, 500–1, 560, 618, 687–92*, 721–22, 865–67, 907–11*, 1117–22, 1230–33, 1317, 1490–91.

friendship (*philia*) **10, 44**, 597–642, 609–10, 658–724, 687–88

funeral procedures 625–35*, 702–5, 818

genealogies 1–5

gods: appearances in tragedy **37**, 1435–89, 1436, 1475–88*; criticized 344–91, 380–91*, 570–71; influence on human affairs **5, 8–10, 12n, 13–15, 17**, 29, 89, 328–29, 477, 639–42, 895–99, 909–11, 987–88, 1084–85, 1234–83, 1317, 1327–1419, 1414–19, 1438–39, 1475–85; statues of 87–88, 222–24, 1041, 1165–67, 1210, 1222–25

hair 50–52, 73, 172–74, 244–45, 285–87, 442–45, 702–5, 811–26, 820–21, 1099–1102. 1147–52, 1236–38, 1276–77

halcyon 1089–1105, 1091

honey 159–66*, 625–35*

hope 414, 721–22

hospitality (*xenia*) 386–91, 947–48

humour **16**, 275–78, 1153–1223, 1174, 1234–83, 1284–1434

hunting 20–21, 77, 282–84, 1163

hymns **39**, 1234–83, 1234–38

INDEXES

iconography **28n**, **29nn**, **32n**, 33n, 20–21, 26–30*, 222–24, 962–63, 1099–1102, 1153–1233, 1250–52. See also 'sarcophagi', 'vase-paintings', 'wall-paintings'.

imagery, metaphor: animal [294], 359–60; architecture 57; birds, flight 843–44, 1089–1105, 1137–42; blooming 300; charioteering 81–83, 191–93, 934; hunting 77, [294], 1163; legal 14; military 1046; music 178–81; sacrifice 552; sickness 531–36, 1018; striking 301–35; topography 399–402, 1089–1105; weapons 136–70; wind 1317. See also 'weddings'.

interpolation 38–41, [59–60], [84], 116–17, 187–88, 197, 225–26, [258–59], [294], [299], [317], [349], 352–53, [363], 463–66, [572–75], 907–8, 957, [1025–26], [1032–33], 1068–[71], [1155], 1346, 1441b, 1478–79

intrigue (*méchanêma*): see 'planning'

irony, dramatic **5**, 42–66, 139–42, 336–39, 350, 456–826, 472–83*, 492–575, 515–16, 550, 569, 579, 612–13, 639–42, 706–7, 1153–1223

keys, key-keeper, **35f.**, 99, 130–32, 1462–63

letter (dramatic device) **2f.**, **10**, **35**, **44**, **47n**, 42–66, 456–826, 578–96, 584, 638–42*, 725–68, 727, 769–97, 811–26

libations 2, **6**, **15**, **34**, **35**, 42–66, 123–235, 159–66*, 625–35

literacy 578–96

lustration (*loutra*) **23**, 42–66, 54, 442–45, 622, 645, 818, 861, 1190, 1222–25, 1316

madness **28n**, **32**, **34**, **45**, 81–83, 260–339, 281–300, 270–71, 285–91, 307, 340–41, 932

marriage **19**, **29f.**, **33**, **48**, 220–24*, 369, 537–39, 818–21*, 1099–1102, 1226–29. See also 'wedding'.

messengers: see 'report speeches'

metaphor: see 'imagery'

monody 123–235, 392, 827–99

music 123–235, 144–47, 178–85*, 366–68, 1089–1152, 1125–27

myth in *Iph. Taur.* **1**, **6**, **7f.**, **11–14**, **15f.**, **17–22**, **23**, **25**, **29–34**, **39**, **40**, **43**, **48**, **49**, 20–21, 902–1088, 1174, 1234–83, 1440, 1471–72

nobility 114–15, 260–339, 321–22, 456–826, 459–62, 578–96, 609–13*, 658–724, 678, 1467–71

nostalgia **38n**, **39**, 392–455, 1089–1152

oaths **36**, 20, 725–68, 747–49, 788–90, 1077

omitted text 113–14, 142, 193–94, 288, 427–29, 780ff., 942–44, 1014–15, 1214, 1236, 1259–61, 1261–63, 1348–53, 1379–80, 1404–5, 1441b, 1467–71

operas **46–48**

paeans 182–85, 1097–1102*, 1234–83, 1403–4

papyri **18n**, **43**, **51**

planning **4**, **10n**, **15**, **35**, **37f.**, **41**, **48n**, 456–826, 492–575, 725–26, 876–80, 902–1088, 1005–6, 1020–27, 1327–1419

plot of *Iph. Taur.* **1–7**, **34n**, **42**, **43**, **44**, **46**, **47**, 42–66, 578–96, 1458–61

pollution **9f.**, **13**, 381–83, 531–36, 940–41, 947–60, 973–75, 1039, 1153–1233, 1161, 1177, 1197, 1459–60, 1207–29*

prayers **10**, **36**, 123, 268–74*, 336–39, 463–66, 1079–88*, 1230–33, 1337–38, 1397–1404*, 1490–99*

prophecy 1234–83, 1254–58, 1282–83. See also 'seers'.

proverbs 57, 288–90, 386–91, 407–21, 759, [1025–26], 1298, 1396

purification **13**, **36**, **48**, 20, 42–66, 54, 255, 381–83, 818, 942–44, 951, 972, 1039–41*, 1192–94, 1216–33*, 1254–58, 1316, 1331–38*

INDEXES

purple 260–64, 303

race-courses 81–83, 436–37

recognition (*anagnôrisis*) 4–6, 9, 10, 14–16, 36, 41, 42n, 44f., 47, 50–52, 172–74, 246–51, 456–826, 467–91, 479, 492–575, 506–8, 565–68*, 578–96, 639–42, 725–68, 769–97, 798–810*, 811–26, 827–99

report speeches 6, 15, 21n, 34f., 41, 236–391, 260–339, 260–64, [294], 301–35, 328–29, 336–39, 459–62, 1208, 1284–1434, 1306, 1325–26, 1327–1419, 1339–43, 1414–19

reversal (*peripeteia*) 4, 5

sacrifices 28, 29f., 8, 16, 20, 38–41, 54, 163, 209–13, 243–45*, 359–60, 442–45, 467–69, 552, 621–22*, 1037, 1337–38; human 2, 6, 8, 10, 12, 13, 19, 22f., 24, 25f., 33, 35, 47f., 49, 20–30*, 35–41*, 75, [258–59], 344–91, 380–91*, 458–69*, 585–87, 702–5, 1113–16, [1155], 1189–90*, 1316–20*, 1458–61. See also Index 3, 'Iphigenia, sacrifice of'.

salvation 33, 35, 48, 20–21, 187–88, 578–96, 905–6, 1490–91

sarcophagi 45, 154n

satyr-plays 16, 21n

seers 20–21, 570–71, [572–75], 662, 711–15, 1128. See also 'prophecy'.

servants 34f., 38, 123–235, 167–68, 456–66, 638, 725–26, 1153–1223, 1204, 1284–1434, 1284, 1327–1419

shame 456–826, 691–92. See also '*aidôs*'.

ships, ships' equipment 10, 116–17, 139–42, 407–10*, 422–38*, 741–42, 1000, 1041–51*, 1110, 1123–36*, 1345–57*, 1377–1402*, 1444–45

silence 123–36, 123, 458, 951–57*, 1056–88. See also Index 2, 'εὐφημία'.

song 2f., 7, 14, 35f., 123–235, 144–47, 178–81, 221–24*, 366–68, 392–455, 427–29, 643–57, 827–99, 856–59,

861–72, 1089–1152, 1091, 1103–5, 1125–27, 1234–83, 1241–44

staging 34–37; entrances and exits 36, 65–66, 67–68, 123–36, 342–43, 386–91, 456–66, 638, 725–26, 1079–81, 1153–1233, 1284–1434, (crane/*mêchanê*) 37, 1435–89, 1488; offstage action 37, 236–391, 638, 1284–1434; onstage action 34f., 67–68, 76, 167–68, 427–29, 798–802, 1089–1152, 1222–25; stage building 34f., 65–66, 75, 1284–1434, 1435–89, 1488

statues: see 'gods, statues of'

stichomythia 492–575, [572–75], 725–68, 902–1088, [1025–26], 1030, [1032–33], 1153–1233, 1203–33

supplication [363], 701, 1068–[71], 1270–72

suspense 5, 42–66, 65–66, 91, 456–826, 492–575, 578–96

sword, sacrificial 8, 26–27, 621, 1190, 1458–61

tragedy, generic features 4, 10, 16f., 23n, 35, 38f., 40, 456–826, 827–99, 1203–33, 1284–1496, 1490–99

ululation 209–13, 366–68, 1337–38

vase-paintings 42, 44, 26–27, 54, 73, 75, 87–88, 99, 456–66, 725–68, 727 1099–1102, 1250–58*

wall-paintings 44f., 26–27, 456–66

water, ritual uses 159–66, 1039, 1192–94, 1254–58. See also 'lustration'.

wealth 407–21*

weddings, wedding imagery 203–5, 214–17, 359–77*, 818–19*, 856–59

winds 8, 15, 20, 29, 423–34*, 1317, 1391–95*, 1487–89

women (lives, conduct) 28–30, 33, 45, 209–13, 221–24*, 366–69*, 482–83, 578–96, 621, 627, 682, 820–25*, 1005–6, 1061–77*, 1097–1102*, 1143–52*, 1197, 1298, 1337–38, 1464–67. See also 'chorus'.

Printed and bound by CPI Group (UK) Ltd, Croydon, CR0 4YY
01/04/2024
14477756-0001